ESSAYS ON PHILOSOPHY, POLITICS & ECONOMICS

ESSAYS ON PHILOSOPHY, POLITICS & ECONOMICS

Integration & Common Research Projects

Edited by

Christi Favor, Gerald Gaus,

and Julian Lamont

Stanford Economics and Finance,
An Imprint of Stanford University Press
Stanford, California

Stanford University Press
Stanford, California

Printed in the United States of America on acid-free, archival-quality paper

Library of Congress Cataloging-in-Publication Data
Essays on philosophy, politics & economics : integration & common research
projects / edited by Christi Favor, Gerald Gaus, and Julian Lamont.
    p.   cm.
    Includes bibliographical references and index.
    ISBN 978-0-8047-6254-0 (alk. paper)—ISBN 978-0-8047-6255-7
(pbk. : alk. paper)
    1. Political ethics.   2.   Political science—Philosophy.   3. Economics—
Moral and ethical aspects.   4. Economics—Philosophy.   I. Favor,
Christi.   II. Gaus, Gerald F.   III. Lamont, Julian.   IV. Title: Essays on
philosophy, politics, and economics.
    JA79.E815 2010
    330.01—dc22

                                                                2009038332

Typeset by Motto Publishing Services in 10.5/15 Adobe Garamond Pro

CONTENTS

ACKNOWLEDGMENTS

The editors would like to acknowledge Sharon Ford, Cheryl Holmes, and the generous support of The Center for Ethics and Public Affairs in the Murphy Institute at Tulane University, and especially its Director, Rich Teichgraeber III, for assistance in preparing the manuscript. We are deeply grateful to Margo Beth Crouppen, our editor at Stanford, for her enthusiasm and support for our project. Of course, above all, we are grateful to our contributors for their fine essays.

ABOUT THE CONTRIBUTORS

H. Sterling Burnett is a Senior Fellow with the National Center for Policy Analysis, a nonpartisan, nonprofit research institute in Dallas, Texas. Dr. Burnett received his PhD in Applied Philosophy from Bowling Green State University in 2001. He specializes in environmental ethics and policy. He has published in *Social Philosophy and Policy, Ethics, Environmental Ethics, International Studies in Philosophy, The Washington Post* and *USA Today.*

Thomas Christiano is a Professor of Philosophy and Law at the University of Arizona and codirects their Rogers Program in Law and Society. He has held visiting fellow positions at All Souls College (2004), the Research School of the Social Sciences at the Australian National University (2007) and the National Humanities Center in 1999–2000. He is coeditor of the journal *Politics, Philosophy and Economics*. He has published papers in ethical theory, distributive justice, political philosophy, and democratic theory. He is the author of *The Rule of the Many* (1996), *The Constitution of Equality: Democratic Authority and Its Limits* (2008), and coeditor (with John Christman) of *Contemporary Debates in Political Philosophy* (2009). He is currently working on a book on the foundations of equality and on a project on global justice.

Christi Favor is a part-time Lecturer at the University of Queensland. She completed her BA in Philosophy and Political Science at Southern Methodist University and her PhD at the University of Arizona, writing on the concept of deserving. Her teaching areas are logic, feminist philosophy, distributive justice, moral theory, and environmental ethics. She also has an interest in philosophy for children, and she has developed and conducted a number of philosophy workshops for children in primary and secondary schools.

Gerald Gaus is the James R. Rogers Professor of Philosophy at the University of Arizona. He was founding editor of *Politics, Philosophy and Economics* and was formerly a coeditor of *The Australasian Journal of Philosophy*. Among his books are *On Philosophy, Politics & Economics* (2008), *Contemporary Theories of Liberalism* (2003), *Social Philosophy* (1999), *Justificatory Liberalism* (1996), and *Value and Justification* (1999).

Russell Hardin is a Professor of Politics at New York University. He has written on a variety of topics in moral, political, and legal theory and in rational choice theory. His books include *Collective Action* (1982), *Morality within the Limits of Reason* (1988), *One for All: The Logic of Group Conflict* (1995), *Liberalism, Constitutionalism, and Democracy* (1999), *Trust and Trustworthiness* (2002), and *Indeterminacy and Society* (2003).

Robert A. Kocis is a Professor of Political Science at the University of Scranton, where he is responsible for the curriculum in political philosophy and constitutional law. He completed his BA at St. Vincent College and has graduate degrees in philosophy and political science from the University of Pittsburgh. He has published articles on Isaiah Berlin, Marx, Mao, liberty, and moral philosophy. He has published books on Isaiah Berlin (1989) and Machiavelli (1998). He is working on an examination of the differing notions of liberty in Bradley, Bosanquet, and Berlin.

Julian Lamont is a Lecturer in Political Philosophy at the University of Queensland. His research interests include moral and political philosophy, applied ethics, economics and philosophy, political economy, legal and professional ethics, and bioethics. He is currently completing books on income justice and (with Gerald Gaus) economic justice.

Edward F. McClennen is a Professor of Philosophy at Syracuse University and the Centennial Professor of Philosophy, The London School of Economics and Political Science. He specializes in decision and game theory, philosophy of political economy, social and political philosophy, and philosophy and public policy. He is the author of *Rationality and Dynamic Choice: Foundational Explorations* (1990) and more than fifty articles on topics in decision theory, game theory, and political philosophy. He is currently working on a book to be entitled *Cooperative Society*.

Calvin G. Normore is a Professor of Philosophy at the University of California, Los Angeles and the William Macdonald Professor of Moral Philosophy at McGill University. His research interests and publications are in the areas of medieval philosophy, early modern philosophy, history of logic, and social and political philosophy. He is a member of the American Academy of Arts and Sciences and a former president of the Pacific Division of the American Philosophical Association.

Daniel Shapiro is an Associate Professor of Philosophy at West Virginia University. His main research interests are social and political philosophy and public policy. He has published articles on a variety of subjects including liberalism, free speech and art subsidies, drug policy, market-based retirement systems, market health insurance, and welfare policy. His recent book, *Is the Welfare State Justified?* (2007), compares major welfare state institutions with more market-based alternatives, as judged by mainstream perspectives in contemporary political philosophy. He argues that these perspectives—egalitarianism, positive rights theory, communitarianism, and many forms of liberalism—actually support more market-based or libertarian institutional conclusions than they realize.

Jeremy Shearmur is a Reader in Philosophy in the School of Humanities at the Australian National University. His primary fields of research are in the philosophy and methodology of the social sciences, social and political philosophy, and the history of political thought. He is the author of *Hayek and After* (1996) and *The Political Thought of Karl Popper* (1996), and joint editor (with Piers Norris Turner) of Karl Popper's *After the Open Society* (2008).

Mark D. White is a Professor in the Department of Political Science, Economics, and Philosophy at the College of Staten Island/CUNY and in the economics doctoral program at the CUNY Graduate Center. He teaches and writes in the intersection of economics, philosophy, and law and has authored several dozen journal articles and book chapters in these areas. He edited *Theoretical Foundations of Law and Economics* (2009) and coedited with Barbara Montero *Economics and the Mind* (2007), with Irene van Staveren *Ethics and Economics: New Perspectives* (2009), and with Chrisoula Andreou *The Thief of Time: Philosophical Essays on Procrastination* (2010).

T. M. Wilkinson is an Associate Professor in Political Studies at the University of Auckland. His primary research interests are in political theory, particularly as it relates to health, justice, and paternalism. In addition to work in health, he has written articles on the minimum wage, paternalism and well-being, age discrimination, rationality in economics, and research ethics. He is the author of *Freedom, Efficiency and Equality* (2000) and is currently writing a book on acquiring organs for transplantation.

Clark Wolf is Professor of Philosophy and Director of Bioethics at Iowa State University, where he also serves in the Department of Political Science and as a faculty member in the Graduate Program in Sustainable Agriculture. His research interests include social and political philosophy, philosophy of law, philosophy of economics, ethical theory, and rationality. He is coeditor with Victoria Davion of *The Idea of a Political Liberalism: Essays on Rawls* (2000), and his articles have appeared in *Ethics, Environmental Ethics, Ethics and the Environment,* and *Philosophical Studies.*

Matt Zwolinski is an Assistant Professor of Philosophy at the University of San Diego and a codirector of their Institute for Law and Philosophy. He has recently published an anthology entitled *Arguing About Political Philosophy* (2009) as well as essays on the morality of sweatshop labor and on the moral significance of the separateness of persons. His current projects include an evaluation of recent developments in libertarian political theory and a monograph on exploitation in markets and politics.

ESSAYS ON PHILOSOPHY,
POLITICS & ECONOMICS

INTRODUCTION

Christi Favor, Gerald Gaus,
and Julian Lamont

As is well-known, the study of philosophy, politics, and economics (PPE) as a combined discipline originated at Oxford University in the first part of the twentieth century, although at Oxford it represented not so much an integration of the three fields as a curriculum that drew on all three. In recent years the number of undergraduate PPE degree programs has increased, and a journal is now devoted to the field. Questions remain, however, as to the characteristics of PPE. Consider two broad understandings. From one view, we are witnessing the rise of a new discipline or perhaps the resurrection of the nineteenth century discipline of political economy. In 1821 James Mill, David Ricardo, Thomas Malthus, and Robert Torrens founded the London Political Economy Club. In 1825 the Drummand Chair of Political Economy was founded at Oxford, which required occupants, such as Nassau Senior, to give a series of lectures. The first economics department in Britain was funded at University College London; John Ramsey McCulloch occupied its first chair of political economy. In 1830 Jean-Baptiste Say occupied the first political economy professorship in France. (Thomas Jefferson wanted to offer Say the chair of political economy at the University of Virginia.) The high point of the discipline of political economy was from this period until the 1870s. The greatest economics text of the nineteenth century, written by John Stuart Mill, was entitled *Principles of Political Economy, with Some of Their Applications to Social Philosophy* (first edition 1848, last edition 1871). PPE as political economy was then a well-defined field, with professional organizations, academic chairs, and textbooks. However, after the "marginalist revolution" led by Carl Menger, William Stanley Jevons, and Leon Walras, economics developed highly formalized, mathematical models of economic life.[1] Jevons, and especially Walras, immediately saw how the idea of diminishing marginal utility allowed for the calculus to be applied to economics. After this, political science and economics (and social philosophy) went their separate ways, developing different professional organizations but, more important, different methods and tools. Some scholars believe we are currently witnessing a reintegration of these disciplines. From this first view, the study of economics and politics and, as Mill would say, their applications to social philosophy, cannot, in the end, be divorced. PPE represents a broad shared subject matter—the developments in the twentieth century may have attempted to divorce them, but it failed.

Although there is certainly something to say for the inherent overlap of economics, philosophy, and social philosophy, we are skeptical of this view as a general reason for the current interest in PPE. The heyday of political economy lasted barely fifty years; the fields have been divided for well over a century. In that time the methods—or what we might call the "toolboxes"—that practitioners of the disciplines share have grown apart in many ways. Therefore, we propose that what we are witnessing today is not so much a general reuniting of the fields, but a complex set of divergences and convergences. Economics today is generally deductive and mathematical, based on rational "*Homo Economicus.*" Public choice economists and political choice political scientists employ these basic assumptions, but their approach diverges from the rest of political science.[2] Economists, political scientists, and philosophers who employ game theory share a great deal in common, but this also separates them from many of their disciplinary colleagues, who are often skeptical of the usefulness of the theory of games. Again, experimental economics—forged most notably by Vernon Smith[3]—has formed links between, on the one hand, economics and, on the other, political psychology and experimental philosophy, but within each of our three disciplines many—perhaps most—have reservations about the usefulness of the experimental approach.[4] More examples can be found. Rather than a general convergence of disciplines, we seem to be witnessing, instead, divisions within disciplines about the best tools and approaches (e.g., disputes about game theory or experimentalism) and instances where selection of the same tools and approaches have united some economists, political scientists, and philosophers (while distancing them from some of their disciplinary colleagues).

This mosaic of divergence and convergence of tools and approaches indicates, we believe, not the emergence of a new discipline, but convergent research agendas in which groups of researchers have agreed that, for specific sorts of problems, certain tools and methods are needed to make progress. These tools and methods are drawn from the separate toolboxes of modern economics, politics, and philosophy. The recent dramatic rise of interest in PPE is, in our view, best understood as driven by specific research projects: The traditional methods and tools of the three disciplines must be drawn upon to tackle questions that are now the core of social and political theory and public policy. It is not so much that we are witnessing the birth of a new discipline as the rise of interdisciplinary research projects in social and political theory. Of course there is truth in both views, but the contributors to this volume stress how, within each discipline, current research projects necessitate that scholars expand their methods and competencies and critically learn from each other.

The work of this volume's contributors is informed by two convictions. First, because policy issues pose value and moral choices, work on public policy questions must be informed by expertise in value theory and theories of justice as well as economics and political science. One of the elements that, we think, has been missing from the toolkits of many economists working on public policy is normative theories relating to desert, fairness, and equality. Many values and action-guiding principles have no place within standard economic analyses; on the other hand, normative analysis uniformed by economic knowledge is apt to be utopian and therefore unhelpful. Philosophers, political scientists, and economists are devoted to a number of similar research projects in which they must learn and employ parts of each others' toolkits. This leads to the second conviction: To make intelligent choices about what tools to employ, we must understand each others' methods and concepts better. Critical examination of central economic notions such as efficiency, preferences, incentives, markets, and so on, are essential if these notions are to play their proper roles in PPE research projects.

The book is divided into six parts, examining: (I) the place of assumptions of rationality and human values in economic analysis; (II) how theories of economic desert may figure into our evaluation of economic outcomes; (III) how the core economic criterion of efficiency relates to other values; (IV) how the basic economic model of humans as choosers relates to the moral ideas of consent and autonomy; (V) how moral standards can be applied dynamically, in the sense that they concern not simply how we act toward present but also future generations; and finally, (VI) how insights from both economics and ethics can help us better frame public policies. Each part explores underlying values, principles, and conceptual frameworks for public policy formation and considers how morality and justice should enter into that formation. The collection as a whole illustrates the value of philosophers' contributions to public policy debates by specifically considering many public policy questions of central importance to contemporary societies. The significance of this collection lies in its role in building conceptual and analytical bridges between philosophy, political science, and economics that will enable each of these disciplines to contribute in richer and more sophisticated ways to debates about fundamental policy issues affecting our societies.

I. THE FOUNDATION: RATIONALITY AND HUMAN VALUES

In the opening chapter, "Utility and Utilitarianism," Edward F. McClennen examines one of the most common moral theories advocated for policy decisions and the founding moral theory for modern economics—utilitarianism. He examines various attempts to derive utilitarianism from axioms of rationality alone and concludes that all attempts to do so have failed. He closes this first chapter by exploring a more promising argument for a utilitarian principle, one grounded on considerations of how to make efficient policy decisions when making repeated decisions over time and under conditions of moderate uncertainty. He argues, though, that on such an account, the utilitarian principle emerges as appropriate only for "middle-level" policy decisions, in which substantial interests are not at stake. It does not serve to establish utilitarianism as a fundamental principle.

In the next chapter, "The Limits of *Homo Economicus*: The Conflict of Values and Principles," Gerald Gaus challenges the claim that *Homo Economicus*—"economic man"—is a general model of rational action, applying, for example, to politics as well as economics. According to Gaus, *Homo Economicus* is a special case of a more general account of rational action, useful in explaining actions in some kinds of environments but misleading when applied in other situations. *Homo Economicus*, he argues, focuses on the choice among competing values, but rational action also concerns the way people act on principles. Gaus develops a model of the way in which rational agents trade off values and principles against each other, and then applies this general model to both market and nonmarket transactions.

Jeremy Shearmur continues the analysis of economic rationality and its application to politics and social life in his chapter, "Preferences, Cognitivism, and the Public Sphere." Shearmur examines both weaknesses and strengths of an "economistic" approach to politics. According to public choice theory, which seeks to explain political behavior through economic models, politics arises because political actors try to satisfy their "brute"—unreasoned—preferences. Drawing on Karl Popper's epistemology, Shearmur explores what he calls "cognitive" preferences: the preferences we hold only because we believe it is correct for us to hold them. Shearmur indicates to the extent politics is concerned with such preferences, it is not simply an arena of "private" brute preference satisfaction, but constitutes a public forum: a socially constituted area, within which ideas face public scrutiny. Shearmur concludes his chapter by examining some difficulties for the approach he has explored, drawing evidence from the history of debates about the commercial and noncommercial supply of blood.

II. THE QUESTION OF ECONOMIC DESERT

Compensation and desert are both concepts that commonly figure in claims of distributive justice, but the proper analysis of each, as well as the relationship between them, is problematic. In "Expressive Desert and Deserving Compensation," Christi Favor explains the challenge posed by standard analyses of desert to a seemingly obvious claim such as, "Miners deserve compensation for work in filthy conditions." Without fundamentally undermining standard and widely accepted features of desert, Favor appeals to the expressive qualities of various deserved treatments to explain how people can coherently deserve compensation.

Many philosophers and others have argued that individuals deserve income, not as compensation, but as a proportionate reward for their productivity or their contributions to others' well-being. A significant problem with this principle is that people's productivity depends partly on their natural abilities, over which people have limited control. Yet most philosophers strongly reject any system distributing income on the basis of other qualities over which people have limited control, such as race, gender, or parental social class. Julian Lamont, in "Productivity, Compensation, and Voluntariness," undertakes a critical evaluation of the productivity principle of income distribution, arguing the alternative "compensation principle" better captures our underlying moral judgments about voluntariness and income rewards for productivity.

In "Discriminatory Privileges, Compensatory Privileges, and Affirmative Action," Robert A. Kocis argues that people would not give their rational consent to a society without affirmative action. In the contractarian device he employs, people are assumed not to know their identities or their group membership, but to be rational agents (1) with a sense of injustice who (2) forge their identities as members of groups, aware that (3) humans are imperfect and so iniquitous beings. Since iniquitous beings who attach their identities to groups would confer preferences upon their own group members, those empowered would be able to foster the life-prospects of their group members in unjust ways. Under Kocis's analysis, affirmative action comes to be a type of compensatory preferential treatment to counterbalance the preferences conferred upon privileged groups.

III. ETHICS AND EFFICIENCY

T. M. Wilkinson, in "Deontic Efficiency and Equality," examines one of the central concepts used in economic approaches to policy: Pareto efficiency. His focus is on a normative conception of Pareto efficiency that directly provides constraints on how the state may act. Wilkinson distinguishes two constraints that follow from this conception. One prohibits harming others, and this apparently conflicts with the redistribution that would be necessary to achieve equality. The other disallows prohibitions of efficiency-promoting acts, and this apparently condemns, among other things, income taxation and minimum wage legislation. Wilkinson argues that, with a proper defence of these constraints and a proper understanding of the values and methods of egalitarianism, deontological efficiency is not in fundamental conflict with egalitarianism.

Thomas Christiano, in "Cohen on Incentives, Inequality, and Egalitarianism," also examines the implications of Pareto efficiency for equality, analyzing G. A. Cohen's argument against the theses of John Rawls and Brian Barry that inequality can be just if it constitutes a Pareto improvement over equality or if it works to the advantage of the worst off by offering incentives to the more talented to work harder. Christiano shows that Cohen's understanding of the role of incentives in generating inequality from equality is indefensible. He also shows how self-interested incentives play an important informational role in generating a productive society. He argues that such incentives and the markets that elicit them will give rise to inequalities that are byproducts of these institutions. Hence, he claims, they are compatible with an egalitarian conception of justice because they are essentially informational and the equalities they give rise to are a necessary concomitant of the productive power of the society.

IV. CHOICE, CONSENT, AND MORALITY

Economics is based on the idea of rational choice. In Part IV, contributors investigate the idea of choice that is implicit in some economic approaches and examine whether choice can also be the ground of morality. In "Behavioral Law and Economics: The Assault on Consent, Will, and Dignity," Mark D. White uses the moral philosophy of Immanuel Kant to examine the intersection of economics, psychology, and law known as "behavioral law and economics." Scholars in this relatively new field claim that, because of various cognitive biases and failures, people often make choices that are not in their own interests. The policy implications of this theory are that public

and private organizations, such as the state and employers, can and should
design the presentation of options and default choices in order to steer people
to the decision they would make, if they were able to make choices in the
absence of their cognitive biases and failures. Such policies are promoted under the name "libertarian paternalism," because choice is not blocked or co-
opted, but simply "nudged." White argues that such manipulation of choice
is impossible to conduct in people's true interests, and any other goal pursued by policymakers substitutes their own ends, however benevolent they
may be, for the people's true ends. Normatively, such manipulation should
not be conducted because it fails to respect the dignity and autonomy of
persons, what some hold to be the central idea in Kant's ethical system, and
which serves to protect the individual from coercion, however subtle, from
other persons or the state.

In "Consent and the Principle of Fairness," Calvin G. Normore examines
the longstanding issue that bedevils all attempts to employ consent to ground
a theory of political obligation: On a plausible view, must a justifying consent
be made voluntarily and explicitly, tacitly, or hypothetically? One avenue for
dealing with this impasse is to ground political obligation in a "Principle of
Fairness," which claims that under certain conditions benefits accepted create
obligations to share in the costs of the practices conferring the benefits. According to Normore, however, we do not necessarily create obligation in others simply by benefiting them against their wills, nor do we necessarily benefit others simply by making them better off than they were. Normore finds
problems with every attempt to formulate a principle of fairness that respects
these considerations. Normore considers an alternative formulation focusing on the obligations created when failure to share the costs could result in
losing the benefit. Such a principle preserves all the intuitive force behind
a principle of fairness, yet is too weak to ground a political obligation for every
citizen of a modern state. Normore suspects, therefore, social contract theorists must reject universal political obligations or introduce them as primitive.

V. THE FUTURE—EQUALITY AND FAIRNESS

The contributors in this part address both the theoretical and practical problems with formulating policy for the future. Russell Hardin, in "The Costs
and Benefits of Future Generations," begins with the question: "How do we

bring future generations under the coverage of moral and political theory?" Hardin examines many of the current moral theories—autonomy; communitarianism; egalitarianism; libertarianism; utilitarianism; and theories of rights, respect for persons, and distributive justice—and finds that none of them is currently up to the task of underpinning and defining our obligations to future generations. He also argues that attempts to treat problems of future generations as trivial are naive. He concludes by outlining which theories he believes offer the best possibilities for addressing the problem.

Clark Wolf, in "Intergenerational Justice and Saving," tackles the issue of a just rate of saving in the context of intergenerational justice. He presents a simple model of saving and intergenerational resources allocation, and an account of sustainability. He also considers some alternative principles of intergenerational distributive justice, particularly John Rawls's difference principle applied to the intergenerational case. Contrary to Rawls, Kenneth Arrow, Robert Solow, and Partha Dasgupta, Wolf argues that an intergenerational difference principle will not prohibit economic progress when the model of saving employed incorporates generational overlap. The case for the intergenerational difference principle is therefore no weaker than the case for its intragenerational counterpart. The overlapping generation model of intergenerational saving offers a promising way to frame questions of intergenerational justice.

VI. POLICY, ETHICS, AND ECONOMICS

In this final part Daniel Shapiro, H. Sterling Burnett, and Matt Zwolinski show how an appreciation of both economics and ethics can shed new light on problems of public policy. Shapiro, in his "Communitarianism and Social Security," compares the United States's Social Security system with a system of compulsory private pensions, recommending communitarians favor the latter. He argues that Social Security produces enormous intergenerational inequities—early generations get a great "rate of return" while later generations do poorly—while a private system avoids these inequities by investing individuals' own contributions. He holds that Social Security fails to keep its promises, and its real functioning is masked by misleading and deceptive rhetoric: Social Security is called social insurance, payroll taxes are called contributions, government IOUs are called trust funds, giving the impression that it is a funded pension plan, rather than a pay-as-you-go system. In contrast, Shapiro concludes, a private system delivers what it promises: a good market rate of return.

In "Rights, Pollution, and Public Policy," H. Sterling Burnett develops a variant of classical liberal rights theory and applies it to pollution problems. He analyzes two different policy approaches to pollution problems: a utilitarian economic approach suggested by the works of Ronald Coase and a common law approach stemming from the application of the classical liberal rights theory developed earlier. Burnett rejects the Coasian approach because it provides no principled defense of rights. Having found the Coasian approach lacking, Burnett examines the complementary nature of liberal property rights and common law protections against pollution. This discussion examines both the historic uses of the common law as a bulwark against pollution and the purported weakness of the common law. Burnett concludes with a discussion of the public policies necessary to reestablish common law protections against pollution.

In the final chapter, Matt Zwolinski examines "Price Gouging and Market Failure." Price gouging occurs when, in the wake of an emergency, the price of some good that is necessary or extremely useful for coping with the emergency is set at what appears to be an unfairly high level. Most people think that price gouging is immoral, and most states have laws rendering the practice a civil or criminal offense. In his provocative chapter, Zwolinski criticizes the philosophical argument underlying the moral condemnation and legal regulation of price gouging. The reason price gouging is singled out as morally problematic in a way that regular price increases are not, he argues, is based on the belief that price gouging occurs in the context of various market failures. But, says Zwolinski, the charge of market failure, even if true, cannot sustain the current condemnation of price gouging. He maintains first, that laws prohibiting price gouging are morally unjustified, and second, that the act of price gouging itself often serves morally praiseworthy ends and should be regarded as morally permissible.

NOTES

1. The key works here were Carl Menger, *Principles of Economics*, translated and edited by James Dingwall and Bert F. Hoselitz, with an Introduction by Frank H. Knight (Glencoe, IL:

Free Press, 1950); William Stanely Jevons, *Theory of Political Economy* (London: Macmillan, 1971); Leon Walras, *Elements of Pure Economcis, or The Social Theory of Wealth*, translated by William Jaffe (London: Allen and Unwin, 1954).

2. Interestingly, public choice political scientists and economists diverge on a number of issues; they also disagree in important ways with economists in general. See Robert Whaples and Jack C. Heckelman, "Public Choice Economics: Where is There Consensus?" *The American Economist* 49 (Spring 2005): 66–78.

3. See, for example, Vernon L. Smith, *Bargaining and Market Behavior: Essays in Experimental Economics* (Cambridge: Cambridge University Press, 2000).

4. See, for example, Walter Sinnott Armstrong's edited three volume collection on *Moral Psychology* (Cambridge, MA: MIT Press, 2008).

PART I

THE FOUNDATIONS: RATIONALITY AND HUMAN VALUES

CHAPTER I

UTILITY AND UTILITARIANISM

Edward F. McClennen

1. INTRODUCTION

The modern concept of utility makes its first appearance in the work of the mathematician D. Bernoulli, where it is employed to "save" a particular decision rule from an embarrassment.[1] The rule in question calls for choosing a gamble that maximizes expected monetary return. The embarrassment arises in connection with a particular gamble, in which the gambler flips a coin repeatedly until heads comes up, and the person who has purchased the gamble receives $\$2^n$, where n is the number of the trial on which heads first occurs. This gamble has infinite expected monetary return and, according to the rule in question, is a good purchase at any (finite) offering price— no matter how large. This is contrary to an intuitive understanding of what counts as a rational choice. Bernoulli's suggestion was to salvage the expectation rule by taking expectation with respect to the utility (value) of the monetary return instead of monetary return itself and by assuming diminishing marginal utility for money.

The link established between a concept of utility, taken as the measure of the value of something, and the salvaging of a simple "sum-ranking" rule for evaluating alternatives (namely, taking the sum of the probabilistically discounted utilities), prefigures the close connection found today between the concept of utility as developed in the work of mathematically oriented economists and decision theorists and different "sum-ranking" approaches to the evaluation of both personal choices and public policies.[2] The modern theory of utility includes a construction, which ensures that the value of any gamble is simply its expected utility, and a natural extension of this construction supports a utilitarian sum-ranking approach to the evaluation of policies. By a careful definition of functions of individual utilities, sets of which define the components on which a social aggregation rule operates, we can hold on to a utilitarian-type sum-ranking rule and also defend it against many standard objections. We can defend a utilitarian-type evaluation procedure from the charge that it is insensitive to deprivation and to inequalities between persons.[3]

To give a historical perspective, utilitarianism came into prominence in the eighteenth and nineteenth centuries, especially in England. As aggressively formulated by Jeremy Bentham, the perception was that it was a needed antidote to a variety of philosophical traditions that allegedly served merely to rationalize different types of vested interests, by trapping them out in the guise of natural laws or eternal truths. Bentham's attack on these vested interests, like the attack that Marxists would subsequently level, had the great disadvantage that it could be used against itself. Utilitarianism, as presented by Bentham, was subject to the objection that it, no less than the doctrines it was designed to replace, spoke to a set of interests (even if not yet vested): the interests of the greater number, the majority. Leaving the problem of ideology to one side, there is still a serious problem with Bentham's argument. He argued that utilitarianism is the only serious alternative to either falling into the anarchy of permitting everyone to judge the issues of public policy from the perspective of personal interests and/or moral commitments or the despotism of supposing that the interests of some one person or group of persons should be regulative for all. This argument proceeds by way of a faulty disjunctive syllogism. If utilitarianism qualifies as an objective, impartial perspective, then there exist other positions as well that are deserving of a hearing.

Within the context of the intellectual development of the second third of the twentieth century, all of this became moot. In general terms, the theory of knowledge that came into vogue, as expressed in the program of the logical positivists for example, rejected any claim to objectivity on behalf of any normative principle. Normative principles could not be objectively valid, since they are neither certifiable by reference to logic or meaning alone (cannot be shown to be true in any possible world), nor are they capable of empirical confirmation (cannot be shown to be true in this world). Such principles are not the bearers of truth-values at all, but simply the objects of an emotional commitment on the part of individuals.[4] This is a doctrine that, it will not escape the observant reader, provides an underpinning for an ideological critique much more sweeping than that envisioned by either the Benthamites or, subsequently, the Marxists.

Even if normative theories in general had not fallen into disrepute, utilitarianism still faced a serious problem concerning the intelligibility, or methodological propriety, of making the requisite interpersonal comparisons of utility. A principle that requires us to choose a policy maximizing the net sum of utilities as distributed to different individuals clearly presupposes that we can meaningfully compare these individual utilities. Within economic theory, however, the trend during this same period toward both an "ordinalist" interpretation of utility and skepticism with regard to interpersonal comparisons of utility served effectively to block any proposal to use the classical version of utilitarianism as a fundamental norm for social policy.[5] The connection between the ordinalist interpretation of utility and the problem of interpersonal comparisons is more complicated than this brief remark might suggest. A person can embrace a "cardinal" conception of utility and still deny the meaningfulness of interpersonal comparisons; or, alternatively, can accept an ordinalist perspective and still insist on the possibility of "level" comparisons from one person to another.[6]

The last few decades have brought significant winds of change with regard to the methodological issues noted above. The theory of knowledge that is now in favor is not in principle as hostile to the suggestion that there might be an objective (or rational) approach to policy evaluation.[7] More recently, the problem of interpersonal comparisons of utility has come to be seen as no longer so intractable.[8] Not surprisingly, the last few decades have witnessed a considerable revival of interest in a utilitarian approach to policy evaluation, a revival that has been encouraged in no small part by the work of economists and philosophers.[9]

What we find in the more formal literature is a variety of ways to underpin utilitarianism as a fundamental perspective on social policy. Some of the arguments proceed axiomatically by way of establishing conditions on what is to count as an adequate social welfare function. Alternatively, we can try to make the perspective of individual choice pivotal and argue that utilitarianism is just the principle to which we should be rationally committed, given that we must make a choice between principles under conditions of substantial uncertainty as to our prospective position in society.[10]

These arguments (unlike the one put forward by Bernoulli with regard to gambling) do not simply beg the question in favor of a simple sum-ranking rule. The power of these contemporary constructions resides precisely in the consideration that they start at least some distance from such a presupposition. The point of these exercises is to provide a formal reconstruction of a simple sum-ranking principle, and one that is antecedently taken by many to constitute the most appropriate way to approach both individual decision-making and the evaluation of alternative public policies. But the sum-ranking rule comes in as a theorem, instead of an axiom.

Despite these interesting developments, there is still a substantial issue that arises in connection with utilitarianism. As my opening remarks suggested, it's the issue of the sum-ranking feature of the utilitarian principle: the presupposition that one collection of individual utilities is as good as another if and only if it has at least as large a sum total of utility (or, alternatively, as large an average utility). Many have questioned this feature on the grounds that it yields an approach to public policy that is not sufficiently sensitive to issues both of deprivation in well-being for some, and inequality. The drift of much of the formal work done in recent decades has been to establish that we can, by one or another device, incorporate such concerns into a sum-ranking approach. I have my doubts as to whether the way in which such concerns are incorporated serves to resolve these issues. But to give this matter even a relatively cursory hearing would double the length of this paper and deflect attention from the equally pressing problem which is my focus.[11]

The focus, then, will be on this question: Granting that there exist valid axiomatic constructions that can exhibit some version or other of the utilitarian principle as a theorem, what can we say by way of defense of the axioms upon which these constructions rest? This is a matter of no small moment. In normative theory, no less than in theories regarding natural phenomena, we are concerned with the soundness and not merely the validity of the arguments we employ. But if we consult the enormous body of work that has been published in the last fifty or so years since the initial publication of John von Neumann and Oskar Morgenstern's *Theory of Games and Economic Behavior* in 1944, we find that little attention has been devoted to the evidentiary status of the axioms employed. In what is to follow, then, I want to review some of the leading axiomatic theories from this perspective.

2. UTILITARIANISM AS A THEOREM

Some of the more recent axiomatic approaches to utilitarianism are connected with Kenneth Arrow's striking theorem concerning the impossibility of a rational principle for the ordering of social alternatives. Arrow's theorem turns critically on a presupposition—buried in a very strong ordering assumption that he introduces, the independence of irrelevant alternatives axiom (IIA)—that the preferences of individuals cannot be numerically represented in a way that makes interpersonal comparisons meaningful. Abstracting from the extraneous feature that rules out interpersonal comparisons, IIA simply requires that the ordering of any two social alternatives is independent of whatever other alternatives happen to be available. It requires that the ordering of any two alternatives depends only on the features of those alternatives. As such, it forms a component of what has come to be known as the weak-ordering requirement.[12] As many constructions have demonstrated, with an appropriately reformulated version of IIA (and some others of Arrow's axioms) and an explicit allowance for different kinds of interpersonal comparability, it is possible to escape the impossibility result. By such means we can defend, as a matter of fact, not only a utilitarian aggregation principle, but also, by a slight modification of the axioms, Rawls's rival lexicographic maximin principle.[13]

Within this more relaxed framework, which permits interpersonal comparisons, the results that can be obtained all involve the appeal to a distinct axiom known as the strong independence axiom. Stated abstractly, as a requirement on the value of any combination of two items, strong independence requires that if A is ranked at least as good as B, then the combination of A and some third item, C, must be at least as good as the combination of B and C. Just where independence enters into these constructions varies greatly. Sometimes it is explicitly introduced as an axiom, but in the extension of the original Arrovian results to a series of possibility theorems, it enters indirectly, as an implication of an assumption that individual utilities are interpersonally unit-comparable, but not level-comparable.[14]

The strong independence axiom also plays a crucial role in a significant pair of alternative constructions due to John Harsanyi, each of which turns on the assumption that individual preferences for social alternatives can be represented by Von Neumann-Morgenstern utility functions.[15] In the first, the axiomatic social choice construction, utilitarianism follows from four quite simple, but allegedly plausible axioms:

1. Individual preferences satisfy the standard Von Neumann and Morgenstern axioms of expected-utility theory (weak ordering, continuity, reduction, and strong independence).

2. Social preferences satisfy the same axioms.

3. If all individuals are personally indifferent between two social options, then the social preference treats those two options indifferently.

4. The linear social welfare function implied by (1)–(3) is symmetric with respect to individual utilities, that is, it treats different individuals equally.

Here strong independence enters three times—in the assumptions about the axiomatic constraints on both individual preference orderings and the social preference ordering, and in a very weak form in assumption (3).

A second construction, the uncertainty choice, turns on supposing that

we must choose among social alternatives under conditions of complete uncertainty as to which position we will end up occupying. By employing a
particular set of axioms, Harsanyi is able to establish that we must proceed
as if we are just as likely to end up in any one position as any other. The
axiom construction employed by Harsanyi does not presuppose, but instead
provides a ground for, the principle of insufficient reason. Many have ob-
jected to this principle, but within the framework that Harsanyi has adopted,
any objection to this way of thinking about uncertainty must focus on the
inappropriateness of one or another of the axioms he invokes.[16] Given these
axioms, Harsanyi is able to show that the person must end up choosing so as
to maximize the sum (or average) of the set of individual evaluations of the
alternatives. In this instance, the explicit assumption is that the individual's
personal preferences with respect to uncertain prospects satisfy the strong
independence axiom.

The Harsanyi constructions are clearly connected in a formal sense with
the expected-utility theorem itself. Explicit recognition of this connection
appears in the work of Eric Maskin and Harsanyi.[17] Harsanyi's uncertainty
choice argument explicitly converts the social choice problem into a problem of individual decision-making under conditions of uncertainty, to which
kind of problem one or another variant of the Von Neumann and Morgenstern approach applies. Even more to the point, the assumption that a person
is just as likely to end up being any particular person as any other neatly
functions in a manner that parallels the way the symmetry condition functions in the axiomatic social choice theorem. Each of these induces the operation of a specific aggregate weighting system, and as such, they are related
to a principle that is central to the subjective expected-utility construction,
namely, that the agent is able to assign well-defined (probability) weights to
all conditioning events, and that these weights are relevant for the evaluation
of options.

All of these constructions connect back to a framework that was originally used to develop a theory of choice under conditions of risk, as explored
originally in the appendix to the first edition of Von Neumann and Morgenstern's *A Theory of Games and Economic Behavior*, and subsequently extended
in a series of discussion papers by Herman Chernoff, Herman Rubin, and
John Milnor, to the problem of choice under conditions of (complete) uncer-

tainty.[18] The crucial independence axiom makes an early appearance in Rubin's discussion paper (and is dubbed "Rubin's Axiom" by R. Duncan Luce and Howard Raiffa, *Games and Decisions*, ch. 13). In Milnor it enters as a column linearity condition.[19] These constructions form, in turn, the intellectual background for the theory of subjective probability that was developed in the 1950s and 1960s.[20]

These early constructions dovetail neatly with two distinct explorations concerning purely formal results in mathematics and in the theory of measurement. First, David Blackwell and M. A. Girschick connected the problem of conditions on a rational preference ordering with a basic theorem for ordering an n-dimensional vector space.[21] Second, the conditions for a rational preference ordering were shown, during the same period, to be equivalent to a set of conditions that were sufficient for a particular numerical representation of an ordering.[22] Consequently, the essentially normative issue of what is to count as a rational preference ordering became bound up with purely technical constructions that have no particular implications for the questions of what is (in a normative sense) the rational thing to do.

This intertwining of issues is worrisome. In the theory of measurement, the task is one of formal reconstruction—of working back from a particular numerical representation to the conditions that must be satisfied if such a representation is to be possible. The demonstration that a given set of conditions suffices, or that some particular condition is necessary, for a particular representation says nothing about the plausibility of the conditions in question, from either a descriptive or a normative perspective. From a descriptive perspective, the question is whether some set of preferences is representable in a clear fashion. That is to be settled by empirically ascertaining that the actual preferences of some individual or other do satisfy the axiomatic constraints. From a normative perspective, the question is whether some substantive constraint plausibly captures how, from a rational point of view, individuals ought to structure their preferences. The point has to be framed carefully here, because it is logically possible that the independence axiom is best understood as nothing more than a purely "technical" assumption, in the presence of which other substantive axioms suffice for a particular constructive result, having either descriptive or normative import.[23] This is the way, for example, that many have interpreted the continuity axiom, which figures centrally in many constructions, and which, in the presence of other axioms, yields the result that choice (social or individual) is representable by a real-valued measure. But the interpretation of continuity as a mere technical assumption is unconvincing. With the addition of continuity to a set of axioms that are otherwise neutral with respect to a utilitarian or a maximum approach to evaluation, the latter has to be rejected. In that context, continuity itself settles what is clearly a substantive issue.

All this is complicated by the consideration that in Von Neumann and Morgenstern's original work, the crucial independence axiom is not even explicitly introduced! It was Edmond Malinvaud who established that the axiom was smuggled in, in the form of a definition of equivalence classes.[24] Once it was identified, no one took it to be a purely technical assumption; instead, questions were immediately raised regarding its plausibility, both as a descriptive and as a normative assumption.

Part of the problem is that many situations exist in which independence appears to fail to characterize the preferences of even careful, thoughtful persons.[25] This suggests that if it is to be invoked, it will have to be as a normative constraint. Matters are complicated by the consideration that one natural way to motivate the independence axiom is by appeal to an analogy to the economic concept of independent goods, in which the value of a conjunctive bundle of quantities of different goods can be represented as an additive function of the value of the quantities of the separate goods that make up the bundle. But independence of this sort can fail to hold (either descriptively or normatively) in the case of preferences for different possible commodity bundles, and this is because of complementarity or value interaction between the different goods in a given bundle. In the proverbial example in which independence does not obtain, the value of a combination of a particular lock and key is greater than the sum of the values of that lock and that key each taken in isolation from the other (since neither alone serves much purpose). In one early discussion of the strong independence axiom, the example cited where independence fails to obtain is that of a mixture of gases with different octane ratings. It turns out that the octane of a blend is not a simple additive function of the octane values of the component gases, even taking into account the proportions in which the gases are mixed.[26]

Two developments in the early 1950s quickly paved the way for the acceptance of the independence axiom, at least as a normative constraint. First, Paul Samuelson offered an argument that appeared to lay to rest the issue of complementarity.[27] Second, and at roughly the same time, Milton Friedman and Leonard Savage suggested a quite distinct basis for understanding the independence axiom, namely, as an explicitly normative principle that invoked the concept of dominance or "sure-thing" considerations.[28]

3. THE SAMUELSON ARGUMENT FOR INDEPENDENCE

What Samuelson proposes is that in the case of preferences for risky alternatives, in which a person ends up getting just one of the disjuncts (one of the alternative possible outcomes), the independence principle has a legitimacy that it does not have in the case of conjunctive commodity bundles. Since you always end up with just one of the disjuncts that characterize the possible outcomes of a gamble (or an uncertain prospect), there can be no conjunction in the context of which the ordinary kind of complementarity could arise. So those who violated the independence axiom must have been keying in on some ephemeral aspect of risky or uncertain prospects that, from a normative point of view, should be ignored.

Samuelson is certainly correct that the nature of a disjunctive bundle precludes there being a complementarity problem of the sort that can arise in the case of conjunctive bundles. But the conclusion he reaches is unwarranted. He offers no argument that rules out the possibility of a distinct kind of complementarity that arises in connection with disjunctive bundles.

That there can be special complementarity problems associated with disjunctive bundles can be shown by appeal to a counterexample that Daniel Ellsberg proposes.[29] Let us suppose someone is offered a choice between a well-defined lottery, G_1, in which the prize is $100 with probability .5 and $0 with probability .5, and two symmetric gambles, G_2 and G_3, based on some binary "black-box" mechanism, which has the same schedule of prizes as does G_1, but where the odds are completely unknown. For example, in G_2 there is a completely uncertain prospect of getting $100 if, say, event E occurs, and $0 if event not-$E$ occurs; and in G_3 the person gets $100 if event not-$E$ occurs, and $0 if event E occurs. Many people declare that they would strictly prefer the gamble G_1 with known odds to either of the uncertain prospects, G_2 and G_3. By appeal to the independence principle, a person would then have to strictly prefer the well-defined lottery, $L = (G_1, .5; G_1, .5) = G_1$ to the following lottery, $L^* = (G_2, .5; G_3, .5)$. But L^* is clearly equivalent in terms of possible outcomes and probabilities to L, for it also promises one $100 with probability .5 and $0 with probability 5. That is, by conditioning symmetric uncertain prospects on events whose probabilities are well defined and symmetrical, the uncertainties are cancelled out. Something, then, must give; and Ellsberg suggests that it should be the independence principle. Ellsberg does not explicitly appeal to the concept of complementarity, preferring instead to argue that the way in which G_2 and G_3 are disjunctively combined in L^*, via the device of the toss of a fair coin, results in a prospect that no longer has any ambiguity about the odds with which you will receive $100 and ends up being strictly preferred to either G_2 or G_3 taken alone. But this is just to say that the two components, G_2 and G_3, exhibit in combination a complementarity relation to each other that renders the independence axiom inapplicable in this case.

Some scholars may object that such problems of disjunctive complementarity will arise at best in cases involving uncertainty (as distinct from well-defined risk), so that the original constructions of Von Neumann and Morgenstern, which employed well-defined gambles, remain untouched. But similar examples can be introduced to show that complementarity problems can arise in the case of examples involving well-defined gambles over well-defined gambles, especially if the agent evaluates risks in terms of a function that takes into account both the mean value of the risk and certain measures of dispersion.[30]

4. THE FRIEDMAN AND SAVAGE ARGUMENT

Friedman and Savage offer a quite distinct case for independence. What they suggest is that independence of the sort required for the expected-utility hypothesis can be secured by appeal to what they characterized as a "sure-thing" or dominance principle. As applied to the evaluation of risky or uncertain prospects, a simple version of dominance requires the following:

If two gambles exist that are conditioned by the same set of mutually exclusive and exhaustive events, and if every outcome of the first gamble is at least as preferred as (weakly preferred to) the corresponding outcome of the second gamble, and for the case of at least one of the conditioning events, the outcome of the first gamble is strictly preferred to the corresponding outcome of the second gamble, then the first gamble must be preferred to the second.

Friedman and Savage speak of this as a normative principle of rational choice that is unrivalled in its intuitive appeal. Interestingly, in the social choice literature a dominance (and an independence) condition is secured by the seemingly plausible assumption that the social ordering should satisfy the familiar Pareto condition:

If two social options exist and if every person in the society regards the first option as at least as preferred as the second option, and at least one person strictly prefers the first to the second, then the social ordering should rank the first as strictly preferred to the second.

The "sure thing" argument has inclined theorists to think that the issue of the status of the independence axiom can be clearly settled in its favor. The consensus in favor of the normative validity of the independence axiom has been so great that, when Mark Machina first presented a theory of utility without the independence axiom, the near unanimous response was that Machina had done a brilliant job of capturing the way that many persons did preferentially order alternatives, but it said nothing whatsoever about what a normative theory of choice should look like.[31] In short, Machina had managed to do no more than neatly capture and formalize a special form of irrational choice behavior.

The Friedman and Savage argument turns out to be no more secure than Samuelson's argument. There is no question that we can formulate a dominance condition that does secure independence. But the requisite condition is considerably stronger than the principle that Friedman and Savage and others have typically offered by way of illustration of the dominance condition. Most theorists have tended to gloss their axiomatic constructions in a manner that can lead the casual reader to confuse a highly intuitive simple dominance condition, dominance with respect to "sure" or "certain" (that is, riskless) outcomes, with a much stronger, and by no means so intuitively secure, extended dominance condition, according to which dominance holds for lotteries over lotteries, and not just lotteries over monetary or other kinds of riskless prizes.

Harsanyi repeatedly explicates the dominance principle in terms of the notion that, other things being equal, a rational individual will not prefer a lottery yielding less desirable prizes to a lottery yielding more desirable prizes. This is, intuitively, a quite secure requirement, if we understand by "prizes" something like "sure outcomes," that is, monetary awards or other sorts of goods. Unfortunately, in its much more general formulation, which is needed for the theorem, it is not so compelling. Ellsberg's counter-example, as discussed in Section 3, clearly challenges an extended version of dominance, although it has no weight against the dominance principle framed with regard to riskless outcomes. Savage, in *Foundations of Statistics*, clearly anticipates this objection but rejects it on the grounds that in the real world every possible prize is itself essentially a lottery, something whose consequences have to be probabilistically characterized.[32] What Savage seems to have missed was that if gambles involve "risk all the way down," we could argue, contra Savage, that there exists no level at which dominance can take hold.[33] In so far, then, as the appeal of independence is taken to rest on its derivability from an intuitively plausible dominance condition, we must conclude that the case for independence is flawed.

The objections rehearsed above can be directed at Harsanyi's version of the social choice construction, in which he postulates that both individual and social preferences are governed by the Von Neumann and Morgenstern axioms, and hence by the independence condition. The history of the controversy over independence conditions for social choice constructions is quite old and complicated.[34] Harsanyi for his part has indefatigably responded to virtually every challenge.[35] I have been unable to locate in his writings, however, any discussion of the problem posed by the need to appeal to an extended version of dominance.

Finally, do we fare any better by pursuing the line of argument that I first mentioned, which modifies the original Arrovian axioms? As Amartya Sen's analysis shows, the results still depend upon invoking independence in a context in which, again, we can intelligibly question its plausibility.[36] In the context of the modified Arrovian framework, the Pareto principle provides one way in which independence can be introduced. The possibility exists to secure a strong enough independence condition by appealing to an extended Pareto requirement, one that is analogous to the extended dominance condition to which Savage appeals. We have only to require that the social ordering respects dominance not when the preferences of all individuals line up in the appropriate manner, but also when, for any arbitrary partition of individuals into subgroups, the social ordering for the whole group respects dominance when the social orderings for all the partitioned subgroups line up in the appropriate manner. But that extended Pareto principle has just as little, if not less, plausibility than does the extended dominance condition.

5. UTILITARIANISM AND UNCERTAINTY

From the perspective of the questions raised, little is to be gained by shifting to Harsanyi's other argument—the argument from uncertainty. This approach gets around any objections that can be raised to invoking independence with respect to the social ordering: The argument goes through on the assumption that the individual's personal preferences are subject to the Bayesian axioms, in this case for choice under conditions of (complete) uncertainty. But this line of reasoning must appeal to precisely the kind of independence axiom that Savage invoked, and so is subject to the objections already raised—both Ellsberg's counter-examples and the more general concern regarding the problematic nature of the extended version of dominance.

To approach the problem of social evaluation from the perspective of what the rational individuals would be willing to accept, from a position of complete ignorance about future position or prospects, leaves a residual problem of no small proportion. Granting that rational persons would embrace this or that principle in such an initial position, we can still ask: What claim does this principle now make upon rational agents, here and now, as they face one another from positions that involve considerably less uncertainty?

This poses a problem not only for Harsanyi but also for John Rawls, who is responsible for a much discussed parallel argument from uncertainty—albeit one that leads him to a quite distinct principle, the lexicographic maximin principle.[37] In recent years, Rawls has tended to respond to this question in the following way: The story we tell about what we would choose behind the veil of ignorance is simply an imaginative way of putting ourselves in mind of what a genuinely impartial moral perspective would require of us. That is, the veil of ignorance argument is just a heuristic device, a way of getting at something implicit in a normative social perspective to which we all, to some extent or other, feel some allegiance.[38] Such a reconstruction, no doubt, can be illuminating. But consider those persons for whom the central question becomes what measure of allegiance is to be accorded to this principle—especially when, given the imperfect world in which we live, it must compete with other interests and even ideals of ours. For such persons, this whole line of reasoning may seem less than fully satisfactory.

The promise held out by constructions such as those of Rawls and Harsanyi is that we might come to understand that our commitment to a particular principle is grounded in something that lies a respectable distance from that principle itself: that the ground is to be found in the notion of rational (individual or social) choice. That is, it promises to do more than simply give us back, albeit in a clarified form, what we already are disposed to believe; it promises an independent and objective ground from which to assess, among other things, our commitments. That promise cannot be fulfilled, if the veil of ignorance argument is merely heuristic.

Harsanyi is clearly not willing to rest content with a purely heuristic interpretation of the uncertainty argument. But that means he is confronted with the problems already discussed. There remains the issue of the plausibility of the extended dominance axiom, and even granting for the moment that a utilitarian principle falls out, as a theorem, from a plausible model of individual choice of a social policy under conditions of radical uncertainty, why should agents structure their relations in accordance with that utilitarian principle, when it is clear that in reality they do not face one another under conditions of such radical uncertainty?

6. WHAT CAN BE SAID IN FAVOR OF UTILITARIANISM

The moral of the story I have told is that there exist many theorems that yield utilitarianism, either directly or indirectly, by utilizing the expected utility axioms that were devised by Von Neumann and Morgenstern or by Savage. But if the fields of decision and social choice theory have been long on theorems, they have been woefully short on careful exploration of the evidential basis for the essential independence axiom. This understanding does not show that utilitarianism is wrong, but it does, I believe, force us to the conclusion that, to date, we have no sound argument that starts at some distance from the utilitarian principle and derives it. The problem is not so much that these constructions yield a principle that is insensitive to two fundamental concerns—the problem of deprivation and the problem of equality. The problem lies elsewhere, in the questionable nature of the kind of independence that is needed to derive the principle. Despite these cautionary thoughts, one interesting line of reasoning can be used to support a utilitarian principle, and it does invoke, albeit in considerably attenuated form, the concept of choice under conditions of uncertainty (or risk). The argument I have in mind is one that can be adapted from the analysis that James Buchanan and Gordon Tullock offer, of conditions under which rational persons would be willing to agree to a majoritarian principle of voting.[39] They argue that the representative individual must expect that if social decisions can be made with less than unanimous consent, then policies will be implemented that work to his disadvantage, whereas under a unanimity rule he has veto power over any policy that would disadvantage him. However, the decision-making costs associated with the operation of the unanimity rule are significant, as measured both in terms of the expenditure of resources to reach compromise agreements that will win the support of all and in terms of opportunity costs. If these decision-making costs are sufficiently high, the individual will find it in his interest to support less-than-unanimity-voting rules. The key argument here explicitly invokes a concept of uncertainty:

Essential to the analysis is the presumption that the individual is uncertain as to what his precise role will be in any one of a whole chain of later collective choices that will actually have to be made. For this reason he is considered not to have a particular and distinguishable interest separate and apart from his fellows. This is not to suggest that he will act contrary to his interests; but the individual will not find it advantageous to vote for rules that may promote sectional, class or group interests because, by presupposition, he is unable to predict the role he will be playing in the actual collective decision-making process at any particular time in the future. He cannot predict with any degree of certainty whether he is more likely to be in a winning or a losing coalition on any specific issue. Therefore, he will assume that occasionally he will be in one group and occasionally in the other. His own self-interest will lead him to choose rules that will maximize the utility of an individual in a series of collective decisions with his own preferences on the separate issues being more or less randomly distributed.[40]

Under somewhat analogous conditions, we suppose individuals might agree to the use of a utilitarian calculus. In so far as the representative individual desires to see his interests promoted but is uncertain as to just what his specific interests will be on any given occasion, he might well find it to his advantage to support the operation of a rule that required the maximization of the sum of utilities (or income, or some other specific measure of value). Recognizing that the operation of such a rule will mean that on some occasions his interests will be sacrificed for the greater interests of others, still he may expect that over the long run he will be a net gainer—that he will be more often on the advantaged than on the disadvantaged side, given the operation of this principle.

To the extent that any such defense of a utilitarian rule for policy decisions could be constructed, it would be subject to precisely the same qualification to which Buchanan and Tullock subject the majoritarian voting principle. It is central to their argument that it is rational for individuals to agree to a constitution, to the specification of different decision-making rules for different classes of policy matters. The rational individual may well be willing to support a simple majoritarian rule for cases in which substantial issues are not at stake but insist on something more approximating a rule of unanimity for cases in which the costs to him of an adverse decision could turn out to be prohibitively high. In that latter category, they suggest, will be policy decisions that modify or restrict the structure of individual human and property rights:

The relevant point is that the individual will foresee that collective action in this area may possibly impose very severe costs on him. In such cases he will tend to place a high value on the attainment of his consent, and he may be quite willing to undergo substantial decision-making costs to insure that he will, in fact, be reasonably protected against confiscation.[41]

By extension, then, we may also suppose that in so far as persons would be willing to agree to the operation of a utilitarian sum-ranking rule, they will also find it prudent to exempt designated classes of policy decisions from

such a calculus. That is, they will regard the rule as appropriate to some policy issues and not for others. Roughly speaking, some version of a utilitarian
type sum-ranking rule might be selected as the appropriate rule for middle-
level decision-making, in which fundamental rights are not at issue in any
substantial way. In this case, we would expect a sufficiently large number
of more or less similar issues to be settled by the use of the rule—issues on
which a person's position is likely to be more or less randomly distributed,
and that, over the long run, things will balance out to the person's advantage. It might be argued that this argument invokes a level of uncertainty
comparable to that invoked by Rawls and Harsanyi and, as a consequence,
that it is subject to the same problem posed in Section 5, that is, how to
bridge the gap back to the real world. I would argue that the Buchanan and
Tullock argument presupposes a much more restricted and "realistic" level of
uncertainty, and one that does not pose this bridging problem.

If this argument is correct, then the utilitarian principle contributes to
a comprehensive approach to public policy, but the range of situations in
which it would be rational to employ the principle will be significantly limited. For this reason, it can hardly be taken, as many philosophers and some
economists have thought, as the fundamental principle for shaping social,
political, and economic policies. The last few decades have witnessed two
extraordinarily articulate and equally thoughtful presentations of the case
against the conception of an unlimited scope for a utilitarian principle, one
set forth by John Rawls and the other by Ronald Dworkin.[42] Many have read
the debate that followed the publication of Rawls's work and find the argument from behind the veil of ignorance is inconclusive. And, again, while
Dworkin's brief for a theory of rights that sets constraints on the operation
of a utilitarian principle is powerfully advocated, still his argument makes
altogether too much of an appeal to intuition.

The line of reasoning I have pursued, based on Buchanan and Tullock's
argument in *The Calculus of Consent*, offers an alternative, much more prag-
matic approach, and one that offers a more secure route to the conclusion
embraced by both Dworkin and Rawls. That is, it provides a ground for
Dworkin's intuitions about rights by appeal to a theory of rational, prudential choice; and it offers a way to reconstruct Rawls's argument from behind
the veil of ignorance so that, while it may not yield Rawls's theory of justice,

it still serves to effectively underline what he finds so worrisome about the utilitarian principle.

NOTES

I am especially grateful for helpful suggestions from Julian Lamont regarding the exposition of many points in the paper that formed the basis of this chapter.

1. D. Bernoulli, "Specimen theoreiae novae de mensura sortis," *Commentaarii academiae scientiarum imperialis Petropolitanae,* Vol. 5 (1738): 175–92. Translated into English by Louise Sommer as "Exposition of a New Theory on the Measurement of Risk," *Econometrica,* 22 (1954): 23–36.

3. J. Broome, *Weighing Goods: Equality, Uncertainty and Time* (Oxford: Basil Blackwell, 1991).

4. C. L. Stevenson, *Ethics and Language* (New Haven, Conn: Yale University Press, 1944).

5. L. Robbins, *An Essay on the Nature and Significance of Economic Science* (London: Macmillan, 1932).

6. A. Sen, "On Weights and Measures: Informational Constraints in Social Welfare Analysis," *Econometrica,* 45 (1977b): 1540–71.

7. This development can be traced back to W. V. Quine, "Two Dogmas of Empiricism," *Philosophical Review,* 60 (1951): 20–43. See, in particular, M. White, *Towards Reunion in Philosophy* (Cambridge, Mass: Harvard University Press, 1956), part III, esp. 254–58, 263, 266f; and also J. Rawls, "Outline of a Decision Procedure for Ethics," *Philosophical Review,* 60 (1951): 177–97; J. Rawls, *A Theory of Justice* (Cambridge, Mass: Harvard University Press, 1971), esp. 576–77.

8. See, for example, the many articles in *Interpersonal Comparisons of Well-Being,* eds. J. Elster and J. E. Roemer (Cambridge, England: Cambridge University Press, 1991).

9. The sense of this revived interest can be taken by consulting, for example, J. J. C. Smart and B. A. O. Williams, *Utilitarianism: For and Against* (Cambridge, England: Cambridge University Press, 1973); H. B. Miller and W. H. Williams, *The Limits of Utilitarianism* (Minneapolis: University of Minnesota Press, 1982); and A. Sen and B. Williams, *Utilitarianism and Beyond* (Cambridge, England: Cambridge University Press, 1982). The latter two also contain excellent bibliographies.

10. By far and away the most ambitious axiomatic defense of utilitarianism is to be found in J. Broome, *Weighing Goods.*

11. Extensive discussions of these issues, however, are to be found in A. Sen, *On Economic Inequality* (Oxford: Oxford University Press, 1973) and E. F. McClennen and P. Found, "Weighing Risk," *Journal of Social Philosophy,* 24 (1993): 155–75.

12. For a fuller discussion of the role of IIA in axiomatic decision theory, see E. F. McClennen, *Rationality and Dynamic Choice: Foundational Explorations* (Cambridge, England: Cambridge University Press, 1990), ch. 2.

13. The constructive results of particular relevance to the present discussion have their roots in a series of papers by P. J. Hammond, "Equity, Arrow's Conditions and Rawls' Difference Principle," *Econometrica,* 44 (1976): 793–800; C. d'Aspremont and L. Gevers, "Equity and the Informational Basis of Collective Choice," *Review of Economic Studies,* 44 (1977): 199–209; R. Deschamps and L. Gevers, "Leximin and Utilitarian Rules: A Joint Characterization," *Journal of Economic Theory,* 17 (1978): 143–63; and E. Maskin, "A Theorem on Utilitarianism," *Review of Economic Studies,* 45 (1978): 93–96. These results are summarized and analyzed in a most perspicacious manner in Sen, "On Weights and Measures." For the relevance of the independence axiom for the rival utilitarian and maximin principles, see also E. F. McClennen, "Constitutional Choice: Rawls vs. Harsanyi,"

in *Philosophy in Economics*, ed. J. Pitt (Dordrecht, Holland: D. Reidel Publishing Company, 1981): 93–109. For a masterful review of these, and more recent, constructions see also P. Mongin and C. d'Aspremont, "Utility Theory and Ethics," in *Handbook of Utility Theory*, eds. S. Barbera, P. J. Hammond, and C. Seidl (Dordrecht, Holland: Kluwer Academic Publishers, 1998), 373–481.

14. See Sen, "On Weights and Measures." For an extended discussion of all the different versions of independence that are invoked in the theory of choice under conditions of risk and uncertainty, see McClennen, *Rationality and Dynamic Choice*, chs. 3, 4.

15. J. Harsanyi, "Cardinal Utility in Welfare Economics and the Theory of Risk-Taking," *Journal of Political Economy*, 61 (1953): 434–35; and J. Harsanyi, "Cardinal Welfare, Individualistic Ethics, and Interpersonal Comparisons of Utility," *Journal of Political Economy*, 63 (1955): 309–21.

16. For a quite accessible discussion of a version of Harsanyi's construction, see R. D. Luce and H. Raiffa, *Games and Decisions* (New York: John Wiley & Sons, 1957), ch. 13.

17. E. Maskin, "A Theorem on Utilitarianism" and J. Harsanyi, "Nonlinear Social Welfare Functions: A Rejoinder to Professor Sen," *Foundational Problems in the Special Sciences*, ed. R. Butts, et al. (Dordrecht, Holland: D. Reidel Publishing Company, 1977).

18. See H. Rubin, "The Existence of Measurable Utility and Psychological Probability," Cowles Commission Discussion Paper, *Statistics*, No. 331. Unpublished (1949); H. Chernoff, "Rational Selection of a Decision Function," *Econometrica*, Vol. 22 (1954): 422–43; and J. Milnor, "Games against Nature," *Research Memorandum* RM-679 (Santa Monica: The RAND Corporation, 1951), reprinted in *Decision Processes*, ed. R. M. Thrall, C. H. Coombs, and R. L. Davis (New York: John Wiley & Sons, 1954), 49–60.

19. A summary of these early papers is to be found in Luce and Raiffa, *Games and Decisions*, ch. 13.

20. See here, in particular, L. J. Savage, *The Foundations of Statistics*, 1st ed. 1954, 2nd rev. ed. (New York: John Wiley & Sons, 1972); and E. J. Anscombe and R. J. Aumann, "A Definition of Subjective Probability," *Annals of Mathematical Statistics*, 34 (1963): 199–205.

21. D. Blackwell and M. A. Girshick, *Theory of Games and Statistical Decisions* (New York: John Wiley & Sons, 1954), sect. 4.3.

22. D. Krantz, et al., *Foundations of Measurement* (New York: Academic Press, 1971); S. S. Stevens, *Mathematics, Measurement, and Psychophysics: Handbook of Experimental Psychology* (New York: John Wiley & Sons, 1951).

23. Sen, "On Weights and Measures." For the role of continuity in expected-utility constructions, see M. Hausner, "Multidimensional Utilities," *Decision Processes*, ed. R. M. Thrall, et al. (New York: John Wiley & Sons, 1954); and J. S. Chipman, "Non-Archimedian Behavior Under Risk: an Elementary Analysis—with Applications to the Theory of Assets," *Preferences, Utility, and Demand*, ed. J. S. Chipman, et al. (New York: Harcourt Brace Jovanovich, 1971).

24. E. Malinvaud, "Note on von Neumann-Morgenstern's Strong Independence Axiom," *Econometrica*, 20 (1952): 679.

25. The literature on utility theory is filled with discussions of empirically documented violations of the independence axiom. See D. Kahneman and A. Tversky, "Prospect Theory: An Analysis of Decision under Risk," *Econometrica*, 47 (1979): 263–91; A. Tversky, "A Critique of Expected Utility Theory: Descriptive and Normative Considerations," *Erkenntnis*, 9 (1975): 163–73; A. Tversky and D. Kahneman, "The Framing of Decisions and the Psychology of Choice," *Science*, 211 (1981): 453–58. For a discussion of some stubborn counter-examples and why they should be taken seriously, see D. Ellsberg, "Risk, Ambiguity, and the Savage Axioms," *Quarterly Journal of Economics*, 75 (1961): 643–69; M. Allais and O. Hagen, *Expected Utility and the Allais Paradox* (Dordrecht, Holland: D. Reidel Publishing Company, 1979); M. Machina, "'Expected Utility' Analysis Without

The Independence Axiom," *Econometrica*, 50 (1982): 277–323; M. Machina, "Generalized Expected Utility Analysis and the Nature of Observed Violations of the Independence Axiom," in *Foundations of Utility and Risk Theory with Applications*, eds. B. P. Stigum and F. Winstop (Dordrecht, Holland: D. Reidel Publishing Company, 1983), 263–93; E. F. McClennen, "Sure-Thing Doubts," in *Foundations of Utility and Risk Theory with Applications*, eds. B. P. Stigum and F. Winstop (Dordrecht, Holland: D. Reidel Publishing Company, 1983), 117–36; E. F. McClennen, "Dynamic Choice and Rationality," *Risk, Decision and Rationality*, ed. B. R. Munier (Dordrecht, Holland: D. Reidel Publishing Company, 1988), 517–36; and McClennen, *Rationality and Dynamic Choice*.

26. A. S. Manne, "The Strong Independence Assumption—Gasoline Blends and Probability Mixtures," *Econometrica*, 20 (1952): 665–69.

27. P. Samuelson, "Probability, Utility and the Independence Axiom." *Econometrica*, 20 (1952): 672–73.

28. M. Friedman and L. J. Savage, "The Expected Utility Hypothesis and the Measurement of Utility," *Journal of Political Economy*, 60 (1952): 463–74.

29. Ellsberg, "Risk, Ambiguity, and the Savage Axioms."

30. See in particular M. Allais and O. Hagen, *Expected Utility*; McClennen, *Rationality and Dynamic Choice*, ch. 4.

31. M. Machina, "'Expected Utility' Analysis." The observation on the significance of Machina's work summarizes remarks made to this author by many decision-theorists, at a conference in Olso, Norway in 1982, at which Machina first presented his work.

32. L. Savage, *Foundations of Statistics*.

33. E. F. McClennen, *Rationality and Dynamic Choice*, ch. 4.

34. For a sampling, see P. A. Diamond, "Cardinal Welfare, Individualistic Ethics, and Interpersonal Comparisons of Utility: A Comment," *Journal of Political Economy*, 75 (1967): 765–66; Sen, *On Economic Inequality*; A. Sen, "Welfare Inequalities and Rawlsian Axiomatics," *Theory and Decision*, 7 (1976): 243–62; Sen, "Utilitarianism and Welfarism;" and McClennen, "Constitutional Choice."

35. J. Harsanyi, "Can the Maximum Principle Serve as the Basis for Morality? A Critique of John Rawls' Theory," *American Political Science Review*, 69 (1975): 594–606; "Nonlinear Social Welfare Functions: Do Welfare Economists Have a Special Exemption from Bayesian Rationality?" *Theory and Decision*, 6 (1976): 311–32; and "Bayesian Decision Theory and Utilitarian Ethics," *American Economic Review*, 68 (1977): 223–28.

36. A. Sen, "On Weights and Measures."

37. J. Rawls, *Theory of Justice*, ch. 3.

38. J. Rawls, "Kantian Constructivism in Moral Theory," *Journal of Philosophy*, 77 (1980): 515–73.

39. J. Buchanan and G. Tullock, *The Calculus of Consent* (Ann Arbor: University of Michigan Press, 1962), ch. 6.

40. Ibid., 78.

41. Ibid., 73–74.

42. J. Rawls, *Theory of Justice*, and R. Dworkin, *Taking Rights Seriously* (London: Duckworth, 1977).

CHAPTER 2

THE LIMITS OF *HOMO ECONOMICUS*

The Conflict of Values and Principles

Gerald Gaus

1. INTRODUCTION

James Buchanan has long insisted that *Homo Economicus* is a general model of rational action, applying, for example, to politics as well as economics. He challenges those who would restrict the application of *Homo Economicus* with the argument from symmetry. Along with Geoffrey Brennan, he writes:

The symmetry argument suggests only that whatever model of behavior is used, this model should be applied across all institutions. The argument insists that it is illegitimate to restrict *Homo Economicus* to the domain of market behavior while employing widely different models of behavior in nonmarket settings, without any explanation how such a behavioral shift comes about.[1]

In this chapter I argue that the economic model of human behavior is inappropriate to important parts of social and political life; I try to demonstrate that it is a special case of a more general account of rational action. As a special, or restricted, instance of the more general theory, it is useful in explaining actions in certain environments but misleading when applied in other situations. I do not offer a general critique; within its proper bounds, I believe *Homo Economicus* yields a variety of enlightening results. So my goal is not simply to point out where it fails, but also where it succeeds and what distinguishes the cases. If I do that—if I can offer a reasoned criterion for the limits of the economic model—then I will have replied to Buchanan's symmetry argument.

The argument proceeds in four parts. I begin by briefly explicating the idea of *Homo Economicus* and showing in what way it focuses on the choice among competing values. I then argue that, in addition to values or goals, almost all rational agents possess principles that are *distinct* from values or goals and are not reducible to them. Section 4 develops a model of the way in which rational agents trade off values and principles against each other, while Section 5 applies this model to market and nonmarket transactions.

2. THE ELEMENTS OF *HOMO ECONOMICUS*[2]

2.1. *Instrumental Rationality*

The core of the economic model is an instrumental theory of rationality. I shall follow Robert Nozick in taking the idea of goal pursuit as the core of instrumental rationality; as he observes, "it is natural to think of rationality as a goal-directed process." So according to the basic "instrumental conception, rationality consists in the effective and efficient achievement of goals, ends, and desires. About the goals themselves, an instrumental conception has little to say."[3]

Let us call the most obvious interpretation of instrumental rationality "rationality as effectiveness":

RE: Alf's action, ϕ, is instrumentally rational if and only if ϕ-ing is an effective way for Alf to achieve his goal, end, purpose, or value, V.

For simplicity's sake, I characterize RE as providing necessary and sufficient conditions for rational action, though this is implausible if we consider other options open to Alf. There may be some alternative action open to Alf that promotes a more important goal; in that case ϕ-ing would not be rational. I consider comparative assessments in Section 2.4.

At first glance RE appears innocuous enough, but it is both too narrow and too broad. To see how it is too narrow, suppose that Alf is a loyal viewer of the Weather Channel, which forecasts a clear day today. Alf, though, is very cautious, so he compares this with the forecasts from the National Weather Service and the local meteorologist, Sam the Smiling Weatherman. They concur; it is going to be a gorgeous day. On the basis of all this information, Alf goes out without an umbrella, gets soaked in a freak thunderstorm, ruins his best suit, and comes down with pneumonia. According to RE, Alf's decision not to carry an umbrella was not rational: It was anything but an effective way to achieve his goals. More generally, RE deems "not rational" any action that harms an agent's goals, no matter how diligent the agent was in getting information and hedging against risks. So any risky action—such as an investment—that turns out badly is not rational.

This judgment seems wrong. That a risky action turns out badly does not show that it was irrational. Whether it was irrational depends on, say, whether the agent took care to inform himself about the risk, whether he had adequate information, and so on. Rationality, including instrumental rationality, is a concept that relates to a person's cognitive processes, and so is not reducible to simple effectiveness. That this is so becomes clearer when we consider the way in which RE is too broad. Suppose that Betty never bothers with weather forecasts of any sort, but consults her horoscope. On the day that Alf gets soaked, Betty's horoscope instructed her to "prepare for an emotional flood." Betty took to heart this reference to flooding and wore a raincoat, thereby preparing for the freak storm. RE deems her action rational: After all, wearing the raincoat was an effective way to achieve her goal (of staying dry). But this really seems like a case of dumb luck, not instrumental rationality.

The inadequacies of rationality as effectiveness lead some philosophers to adopt a subjective test for effectiveness, as in subjective rationality:

SR: Betty's action, φ, is instrumentally rational if and only if, (1) given Betty's beliefs and (2) if these beliefs were true, then (3) φ-ing would be an effective way to promote her goal, end, purpose, or value, V.

SR can show that Alf was instrumentally rational when he got soaked despite all his precautions. But it also indicates that Betty was rational when she consulted her horoscope. According to SR, Betty would be instrumentally rational even on those days when she consults her horoscope and gets thoroughly soaked. After all, if her beliefs about the accuracy of horoscopes were true, then doing what they say would be an effective way to pursue her goals.

We could say more about these matters, but an account of instrumental rationality must include reference to the well-groundedness of the beliefs on which the agent acts.[4] Alf is instrumentally rational even though he fails to achieve his goals because the beliefs on which he acted were well grounded; Betty, even though she succeeds in achieving her goals, is not instrumentally rational because her beliefs are, from an epistemic point of view, terrible. An adequate characterization of instrumental rationality, then, must go something like this:

IR: Alf's action, φ, is instrumentally rational only if Alf soundly chooses φ because he believes it effectively promotes his goals, values, ends, and so on.

An agent who is instrumentally rational acts in light of his goals; the decision must be based on minimally sound beliefs (ones that are not grossly defective from an epistemic viewpoint), and the deliberation leading to action must not be grossly defective. For now, I shall employ the admittedly vague ideas of a "good reason" and a "sound choice" to cover these minimal epistemic requirements. For present purposes, abstract formulations are preferred to more definite ones. As my aim in this chapter is to show that *Homo Economicus* is a case of a more general theory of rational action, I wish to focus on its most abstract plausible formulation.

2.2. Consumption Rationality

It is tempting to characterize *Homo Economicus* simply in terms of instrumental rationality, and in Section 2.3 I argue that instrumental explanations are the preferred mode for *Homo Economicus*. But we cannot restrict *Homo Economicus* to instrumental reasons to act, for if we do, we cannot adequately explain consumption behavior. For example, Betty is eating ice cream, and she explains her behavior by proclaiming, "I like ice cream." A hedonist might explain Betty's action by saying that it was an instrumentally effective way of achieving pleasure. If pleasure is the sole end, and if human nature always results in the pursuit of pleasure and the avoidance of pain, then all action is instrumental to this end. Classical economists such as Nassau William Senior adopted this hedonistic criterion and acknowledged that wealth maximization as a value was derived from it. "Wealth and happiness," he observed, "are very seldom opposed."[5] But if we leave hedonism behind, this interpretation of Betty's ice cream eating loses plausibility. In general, consumption activity is noninstrumental: it does not seek to achieve some goal that is distinct from the consumption activity itself.

But this raises the specter of entirely vacuous explanations of people's actions. We see Betty φ-ing and we "explain" it by saying that "Betty likes φ-ing." If we then explain "likes" in terms of a feeling state, then the account would not be empty; but if we adopt a notion of revealed preference, explaining "likes φ-ing" as "is observed to φ," then our explanation takes this form:

Explanandum: (1) Betty φ-s.
Explanans: (2) Betty's reason for φ-ing is that she likes φ-ing.

The revealed preferences account of liking would then yield:

   (3) Betty φ-s because she is observed to φ.

This reasoning does not seem promising as a way to explain her action; the explanans is a restatement of the explanandum.

Although it is tempting to revert back to a thoroughly instrumentalist account of *Homo Economicus* and not worry about consumption, we can resolve the problem by an appeal to general dispositions. We can explain Betty's act, φ, (as opposed to merely restating it) if the act is an instance of a general disposition to φ, or engage in Phi-type acts—that is, a disposition to engage in actions of a given type.[6] Thus, for instance, when Betty explains eating ice cream by saying, "I like it," this counts as an explanation if Betty is generally disposed to eat ice cream. The explanation here is one of token and type, or specific instance and general kind. This explanation is not altogether empty. Consider:

Explanandum: (1) Betty φ-s.
Explanans: (2) Betty's reason for φ-ing (in this instance) is that she likes Phi-type acts.

The revealed preference account of liking would then yield:

> (3) Betty's reason for φ-ing (in this instance) is that she
> is observed to engage in Phi-type acts.

In this case, what is doing the explaining is not a restatement of the thing we need to explain; we explain the act by showing it is an instance of a general type. Again, one may be tempted to reduce this to an instrumental explanation: Betty φ-s as a way to bring about her goal of Phi-typing. But this really is to get the relation of the specific act and the general type wrong: φ-ing is not a means to Phi-type acts, it is an instance of it.

We can therefore complement the idea of instrumental rationality with that of consumption rationality:

CR: Betty's action, φ, is consumptively rational only if it is an instance of Phi-type activity, a general value or end of hers.

If we wish to be careful, we might say: Betty's action, φ, is consumptively rational only if she soundly believes it to be an instance of some general valuing of hers. But the epistemic considerations that are important in evaluating instrumental rationality do not seem to pose much of problem for consumption. For simplicity's sake, I will leave them aside.

Let us now combine IR and CR for a preliminary account of economic rationality:

ER: Charlie's action, φ, is economically rational only if it is (a) instrumentally rational or (b) consumptively rational.

Note that ER provides necessary but not sufficient conditions for economic rationality. It does not, for example, determine what is economically rational for Charlie to do if he must choose, say, between two consumptively rational acts—Phi and Chi. We shall turn to that problem in Section 2.4.

2.3 Instrumentalism as the Preferred Explanation

Although the full explication of *Homo Economicus* must allow for both instrumental and consumption rationality, its power and persuasiveness stems from instrumental explanations. *Homo Economicus* rests much of its claim to our allegiance on the "almost unbelievable delicacy and subtlety"[7] of its analysis of the market. And this analysis shows that individuals with diverse preferences engage in some kinds of economic activity because they believe that such activity is instrumentally effective in achieving their values. For instance, the economic model can explain the choice of medicine as a career by citing relative costs of training, opportunity costs, and so on, and showing how occupational choices are instrumentally rational in achieving an agent's ends. For some economists, the crux of the economic model is to explain how different actions in different situations are instrumentally rational to satisfying a stable set of preferences.[8] Choices, such as the choice of an occupation, are ways of achieving the satisfaction of a stable set of preferences in different circumstances. Such economists, then, would not explain occupational choice by appeal to a brute preference (say, to be a doctor) but, instead, as a way to satisfy one's stable preferences for income and prestige given one's opportunity costs.

However, note that citing the brute preferences of people to be doctors does not abandon the notion of economic rationality: After all, people must have brute preferences if the economic model is to work. But direct appeal to a preference to Phi-type as a way to explain φ-ing is not the preferred mode of economic explanation. We might say that it is an explanation of the last resort, for while it is not empty, it does not explain as much. The preferred explanation is to show that action φ is instrumentally rational for agents with a wide variety of preferences, preferences that are not directly about the merits of φ-ing. Thus, the tendency I cited previously to identify *Homo Economicus* with instrumental rationality is not entirely off the mark: Although economically rational agents have access to other reasons besides instrumental ones, *Homo Economicus*, as a model of rational action, prefers explanations in terms of instrumental rationality.

2.4 Four Fundamental Features of Economic Rationality

We can identify four further features of economic rationality.

More is better than less. (F1) Faced with a choice between quantity p of value V and quantity q, where $p > q$, a rational agent almost always has reason to act to obtain pV instead of qV. Feature 1 is fairly straightforward: For almost any value or goal, given the option between satisfying it to a lesser and a greater degree, an economically rational agent will choose to satisfy it to a greater degree. If we interpret the value V as "utility" or even "happiness" then F1 is true without exception. But when we consider more specific goods, we can discover anomalies. Some values or goals manifest satiation; the goal of eating a big steak, for example, reaches satiation at some level of fulfillment; most of us prefer a two-pound to a ten-pound steak for dinner. In this case, if we redefine our goal in terms of, say, pleasure or satisfaction, then the anomaly disappears, for the bigger steak does not, presumably, bring about more pleasure. Although we need not adopt hedonism, it probably is the case that goal rationality conforms to F1 far better when we understand values not as specific goods, but as more abstract aims, ends, and states of being. But even if values are understood as specific goods, it will generally be the case that a value-pursuing agent does not have a hard time deciding whether to opt for more or less of a good. If the value is understood in terms of specific goods, lumpiness can also be a problem; it may well be that we only have use for value V in some "lumpy" increments, and an extra amount that does not get us to the next increment is of no use.

Decreasing marginal reasons. (F2) Reasons to obtain more of a value or goal increase (as stated by F1) as the amount of the value or goal achieved increases, but the rate of increase diminishes from the nth to the $n+1$ unit of a value. The justification for this feature will differ depending on the theory of value. A subjective theory of value, for instance, might claim that as V increases from the n to the $n+1$ unit, the rate of increased satisfaction slows as we obtain more of the value. I will avoid commitment to a specific account of value; for a theory of rationality, the important point is that other things being equal, a person's reason to ϕ increases as the amount of V achieved by ϕ increases (F1), but this rate of increase slows down as the person achieves more of the value (F2). I will treat decreasing marginal reasons as an empirical generalization instead of as a law.[9] Nevertheless, it seems to characterize almost all our values or goals. Suppose, for example, that the goal is to become rich and famous. Although there is always some reason to choose being yet richer and more famous (F1), when a person has become extremely rich and extremely famous, the reasons to seek yet more are going to be pretty weak. If someone seeks riches simply as a sign of status, and he is the richest person around, then that person will seek more and more riches as others begin to catch up. Here the value sought is status, a good that is easy to lose. But even status is subject to F2; if one has it and is not in danger of losing it, one's efforts are apt to switch to the pursuit of other values. Again, we can imagine anomalous cases where people not only "cannot get enough," in the sense they are not satiated (which is consistent with F1), but whose reasons to pursue a value or goal are just as strong no matter how much of it they obtain. However, cases like this often suggest an alternate explanation in terms of neurotic instead of effective instrumental behavior; someone who cannot get enough in this sense may be looking for satisfaction where it is not to be found and thus his seeming obsession may well be an indication that he is not really achieving his value at all.[10]

Completeness of Goal Comparisons. (F3) Fully economically rational individuals possess a system of trade-off rates between all their values or bundles of values. They are always able to determine whether q amount of V_1 is better than, worse than, or just as good as, p amount of V_2. This is equivalent to the standard requirement in decision theory that one completely ranks one's preferences.

"Downward sloping demand curves." (F4) Given F3, as the cost of V_1 (in terms of V_2) increases, economically rational agents have less reason to undertake acts seeking to bring about V_1. This is one way to interpret the idea that the demand curve for V is downward sloping.[11] (This feature is distinct from F2. According to decreasing marginal reasons, if we hold constant the cost of obtaining V, our reason to secure it decreases as we obtain higher levels; according to F4, holding constant the level of V, our reasons for pursuing it decrease as the cost of obtaining it rises.) A rational agent, then, not only is able to resolve conflicts between his ends, but also must do so through a system of trade-off rates (a utility function)[12] according to which the "demand" for a value/goal/end decreases as its cost relative to other values/goals/ends increases. Again, anomalous cases occur, as with Giffen goods, for which demand increases as their costs rises. As Robert Giffen pointed out, when the price of bread rises, the very poor may purchase more of it; the increase in the price of bread has a significant effect on the poor person's real income, causing them to substitute bread for more expensive foods they can no longer

afford, thus increasing the total amount of bread they consume. Status goods also are exceptions to downward sloping demand—if they do not cost a great deal, they do not serve their purpose of showing that you can afford them.

2.5. Are Economic Agents Egoistic?

Geoffrey Brennan and Loren Lomasky insist that economically rational agents are egoists.[13] And it is correct that the core of the "economic approach" to society has been the explanatory power of self-interest.[14] It is precisely this aspect of *Homo Economicus* that has attracted so much criticism from social scientists resisting the economic approach.[15] It remains, though, a matter of dispute whether the assumption of egoism is basic to the economic conception of rationality or whether it is a simplifying assumption that allows for more determinate applications of the model. The latter, I think, is plausible. Philip Wicksteed is quite right that "[t]he specific character of an economic relation is not its 'egoism,' but its non-tuism."[16] That each party to an economic relation is seeking to advance his or her own values and not the values of the other party is certainly fundamental; economics is not a study of transactions among altruists, but of non-tuists. But the idea of a market transaction does not require us to suppose that the values of the agents are egoistic, though we may well find that supposing egoism is necessary to get very far in developing some economic models.

As I have stated, my concern is to show that even a broad understanding of *Homo Economicus* is too narrow. If *Homo Economicus* is always an egoist, not to mention a personal wealth maximizer, it is even narrower than I take it to be, thus reinforcing my thesis.

3. REASONS OF FIDELITY

3.1 Do Instrumental and Consumption Reasons Exhaust Rationality?

Given our broad characterization of economic rationality, it may seem inconceivable that an act could be rational and yet not economically rational. Consider the paradigm of a supposedly non-economically rational act: acting according to duty. Suppose a Kantian argues that Betty has a reason to ϕ in circumstances C simply because there is a justified moral principle P, such that P requires ϕ-ing in C. This action may seem genuinely non-economic.

But once we have rejected the narrow interpretations of economic rationality as egoistic or simply instrumental, this also appears economic. Recall our characterization of consumption rationality:

CR: Betty's action, ф, is consumptively rational only if it is an instance of a general value or end of hers.

So a Kantian Betty has a general valuing of, or preference for, acting on P, and ф is an instance of this preference. The dutiful act appears to be simply "moral consumption."

I have stressed that CR only provides a necessary condition for consumption rationality; Features 1–4 (§2.4) are necessary, too. Most analyses of dutiful action fail to meet F1. If duties are what Robert Nozick calls "side constraints," people can have a conclusive duty-based reason to ф today, even if that means the ability to ф in the future will be seriously impaired.[17] Thus, Nozick indicates, if you have a duty to respect the rights of another, this gives you a reason to respect those rights, even if you know that it means in the future you will not be able to respect such rights. A variety of stories are constructed to show how this could be the case; let us begin with a real case to develop the point.

3.2 Lewis's Reluctant Judgment

Consider the reluctant judgment of Lewis J. in the case of *Daniels and Daniels v. White & Sons and Tarbard*.[18] In this case, Mr. Daniels purchased a bottle of *R. White's Lemonade* at Mrs. Tarbard's pub. Taking it home, he and his wife had a glass, and both became ill. Carbolic acid, as it turned out, had contaminated the lemonade, and the Daniels sued both the manufacturer and the publican. Lewis J. concluded that the law was such that the manufacturer was not liable, but Mrs. Tarbard was, despite the fact she was entirely faultless. Mr. Daniels asked her for a bottle of *R. White's Lemonade*, and that was precisely what she gave him. Lewis J. thus summed up:

I therefore find that this was a sale by description, and therefore hold—with some regret, because it is rather hard on Mrs. Tabard, who is a perfectly innocent person in the matter—that she is liable for the injury sustained by Mrs. Daniels through drinking this bottle of lemonade. However, that as I understand it, is the law, and therefore I think that there must be a judgment for Mr. Daniels.[19]

Lewis J.'s reason for the judgment is that, as he understands it, the law requires it. Lewis concluded he "must" direct Mrs. Tarbard to pay because "it is the law." The law requires it. And there is nothing unusual about this kind of claim. In a wide variety of legal and moral contexts, people claim that they act in a given way because a norm requires it.[20] As H. L. A. Hart stresses, "[i]n any large group general rules, standards and principles" are the primary mode of regulating social life; the rules identify general classes of action and require or prohibit acts falling under these general descriptions.[21] I will call this a reason of fidelity:

RF: Doris has a reason of fidelity to (or not to) φ if (1): she accepts some norm, principle or rule R; (2) R requires (or prohibits) Phi-type acts; (3) φ is an instance of Phi-type acts.

This characterization of reasons of fidelity highlights three features of rule following. First, an account of rational rule following must clarify what is meant by embracing or internalizing a norm or a rule, a phenomenon that sociologists and psychologists have studied.[22] Rule rationality is not simply behavior in conformity to rules; it is action performed because rules are accepted. Second, rules are generalizations that identify types of actions;[23] because of this, third, an act required (or prohibited) by a rule stands to the rule in something like a token-to-type relation; to φ because of a rule is to do it because it instantiates Phi-type, that is, it is an instance of it.[24]

Recall that the notion of a token-to-type relation was basic to the notion of consumption rationality (§2.2). We can explain an act of consumption by showing that it instantiates a disposition to consume some type of thing. It might appear then, that we can understand Lewis's decision as act of "judicial consumption": Lewis values acting on general principle P and his finding here is an instance of that valuing. But this appears to be the wrong analysis. Suppose that Lewis knew that he would be removed from the bench for this unpopular and in many ways unjust decision. If that occurred, his future ability to act on P would be greatly impaired. If his action here is a simple act of economic consumption, F1—more is better than less—would indicate that he should forgo consumption in this case in order to allow him opportunity for consumption in the future. But if we presented this argument to Lewis as a reason to change his opinion, he would understandably conclude that we had no idea what principled judicial reasoning was all about. Whether he

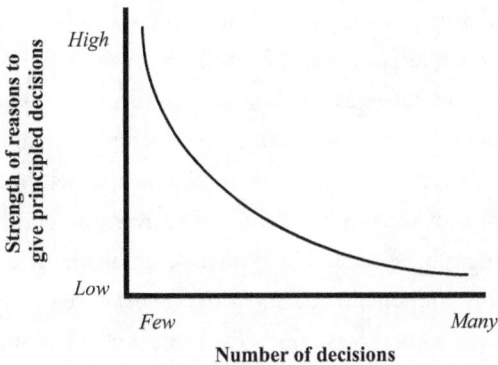

FIGURE 2.1. Marginal decreasing reasons applied to principles.

would face removal from the bench has nothing to do with whether he has a reason to find for Mr. Tabard.

We also should note that F2 (§2.4) does not characterize Lewis's judgment: Lewis's reason to act on principles does not decline as his "consumption" of principled action increases. If Lewis's action was a mere act of consumption rationality, it ought to be the case that his reasons for further consumption are marginally decreasing: He should have less additional reason to make the nth+1 principled decision than he had to make the nth. As Figure 2.1 indicates, if consumption rationality was the right explanation for judicial behavior, a judge who made many principled decisions should have very little reason to make yet another.

3.3. Economic Analyses of Reasons of Fidelity

What else might an advocate of *Homo Economicus* say about reasons of fidelity? Let me very briefly comment on several familiar strategies, and say a word about why I think they are either mistaken or, at best, implausible.

The first, and I suppose most straightforward, response is simply to insist that so-called reasons of fidelity are never reasons at all; only some sort of rule-worshiping confusion would make us think "The rule required it" could be a reason for action. Some may say this, but the theory of practical rationality underlying such a sweeping claim would be highly revisionary. I do not want to claim we must reject highly revisionary theories of practices out of hand, but it does seem there is a strong presumption against them. If a theory of practical reason tells us that so much of what we take as central to reason-giving is simply wrong-headed, it does not really enlighten us about our existing practices. In any event, I think that economic theories of reasoning rarely depict themselves as revolutionary in this way; instead, they depict themselves as powerful explications of current practices. And if the advocates of purely value-driven reasoning wish to defend this self-image, they must give some account of reasons of fidelity. Moreover, the sensibility of token-to-type reasoning is presupposed by economic rationality itself (§2.2).

Second, many proponents of *Homo Economicus* seek to ground reasons of fidelity on instrumental reasoning. The most obvious tack is to claim that all norms are what J. S. Mill called "rules of art."[25] Mill held that an "art" proposes an end or value, and then searches for means to achieve it. Science helps the art by considering what combination of circumstances is required to produce the end. If the art finds these conditions practical, it converts the advice of science into a rule. But Mill insisted that such rules always admit of exceptions. A "practitioner, who goes by rules rather than their reasons . . . is rightly judged to be a mere pedant, and the slave of his formulas."[26] On such a view, Lewis J. would seem liable to the charge of pedantry: He acknowledges that his judgment against Mrs. Tabard is "rather hard" since she is a "perfectly innocent person in the matter" yet he insists that the judgment must be given because it is required by the law. On almost any plausible analysis of the point of legal rules—be it justice, predictability, coordination, promotion of the general welfare, or whatever—holding Mrs. Tabard liable seems inconsistent with that end. Yet it is implausible to insist that in such a case Lewis J. had no reason at all to find against Mrs. Tabard. After all, the law required it.

Even a moderately gifted economic theorist can concoct all sorts of other, more idiosyncratic values that Lewis may have been pursuing. Perhaps Lewis values being a good judge, and a good judge must find against Mrs. Tabard. So reasons of fidelity are, after all, instrumental—they are ways of being a good judge. I think we should be cautious about accepting this type of account—whether Lewis valued being a good judge or not is quite irrelevant to whether he has a reason to find against Mrs. Tabard just because it is the law. I have to confess that this sort of account strikes me as getting things precisely backwards. Jurisprudential goodness just is acting on reasons of fidelity—to know what a good judge is, we must know what a reason of fidelity is. Reasons of fidelity thus seem logically prior to the notion of a good judge; they cannot, then, be instruments to achieving the value of judicial excellence. Saying that acting on such reasons is an instrument to achieving the value of being a good judge is akin to claiming that recognizing a reason to tell the truth is a means to veracity.

At this point a sort of Humean line is possible: Unless Lewis had a desire to apply the law in this case, he simply could not have had a reason to do so. Thus, insofar as every act aims at satisfying a desire, all action is instrumental. Or, to be bald, if Lewis did it, he must have had a preference to do it, so it did satisfy an end after all. I have elsewhere argued against this theory, and I will not say much here. [27] But note that this account does not conform to our analysis of consumption rationality: An act, ϕ, can be explained as rational consumption only if it obtains a value that is distinct from ϕ-ing. If Lewis's action was instrumental because he had a desire (goal) of so acting, it fails to meet the distinctness requirement.

Finally, we could simply reply that Lewis had a disposition to give rule-worshiping decisions: He valued them. This would meet the requirements of consumptive rationality. But then we meet the problem of Lewis insisting that he has a reason to find against Mrs. Tabard even if this means his removal from the bench, and so impairs his future ability to act on this disposition. According to FI (§2.4), this would be an economically irrational consumption decision; but it appears to be a reasonable judicial attitude.

3.4 Another Reason for Resisting the Reduction of Fidelity to Economic Rationality

I do not suppose that this quick review of several familiar attempts to reduce reasons of fidelity to instrumental considerations is decisive; much more can, and has been, said, and theorists could advance even more ingenious proposals.[28] A paradigm such as *Homo Economicus* can account for just about any phenomenon if it is willing to add enough epicycles. In the remainder of this chapter I wish to take a different approach. As I have said, much of the attraction of *Homo Economicus* stems from its great success in explaining market behavior. On the other hand, in several areas central to politics and ethics—especially those that raise free-rider issues—it has led to seemingly intractable problems. What I wish to suggest here is that a broader conception of practical rationality—one that admits reasons of fidelity as independent reasons for actions—can preserve the insights of a *Homo Economicus*-based analysis of the market while permitting progress on these other problems. That is, I argue that several persistent puzzles in ethics and social theory dissolve if we resist the attempt of *Homo Economicus* to reduce all rationality to economic rationality.

4. TRADING OFF VALUES AND PRINCIPLES

4.1 The Conflict of Principles and Values

Before turning to the explanatory power of a broader conception of practical rationality, we need first to consider its major drawback: It not only has to handle, as does *Homo Economicus,* the conflict of values (or goals), but it also must make sense of the conflict of principles with each other, and the clash of principles and values. However, as Stanley Benn showed, these conflicts can be analyzed by employing the same apparatus that *Homo Economicus* utilizes for trading off values against each other.[29] Economically rational agents, we saw above, must have a system of trade-off rates such that they are always able to determine whether q amount of V_1 is better than, worse than, or just as good as p amount of V_2 (F3, §2.4). Benn applied the same analysis to a conflict of principles. His preferred example was the case of Lucius Junius Brutus, who acted in accordance with his civic duty and so sentenced his sons to death. Let us understand this as a conflict between reasons of fidelity (to the duties of his judicial office) and his valuing the welfare and happiness of his family. Benn stressed that even though in this critical case (let us call it Case 1) Brutus acted on his judicial reasons instead of on his family values, it does not follow that a rational Brutus must do so in every case of conflict. For just as the family values may be either marginally or critically affected in a given situation—the "amount" of the good to be had may vary—so too principles are implicated to different degrees in different situations. For example, Benn considers another possible situation in which Brutus's judicial principles and family concerns may clash. According to Case 2, on his way to a Senate Committee meeting, Brutus sees that one of his sons (not a rebellious one) is drowning in the Tiber and needs his assistance. If he saves his son, Brutus will be late. As Benn observes, Brutus may take an "ultra-Kantian view, that since his reason for [consular] action is that it is a duty and not, for example, a consequentially valuable action, any dereliction would be just as bad as any other."[30] But, as Benn says, "this would be an extreme and somewhat austere judgment."[31] In this second case, Brutus may well choose to save his son instead of act on his consular duty. And he need not be open to the charge of inconsistency. Instead, in the second situation, the consular commitments are less "at stake" than in the first, historically famous, case. Brutus may reasonably hold that a consul who ignores proof of guilt and lets his sons go free would demonstrate contempt for judicial principles, whereas being late for a meeting to save a son is a minor infraction, one that is consistent with taking principles seriously.

We thus can analyze Brutus's various judgments in terms of trade-off rates. In a conflict between Principle P and Value V, Brutus's choice will depend on two variables: (1) how weighty, in his system of beliefs, principles, and values P and V are and (2) to what extent, in any situation, P and V are at stake. This second factor, salience, can vary for two different reasons. First, though the goal or rule may be relevant, it might be uncertain which action is called for. Consider H. L. A. Hart's famous example of a rule that forbids vehicles in a park. Even if a bicycle rider places great weight on this rule, if she is uncertain whether it applies to bicycles, the rule will be less salient for her than in cases where its requirements are clear. The same can apply to the pursuit of a value; no matter how important a value is, if we cannot decide which of two alternative actions better promotes the value, it will not be salient in the choice. A second type of variation in salience occurs in cases where a goal or rule is relevant, and we know how an action impacts on it, but the extent of this impact is modest. Brutus, for example, may know that it his civic duty to attend consul meetings, and he also knows that saving his son from drowning will definitely impact that duty by making him late; but being five minutes late for a meeting does not have a significant impact on his duty, so the demands of duty will be less salient in his decision. We can also say that as the cost of procuring P in terms of V forgone increases, Brutus's "demand" for P—his propensity to act on P—will decrease (and the same applies to V relative to P). This is a simplification. Thresholds are possible, in which no matter what the costs in terms of V, Brutus demands a minimum satisfaction of P. A more careful formulation would be that, as the

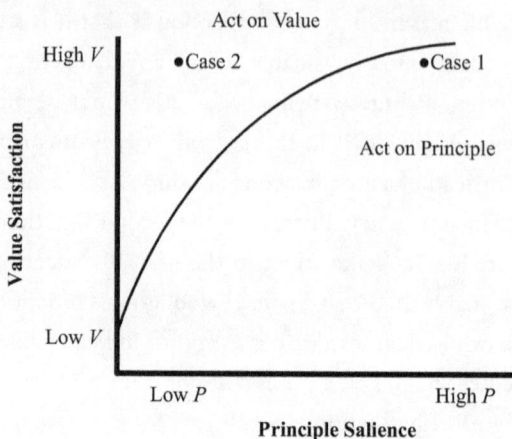

FIGURE 2.2.   Principle-value trade-offs.

costs of procuring satisfaction of P in terms of forgone V increases, the demand for P will never increase and will typically decrease. I will not pursue
that complication here.

Figure 2.2 depicts Brutus's trade-off rates. ("High P" signifies that principle P is greatly at stake, "Low P" that it is not much at stake. Similarly
for "High" and "Low" V.) As depicted in the account of the Roman his-
torian, Livy, Brutus heavily favors reasons of fidelity over family values; he
only begins to take family values seriously once reasons of fidelity are not
much at stake. In the area below the curve Brutus resolves conflicts of the
principle and value in favor of the principle, while in the area above he acts
on the value instead of the principle. We thus see that even Brutus, who is so
strongly committed to reasons of fidelity can, given his trade-off rate, consistently act to save his son and ignore his consular reasons in Case 2, while in
Case 1 condemning his sons because it is demanded by reasons of fidelity.

This analysis suggests that measuring personal consistency in decision-
making is apt to be more difficult than personality theorists have sometimes
thought. Students of personality have long sought to measure personality
traits such as "honesty," for example in measuring children's resistance to
theft or lying. As is well known, considerable controversy exists as to whether
such personality traits allow prediction from one situation to the next; some
have insisted that they have very low predictive value.[32] We can now see,
though, that Brutus may act consistently even though sometimes he chooses

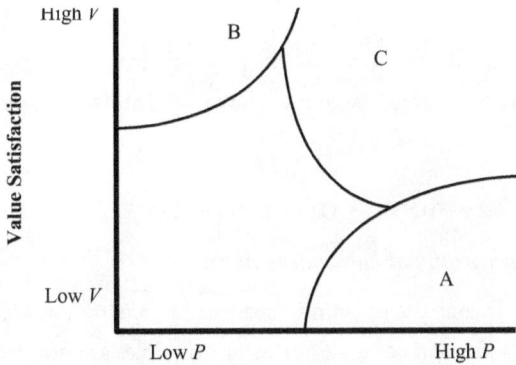

FIGURE 2.3.   Three trade-off areas.

to save his sons while at other times he condemns them. And even when the same principle/value conflict occurs, behavioral "inconsistency" can emanate from consistent trade-off rates.

4.2 The Notion of a Typical Agent

Few people will have trade-off rates similar to those of Brutus. Many would consider his decision to condemn his sons as giving too much weight to consular reasons. And, in a similar vein, some would insist that Lewis J. gives too much weight to reasons of fidelity in finding against Mrs. Tabard, even though she is obviously and entirely innocent in the matter. Most of us lie somewhere between Brutus and Kant, who rarely are willing to trade principles to obtain values, and *Homo Economicus*, who only acts on values.

Suppose we were trying to construct a trade-off rate between a principle and a value for an average or typical agent. Is there anything that we could confidently predict? I believe so. In two areas we could predict a person's trade-off rate with a high degree of confidence: (A) conflicts between a principle that is greatly at stake and a value that is not significantly implicated; (B) situations in which a conflict occurs between a value that is importantly at stake and a principle that is not sufficiently implicated. In such "low/high" conflicts we would expect a reasonable agent to act on what is crucially at stake and bear the small cost of forgoing what is not crucially at stake. Figure 2.3, then, identifies these two areas (A and B) plus a third.

In area B it appears that the typical agent will act to pursue his or her values. The principle is not significantly at stake, while the value is crucially involved. Area A is the opposite case; here we can predict with considerable confidence that an agent will act on the principle instead of the value. Area C is much more complicated; I will say a few words about it before I close.

5. THREE SUB-MODELS OF RATIONALITY

5.1 The Proper Realm of Homo Economicus

My hypothesis is that the economic model of behavior is most enlightening when, in the agent's perceptions, norms or principles are not deeply involved, but values (goals, aims, etc.) are (area B). This, after all, is the standard case with consumer behavior. Typically, though by no means always, consumers act to pursue their values, and they do not typically see principles as relevant. They are relevant as background conditions, as classical economics well recognized. Laws of property and rules against fraud are crucial to the normative background. But if we wish to explain the behavior of consumers against such a background—that is, we suppose that people are honoring the background principles—we can assume that consumers reason purely as economic agents. Many actions other than consumer behavior fit this pattern as well. The everyday coordination problem of what side of the road to drive on is another example: Here we all are pursuing our values, with very little of our action guided by reasons of fidelity. My hypothesis, then, is that these are the cases where we can expect the economic approach to behavior to be most enlightening.

5.2 Homo Ethicus

5.2.1 Instrumentalist Analyses of Voting. In his *Economic Theory of Democracy,* Anthony Downs sought to apply *Homo Economicus* to political behavior, to explain why people voted in some ways, and why some configurations of political parties resulted.[33] This was highly controversial in democratic theory: It seemed to reduce what John Stuart Mill saw as a public-spirited, educational experience into something akin to shopping at Kmart. But putting that aside, if we focus on Downs's own theory, we see that though he did advance an elegant and, in my mind, enlightening account of why, once in the voting booth, people marked their ballots in one way instead of another, he had tremendous difficulty accounting for their being in the voting booth at all. The problem is that, based on instrumental theory, voting is almost surely an irrational act when there is no penalty for not voting. It costs to vote. It costs in terms of time and acquiring information. Sometimes it costs because you will get wet on a rainy day. These costs may appear so small that they could not possibly make a difference; how much cost is involved in missing fifteen minutes of TV, getting into the car, and going out to vote? Although these costs are very low, they are not so small as are the expected returns from voting. Even if it matters to you a great deal who wins the election, the probability that your vote will make a difference is so minute that it is almost impossible to appreciably advance your values by voting. As Brennan and Lomasky demonstrate in their work on democratic theory, "The chance of one's own vote being decisive in a large election is vanishingly small. This means that the expected payoff . . . is also minute."[34]

Some say that this argument does not demonstrate that voting is instrumentally irrational, only that voters must have some very odd beliefs. Voters, for example, may drastically overestimate the effect of their votes or somehow assume that if they do not vote, it will causally affect others in a way that no one else will vote. So, at best Brennan and Lomasky's argument could only show that voters with completely sound beliefs would not vote. But we rejected the subjective theory of instrumental rationality in Section 2.1: Voters impugn their rationality when they act on very odd beliefs and resist the correct ones when informed of them. The analysis of the market does not presuppose all sorts of odd beliefs on the part of consumers, but judges consumers to be fairly good at getting information and properly responding to it. But, on some views, when these consumers enter politics, they suddenly lose their ability to form sound beliefs. If they do so, I have argued, they are not instrumentally rational.

Neither can the instrumental rationality of voters be defended by pointing out that, as a whole, those who participate in politics have their interests better protected than those who do not. The conception of instrumental rationality as mere effectiveness did not pay sufficient attention to the beliefs on which the agent is acting. Given IR, it appears impossible to avoid the conclusion that voters are not instrumentally rational.

This is but a single example of an entire class of problems, often called

Others ⟶ You ↘	Vote	Not Vote
Vote	Your candidate is elected; you pay.	Your candidate is not elected; you pay.
Not Vote	Your candidate is elected; you do not pay.	Your candidate is not elected; you do not pay.

FIGURE 2.4.   A voter's dilemma.

public goods problems. In order to stress the strategic nature of public goods interactions, public choice theorists often employ the language of games. As in a game, your best move typically depends on my best move, and vice versa. Figure 2.4 provides the matrix for the famous Prisoner's Dilemma game, which could characterize the decision whether to vote.

You can imagine that you are playing a game against all other voters. Again, this supposes no penalty for failing to vote. Because it is so vanishingly small, I leave out of account the minute probability that your vote will be the decisive ballot.

Now, as an instrumentally rational person, you are trying to figure out what to do, given what others do. First suppose that enough others do vote for your candidate. Well, if you vote, your candidate wins though you had to pay a very small cost. Suppose that you did not vote; if enough others vote, then your candidate still wins, so you get your result for free. If you are instrumentally rational, then, you will not vote if enough others vote for your candidate. What if enough others do not vote for your candidate? Well, if you vote, then you pay the cost and do not receive any benefit; if you had stayed home, you would not have incurred any costs. So, if not enough others vote for your candidate, then you should not vote. We can see that no matter what other people do, you should not vote if your vote is not the decisive vote. And since it is wildly improbable that your vote will be decisive, you should not vote. But, and here is the rub, if everyone reasons like this, no one will vote. Perfectly rational instrumental agents, all deciding where their own interests lie, will fail to secure the public good.

5.2.2 The Backup Explanation: Voting As Consumption. If this discussion seems terribly familiar, that is because it has fueled something of an industry in offering solutions or explaining why it is not really a problem.[35] What I wish to stress here is that the rationality of such low-cost cooperative action remains a puzzle to theorists who rely on instrumental rationality. Perhaps, then, the problem is that voting has been analyzed as instrumentally rational instead of as a consumption activity. If voting is a consumption activity, it still falls under the economic model of rationality, though such explanations are not in the preferred, instrumentalist, mode.

Geoffrey Brennan and Loren Lomasky have offered such an analysis, distinguishing instrumental from expressive behavior. Their model of expressive behavior is a fan at a ball game. "The fan's actions," they stress, "are purely expressive. Revealing a preference is a direct consumption activity, yielding benefits to the individuals in and of itself."[36] Expressive reasons are genuinely non-instrumental, though they are certainly not reasons of fidelity. Voting is a consumption activity that directly yields benefits.

Although their attempt to apply the economic model in this way leads, as we shall see, to some real insights, on the face of it voting does not seem a case of consumption behavior. Over a wide range, consumers prefer more and not less of a good. Although, given marginal decreasing utility, the demand for a good decreases the more one has of it, voting appears to have a very odd demand curve. In parliamentary systems where governments decide when to call an election, for example, governments may be "punished" for calling an early election, even by just a year. Now in Brennan and Lomasky's view this reaction is puzzling. As they see it, those who vote are those who enjoy voting for their "team"—they are already a self-selecting set of citizens who have a pretty high demand for expressing their attitudes through voting. It would seem that, if anything, they should reward governments for frequent elections, since they enjoy voting and they can distribute the costs of elections over the whole population, subsidizing their consumption.

Much the same applies to other low-cost cooperative activity. We may recycle our used soda cans at some cost to ourselves, but it is not at all obvious that recycling is a consumption activity. Perhaps to some it is. Many of us recycle, though, but are only too happy to avoid it, and would be happy if we never had to again. If so, it is a strange consumption good—one that we cannot get too little of.

5.2.3 Fidelity and Voting. My proposal is that in these cases, significant reasons of fidelity confront actors, and these can be satisfied at quite modest costs to their values (Figure 2.3, area A). For the most part their values are not really relevant as costs are minute. But, although their values are not really relevant, reasons of fidelity are: The requirements of civic duty and citizenship, a commitment to the best candidate, or devotion to your ideology seem manifestly relevant. In these cases we should expect compliance with principles or norms despite its economic irrationality. Note that I am not claiming that voting is an effective way to further good citizenship or even secure the election of the better candidate. It is not. But, like Lewis, many believe that their political commitments require that they vote, and that is their reason for it. And small costs plus high relevance of principle makes for compliance. As long as we insist on applying the economic model to such cases, however, this very modest public-spirited behavior will seem anomalous.

5.2.4 Decisiveness and Non-Instrumental Action. Although I am skeptical of Brennan and Lomasky's claim that voting is a type of consumption behavior, their analysis points to when we can expect people to act on instrumental reasons and when we can expect them to act on non-instrumental reasons. They write:

The relative price of expressive elements in any act of choice, measured in terms of instrumental benefits forgone, is higher in markets than in electoral settings. As we move from the marketplace to the ballot box, all other things equal, the relative significance of expressive elements increases by a factor equal to the inverse of the probability of being decisive.[37]

The idea of decisiveness is fundamental to their analysis. In the market, a person is typically decisive in the sense that the choice to act to obtain V_1 entails forgoing V_2. In the market, I am decisive in the sense that if I buy a computer, I obtain it, but I also forgo the opportunity to use that money to go on a vacation. But Brennan and Lomasky stress that this is not the case in voting. I might really think that my values would fare much better under a moderate government, but I like the idea of venting my anger by voting for the fascists. Because my vote is insignificant in determining the outcome, I can indulge my preference to support the fascists (that is, I vote for them) because I know this single vote will not impact on my values. Voting fascist does not entail that I will obtain a fascist government, and so it does not mean that I forgo the opportunity of having a moderate government. If, on the other hand, my vote were decisive—if I knew that my vote for the fascists would cause their election—my vote for the fascists would entail the opportunity costs of not having a moderate government, and so I would have excellent instrumental reason to vote for the moderates.

This is a real insight, though Brennan and Lomasky are apt to put far too much stress on its dark side—the way in which voters may vote out of malice and perversions against their own better interests.[38] Decisiveness is relevant because it affects the probability that the action will produce a result, and that in turn affects the extent to which the agent's values are really at stake in his decision about how to act. Any factor that decreases the overall salience of Betty's values in the decision will push her toward area A in Figure 2.3, inducing her to act on principled instead of instrumentalist concerns. And the salience of the values may be low for two reasons. (1) As Brennan and Lomasky stress, though the value may be important, the probability that the agent can do anything to promote it may be minute, or (2) the value itself may be relatively unimportant, even though the person is in a position to decisively achieve it. Both paths to low-salient values are at work in voting. In the decision of how to vote, lack of decisiveness massively discounts instrumental concerns. On the other hand, one is decisive concerning the decision whether to go out and vote: If one does vote, one will bear the opportunity costs of doing so. But here values are not salient because the costs of voting are so extremely low—one bears the full opportunity costs of voting, but "full" here is quite modest.

5.3 Homo Politicus?

5.3.1 The Conflict of Values and Principles. If I am right, Homo Economicus will tell us a lot about actions in area B, while principled theories of action will allow us to make headway in area A, a source of constant difficulties to Homo Economicus. Let me conclude with a few observations about the complicated area C. Here the satisfaction of values (ones not discounted because we have little probability of attaining them through our actions) clashes with the satisfaction of principles. It is of interest that many political theorists have thought that such situations are of fundamental importance to political life. I have in mind here the commonly called "problem of dirty hands in politics." The notion can be traced back to Machiavelli and probably further. In *The Prince*, Machiavelli writes:

[H]ow we live is so far removed from how we ought to live, that he who abandons what is done for what ought to be done, will rather learn to bring about his own ruin than his preservation. A man who wishes to make a profession of goodness in everything must necessarily come to grief among so many who are not good. There- fore, it is necessary for a prince, who wishes to maintain himself, to learn how not to be good, and to use the knowledge and not use it, according to the necessity of the case.[39]

Others, such as Max Weber, have also stressed that in politics we cannot af- ford to follow absolute principles of right and wrong, but must be ready to sacrifice those principles to achieve great values.[40]

Now, on the face of it, this would seem to fit nicely with the instrumental view: We should follow moral norms only when they get us where we want to go, otherwise we should discard them. From Machiavelli to Downs and Buchanan, political theorists have insisted that those who know what they are doing in politics are pursuers of values. It would seem, then, that *Homo Economicus* points to a science of politics.

But such accounts have a mixed record for two reasons. First, we cannot confidently predict that rational agents will have trade-off rates that so heav- ily discount principles relative to values. Machiavellians, of course, insist that anyone who has any business in political life should have this type of trade-off rate—one in which devotion to great goals and values almost always outweighs fidelity to principles. And so-called "political realists," following Machiavelli, have claimed that real politicians are single-mindedly devoted to goals or in- terests in this way. But, as an empirical claim, this is dubious.[41] Although some politicians are Machiavellians, others give considerably more weight to rea- sons of fidelity. Though realists disparage Gladstonian and Wilsonian foreign policy, it is hard to deny that such creatures have, and perhaps still do, exist.

Several political theorists insist that the conflict of principles and values is at the core of political life. To see their point, consider a famous example presented by Michael Walzer:

[C]onsider a politician who has seized upon a national crisis—a prolonged colonial war—to reach for power. He and his friends win office pledged to decolonization and peace; they are honestly committed to both, though not without some sense of the advantages of the commitment. In any case, they have no responsibility for the war; they have steadfastly opposed it. Immediately, the politician goes off to the colonial capital to open negotiations with the rebels. But the capital is in the grip of a terrorist campaign and the first decision the new leader faces is this: He is asked to authorize the torture of a captured rebel who knows or probably knows the location of a number of bombs hidden in apartment buildings around the city, set to go off in the next twenty-four hours. He orders the man tortured, convinced that he must do so for the sake of the people who might otherwise die in the explosions—even though he believes that torture is wrong, indeed abominable, not just sometimes, but always. He had expressed this belief often and angrily in the campaign; the rest of us took it as a sign of his goodness. How should we regard him now? (How should he regard himself?)[42]

Walzer insists on three points. (1) Public office holders and public servants regularly face problems of this type, though not always quite as dramatic. But as demonstrated by the British decision (pressured by the Americans) to accede to Stalin's demand for repatriation of Russians and Ukrainians, some but not all of whom fought for the Nazis, politics is not short on such examples.[43]

Also (2), Walzer insists that anyone who has any business in politics must sometimes choose do what is wrong, or even awful, if he is to achieve his goals. Someone who refuses to ever get his hands dirty, says Walzer, will accomplish little, and only betrays his supporters. As Machiavelli says, the prince who is good in a world where so many are so far from being good, will only come to grief. This was precisely the point that Sartre made in his play, *Dirty Hands* (French: *Les Mains Sales*), that gave the name to this debate. In the play, Hoerder, the experienced revolutionary, replies to the young, moralistic Hugo, who insists on staying pure:

How you cling to your purity, young man! How afraid you are to soil your hands! All right, stay pure! What good will it do you? Why did you join us? Purity is an ideal for a yogi or a monk. You intellectuals and bourgeois anarchists use it as a pretext for doing nothing. To do nothing, to remain motionless, arms at your side, wearing kid gloves. Well, I have dirty hands. Right up to the elbows. I've plunged them in filth and blood. But what do you hope? Do you think you can govern innocently?[44]

But Walzer also (3) is adamant that the instrumentalist view of the broken rules is fundamentally wrong. Suppose that in this case, or one like it, one finally is willing to accept that, perhaps, torture is the only way out; too many lives will be lost by keeping one's hands clean. But, if you are an instrumentalist, your view will be, "Well, since in this case the rule against torture does not advance my values, there is no reason to follow it; it would be stupid to follow it; so forget about it and let the torturing begin." This, Walzer and others argue, fails to appreciate that the norms continue to pull us, even when we must go against them. They possess an independent validity, and it is always a cause for regret when they have to be put aside. Max Weber, for example, wrote of the statesmen sacrificing his integrity for the sake of his political values; even Machiavelli indicated that politicians may lose their souls for the good of the community.

Though this all sometimes gets more than a little romantic, Walzer's point is sound: Values and goals alone cannot explain political life. In contrast to the economic analysis of market behavior, in politics we must not assume the normative constraints are part of the background. They are themselves a matter of dispute. The stuff of politics is the constant need for a choice between crucial norms that demands compliance, and important political values that require breaking the rules. Walzer argues that the result is the cruel paradox of political life:

Sometimes it is right to try to succeed, and then it must also be right to get one's hands dirty. But one's hands get dirty from doing what it is wrong to do. And how can it be wrong to do what is right? Or how can we get our hands dirty by doing what we ought to do?[45]

To be a successful politician, or high level public servant, one must sometimes do what is wrong, but that does not make it any less wrong.

I do not wish to endorse Walzer's conclusion that we are wrong or tainted no matter what we do. Instead, I want to stress that both Machiavellian and more moralistic versions of politics agree that area C—where values and principles are both crucially at stake, and where they regularly clash—is the central stuff of politics. The difference is the way the conflict is resolved. The Machiavellian, and more generally the realist, traditions insist that disputes in area C should be resolved in favor of whatever course best promotes the politician's values. In contrast, the liberal or Gladstonian view of politics argues that sometimes choices in area C should be resolved in favor of principled behavior, even at a cost to important interests. Walzer has a more complex position. He believes that politicians are typically obliged to pursue the Machiavellian course, acting as if in area C only values were at stake, but since this is not the case—because principles need be set aside to pursue these goals—some form of remorse is in order.

5.3.2 The Limits of Instrumental Reasoning. Machiavellians insist that the liberal or Gladstonian view of politics is deeply confused—if liberals understood the great values at stake in politics, they would not be so self-indulgent as to keep their hands clean by sticking to their cherished principles. However, I hope it is now clear that even when great values are at stake agents may find themselves in area A instead of C. We saw that in an election, a voter may agree that her values are crucially at stake, but since there is little she can do to determine the outcome, she may still find herself in A, the area of principled behavior. What realists have always overlooked is that governments often find themselves in a very similar situation in matters of high policy. Successful policy requires that policymakers be able to make accurate predictions—concerning both the effects of a policy and how the world would have gone if the policy were not implemented. Theorists and politicians believe they have a good handle on large-scale social developments, and can accurately make these kinds of predictions, but, as I have argued elsewhere, there is good reason to think they are mistaken.[46] Indeed, as Philip E. Tetlock's recent masterful study of expert policy prediction has revealed, the predictions of experts about macro political and economic developments—from whether there will be an increase, decrease, or no change in the incidence of wars, and democratization to changes in inflation, unemployment, and interest rates—is distressingly near to random. In some respects a monkey throwing a dart at a board divided into spaces labeled "variable will go up, variable will go down, variable will stay the same" would outperform experts.[47] Over a wide range of "grand policy"—which includes much foreign policy, social policy, and, alas, economic policy—great values are relevant, but because of our gross inability to predict social developments, they are not really salient. Consequently, it is anything but obvious that rational policy makers should seek to act in a purely instrumental way.

6. CONCLUSION

I have tried to do three things in this essay. First, I have sought to reply to Buchanan's symmetry argument by showing that *Homo Economicus* is not a general, but a special, model of rational action. If, so, we should not expect it to be applied to all situations; in fact, I have tried to quickly sketch some situations in which devotion to *Homo Economicus* leads us astray. But, second, I not only wanted to show why *Homo Economicus* has limits, but also to give some idea why, within those limits, it has been so powerful. The paradigmatic market relation is precisely the case in which we would expect agents to behave in the purely value-drive way predicted by *Homo Economicus*. Last, I have tried to indicate why Buchanan's main proposal—that we apply *Homo Economicus* to politics as well as economics—has been one of the persisting disputes in the study of politics, going back to Machiavelli and beyond. In politics, values and principles regularly conflict. If Machiavelli is right, and the conflicts are always resolved in favor of values, then politics is not so very different than economics. But if political actors sometimes sacrifice important values for the sake of fidelity to principles, then the application of *Homo Economicus* to politics will have, at best, mixed success. And, I have suggested, given our gross inability to predict large-scale social developments, or to discover the causes of current social problems, it is hard to avoid the conclusion that rational political actors will often act on principles instead of values.

NOTES

1. Geoffrey Brennan and James M. Buchanan, *The Reason of Rules: Constitutional Political Economy* (Cambridge, England: Cambridge University Press, 1985), 50.

2. This section draws on my *On Politics, Philosophy and Economics* (Belmont, CA: Thomson-Wadsworth, 2008), chap. 1.

3, Robert Nozick, *The Nature of Rationality* (Princeton: Princeton University Press, 1993), 164.

4. *Cf.* Jon Elster, "The Nature and Scope of Rational-Choice Explanation" in *Actions and Events: Perspectives on Donald Davidson,* eds. E. LePore and B. McLaughlin (Oxford: Blackwell, 1985), 60–72.

5. Nassau William Senior, *An Outline of the Science of Political Economy*, 5th ed. (Edinburgh: Charles Black, 1864), 187–88.

6. *Cf.* Donald Davidson, "Actions, Reason and Causes," in his *Essays on Actions and Events* (Oxford: Oxford University Press, 1980).

7. George J. Stigler, *The Economist as Preacher* (Chicago: University of Chicago Press, 1982), 21.

8. Gary Becker, *The Economic Approach to Human Behavior* (Chicago: University of Chicago Press, 1976).

9. *Cf.* Daniel M. Hausman, *The Inexact and Separate Science of Economics* (Cambridge, England: Cambridge University Press, 1992), 32; Ludwig von Mises, *Human Action: A Treatise on Economics*, 3rd ed. (Chicago: Contemporary Books, 1966), 125.

10. Sigmund Freud, "The Disposition to Obsessional Neurosis" in *On Psychopathology*, ed. A. Richards (Harmondsworth: Penguin, 1979), 134–44. *cf.*, Thomas Hill Green, "On the Different Senses of 'Freedom' as Applied to the Will and to the Moral Progress of Man," in *Lectures on the Principles of Political Obligation and Other Writings*, eds. Paul Harris and John Morrow (Cambridge, England: Cambridge University Press, 1986), 228.

11. Brennan and Lomasky, *Democracy and Decision*, 9.

12. See Stanley Benn, *A Theory of Freedom* (Cambridge, England: Cambridge University Press, 1988), ch. 3.

13. Brennan and Lomasky, *Democracy and Decision*, 9–10.

14. Stigler, *The Economist as Preacher*, 21. *Cf.*, Becker, *The Economic Approach to Human Behavior*, ch. 13

15. *Beyond Self-Interest*, ed. Jane J. Mansbridge (Chicago: University of Chicago Press, 1990).

16. Philip H. Wicksteed, *The Common Sense of Political Economy*, 2 vols, ed. Lionel Robbins (London: George Routledge & Sons, 1946), vol. I, 180.

17. Robert Nozick, *Anarchy, State and Utopia* (New York: Basic Books, 1974), 26ff; Gerald F. Gaus, "Goals, Principles and Symbolic Expressions. Nozick's Theory of Practical Rationality" in *Robert Nozick*, ed. David Schmidtz (Cambridge, England: Cambridge University Press, 2002), 105–30. For a recent excellent treatment of deontic constraints and the rationality of rule following, see Joseph Heath, *Following the Rules: Practical Reasoning and Deontic Constraint* (Oxford: Oxford University Press, 2008).

18. [1938] 4 All E.R. 258. See Neil MacCormick, *Legal Reasoning and Legal Theory* (Oxford: Clarendon, 1978), 19ff.

19. MacCormick, *Legal Reasoning and Legal Theory*, 21.

20. Frederick Schauer, *Playing by the Rules* (Oxford: Clarendon Press, 1991).

21. H. L. A. Hart, *The Concept of Law* (Oxford: Clarendon Press, 1961), 121.

22. See Talcott Parsons, *The Social System* (London: Routledge and Kegan Paul, 1965), 207ff; Viktor J. Vanberg, *Rules and Choice in Economics* (London: Routledge, 1994), 14; Jerome Kagan, *The Nature of the Child* (New York: Basic Books, 1984), ch. 4.

23. Schauer, *Playing by the Rules*, ch. 2; Vanberg, *Rules and Choice in Economics*, 16ff.

24. Schauer, *Playing By the Rules*, 54ff, 72, 77, 113; Benn, *A Theory of Freedom*, 24.

25. See my "Mill's Theory of Moral Rules," *Australasian Journal of Philosophy* 58 (September 1980): 265–79.

26. John Stuart Mill. *A System of Logic* (London: Longman's, 1947), book VI, ch. xii, sect. 2.

27. S. I. Benn and G. F. Gaus, "Practical Rationality and Commitment," *American Philosophical Quarterly* 23 (July 1986): 255–266. See also my *Value and Justification*, 84–101.

28. See Robert Nozick, *The Nature of Rationality*, ch. 1.

29. Benn, *A Theory of Freedom*, ch. 3.

30. Ibid., 51.

31. Ibid., 52.

32. Lee Ross and Richard E. Nisbett, *The Person and the Situation* (Philadelphia: Temple University Press, 1991), esp. ch. 4; *Cf.* Derek Wright, *The Psychology of Moral Behaviour* (Harmondsworth, England: Penguin, 1971), 51ff.

33. Anthony Downs, *An Economic Theory of Democracy* (New York: Harper & Row, 1957).

34. Geoffrey Brennan and Loren E. Lomasky, "Large Numbers, Small Costs: The Uneasy Foundation of Democratic Rule," in *Politics and Process: New Essays on Democratic Thought*, eds. Geoffrey Brennan and Loren E. Lomasky (Cambridge, England: Cambridge University Press, 1989), 48.

35. S. I. Benn, "Rationality and Political Behaviour," in *Rationality and the Social Sciences*, eds. S. I. Benn and G. W. Mortimore (London: Routledge, 1976), ch. 10.

36. Brennan and Lomasky, *Democracy and Decision*, 33.

37. Ibid., 24.

38. Ibid., e.g., 157ff.

39. Niccolò Machiavelli, "The Prince," in *The Prince and Discourses* (New York: Modern Library, 1950), ch. XV, 56.

40. S. I. Benn, "Public and Private Morality: Clean Living and Dirty Hands," in *Public and Private in Social Life,* eds. S. I. Benn and G. F. Gaus (New York: St. Martin's, 1983), ch. 7.

41. John W. Kingdon, "Politicians, Self-Interest and Ideas," in *Reconsidering the Democratic Public,* eds. George E. Marcus and Russell L. Hanson (University Park, Penn: Pennsylvania State University Press, 1993), 73–89; Charles R. Beitz, *Political Theory and International Relations* (Princeton: Princeton University Press, 1979), part 1; Paul Knapland, *Gladstone's Foreign Policy* (London: Frank Cass, 1970).

42. Michael Walzer, "Political Action: The Problem of Dirty Hands," *Philosophy & Public Affairs*, 2 (1973): 166–67.

43. See Benn, "Clean Living and Dirty Hands": Gerald F. Gaus, "Dirty Hands" in *The Blackwell Companion to Applied Ethics*, eds R.G. Frey and Kit Wellman (Oxford: Basil Blackwell, 2002), 339–62.

44. Quoted in Benn, "Clean Living and Dirty Hands," 160.

45. Walzer, "Political Action," 164.

46. I have argued this "Is the Public Incompetent? Compared to Whom? About What?", *Critical Review: A Journal of Politics and Society,* vol. 20 (2008): 291–311 and in "Social Complexity and Evolved Moral Principles," in *Liberalism, Conservatism, and Hayek's Idea of Spontaneous Order,* ed Peter McNamara (London: Palgrave Macmillan, 2007), 149–76.

47. See Philip E. Tetlock, *Expert Political Judgment* (Princeton: Princeton University Press, 2005).

CHAPTER 3

PREFERENCES, COGNITIVISM, AND THE PUBLIC SPHERE

Jeremy Shearmur

1. INTRODUCTION

This chapter is, by intention, exploratory. In it, I am concerned with various ways in which one might take what could be called a "cognitivist" approach, and in particular one that involves openness to inter-subjective criticism, toward our preferences. The kind of criticism with which I am concerned is limited, if, for instance, it is compared to that suggested by Habermas's later work. The reason for this limitation is that I would not wish to commit myself to his particular substantive—and in my view contentious—ideas. In addition, I do not suggest a general theory as to how we should distinguish between what is and what is not open to such criticism. The reason for this is that it can be up to an individual's decision as to what status he or she wishes to claim for something, and thus the kind of scrutiny to which it is appropriate that it be subjected. In addition, the kind of scrutiny that is appropriate may also depend on what our aims or goals are.[1]

2. ON PREFERENCES AND CRITICISM

Economists tend to take preferences as given. Within economics, and given the kinds of problems with which economists are often concerned—such as how people will react to incentives—this approach may not be controversial. (This understanding does not discount the approach of, for example, Gary Becker.[2] But issues raised by his work on the explanation of tastes do not affect the argument of this chapter.) More interesting, and more obviously controversial, is the extension of "economic" approaches to less-familiar subject matter, where they may also properly receive a kind of scrutiny that they do not receive on their home ground. This may serve to illuminate issues that are real but not as obvious when economists are practicing economics. Accordingly, the fate of public choice theory, conceived as the attempt to extend "economic" approaches to subject matter more traditionally studied by political science, may throw an interesting light upon economics and upon ideas that economists take for granted. Problems may arise within political science topics that are not as apparent when economists are doing only economics. When we extend the economic approach into a field such as politics, it may also have to argue for itself in a way it does not within economics.

Sometimes the core ideas of an academic discipline do not appear to its practitioners to call for scrutiny. As Thomas Kuhn stressed in his treatment of "paradigms," they are something into which people are socialized as a result of their professional education (and the education of an economist fits remarkably well with what Kuhn says about the training of a "normal scientist."[3]) The academic discipline of economics is, to a considerable extent, just a matter of what economists do. At the very least, economists do not need, in the course of their everyday practices, to produce arguments for what they are doing. Although dissent exists within the profession of economics, it takes place largely at the fringes of the discipline, and it is not something with which successful economists have to concern themselves, unless they choose to do so.

The situation is different when economists move into another field. When, like some barbarian hordes of old, economists sweep down onto what they perceive as fertile yet inadequately tended fields, to pillage, rape, and, eventually, settle and tend the land more intensively (and they believe more fruitfully), they may actually encounter some resistance. They may find themselves forced to give an account of what they are up to. And they are likely to encounter detailed critical scrutiny from academics already there.[4] Problems may be articulated that, while present, are not as obvious within economics itself. This illumination may be because, within economics, the questions customarily posed may be the very questions amenable to the approaches usually used within economics. As Kuhn suggested, within an established discipline, what may be seen as a problem is, sociologically, better seen as a puzzle—as something that is expected to be resolved in terms of the paradigms within which people are working. The varied reactions to issues in the methodology of economics by writers as different as the falsificationist Mark Blaug and Daniel Hausman from his John Stuart Mill-influenced position, provide some support for such an account. Each of them suggests that the usual practice of economics is almost self-contained, not looking for external justification in terms, for example, of the success of its predictions.[5]

Things look different when we apply the economic approach to the subject matter of political science, in which it cannot as easily set its own agenda. Even some of those most closely associated with the initial development of public choice theory have later expressed doubts about its value as an explanatory tool within politics.[6] In recent work, Geoffrey Brennan—a one-time collaborator with James M. Buchanan—has, in effect, thrown in the towel with regard to what might have been public choice theory's programmatic approach to the explanation of voting. In his work with Loren Lomasky, Brennan has joined those who criticized public choice theory's analysis of voting on the grounds that it is expressive instead of instrumental in its character.[7] (At the same time, Brennan and Lomasky have brought the tools of rational choice theory to bear on this non-public-choice approach. But we should not, I think, characterize this work, however interesting, as a "progressive" development of rational choice theory, just because it departs from that approach's core ideas.[8])

Economists operating outside their usual fields may also provoke the articulation of an alternative approach. In this connection, Jane Mansbridge's "The Rise and Fall of Self-Interest in the Explanation of Political Life" is interesting because of her discussion of deliberative democracy as an alternative to public choice theory's treatment of politics as only a matter of interest and preference.⁹ But deliberative democracy as an ideal might be thought problematic. It tends to invoke images of portly men in togas engaged in elevated conversations about philosophy and public affairs in the fora of small city-states. Not only is it unclear how this aspect of the classical republican ideal was ever to be extended to large societies in which there was an extensive division of labor, but the ideal itself would for us today conjure up counter-images. We think instead of the exclusion of women from the fora of the classical world and of the slave labor supporting the whole society within which such elevated discussions took place. I do not wish to argue in favor of deliberative democracy in any extended sense, still less for political participation. I also do not wish to enter into discussion of the pros and cons of modern interpretations of "republicanism," interesting though they are.¹⁰ There is, though, one element from the tradition of deliberative democracy that I think is of pressing significance in the present context. It relates to the question of preferences and to the issue of whether they are given—in the sense of being beyond inter-subjective scrutiny.

A useful point of departure is with Harry Frankfurt's "Freedom of the Will and the Concept of a Person" and A. Sen's "Rational Fools." In each case, the author has claimed that we should recognize that people might have preferences about their preferences. People may wish they did not smoke, did not like to eat or drink too much, or did not feel quite the way they do about some members of the opposite sex to whom they are not married. The recognition of such higher-level preferences may lead them to prefer procedures or institutions of a distinctive kind. So those who are worried about smoking may purchase cigarette containers that release cigarettes only at timed intervals; those who worry about their weight may adopt a rule that they do not enter all-you-can-eat fixed-price restaurants. At a collective level, those who are worried that they, or those for whom they will vote, may approve measures in the heat of the moment that are at odds with things for which they have a deeper concern, may favor forms of constitutional constraint.

I have suggested these ideas as a starting point, not because I wish to endorse them uncritically, but because they are useful for critical discussion. As Gerald Gaus has suggested to me in a private communication—a suggestion with which I heartily concur—such higher-level preferences may sometimes be very much against the interests of those unfortunate enough to have them. Individuals have sometimes had their lives ruined by "higher-level" disapproval of their tastes or preferences when these preferences are both innocuous and also not easily subject to change. Further, within the accounts of both Frankfurt and Sen, the higher-level preferences are still what I will call "bare" or "brute."[11] People may have this hierarchy of preferences; there may be no *reason*—aside from the fact that this is how people happen to feel—that the "higher" ones are to be weighted more heavily than others when they clash. The idea of such a rational hierarchy, however, may run into problems.

The first is an argument based on the difficulties of explicating what characterizes the "better" preferences as better. It might be tempting to say that what is called for is a justification for them. The trouble about this approach is that it would generate a vicious regress of justification. At any one level, it might be possible to furnish such an argument. But then the terms for advancing such an argument would, at the next level, figure as bare unjustified preferences, unless a further argument were offered for them in its turn. And this process would continue until argument runs out—at which point the original problem would remain: that of bare preferences. (Compare, for a discussion of this issue in the context of rationality, W. W. Bartley III's *Retreat to Commitment*.[12])

The second problem with rational hierarchy would be that, although ideas about what is better exist, those ideas could amount to other people's preferences and their internalization by us in the social constitution of our selves. Why do we go along with the idea that it is desirable to be thin? Because, according to this view, insofar as this goes beyond considerations about health, this happens to be a widely shared prejudice in our society. Go back one-hundred-fifty years, and people would commend me for looking like John Bull, instead of tut-tutting me for being obese. And if I am worried about this myself, then it might be argued it is because I have internalized judgments made by others. The "voice within the breast"—and what appears to give normative force to the content of my "higher" preferences—is the product of the brute judgments of others that I have taken into myself.

I think this latter idea offers a lot, *qua* sociological description. But more *may* be going on when we are involved in such exercises. Popper's critique of "justificationist" epistemology suggests that we may understand rationality in terms of inter-subjective critical scrutiny. This approach also offers us an escape from the vicious regress of justification to which I referred earlier.[13] If we accept such an approach, it allows us on the one side to note that more may be involved in the judgments of others and their internalization than the sway of fashion. For, as Adam Smith noted in *Theory of Moral Sentiments*, we may reflect on and refine those judgments, and we may come to care not so much about the judgments that people are making as for those an impartial spectator would make. We may, further, follow Smith into a concern for that conduct of which spectators should approve—and so into a concern for what is right and what is true, even in the face of dissent from spectators (see, on this, also Knud Haakonssen's discussions of Smith, voluntarist natural law theory, and moral realism[14]). Yet at the same time, our concern is with what can pass inter-subjective scrutiny, instead of with what appears self-evident, or even unproblematic, to us as individuals.

If we now turn back from these heady heights to our starting point, we can say something significant. For we make some judgments and have some preferences only because we believe them to be correct, in the sense of their being appropriate for us to have given who we are and the situation that we are in. These are preferences and ideas about our identity, the character of which implies that we could and should submit them to (judicious) inter-subjective scrutiny. They include matters where we might be sorry about what might turn out to be the rational verdict of others. For example, they might be able to furnish good arguments to the effect that preferences we currently have are ones we should not have, where we would like to be able to retain them. Insofar as such preferences and the need for such scrutiny are important to us, we may wish to build a concern for them into the design of our institutions. If we think that our preferences may require correction by the critical input of others, we may wish to ensure that what happens (either to us or to our society) does not reflect our bare preferences too easily. We may choose institutions that submit our preferences, or even our selves, to various forms of deliberative control, which may mean that we do not get to act on, or even get to contribute into the process of collective decision-making, the "bare" preferences that we had initially.

Such a view contrasts, in a useful way, with that of people who see politics as only consisting of the realization of preferences. Consider, for example, the contrast between the approaches to the character of constitutions in the quite different views of Jean Jacques Rousseau and James M. Buchanan.[15] Buchanan allows for constitutional constraints; but the point of them is to allow individuals to do the best they can in terms of the satisfaction of their bare preferences. From Buchanan's perspective, much in Rousseau's work looks perverse and involves an illegitimate shaping of people and their preferences by the concerns of others. In Rousseau's view, it is only when people allow themselves to be shaped by the general will that they are free and (as we are talking in Rousseau's political writings of men, I can say) masters of themselves, in the sense of enjoying moral freedom.[16]

There is a danger, if we take the economist's usual approach, that what I call "cognitive" (as opposed to bare) preferences and institutions that make sense in relation to them can disappear. By cognitive preferences, I mean preferences that are open to inter-subjective scrutiny of the kind that I have described. Although so far we have approached this problem by looking at what happened to an economic approach when it encountered political subject matter, the issue raised holds true more generally as well. Cognitive preferences also exist in the realm of the economic, and we may need distinct institutions to help us deal with those cognitive preferences too; for example, regarding the character of advertising. At the same time, balance is needed. Not all of our preferences are of this cognitive character. We are happy to hold some things as bare preferences; and there is much that, I think quite properly, we would not wish to have submitted to open-ended inter-subjective scrutiny. Many things exist about which we may wish to say only that we happen to like them. Much in our day-to-day lives involves the telling of stories that can aspire only to very local validity. There is also much about us as human beings that is only compatible with restricted scrutiny. To live out in the open all the time is hardly compatible with being human. And those accounts, from the theological to the social, that would try to force such accountability onto us appear to me gravely mistaken as a vision of what human beings are or might become, and, if people take them seriously, recipes for misery to boot.

Accordingly, while I am breaking a lance for those who are critical of economists, I would not wish to be misunderstood. I think that we should make room for the cognitive considerations with which I have been (and will be) concerned. But I also think that it would be a disaster if we were to give them too much room or to treat them as if they were the only legitimate kind of preference. While I am critical of economists' assumptions that all we have are bare preferences, I do think that, at one level, they are on to something. We need to be able to secure a private realm and to tell the intrusive scrutinizer—from an all-seeing God to the would-be director of Jeremy Bentham's Panopticon to recent feminist critics of the private sphere—to go away, if we are to be able to live human lives. (I should stress, in this context, that my comments relate to self-regarding actions; further, as should be clear to readers of John Stuart Mill's *Subjection of Women*, liberals—as opposed to conservatives—typically wished to safeguard from such scrutiny individual freedom of action, not to preserve a domestic sphere within which men could tyrannize over women.) In addition, the existence of markets in which we can express our bare preferences, and others can respond to them as such, appears to me of the greatest possible importance for human well being.

There is also another sense in which our preferences may be open to inter-subjective scrutiny, as Kelvin Lancaster has explored in his "New Approach to Consumer Theory," and as Gary Becker has taken further.[17] My concern is with the appraisal of preferences as appropriate as such. But we may also appraise a preference in light of whether it is instrumentally effective in the satisfaction of more basic underlying (bare) preferences. Behind preferences that we may exhibit for goods in a supermarket, for example, are underlying preferences that may be satisfied more effectively by other goods. Considerable room is available for the inter-subjective scrutiny of our existing preferences on a purely instrumental basis. Institutions of various kinds, from some types of advertising to the publications of consumer associations to scrutiny from family, friends, clergy, and social workers, doubtless play an important role in supplying it. The issues to which I have just referred also open many opportunities for discussion of the extent to which we, as individuals or as members of collective bodies, have a responsibility for improving the satisfaction of other people's underlying preferences; and, if we do, what institutions would be most effective in discharging this responsibility.

At the same time, let us not overlook two considerations. The first is that what such preferences might amount to is largely a matter of conjecture. It is not obvious what deeper preferences might underlie the more specific prefer-

ences that we might exhibit in a supermarket (or if any such preferences do—
the preference that we exhibit might itself be "basic"). The second criticism
that is apparently offered on this instrumental basis may well be criticism of
the cognitive kind, with which I am concerned in this chapter. Well-meaning
persons may criticize others for having inappropriate preferences; for example, for goods that are flashy, widely advertised, and of poor functional
quality, instead of things that are good and solid. But such criticism would
be valid as instrumental criticism only if the critic has correctly identified
what other people's underlying preferences are. At the level of bare preference, a variety of preferences may have been involved. The well-intentioned
instrumental criticism may indeed be correct if the functional preference
that it identified was all that was involved. But there could have been other
preferences that led to the original preference for something flashy. Such
preferences may themselves give rise to criticism. The criticism is more likely
to be cognitive rather than purely instrumental. The criticism is likely to be
that the preference is inappropriate, instead of that what has been chosen is
not instrumentally effective in the satisfaction of the (underlying) bare preferences. Accordingly, I wish to turn back to the cognitive issues relating to
preferences that are the focus of this chapter. (It might be open for debate
that what I am calling "cognitive" is, at a deeper level, explained in purely
instrumental terms—as Tyler Cowen has urged upon me. But this is not an
issue that I will pursue here.)

Before I go further, it might be useful to say a little more about cognitive
preferences. They are preferences that are open to non-instrumental inter-
subjective appraisal along the lines I indicated earlier by referencing Karl
Popper's work. Such appraisal will often be in terms of its appropriateness for
an individual to have in a given situation. To illustrate: We may have tastes—
for example, for white chocolate—that we are happy to regard as matters of
bare preference. We could imagine ourselves not feeling this way about white
chocolate and think our situation not much the worse. We might make a
passionate case for our freedom to indulge in this taste. But it would be in
terms of the (harmless) pleasure that it would give us; or that people should
be free, within limits, to use their time and resources in the pursuit of such
pleasures, and so on. There may be other preferences—for example, for some
kinds of music, wine, or writing—which we may not be happy to defend in

such terms. We might argue that we *would* be the worse if we did not have them; that it would not be good if we had other such tastes, and so on. Such judgments, and associated aesthetic, moral, or factual judgments, could be open in principle to the critical scrutiny of anyone. We may take such judgments to be ones that are in principle open to such criticism. Should anyone offer criticism in a form that we cannot eventually answer, we might consider ourselves to be committed to changing our view of the status of our preference, or possibly even the preference itself. Higher-level judgments may also be open to such scrutiny. A pedophile might wish that he were not attracted in that way to small children. Or he might claim that it is all right—on a par with any other taste. Or he might claim that there is something elevated, even spiritual, about it. He might think the world would be less rich if such tastes were absent from it, and that it is appropriate that he should have them and indulge in them in his current manner. These claims would be open to inter-subjective scrutiny; and we might imagine that the latter claims would swiftly face telling criticism.

What this example amounts to is the suggestion that, once criticisms are raised, we may wish to make different claims with respect to our preferences and tastes. In some cases, our claim may be modest: The only inter-subjective appraisal we require is that nothing about the claim is judged problematic in terms of its impact on the legitimate and protected interests of others in our society. In such cases, arguments about whether we should be free to indulge such tastes are likely to rest on other considerations; for example, more general claims about rights or utility in the context of social theory. In other cases, we may make stronger claims for a preference: This preference is fitting for us to have and we would judge ourselves poorer if we did not have it. Here, the having of the preferences and our being able to act on the basis of them directly faces inter-subjective appraisal.

What is involved is an approach that, while acknowledging that preferences may be of different kinds, takes seriously the idea that cognitive and bare preferences exist. *Cognitive* is a matter of these preferences being open to inter-subjective appraisal (as such, not just in instrumental terms). The approach may be contrasted with Richard Brandt in *A Theory of the Good and the Right*, which, from my perspective, does not offer a cognitivist approach to preferences. I will spare the reader a fuller account of the details of these views about inter-subjective appraisal.[18] They may be understood as a generalization of Karl Popper's critical rationalism and as having parallels to Adam Smith's ideas in *Theory of Moral Sentiments*. They are also in some respects close to David McNaughton's approach to ethics in *Moral Vision*.[19]

As it is significant for what follows, I would stress that cognitive preferences, at their strongest, are ones that we would claim to be the correct or appropriate ones for us to have in the situation that we are in. (Alternately, we may wish to claim, more weakly, that they are members of a set of such preferences, such that it is appropriate for us to have any one of such preferences, but that we can legitimately have one or other such preference, within this set, indifferently.) When we exhibit cognitive preferences, we open ourselves in principle to inter-subjective criticism. Usually, this criticism will come from the people with whom we regularly interact: our family, friends, and workmates. But their appraisals may not furnish us with the kind of criticism that these preferences call for. Because of our implicit claim concerning the cognitive status of the preferences, it is as though we are claiming them as analogous to truth. We are implicitly claiming that it is appropriate for us, in our situation, to have such preferences. We are asserting that our preferences are, in principle, open to criticism from anyone and have the normative standing of something claimed to be correct. In this respect, we are making the claim for everyone, although what we are saying for them is that this preference is appropriate for us as individuals in the situations that we happen to be in. The argument I outlined above suggests that the ordinary patterns of interaction with our friends, family, and colleagues may be inadequate as a basis for the appraisal of such claims. Instead of functioning as critics, they may function as a faction as defined by Hume; that is, as people who do not appraise but act more like cheerleaders. We may need to construct or maintain institutional arrangements for the purpose of submitting such ideas to criticism.

Nicole Mitchell has explored factions and creating critical institutions in unpublished work on Hume's politics. The problem of faction, which Mitchell has discussed along with its adverse effects on the processes of inter-subjective appraisal, suggests that Habermas is mistaken in suggesting that New Social Movement can be expected to redress the balance between instrumental and more cognitive, consensual, and inter-subjective concerns.

New Social Movements would appear to be the epitome of factions in Hume's sense. They would appear to be organizations whose very character tends to make their members impervious to criticism from nonsympathizers—and, in my view, to rationality. Alasdair MacIntyre makes a similar point in his comments in *After Virtue*, on what, from the perspective of this chapter, may be termed the noncognitive character of much political protest.[20]

In the case of purely personal matters, all this discussion may indicate that ways exist in which our preferences could be subjected to criticism, should we wish to hold them in such a form that this may take place. But we may have other pressing reasons not to be too interested in such appraisal beyond a certain point, and other people may have little interest in making the appraisal for us. In other cases, our preferences and actions may be of greater moment; notably when they not only affect others but also shape the general character of the environment (social, political, and physical) within which we all live and which shapes us. In this momentous situation, issues of intersubjective appraisal and the question of where—through what institutions—it takes place, may become pressing. I will return to this problem in the fourth section of this chapter.

Before that, in the third section of the chapter, I will explore one implication of the recognition of cognitive preferences: They enable us to move beyond the approach to the understanding of political arrangements that is possible for those who see individuals as having only bare preferences. I have elsewhere described and criticized an approach that I dubbed "prudential liberalism"—the attempt to derive liberal conclusions from a noncognitivist, economistic starting point.[21] In this chapter, I suggest that the recognition of cognitive preferences may furnish us with an additional resource and an additional line of argument, one that is significant in the context of political argument.

3. ON DIALOGUE AND RIGHTS

When political philosophers look at the way in which economists typically address welfare-related issues, what strikes them as strange is that economists often approach issues as though the individuals with whom they are dealing had rights in their persons and to their property of the kind favored by a rights-based classical liberalism. For example, economists typically assume that we should work within the framework of voluntary exchange and with the exchange of things that people own; we should not work under the notion of some people simply taking things from others. Further, if redistribution (it is usually assumed that government, not other individuals, does the distributing) is to take place and be evaluated, it is assumed that each individual should be treated equally and as though his or her well-being counts equally with that of each other person.

Such a view of how the process can work may present the economist as philosopher king, looking down with benevolence upon an entire society. But it is not clear that the view actually represents the perspective of individuals within that society. This notion is significant when we are exploring an approach that gives primacy to those individuals and their preferences. The key problem is as follows: Economists take for granted a framework of analysis in which each person has rights, including rights to their property, that others are believed to respect. But why should economists work within that framework? Let us consider three answers to this question.

First, the framework is something that many economists think *should* exist, either because they believe in rights theory or because they favor utilitarianism and think that such rights are conducive to social utility. Economists may hold these ideas explicitly; they may have absorbed the ideas unconsciously, as part of their education as economists; or they may have developed the ideas through the broadly liberal cultures they live in. Views of this kind are problematic for two reasons: (1) because economists typically present themselves as undertaking a positive rather than a normative analysis, and (2) because many economists espouse a noncognitivist view of values. They wish to treat values as though they were only a kind of bare preference. But this would make the key role played by what turn out to be their own preferences in their analysis of society odd, to say the least.

The second answer is that economists might argue that these are views held by the people whose actions they are discussing. Such a view has, in most Western countries, some plausibility. It would also appear more appropriate to deal with the actual ideas of the people whom they are analyzing instead of importing the economists' own normative preferences. I see two problems with the economists' second argument: (1) As far as I know, we have no evidence that economists have much interest in trying to discover whether people do, in fact, have such views and what the contours are. (2) In many of the Western countries where the economists live and work, there is casual evidence that people believe a fair measure of redistribution from the rich to the poor, the fortunate to the unfortunate, and so on should be in place. If ordinary people hold such views, economists are mistaken concerning the basis upon which they are working, if it is taken as an account about how individuals in the societies that they are studying think that the institutions of business, the law, and government as a whole ought to work, or even (given the existence of various forms of redistributive taxation) do work.

The third argument is that the framework within which economists work is what is in the interests of all people. In this sense, if people did not have this framework, it would be in the interests of even self-interested individuals to set one up. This is an interesting claim, and I think it is the only basis on which we might combine economists' proto-classical-liberalism with their noncognitivism. Further, striking attempts to show that this would indeed be the case exist, from James Buchanan's work (at those points when he is not also invoking Kantian concerns for the value of each individual) to David Gauthier's to those of Jan Narveson.[22]

Such argument would be impressive to the extent to which it started with economists' ordinary points of departure (such as self-interest or non-tuism) and then delivered the goods. It would not be impressive, in this context, to produce liberal rights out of this hat if they were placed there by surreptitious means to start with; for example, by way of an ad hoc assumption that individuals happened to have noncognitive moral preferences of just the kind as would lead to liberalism. It will also not do for the theorists to introduce their moral principles on an ad hoc basis. In this context, Buchanan's occasional, if morally understandable, Kantian lapses must go, but so must any appeal to utilitarianism. We must let go of any view that puts the interests of others with whom one is engaged in commercial transactions above those of the self-interested individual, and let go of views that in any way suggest that such individuals must treat others as they would themselves wish to be treated, unless it is to their advantage to do so. Starting from such— reasonable and humane—moral assumptions, it may not be difficult to derive liberal views. But that is because we started with proto-liberal assumptions; assumptions to which we are not entitled if we are supposed to start from the economist's usual starting point.

The problem is that it is not clear that such a basis, understood in noncognitivist terms, can support liberal ideas. If I am right, this assumption poses a problem for those who would wish to defend liberalism on a purely prudential basis. Further, if I am right that economists often tacitly presuppose liberal ideas as a framework for their analysis, it suggests that they may face a more general difficulty—namely, an incompatibility between their starting point and the consequences of their assumptions. I will not rehearse all the details of what is, in light of the details of Gauthier's work, a complex if fairly obvious argument.[23] But briefly, just as Hobbes noted that there could be precontractual coalitions of the weak against the strong, so there may be such coalitions of the strong against the weak. They may offer the weak cooperation, but only on terms under which they do not enjoy constitutional equality. And if the weak have tenuous hold over things that the strong want, and if the strong can take them by force, the strong may realize that it is in their interest to do this and to kill the weak. This action is especially compelling if the strong are worried that the weak might be a threat at some time in the future. For there is no reason why, in general, the gains from present and future cooperation should be greater than the gains from expropriation and murder. This reasoning will be especially telling if the weak are members of ethnic or social groups that are (or can be) marginalized, so that the behavior of predators toward them does not have a feedback effect upon how other nonmarginalized people will expect them to behave. If people are self-interested, they will not be subject to moral constraints when making such prudential evaluations. All told, real problems exist with regard to the relationship between the framework and the assumptions of self-interest or of non-tuism on which economists base their analysis. What I believe is crucial is not the self-interest or the non-tuism as such, but those ideas combined with a noncognitivist view of preferences. For, as I will argue below, a cognitivist view of even narrow self-interest may help us avoid the problem that we have just generated because a cognitivist view requires that, at some level, we treat others as something akin to ends in themselves—because we need them, in this capacity, to appraise our cognitive claims.

In my view, there is also a more general problem facing any liberalism that starts from the preferences and concerns that citizens actually have; something that, I believe, is our only proper starting point. (For a discussion of a range of alternative starting points, see James Fishkin's *The Dialogue of Justice*.[24]) The problem is posed by the fact that people typically moderate their concerns for themselves with nepotism; they are inclined to promote the interests of their families, their friends, and the groups with whom they identify.[25] In this context, what is problematic about liberalism is its attachment to moral universalism, a universalism that I personally would wish to be able to uphold. Historically, this moral universalism looks like a product of philosophical and religious ideas, such as Stoicism and Christianity. Moral universalism is also something that often goes with multinational empires—institutions that, in recent years, have perhaps had unjustifiably bad press. I see a significant intellectual task facing contemporary liberalism; namely, to try to find ways to make telling people whose attachments are more local why they should treat everyone, to a limited degree, as ends in themselves—and to do so in a context in which appeals to Stoicism or Christian ideals will not carry much weight in a public forum.

Two resources may be important in this context. The first is the "douce commerce" thesis. It relates to themes with which earlier theorists of commercial society were much concerned: Commercial relations may themselves have a civilizing influence on those who engage in them.[26] We might also refer to the theme, celebrated in the Manchester School's slogan of "Peace and Free Trade," that developing a network of commercial interpenetration may mean that war and predation become obviously against the interests of all concerned. From this perspective, our problems would be resolved if we could get all people into commercial society and then persuade them to pursue their self-interests instead of embarking upon moral crusades. The interpenetration idea draws strength from recent analysis of the way in which reputation, and the development of markets in information about reputation, may serve to keep people on the straight and narrow.[27] If there is any truth in this line of argument, it would suggest (against the wisdom of our age) that individuals who care about the fate of marginalized and disadvantaged aboriginal peoples should do everything they can to bring them as fully as possible into the networks of commercial societies. For insofar as marginalized peoples are not part of commercial networks, they may remain open to predation by the narrowly self-interested. More than external structures based on self-interest, commercial networks may transform the characters and dispositions of those involved in them. (Studying the treatment of people within commercial organizations can illuminate a parallel problem. If those people are seen as the bearers of fallible and disaggregated knowledge, rather than as operatives and bearers of information, they may be treated once more like people who have rights.[28] Yet not only may such rights be misused—compare the conclusion to this chapter—but circumstances may also exist in which it would be advantageous for a company to treat its employees instrumentally instead of as sources of knowledge.)

Another possible line of argument is particularly significant in the context of this chapter because it draws upon the cognitivist theme we explored previously. It is an argument—which I believe may be found in the work of Karl Popper—that our cognitive concerns as such may give us a reason to treat people as something like ends in themselves. The key idea is as follows. Suppose that we are interested in truth or in the correctness of a moral or aesthetic judgment. The epistemological argument to which I referred in Section 1 suggests that we should hold our view open to inter-subjective criticism. But this idea is, itself, morally and politically significant. On the one side, criticism might come from anywhere. This idea is suggested by Popper's Kantian theme of the "rational unity of mankind," when interpreted in light of his epistemology.[29] His idea is that any person is a possible source of criticism; so we have, on this basis, a source of concern even for strangers and those with whom we are not in face-to-face contact. On the other side, it leads us toward liberal concerns about the autonomy or the independence of others. People can only offer us criticism insofar as they enjoy a kind of autonomy or independence. In *Subjection of Women*, John Stuart Mill commented that, if women were subservient to their husbands in that they did not have an independent existence in law or have property rights in their names, then they would suffer from a kind of dependency. As a consequence of this dependence, their husbands could not be sure that they understood their wives' views about things (see the last few pages of his chapter 1). Under those circumstances, if a husband were to ask his wife, "Are you content?" Mill's argument was that the husband could no more trust what was said in response, than if a master were to ask his servant, "Am I a good master?"

As Jeremy Waldron has suggested in the context of arguments about political participation, such considerations may cut in different ways.[30] It was with an eye to such considerations that those who, historically, favored republican ideals had typically restricted citizenship to people who were considered independent: people who were not subservient to others. Waldron himself argues that given unrestricted democracy as a sociological fact, this argument may offer a basis for Marshall-style citizenship rights, as these would guarantee to all citizens the kind of independence that the republican tradition requires. [31] In our context, a concern for truth and for the validity of moral and aesthetic claims will of itself lead us to value the autonomy of others in general. This autonomy would be extended not just to those who are close to us, whose interests may be included within tendencies toward nepotism, but to people who are not members of groups with which we identify. A claim to truth or the correctness of some moral or aesthetic judgment can fall with one good counter-example. And this counter-example might, in principle, come from those with whom we do not identify.

Just what we can—and cannot—get out of such an argument, I will not explore further here.[32] But I have raised this concern for two reasons. First, because it suggests a link between our cognitivist concerns and that respect for others in the tradition of classical liberalism that I have suggested is a problem for economists if they take a noncognitivist perspective, albeit one of which they may not usually be conscious. And, second, because it suggests that James Buchanan has got things badly wrong when he argues that an approach toward politics that sees it as concerned with truth is pernicious in its political consequences, as compared with one based on noncognitivism.[33] For provided that a person is a fallibilist, then it is a concern for truth and for the validity of moral and aesthetic claims that gives that person reason to listen to others and to respect their autonomy. This would be true even if our moral claim is that we are entitled to act in a narrowly self-interested manner. For this claim, if held in a cognitivist form, calls for inter-subjective appraisal from other people who enjoy a form of autonomy. While those who act on the basis of their unquestioned preferences held in a noncognitivist manner may well end up taking attitudes toward others that are predatory if not homicidal.

4. THE PUBLIC FORUM

Someone could suggest that I have been unfair to the writers of whom I have been critical. For it is clear enough that, while Buchanan and Narveson may

be noncognitivists with regard to preferences and take a prudential understanding of morality, at another level they are cognitivists. Their writings
attempt to appeal to people's understanding and reason and not their emotions. They are advancing arguments and are expecting evaluation of them as
such. This could, I suspect, itself be the basis for a case like that developed in
the previous section. Insofar as they are interested in the correctness of their
arguments, they have an interest in the people appraising those arguments
being treated as something like ends in themselves, instead of as the subject
matter for the fulfillment of their bare preferences. My concern in this section, however, is quite different. It asks the question of where such appraisal
is to take place, which might appear strange. But it is worth asking because
economic analysis undertaken on the basis of a concern for what would best
satisfy people's preferences has, understandably enough, led us in the direction of privatization. Let me explain the issue toward which this argument
leads and why privatization is relevant.

The Washington D.C.-based Cato Institute, a leading public policy think
tank with a Libertarian orientation, put out, a few years ago, a Christmas
card that depicted the Capitol building being covered completely in snow.
It was a nice joke. But it raises an interesting question; namely, what would
happen to the Cato Institute if the United States federal government disappeared? It's no accident that the Cato Institute is located in Washington,
D.C. (Note that they moved there from San Francisco in order, presumably, to become a more effective voice in the making of public policy.) When
people in the United States are interested in having a voice in public policy at
the federal level, it behooves them to be in or near the District of Columbia.
A forum is created for the discussion of public policy (and for the development of something akin to an informed public opinion, or bodies that can
reflect upon and debate with those involved more directly in the formation
of government policy) as a result of the interactions between government and
various activities that take place round it. Should government disappear, this
forum would also disappear. Yet it would be naive to think that discussions
of public policy, in the sense of the need to reflect on our shared situation
and to discuss how we might best respond to it, would disappear if there
were no government—if people kept all their taxes and just made private
decisions about how their funds were to be spent, including on the private
provision of "public goods." We need to explore the likely consequences of

doing things in one way instead of another. We need also to reflect on the character of problems as they arise, so that we will know what kinds of commercial or voluntary initiatives it will make sense to take, in the face of them. As things stand, much of this discussion goes on around government. But we would still need a fair bit of it, even if all action were private and undertaken by commercial, charitable, or other cooperative bodies, or by individuals. A public forum—a public sphere—is a mirror in which we may come to see ourselves and an area within which we can receive inter-subjective appraisal of our ideas and conjectures. Complete privatization, in the sense of the abolition of government, would, I suspect, be fatal to the Cato Institute. Yet we would still need a public forum of some sort, and institutions like the Cato Institute would play a role in that forum, one that we would need to re-invent in order to address issues of public policy. But we would need it for other reasons, too.

In the United States Declaration of Independence, Thomas Jefferson stated, "We hold these truths to be self-evident," and then he proceeded to list several claims of a broadly classical liberal character. If such truths were self-evident, and if other people recognized them to be such, then politics would, in some respects, be a fairly easy matter. But such claims (and also the theses of writers like Buchanan and Narveson regarding what moral and constitutional arrangements are in the interests of self-interested individuals) are in need of discursive elaboration and defense. But this, again, poses the question of where such elaboration, defense, and the popular dissemination of the products of such deliberation would take place. Where do we explain this material, and by what means do we put the results of more specialized deliberation before people who would use them when they are thinking about how to make moral and political decisions?

We are, I believe, led again to the idea of a public sphere, constituted on the basis I indicated previously. I would now like to draw attention to an additional problem concerning the public sphere, raised by the path-breaking early work of Juergen Habermas.[34] He described the way in which a public sphere developed within London coffee-houses, where merchants gathered, conversed, and formed opinions on issues of the day. They reflected on what government was doing at the time. (Nothing rests, in my account here, on how close such fora were to an ideal exemplification of unrestricted dialogue.) Habermas then recounts a long and interesting story about the decline of such fora in the face of increasing democratization.

An important lesson from this history is relevant today. The public sphere we are familiar with is a creature that lives in a space between government and private activity. Government gives the public sphere its focus, both geographic and thematic, and it also provides a variety of fora that it inhabits and that form from people and organizations participating in them. But the public sphere is also typically constituted by all kinds of private activity; often (and this is, in my view, a crucial point) as a by-product of people's other concerns. Let us return to Habermas's coffee houses. Their owners were in business not to provide the space for a public forum, but to make a living by selling coffee. Newspapers and television stations today are in the business of making money by selling newspapers and attracting an audience for advertising, not by creating a public sphere. Public policy institutes often receive funds from people who are interested in pursuing personal interests or self-aggrandizement rather than in creating space for debating issues on their merits. And yet, if we are lucky, things work out. But, and here is the rub, there appears to be no special reason why these private/public spheres should continue to work as well as they do. I am not concerned with the corruption of the media by sinister private interests (although it is striking how much of the editorial material of even distinguished newspapers is little more than a fawning backdrop within which advertising can be located). Instead, my concern is with the likely impact of our choices as *consumers* upon such fora.

Robert Putnam, in his "Ithiel de Sola Pool" lecture at the American Political Science Association in 1995, argued that the decline of civic institutions, which had been an earlier topic of discussion (especially in "Bowling Alone"), was to be attributed to our willingness over successive generations to watch increasing amounts of television. I do not know if his claims are sustainable, [35] [36] [37] but I think his argument highlighted something of real importance. Interesting tensions may emerge between what we choose, in the sense of what realizes our preferences, its consequences, and the maintenance of institutions that we value. Consider, for example, the development of narrowcasting on television and the Internet. We may find it extremely attractive to watch material that fits our interests (given that what we are offered does not consist entirely of reruns interlarded with vast periods of substandard advertising). But if we each follow our different preferences, and hitherto general fora dissolve into narrowcasting targeted at individual interests, we may start to lack common concerns. We may lose touch with material pertaining to a view of the world that we share with our fellow citizens. Further, there is a risk that we will miss the critical debate that can help inform us of what the pros and cons of different political positions are, ours included. If our opinions are not formed—and informed—by interaction with contrasting perspectives within a public forum, how can we tell the claim of the extremist or the fanatic from the claim that makes sense, unless it falls within our area of ever-narrowing expertise?

All told, we need institutions that will play a cognitive role for us. But there is a real problem—the institutions that play this role are, in large part, created primarily in order to meet other preferences. Few of us, outside those working in universities, are likely to buy specialized books on political institutions and how they function. The rest of us will typically pick up our ideas from media whose prime concern is other matters (advertising) and who are in competition for our dollars with other institutions that will bid for them more directly. Insofar as our institutions become more responsive to our bare preferences, and insofar as they become more narrowly targeted at satisfying our tastes, there is a risk that they may no longer fulfill the cognitive function that, I have suggested, even our constitutional economists need them to fulfill. Yet recent tendencies, for example the opening up of broadcasting to commercial pressures, not least because of the impact of economic analysis on public policy discourse, are making our institutions more responsive to our bare preferences in just these ways.

Someone might claim that my argument in this section is ambiguous, for the ideas about publicity to which I have referred might be interpreted in two different ways.[38] The first is that of testing our views by way of criticism from anyone who happens to come along. The second, is that we claim to speak for everyone. But are institutions that are public in the latter sense needed for public life? My response goes back to the notion of cognitive that I developed earlier in the chapter. The sense of cognitive with which I am concerned pertains to the claims of individuals or organizations as to what is true, good, beautiful. It also pertains to claims about what others should give weight to, or as to what is in their interest. Such claims are understood as being made in such a way that they should be recognized as legitimate by everybody—and, to this end, as in principle open to criticism by anybody. This approach does not mean we need to ask all people if they have a view about the claims. That would be pointless, in part because many people would have nothing to say or would merely repeat points that have been made by others. In another way it would be pointless because the benefits of what we might learn are likely to be outweighed by the sheer cost of asking. We also cannot assume that our cognitive concerns will be taken care of automatically through the media or through informal exchanges with family and friends. The latter may be too close to our perspective to offer effective criticism. Further, the criticism in question is criticism that we may need but not welcome. All told, we may need to give thought to how to create and maintain the institutions that we need for this criticism.

5. ON HAZARDS OF COGNITIVISM IN PUBLIC POLICY FORMATION

So far in this chapter, my argument has been for the significance of a cognitivist approach; and I have offered it, in broad measure, as a corrective to the approach that economists would often offer toward issues of public policy. But the balance of the argument is not all on one side. Toward the end of Section 1, I indicated that I had reservations about a cognitivist approach, and I would like to conclude by addressing them. My concerns here arise from research that I was undertaking near the same time I developed the ideas presented in this chapter. Some implications of this research for the point of view that I have explored in this chapter came as quite a shock.

My preference is for what we might call a "minimal cognitivism"—one that allows for discourse about rights, reflection on public policy issues, the use of people's knowledge within organizations, and so on, but one that also gives the greatest possible scope to private decision-making. I will offer one argument here, drawn from problems involving the blood supply, intended to encourage critical reflection on any promiscuous enthusiasm for cognitivism the earlier part of the chapter may have generated.[39] This concrete example should, however briefly, illuminate my reservations.

In 1970 Richard Titmuss published *The Gift Relationship*.[40] This work was both a comparative study of the supply of blood in the United Kingdom and the United States and a polemical work in social philosophy. Titmuss advocated a system of voluntary blood donation in which gifts are given without recompense by anonymous others. He opposed the complex system, then current in the United States, that that rested in part on the purchase of blood from skid-row storefront collection agencies. Titmuss argued for both the moral and the practical preferability of a U.K.-style system resting on voluntary donors that was also championed in the United States by the Red Cross.

Titmuss argued it was desirable for our social institutions to foster this anonymous altruism. And, at the same time, he argued that a volunteer-based system worked better. Not only—he claimed—was it more efficient, but it also overcame a significant problem associated with the sale of blood. Specifically, people who were desperate enough to sell their blood in storefront collection agencies were likely to be in relatively ill-health, and they were more likely to lie about their medical status and infection-risking behavior. Since there were (and probably always will be) blood-borne diseases for which tests didn't exist and "windows" between the point of infection and the point at which tests may be effective, there is every reason to prefer voluntary donors as sources to people who would sell their blood.

The system of payment for whole blood is now almost unknown in Western countries. (While writing this paper, I discovered an appeal: "Blood donors needed. Immediate cash! Free health check & mention this ad for a FREE T-SHIRT when you donate blood at Continental Blood Bank . . ." on the Internet.[41] It is almost certain that the organization in question was after blood plasma—which is still a largely commercial operation—instead of whole blood.) Alongside the now volunteer-based system for whole blood, the United States has a sizeable, commercial blood plasma industry that operates by purchasing blood plasma from donors. Blood is drawn from them, centrifuged, and the red cells are returned to the donors, while the plasma is used, notably, for the manufacture of a variety of pharmaceutical blood products, including blood clotting factors and various specialized reagents.[42] Historically, plasma purchase made sense because donors can give it more frequently than they can whole blood, and because, until the late 1980s, the process of taking blood, centrifuging it and returning the red blood cells was time-consuming. For reasons of medical safety, using as few donors as possible is an advantage. And the combination of these factors led to the frequent use of paid donors instead of volunteers.

Relative to blood donors—whose concerns and motives have been mapped in extensive detail—those who sell their blood plasma have not been the subjects of as much study.[43] But such work as I have come across—of an ethnographic character—suggests an interesting contrast with blood donors. While blood donors are treated in a particularly pleasant and gentle fashion, those selling plasma have, historically, been treated in an extremely tough manner.[44] As one study commented, people were treated as though they were trying to conceal medical problems and a history of drug taking. (My comments here oversimplify slightly; there appear to have been two different groups of paid plasma "donors"—students and poor adults—who were treated somewhat differently.)

We have here, if we compare whole blood donors and paid plasma donors, almost ideal types of two different kinds of relations. One involves the almost purely instrumental use of human beings. The other operates with kid gloves, is concerned for people's sensibilities, and—at the level of policy—was consulted extensively with relevant interest groups and maintained a government-like concern for consensual policy-making in a public forum: The treatment of volunteers illustrates the kind of relationship we might see as flowing from a cognitive approach. (This conduct appears, in part, to have been due to the fact that these donation centers needed to maintain good relations with donors, in part because they had an interest in stressing their public character as a way of avoiding liability claims.)

It is interesting to see what occurred in the face of increasing cases of HIV-AIDS infection.[45] The commercial plasma companies reacted more speedily, by introducing detailed questioning about the seller's sexual behavior, than did the Red Cross and the blood banks. The reason was that the commercial companies in question were driven by concerns about the promotion of the merits of their brands, in competition with others, and presumably by concerns about commercial liability. Once a test was introduced by one company, it was taken up by others. It was also unproblematic for them to introduce the detailed and intensive questioning of the plasma sellers because the buyers were not committed to respecting the sellers' feelings or self-image.[46] By contrast, the blood banks and Red Cross were slower because they did not wish to disrupt their relationships with clients and also because they were committed to consultation with the spokespeople of relevant interest groups.

The later introduction of detailed questionnaires about sexual behavior did elicit some hostile reactions from elderly blood donors. And, in the early part of 1983 (well after those purchasing commercial blood plasma had introduced screening with regard to sexual behavior) spokespeople for gay groups were arguing against the introduction of direct questioning about the sexual behavior of blood donors on the grounds that it would be stigmatizing. They also contested whether the links existed, upon a belief in which the plasma purchasers had already acted.

This argument is not, I should stress, directed against the spokespeople for the gay groups in question. It was reasonable for them to argue as they did, given the institutional setting within which they were acting. It is, instead, an argument against the idea that dialogue-based, consensus-directed decision-making is always the best way to operate. There is a problem with dialogue: Even when the weight of the argument is against you, you can, in good faith, argue a case for a position because you are compelled to by your perceptions of your concerns and interests or by your perceptions of the concerns and interests of those you represent.

A case often becomes overwhelming only after a fair amount of discussion has taken place. And even then, because our knowledge is fallible, it will still be possible for people to argue the other side in good faith. Decision-making on the basis of consensus, in such cases, may be unduly slow. There is also a sense in which those participating in the discussion but not actually responsible for the outcomes may have a kind of power without responsibility that is dangerous. (My colleague David Adams has drawn my attention to comments made by Sir Geoffrey Vickers in which he expresses reservations about "the need for consensus and the vulnerability of that consensus to the resistance of protesting or predatory minorities."[47]) Further, while we may favor the kind of treatment accorded to blood donors, as opposed to the way in which disadvantaged people who sell their blood plasma were treated, cases exist—and this is one—in which the outcome is more important than how it is arrived at. In such cases, an insistence on deliberative democracy and its analogues, as opposed to commercial relationships, the commercial assessment of risk, bare preferences, and the treating of others as a means to an end, may be a devastatingly mistaken path to follow. As this example illustrates, it is not always for the best that people be treated as they would want to be treated by others; for it was, in this instance, the more humane path—in which there was consultation and in which people's voices were heard—that was the wrong path. At the same time, subsequent actions in dealing with the transmission of HIV-AIDS may have depended crucially upon information obtainable only in dialogue with members of the gay community.

6. CONCLUSION

My conclusion is fairly simple, although it opens up problems instead of re-solves them. If I am correct in the argument offered in this chapter, we need to take into consideration that both cognitive and bare preferences exist. Once we recognize this coexistence, we may need to treat these preferences in different ways. We may need to create or foster institutions of different kinds to cope with them. The maintenance of such institutions may pose many interesting problems, not least because of the way in which different institutions typically serve many different functions and are subject to differ-ent forms of accountability that, in the ordinary way of things, may operate other than with an eye to some functions in which we may be interested.

I also argued that the recognition that cognitive preferences exist may lead us to treat one another in a different way. Paradoxical as it may sound, a recognition of cognitive preferences may lead us to treat other people as something like ends in themselves, albeit for the instrumental reason of the role that they can possibly play in the appraisal of such preferences.

Finally, the story with which the chapter ends may suggest that, if what I have called cognitive preferences and their significance are recognized, we should not be too ready to demand that we—or others—should be treated as ends in ourselves, or with whatever dignity we feel that we, or they, deserve, and make our decisions on the basis of models of deliberative democracy. For we need to be aware of what the consequences of this will be and of the strik-ing ways in which commercial accountability and market mechanisms that may not always treat us as we might like to be treated can achieve goals that would be difficult to achieve by other means. Thus, there may be a strong moral case for sometimes treating us in ways that, if we take a cognitive perspective, we may think are unethical, and in ways that economists are inclined to picture us as being treated all the time.

NOTES

Some of the research that feeds into this chapter was undertaken while I was a Visiting Scholar at the Social Philosophy and Policy Center, Bowling Green State University, Ohio. I would like to thank the Center for its hospitality and its supporters for making my visit there, and in consequence this work, possible; the members of the Departmental Seminar in the Department of Philosophy, Faculty of Arts, ANU, for their comments on a paper upon which I have drawn in the latter part of this material; Gerald Gaus, Julian Lamont, and Glenn Worthington for their comments upon an earlier version of this paper, and David Adams, Tyler Cowen, Dan Klein, and Robert Taylor for discussion.

1. *Cf.* Jeremy Shearmur, "The Logic of Scientific Discovery," in *Central Works of Philosophy: Volume 4: The Twentieth Century: Moore to Popper,* ed. J. Shand (Chesham: Acumen, 2006), 262–86.

2 . Gary Becker, *Accounting for Tastes* (Cambridge, Mass: Harvard University Press, 1996).

3. *Cf.* Thomas Kuhn, *The Structure of Scientific Revolutions* (Chicago: University of Chicago Press, 2nd edition, 1970).

4. *Cf. Beyond Self-Interest,* ed. Jane J. Mansbridge (Chicago: University of Chicago Press, 1990); and Donald P. Green and Ian Shapiro, *Pathologies of Rational Choice* (New Haven, Conn.: Yale University Press, 1994).

5. Mark Blaug, *The Methodology of Economics* (Cambridge, England: Cambridge University Press, 2nd edition, 1992); and Daniel Hausman, *The Inexact and Separate Science of Economics* (New York: Cambridge University Press, 1992).

6. Geoffrey Brennan and James Buchanan, "The Normative Purpose of Economic 'Science,'" in *Economics: Between Predictive Science and Moral Philosophy,* ed. James Buchanan (College Station: Texas A&M University Press, 1987), 51–65.

7. Geoffrey Brennan and Loren Lomasky, *Democracy and Decision* (Cambridge, England: Cambridge University Press, 1993).

8. *Cf.* Imre Lakatos, *The Methodology of Scientific Research Programmes,* eds. John Worrall and Gregory Currie (Cambridge, England: Cambridge University Press, 1978); and Jeremy Shearmur, "Popper, Lakatos and Theoretical Progress in Economics," in *Appraising Economic Theories* eds. Neil de Marchi and Mark Blaug (Aldershot, England: Elgar, 1991), 35–52.

9. Jane J. Mansbridge, "The Rise and Fall of Self-Interest in the Explanation of Political Life," *Beyond Self-Interest,* ed. Mansbridge, 3–22.

10. *Cf.* Philip Pettit, *Republicanism* (Oxford: Clarendon Press, 1997); and Quentin Skinner, *Liberty Before Liberalism* (Cambridge, England: Cambridge University Press, 1998).

11. *Cf.* Gary Watson, "Free Agency," *Journal of Philosophy* (April 24, 1975), 72(8): 205–20.

12. William Warren Bartley III, *Retreat to Commitment* (La Salle, Ill: Open Court, 2nd edition, 1984).

13. *Cf.* Bartley, *Retreat to Commitment*; and Karl Popper, "On the Sources of Knowledge and of Ignorance" (1960), now the "Introduction" to his *Conjectures and Refutations* (London: Routledge, 1963), 3–30.

14. Knud Haakonssen, *Natural Law and Moral Philosophy* (Cambridge, England: Cambridge University Press, 1996).

15. *Cf.* James Buchanan, *The Limits of Liberty* (Chicago: University of Chicago Press, 1975); and Jean Jacques Rousseau, *The Social Contract.*

16. See Rousseau, *The Social Contract,* conclusion to Book 1, ch. 8.

17. Kelvin Lancaster, "A New Approach to Consumer Theory," *Journal of Political Economy* (April 1966): 132–57; see esp. 151. *Cf.* also George Stigler and Gary Becker, "De gustibus non est disputandum," *American Economic Review,* 67, no.2 (March 1977): 76–90.

18. Richard Brandt, *A Theory of the Good and the Right* (Oxford: Clarendon Press, 1979).

19. David McNaughton, *Moral Vision* (New York: Blackwell, 1988); see also Jeremy Shearmur, *The Political Thought of Karl Popper* (London & New York: Routledge, 1996).

20. Alasdair McIntyre, *After Virtue* (Notre Dame: University of Notre Dame Press, 2nd edition, 1984), 71.

21. Jeremy Shearmur, "The Scope and Status of Prudential Liberalism," *The Review of Politics,* 54, no.2 (1992): 211–30.

22. *Cf.* David Gauthier, *Morals by Agreement* (Oxford; Clarendon Press, 1986); and Jan Narveson, *The Libertarian Idea* (Philadelphia: Temple University Press, 1988). See also Shearmur, "The Scope and Status of Prudential Liberalism."

23. *Cf.* the details of Gauthier, *Morals by Agreement,* and Shearmur, "The Scope and Status of Prudential Liberalism."

24. James Fishkin, *The Dialogue of Justice* (New Haven, Conn: Yale University Press, 1992).

25. *Cf.* Robert Wright, *The Moral Animal* (New York: Pantheon, 1994); and, for the argument in historical context, Jeremy Shearmur, "From Divine Corporation to a System of Justice," in *Economics and Ethics?* ed. Peter Groenewegen (London: Routledge, 1996), 46–67.

26. Albert Hirschman, "Rival Interpretations of Market Society," *Journal of Economic Literature,* 20 (December 1982), 1463–84; and *Reputation* ed. Daniel Klein (Ann Arbor: University of Michigan Press, 1997).

27. See *Reputation,* ed. Klein.

28. Jeremy Shearmur, "The Use of Knowledge in Organizations," *Knowledge Technology & Social Policy,* 13, no.3 (Fall 2000): 30–48.

29. Karl Popper, *The Open Society and Its Enemies* (London: Routledge & Kegan Paul, 1945). See also Jeremy Shearmur, *Hayek and After* (London & New York: Routledge, 1996); and Shearmur, *Political Thought of Karl Popper.*

30. Jeremy Waldron "Social Citizenship and the Defense of Welfare Provision," *Liberal Rights* (Cambridge, England: Cambridge University Press, 1993), 271–308. *Cf.* also T. H. Marshall, "Citizenship and Social Class," (1949), for example, T. H. Marshall and Tom Bottomore, *Citizenship and Social Class* (London: Pluto Press, 1992).

31. See, more generally, Pettit, *Republicanism.*

32. See Shearmur, *Hayek and After* and *Political Thought of Karl Popper,* for further discussion. But also, for some criticism, Frank Michelman, "From Dialogue Rights to Property Rights: Reply to Shearmur," *Critical Review: A Journal of Politics and Society,* 4, Issue 1, 1990: 133– 43.

33. *Cf.* James Buchanan, "From Private Preferences to Public Philosophy," in *The Economics of Politics,* ed. J. Buchanan and others (London: Institute of Economic Affairs, 1978), 3–20.

34. Juergen Habermas, *The Structural Transformation of the Public Sphere* (Cambridge, Mass: MIT Press, 1989). See also Craig Calhoun, *Habermas and the Public Sphere* (Cambridge, Mass: MIT Press, 1992).

35. Robert Putnam, "Tuning In, Turning Out: The Strange Disappearance of Social Capital in America," *PS: Political Science and Politics,* 28, no.4 (December 1995): 664–83.

36. Robert Putnam, "Bowling Alone," *Journal of Democracy*, 6, no.1 (Jan 1995): 65–78.

37. See, for Putnam's responses to critics, Robert Putnam, *Bowling Alone: The Collapse and Revival of American Community* (New York: Simon & Schuster, 2000).

38. Stanley Benn and Gerald Gaus (eds.), *Public and Private in Social Life* (London: Croom & Helm, 1983).

39. *Cf.* Jeremy Shearmur, "Blood, Altruism and Money: The Gift Relationship Re-visited" (unpublished paper delivered at Bowling Green State University, May 1997); and "Trust, Titmuss and Blood," *Economic Affairs*, 21, no.1 (March 2001): 29–33.

40. Compare Richard Titmuss, *The Gift Relationship*, eds. Ann Oakley and John Ashton (London: LSE Books, 1997).

41. See http://www.clo-sfl.com/classifieds/data/135.htm; initially consulted 11/22/98.

42. See, for a useful overview, Judith D. Weber, *Blood Banking and Plasma Products Markets* (Mountain View, Cal: Market Intelligence Research Co, 1990).

43. See for example Jane Piliavin and Peter Callero, *Giving Blood: The Development of an Altruistic Identity* (Baltimore: Johns Hopkins University Press, 1991).

44. Compare Wendy Espeland, "Blood and Money: Exploiting the Embodied Self," in *The Existential Self in Society* eds. Joseph A. Kortaba and Andrea Fontana (Chicago: University of Chicago Press, 1984), 131–55; and Martin J. Kretzmann, "Bad Blood: The Stigma of Paid Plasma Donors," *Journal of Contemporary Ethnography*, 20 (January 1992): 416–41.

45 See, for example, Harvey Sapolsky, "AIDS, Blood Banking and the Bonds of Community," in *Living with AIDS*, ed. S. Graubard (Cambridge, Mass: MIT, 1990), 287–305; *HIV and the Blood Supply*, eds. Lauren B. Leveton *et al.* (Washington: National Academy Press, 1995); Sherry Glied, "Markets Matter: U.S. Responses to the HIV-Infected Blood Tragedy," *Virginia Law Review*, 82 (1997): 1493–1509; Shearmur, "Blood, Altruism and Money;" and Kieran Healey, *Last Best Gift*, Chicago: University of Chicago Press, 2006.

46. See Espelund, "Blood and Money," and Kretzmann, "Bad Blood."

47. Geoffrey Vickers, *Value Systems and Social Process* (Lozndon: Tavistock, 1968), 46.

PART II

THE QUESTION OF
ECONOMIC DESERT

CHAPTER 4

EXPRESSIVE DESERT AND DESERVING COMPENSATION

Christi Favor

At first glance, the answer to the question "Can compensation be deserved?" seems a straightforward "Yes." "Harry deserves compensation—a reckless driver smashed his car" seems a nonproblematic claim in everyday conversation. Such claims occur throughout the legal and distributive justice literatures: "Miners deserve compensation for work in filthy conditions," "The police deserve compensation for dangerous jobs," "Nurses deserve higher compensation for irregular hours."[1] Claims of this form also arise in the context of redressing past injustice: "Holocaust victims and their families deserve compensation for the horrors of the World War II genocide," "Victims of violent crime deserve compensation for harm and trauma." In all these cases, the argument for compensation partly appeals to the fact that victims of such wrongdoing deserve compensation.

These claims demonstrate the familiar and natural role of appeals to desert in political and cultural contexts about justice; they also provide a convincing case that justice often requires compensation. But the relationship

between desert and compensation has received little attention in the philosophical literature on justice, which is striking given that standard analyses
render the logic of all these claims puzzling, if not incoherent. An analysis
of the sense in which compensation can be deserved, if it can be, would help
us understand what sort of justifications can be given for politically divisive
claims such as those above. Clarification of the relationship between desert
and compensation would also contribute to a greater understanding of some
distinctive proposals for justice in income distribution, which depend on the
plausibility of deserving compensation.[2] In this chapter, I explain the reasons why such apparently familiar political demands pose a puzzle for the
philosopher. Then, without undermining standard wisdom regarding desert,
I show how considerations of desert are sometimes, but not always, a coherent and significant part of the justification for compensation. Many of these
desert claims are misleading because they usually misidentify the true basis
for deserving compensation. The relationship between desert and compensation is clarified in a way that is consistent both with the standard analysis of
desert and with the plethora of ordinary claims appealing to desert to defend
compensation. To achieve this result, I employ an analysis of the relationship
between desert and entitlement and a conception of desert emphasizing the
expressive function of deserved treatments.

1. COMPENSATION CLAIMS AND THE
STANDARD ANALYSIS OF DESERT

Do holocaust survivors deserve compensation, and by whom? How much, if
any, additional pay do miners deserve as compensation for dangerous conditions? Although claims such as these may provoke hot disputes, we rarely see
the claimants' demands dismissed as conceptually incoherent. With such a
plethora of apparently ordinary cases, what is the motivation for questioning
whether desert can provide a coherent basis for compensation?

Primarily, the motivation is that compensation appears to be excluded as
a deserved treatment in most philosophical analyses of desert, in which the
following claims are usually either explicit or implicit elements:

1. A three-part relation: Desert claims such as "Smith deserves to be ex-
   pelled for cheating" include a deserving agent, a way of treating or re-

sponding to the person, and a basis for desert, that is, a characteristic or action in virtue of which the agent should be treated as specified in the claim.

2. Desert requires a basis: The desert basis provides a reason or explanation for the desert and must be a characteristic or action of the deserving agent.

3. Fitting responses: To say "Smith deserves to be suspended for cheating" is to say "suspension" is a fitting or appropriate response to cheating. When the basis is negatively valued (disobedience, theft), the treatment will be a negative or undesirable response (scolding, prison). Similarly, when the basis is positively valued (academic excellence, hard work), the treatment will be a positive or desirable response (a grade of A, a promotion).[3]

Claiming to deserve compensation contravenes this widely accepted analysis in two ways. First, compensation claims often take the form that a person deserves compensation because of what a different person has done, contrary to the requirement in (2) above, that the basis for desert be a characteristic of the deserving agent. Contrary to (3) above, compensation is usually a positive treatment, while the basis for the compensation is usually negative (an injury, loss, hardship, etc.). These violations of the standard analysis have led theorists such as David Miller and William Galston to reject the conceptual propriety of arguing for compensation on grounds of desert, providing the motivation for my inquiry here.[4] I accept the standard analysis of desert (with a minor qualification) and defend it against two complaints raised by Geoff Cupit and Fred Feldman.[5] I only partially agree with Miller. I argue that, appropriately interpreted, some but not all claims to deserve compensation are conceptually inappropriate. In many cases, desert is a crucial part of the justification for compensation. By providing a better understanding of desert claims, I can also explain why the tendency to describe compensation as deserved has evolved, even in cases where desert is conceptually not the most appropriate ground for justifying the compensation claim.

First, a few comments about methodology are in order. Claims to deserve compensation are problematic because they seem both (1) commonly described as desert claims in everyday contexts and in philosophical and legal literature, and (2) contrary to an uncontroversial, standard analysis of desert in the two ways mentioned previously.

We could address such a puzzle by rejecting the standard analysis of desert. Fred Feldman takes this approach.[6] Unlike Miller, Feldman takes claims to deserve compensation at face value and rejects the standard analysis on the grounds that cases such as those listed above are counterexamples to it. Feldman offers no extended discussion of how to modify the standard analysis to be consistent with counterexamples, of how to reinterpret the counterexamples for more consistency with the standard analysis, or of how to weigh relative strengths and weaknesses of the standard account and the counterexamples to determine which to reject. Given the wide variety of cases consistent with the standard analysis, and given the distinctiveness that analysis achieves for the concept of desert in relation to other moral concepts, we should not reject the account without a more complete discussion. I undertake such a discussion here, concluding that the standard analysis can accommodate the so-called counterexamples.

In a second challenge to the standard analysis, Cupit discusses a rowing team that has a tradition of throwing its best rower in the river at the end of each racing season. In this example, a team-member deserves to be thrown in the river in virtue of being the best rower. Here, a positive quality is rewarded with a treatment ordinarily considered negative or undesirable, apparently contradicting the fittingness element of the standard analysis.[7] Cupit believes this example demonstrates that the third component is a usual but not necessary feature of desert. I discuss this claim further later in the chapter; I believe it constitutes only a minor qualification to the standard analysis and one that is consistent with the expressive account I propose. Though this qualification will not itself solve the compensation puzzle, a deeper understanding of the expressive features of deserved treatments explains why they usually, but not necessarily, conform to the standard analysis. This same appeal to expression is ultimately the key to understanding deserved compensation.

2. THE EXPRESSIVE THEORY OF DESERT

In this section, I propose a three-part account I call "expressive desert," providing the framework for my treatment of deserved compensation. According to the expressive theory, any assertion represented by the schema "S deserves T in virtue of b," implies three claims:

1. S is, has, or did b. Here, b is an action performed by or a characteristic of S.

2. Some evaluative attitude about S is warranted in virtue of b (an evaluative attitude such as admiration, gratitude, resentment, marvel, respect) or that b is a good, bad, wrong, evil, or valuable attribute or action.

3. T (a treatment) is an effective expression of the evaluative attitude referred to in (2).

According to this account, each desert claim implies three separate claims. "Judy deserves a standing ovation for her dramatic interpretation," communicates three ideas: (1) Judy's performance demonstrates dramatic skill, (2) the demonstrated skill is superb and worthy of great admiration or appreciation, and (3) a standing ovation would effectively express great admiration or appreciation.

A question that immediately arises with regard to the expressive account is, "What counts as effective expression?" Is expression effective from the point of view of the whole society, some smaller more relevant audience, or just the deserving agent?

I propose three (sometimes conflicting) factors relevant to the effectiveness of a treatment:

a. Effectiveness to the agent: The likelihood that the response will express the right evaluative attitude to the deserving agent.

b. Effectiveness to the public: The likelihood that the response will express the right evaluative attitude to the relevant audience.

c. Effectiveness to the expresser: The satisfaction in the communicator that the response effectively expresses the right evaluative judgments or attitudes.

I do not say each is necessary, or that any one is sufficient, for a treatment's being effective enough to count as deserved. I do not have a strict formula, and I suspect none exists, for which consideration is the most important or how to weigh each when they conflict. But the inexactness of this account is not an overwhelming weakness of it. We would only expect to find a precise formula for measuring effectiveness if our intuitions about which treatments are deserved were exact, but typically, we are willing to assent to numerous desert claims recommending quite different treatments for an agent's action, and we're unable to rank the treatments precisely according to which are the most deserved.

The second evaluative component in the account of desert works with the expressive component to explain why some treatments and not others are fitting responses to specific bases of desert. It also explains why positive bases usually go with positive treatments, why they sometimes do not (as with the rowers), and why desert can be part of a coherent justification for compensation.

People value many characteristics or behaviors: intelligence, agility, strength, honesty, clarity, reasonableness, diplomacy, compassion, artistic expression, or beauty. Other traits and actions we disvalue: selfishness, deception, disregard of others, carelessness, or aggression. Values such as these determine desert bases. The feature or action specified as the basis of desert is just the feature or action that is valuable or disvaluable. The value component is also relevant in determining a fitting response to a desert basis, since treatments express these values. We respond well to honesty, express hurt or anger when deceived, imprison people who intentionally harm others, behave graciously for kindness shown us, and so on. An appropriate and fitting response will be one that is apt, given its conventional meaning and effects on well being, to give expression to our values and communicate them to the public and/or the deserving agent.

Recall that on the standard analysis, positively valued traits go with positive treatments. On the expressive theory, the treatments that are fitting responses to positively valued traits in people are those treatments effectively expressing the positive evaluation. Usually these treatments will be pleasant and desirable, because usually we express gratitude, respect, appreciation, or admiration by treating people in pleasant, desirable ways. But expression is necessarily conventional, and treatments take on special expressive effects in unique contexts or cultural settings. We would not expect the treatment most people find enjoyable or pleasant in one culture to be the same in another, even if much the same behavior warrants pleasant treatment in both cultures. Even if the behavior or characteristics that warrant deserved treatment are not culture specific, the treatments that count as fitting responses are sensitive to cultural interpretation.

In Cupit's rowing case, throwing a team member into the river as part of a team tradition carries a special, and unusual, message. That is, it expresses something different in this special team culture than it would elsewhere in the general population. Perhaps it demonstrates familiarity, respect, playfulness, membership, or recognition of ruggedness, alongside esteem for exceptional talent and skill. Medals and trophies would more effectively express the public's esteem for rowing talent and skill, but throwing a teammate in the river better expresses the team's esteem—a special form of admiration among one's friends and rowing peers—even if the treatment appears peculiar outside the team culture.

Thus, expressive desert provides a deeper understanding of that component of the standard analysis that says positively valued desert bases tend to go with positively valued treatments (because positive treatments usually express a positive evaluation); at the same time, expressive desert is able to explain Cupit's example as one in which expression of positive evaluation is best achieved by a treatment, ordinarily considered mildly unpleasant, that has taken on a special meaning in a specific social context. Cupit is right to urge that the fit between positive desert bases and positive treatments, or negative desert bases and negative treatments, is usual, but not necessary. What is necessary, on the expressive account, is that the deserved treatment be one that effectively expresses the evaluation in question.

Treatments can be effective expressions to a degree, and deserved, if they are effective expressions to most people most of the time, even if some individuals are unusual in what they find pleasant or unpleasant treatment. For example, trophies generally express recognition and admiration effectively because most people enjoy receiving and displaying them. In virtue of their established role in public bestowals of admiration, they are effective expressions, even to those individuals who happen not to enjoy the ceremonial receiving of them or who find the trophies themselves aesthetically displeasing. Similarly, if most people on the rowing team found the ceremonial throwing into the river a fun, playful activity, then the fact that some rowers hate the experience would not undermine its expression. However, if a toss into the river were not only mildly unpleasant, but horribly so, the tradition would probably not have developed as it did.

The above discussion permits us to address the question of whether, and in what sense, deserved treatments are relative or have objective constraints. Since deserved treatments are partly a matter of expressing values, and expression is culturally influenced, what treatments are deserved will depend partly on their cultural context. However, there are two objective constraints on what can count as a deserved treatment. First, cultural differences may still be subject to particular objective constraints; for example, what humans are able to sustain and understand as treatments. So, no matter how well-engrained the rowers' tradition of honoring their teammates with a toss in the river, such expression would be ineffective in dangerously freezing temperatures, an objective constraint on cultural expression. Second, what the treatments express is a valuing of the characteristic in question, such as hard work or honesty, and a view that the deserving agent exhibits this value. At least some of the values themselves (unless one is a relativist about all value), and whether the agent actually exhibits them, are objective matters.

My solution to the puzzle of deserved compensation appeals to what can be expressed when we either agree or refuse to compensate people for harms they suffer. What compensation expresses, however, is not so straightforward as the rowing case, explaining why the relationship between desert and compensation has proved so confusing. As a bonus, Feldman's complaint that compensation cases violate the desert basis feature of the standard wisdom also disappears.

3. THE INTERPRETATION OF COMPENSATION CASES

I will explain how compensation can coherently be deserved in three stages. First, I agree with Miller that despite appearances and common usage to the contrary, some claims to deserve compensation are conceptually inappropriate and hence, not really cases of desert. In these cases, entitlement is a better justification for the compensation. Second, and contrary to Miller, I argue that compensation is sometimes deserved, but I urge that, despite appearances, these claims are compatible with the standard analysis of desert. Finally, I show that even in cases for which entitlement offers the more appropriate structure, often a justification of desert is lurking behind the institutional scheme, giving rise to the entitlement claim. However, standard formulations of compensation claims in ordinary social and political discourse are misleading because they do not reveal the whole justification for the compensation, or the true bases of desert, which explains why they have previously appeared incoherent.

Consider this ordinary case of desert:

Harry deserves compensation for auto repairs; Tom was reckless when he hit Harry's car. Harry was driving properly and is in no way at fault.

This claim allegedly contravenes the standard account in two ways: (1) Reckless driving is not Harry's action but Tom's. On the standard account, a person cannot deserve treatment for another's actions. (2) Receiving money is a positive treatment, but not in response to a positive feature of the deserving agent, as the standard account requires, since having suffered property loss is not a positive feature of Harry.

Is this type of compensation claim really a case of desert? Because people sometimes say "S deserves T" when they mean only "S ought to receive T," the relationship between ought and desert should first be clarified. Legitimate claims of desert generate prima facie ought claims. To say George deserves T usually implies, ceteris paribus, that George ought to receive T. Other types of moral claims often compete with and sometimes outweigh considerations of desert. Entitlements, rights, and some forms of needs claims, for example, similarly have this feature, but each is distinct from desert. The reverse does not hold: To say Mary ought to receive T does not imply, even prima facie, that she deserves it (since some other moral consideration might serve to justify the oughtclaim).

With these distinctions in place, the next step is to query whether any of these non-desert considerations are behind the claim that Harry ought to receive compensation. A likely candidate is entitlement. Perhaps Harry ought to receive compensation not because he deserves it (not because he has demonstrated some feature worthy of this money), but because he is entitled to it. Standard features of many legal systems do entitle those who have suffered loss at the reckless hands of another to remedy for the loss. Someone who urges compensation for Harry may have in mind that Harry is entitled to compensation under the existing rules of an institutional or legal structure, the purpose of which is to ensure harms suffered at the reckless hands of another are compensated. Such claims would be more clear using "ought to receive," "is entitled to," or "has a right to compensation," instead of "deserves compensation."[8]

Making such conceptual distinctions is significant from a philosophical point of view. Few philosophers treat desert and entitlement as the same concept, having the same logical structure.[9] One of Joel Feinberg's motivations in developing the standard analysis of desert was to remedy widespread confusion caused by the failure to see desert as a special kind of ought statement, distinct from entitlement. Feinberg shows that desert and entitlement are distinct with his example of the runner. The runner who crosses the finish line first is entitled to the prize. Generally those runners who finish first also deserve the prize, but this correlation sometimes fails, as when the fastest runner "turns up lame," or has her path crossed by another runner, in which case the runner who crosses the finish line first is entitled to, but may not deserve, the prize.[10] This example suggests the two concepts are distinct. The distinct structures and justifications for these claims are lost when people use "ought to," "has a right to" or "is entitled to" interchangeably with "deserves."

4. THE SENSE IN WHICH COMPENSATION CAN BE DESERVED

That a significant number of claims to deserve compensation are nothing more than claims to entitlement is the first stage of my argument, but something unsatisfying remains in saying that those people who claim compensation is deserved are simply confused, while those using the language of entitlement and rights are not. So far our only explanation for people making such desert claims is that they are being loose in their use of conceptual categories. In this section, I rely on the account of expressive desert to demonstrate coherent versions of the claim to deserve compensation, as opposed to being entitled to it.

First, let us consider two cases in which someone is entitled to, but not deserving of, compensation. The coherence of such cases suggests the possibility, by contrast, of being both deserving of and entitled to compensation. If so, the appeal to entitlement cannot replace all claims to deserve compensation.

Imagine Reckless Rick, who is well accustomed to taking chances on the road. On a regular basis, he is too fast, reckless, under-cautious, rude, and a real risk to others. Moreover, Rick makes no attempt to improve his driving and is instead exhilarated by the danger he creates. Although Rick has, due to sheer luck, narrowly avoided countless accidents, this day, through no fault of his own, Rick is bumped from behind by Oblivious Owen (who is paying no attention). Under a system of strict liability, Rick may be entitled to compensation to restore his damaged bumper, although he does not deserve it. But Rick deserves to lose his car (and license) for his constant disregard and reckless endangerment of others. Rick's usual behavior warrants negative responses, not positive ones.

Take as a second example Bob, whose job is to cut wood for a lumber company that is in violation of the law regulating safe working conditions for its employees. Bob has an accident at work and injures his back. Since his lawyer is able to prove the company did not provide safe working conditions, under the law he is entitled to compensation from the company. But suppose Bob's accident was not at all a result of the otherwise unsafe conditions in his workplace. Suppose Bob has developed an illness that causes him to lose his balance on a regular basis, and the illness was the cause of his accident. He has known about the illness, and the danger it poses both to himself and to his workmates, for months. His doctor has been urging him to find more suitable employment. Although Bob knows the company would offer him a desk job that would be safer for someone in his condition, he has failed to inform them of his illness because his position as a woodcutter is central to his self-image. In this case, although Bob is entitled to compensation because the company did place him in dangerous conditions, his foolishness (which is the real cause of the accident) would lead many to judge him undeserving of it.

Consideration of such cases suggests that something more than or independent of entitlement is often behind the claim that Harry, a good driver by contrast, or Jack, a woodcutter whose injuries are due entirely to unsafe working conditions, ought to be compensated. Can we appropriately classify this something as desert, as that concept usually functions? The second stage of my argument offers an interpretation of some compensation claims yielding genuine desert claims (distinct from entitlement claims), consistent with the spirit of the standard analysis.

According to expressive desert, desert claims are a means by which people in everyday contexts express how the world should be.[11] One of the distinctive features of using desert claims for this purpose is that they express the idea that people should fare well or badly in proportion to how good or bad they are. This goodness and badness is not restricted to moral goodness and badness. The claim "Carl Lewis deserved to win the 1988 Olympic 100 meters" is made on the grounds that his sprinting was the best in the world. Goodness and badness here range over the full spectrum of what people find valuable. The fittingness requirement of the standard analysis of desert captures this feature. With this basic feature of desert in mind, let us explore the case of Australia's "Stolen Generation," who have demanded compensation for years of trauma suffered as a result of Australia's cultural assimilation strategy in the first half of the twentieth century.

The Stolen Generation in Australia refers to the now adult members of Australia's aboriginal community who were taken as babies from their parents and placed in government or church-sponsored institutions (with government knowledge and permission), as part of a policy of socializing aboriginals into the lifestyle and culture of the British and Europeans who had settled and established themselves in Australia. Once the documents proving a government role in this injustice surfaced, the Stolen Generation demanded an official apology and compensation for their years of suffering and harm. An official commission was established to determine exactly what had happened, by whom, to what extent the government was involved, and what harms resulted for these people. Part of the commission's task was also to determine whether compensation ought to be paid to the victims.[12] The commission explored whether any existing legal and institutional imperatives entitled the victims to compensation. Yet surely a separate consideration in the minds of both victims and the general public was that anyone treated in this way for no good reason deserves compensation, even if existing institutional imperatives do not require it.

On the expressive account, this consideration has a coherent and distinctive place. In so far as we think the world should be a place where the bad things that happen to people (particularly as a result of the actions of others) are responses to their faults (that is, a world where desert reigns), then the losses these people suffered seem wrong to us. This is partly because their losses cannot possibly be seen as what they deserved. Hence, if we want desert to reign (at least to a reasonable degree in some social spheres), then our social institutions should treat people in ways that to a reasonable degree reflect (and in any event are not inconsistent with) what people deserve.

From this perspective, compensating people for losses that cannot be explained or justified according to desert is a way of giving people what they deserve. Although no world, and no social system, does or should seek to make sure all gains and losses in people's lives are a reflection of their deserts, to see compensatory treatments as deserved is to see them as functioning to increase the range in our lives in which desert, rather than luck or something else, determines our outcomes. By way of addressing an objection raised by Cupit against the strategy I take here, I will be more specific about how the consideration raised above is captured in the structure of desert claims for compensation.

To say that the treatment of indigenous Australians cannot be explained according to desert is ambiguous between two interpretations. On the first interpretation, the treatment and resulting harm was undeserved. On the second interpretation, indigenous Australians deserved not to receive the treatment and resulting harm they suffered. Determining which of these interpretations is at issue is necessary in order to evaluate the following objection raised by Cupit, against employing desert in compensation cases:

It is often held that those who suffer through no fault of their own—and especially those who suffer as a result of another's fault—deserve compensation . . . it may seem that we may argue as follows. People who suffer through no fault of their own deserve compensation simply because they do not deserve to suffer. Thus deserving. compensation cannot run counter to the status requirement for, since no positive desert claim is made, no desert basis (status-affecting or otherwise) is presupposed.

But this argument is a non sequitur. We may agree that those who suffer through no fault of their own do not deserve to suffer. But to say that someone deserves compensation is to say that that person deserves not to suffer. The argument, then, requires us to move from the claim that a person does not deserve to suffer to the claim that the person deserves not to suffer. But the latter claim does not follow from the former. To say that a person does not deserve to suffer is to say that there is no reason (of a desert-generating type) for that person to suffer. To say that a person deserves not to suffer is to say that there is a reason (of a desert-generating type) for that person not to suffer. And clearly, it does not follow merely from the fact that there is no reason, of a desert-generating type, for a person to suffer that there is a reason, of a desert-generating type, for that person not to suffer . . . The conclusion we require is not that people should not suffer, but that they deserve not to suffer.[13]

It may appear that my argument regarding the sense in which compensation is deserved is a non sequitur, since I have argued that support for the claim "Aboriginal victims of Australia's Stolen Generation deserve compensation for their suffering," may come from the feeling that "The Stolen Generation's suffering was undeserved." As Cupit rightly claims, "not deserving a loss" is not logically equivalent to "deserving not to have a loss." Yet the aboriginal claim to compensation is not undermined by this kind of objection for two reasons, both deriving from the expressive nature of treatments genuinely supported by considerations of desert.

First, we have good justification for interpreting the aboriginal claim according to the second stronger interpretation, "Indigenous Australians deserved not to suffer the treatment and harm they endured under Australia's cultural assimilation policies." Cupit's reason for questioning this interpretation is that "losses are not ordinarily thought to affect one's status."[14] That is, he does not believe that losses are generally taken to indicate that something about the person who suffered the loss made the loss appropriate. If this is true, then neither suffering a loss nor not suffering a loss expresses or reflects any evaluation of moral worth, status, characteristics, value, or so on.

On the expressive account, we build a case for the claim that someone deserves not to suffer a particular treatment by analyzing what is expressed in the treatment or in withholding the treatment. Many losses are merely undeserved, and consequently, do not support the stronger claim that people deserve not to suffer them. For example, the loss experienced when a loved one dies of natural causes at the end of a long life is an undeserved loss. Odd would be the claim that some warranted evaluation of the deceased or the deceased's family members is effectively expressed in the death and so provides justification for it. The loss of a loved one under these circumstances is undeserved. However, equally odd is the claim that people deserve not to experience such losses. Mortality is part of human nature. To enjoy a long life and die of natural causes at its end is all anyone may expect. The loss we experience when loved ones die is a natural part of human existence, and one none can avoid. This inevitable suffering expresses no evaluation of us, rendering the language of desert out of place here.

By contrast, when someone dies or loses a family member prematurely as a result of someone else's recklessness or wrongful treatment, the claim that the person deserved not to die, or that his family members deserved not to lose him, is appropriate. This would not be true if the deceased himself had died as a result of participation in violent crime; but as an upstanding citizen who treats others with respect and fairness, he deserved not to die from wrongful treatment. Such considerations may coherently underpin a compensation claim for his family members. Similarly, aboriginals deserved not to have their families separated for the purpose of cultural assimilation, merely for being part of a different cultural background than that favored by British or European colonists. Equivalently, aboriginals deserved the respect as individuals and as a culture that would prohibit such cruel practices as forcibly removing children from their parents, on the sole condition of being aboriginal. In this context, compensation is deserved, because in so far as compensation can go some way toward making up for the harm aboriginals suffered, it expresses that aboriginals deserved not to suffer that harm.[15]

I now want to argue that in the context of a society in which institutions exist with the capacity to compensate undeserved losses, a decision not to compensate victims of undeserved losses can also express evaluations of those people. This is especially true when loss or harm occurs at the reckless or morally wrongful hands of the society's own citizens, or worse, its authorities. The tendency to express negative evaluations of people by not compensating is even stronger when the victims are members of a group historically undervalued or discriminated against in the society. According to expressive desert, treating people in accordance with desert is a means by which we express evaluations of people, their characteristics, and actions. We do this both as individuals and as members of a community, in which social institutions also express evaluations in their treatment of people.

In the case of Australian aboriginals, when the compensation demand was denied, much of the outrage felt among members of the Stolen Generation was due to the fact that they understood the failure to compensate as a negative and unwarranted judgment of them as people. The outrage was not merely due to the fact that their loss and harms would be left unrestored. The message they took was understandable because the treatment leading to the harms in the first place was an expression of an unwarranted negative evaluation of them and their culture. Compensation would serve as a partial rejection, on behalf of all Australians, of the evaluations relied upon to motivate the original policy of social assimilation. In so far as compensation would express that these people are of equal status and equal worth, with the same rights as other Australians to choose cultural practices, and in so far as compensation is a possible option for this institution, Aboriginals understandably take the decision not to compensate as a continued expression of unequal status.

The situation might be different if the injustice did not take place in the context of a society in which institutions exist with the authority and purpose to handle such claims. Where losses are undeserved in a context in which no relevant institutions exist, then failures to compensate may not express anything at all. But where it makes sense to claim that compensation is deserved, my argument is that the compensation and the decision not to compensate can express evaluations of the victims involved. Where the failure to compensate expresses unwarranted negative evaluations, the denial of compensation is undeserved; where compensation expresses evaluations that are warranted, it is deserved. Decisions must be made as to whether the resulting desert claims generate overriding reasons to act, given their relative importance alongside other goals of the relevant institutions and other claims on their resources.

Cupit considers, but rejects, a reply similar to this: "But to fail to compensate is not in itself to treat a person as deserving to suffer."[16] I have argued that failures to compensate can express negative and unwarranted evaluative judgments. In this case, failure to compensate reinforces the expressions in the original injustices. This is not the same injustice as taking them from their families in the first place, but it is a serious injustice nonetheless. If expressions of this kind occurring in the actions of our social institutions were not sources of justice or injustice, the social support or outrage such treatments elicit would be inexplicable.

This point about how compensatory treatment, or the denial of it, is even more likely to have an expressive function in the context of social institutions brings me to the third stage of my argument. I have argued that some compensation claims are best formulated in terms of entitlement, but that desert does play a coherent and distinctive role in the justification for a number of other compensation claims. I now want to show that desert claims sometimes even underpin the institutions giving rise to entitlements for compensation. To do this, I need to explain the sense in which desert can be pre-institutional, or logically prior to institutional structures.

5. HOW DESERT CAN BE PRIOR TO INSTITUTIONAL ENTITLEMENT

The expressive account of desert helps clarify the relationship between desert and entitlement, where entitlement arises out of institutionally established rules and conventions. Not only are these two notions distinct, but also sometimes considerations of desert are prior to claims of entitlement, in the sense that the bases of desert and the values determining them are one (but only one) moral constraint in the choice of entitlement conditions. That is, the conditions making someone entitled to a prize (crossing the finish line first) are partly determined by our values regarding running (speed) and the bases they pick out (being the fastest runner). Given this relationship between desert and entitlement, we may believe both that Harry is entitled to compensation because of the legal and insurance institutions governing traffic incidents, and also that these laws are legitimate in part because people in Harry's circumstances deserve compensation for their losses. If so, appeals to entitlement can often be supplemented with considerations of desert, where the justification for the institution giving rise to the entitlement claim is itself justified in terms of desert. That is, desert is one (but not the only) pre-institutional moral consideration providing justification for institutional entitlement.

Desert may be described as pre-institutional in the sense that considerations of desert may provide criticisms or moral constraints on our institutions. The value component of expressive desert allows a richer explanation than has so far been given of the pre-institutional force of desert. Legal or rule-governed entitlement arises out of institutional frameworks that specify entitlement conditions in the rules of the practice. The institutions themselves are typically developed in response to the values, attitudes, and aims of the community, and their desire to express these in their treatments of people who exhibit valuable qualities. Institutions rewarding sport, for example, arise out of the value of sport to the community. These values in turn determine the specific bases of desert (such as speed in running), which in turn determine entitlement conditions (such as crossing the finish line first). The institution in general allows the community more efficient and effective expression and celebration of its values, yet necessarily the institution will sometimes generate entitlements that fail to coincide with desert. In an institutional setting, entitlement conditions generate distinct moral considerations, such as those that arise from legitimate expectations, that should usually coincide with desert but sometimes compete with it. Desert offers normative constraints on institutional structures in the sense that desert claims (and the values implicit in them) motivate and provide normative support for the institutions and can also be offered as grounds for revising the institution's methods when the entitlement conditions fail too often to reflect the values on which an institution is based.[17]

Drawing on this account of pre-institutional desert, the expressive theory of desert and the three stages of the argument in this chapter should clarify claims to deserve compensation in a range of cases. I hope, for example, it will be particularly useful in debates about the justification of income. Desert is a common, and particularly compelling, justification for differentials in income for labor. However, theorists who strongly believe some people deserve more income than others for their work disagree about the basis for deserving higher and lower income, that is, whether higher incomes are deserved as a reward for a more valuable contribution to the social product or as compensation for greater losses incurred in the work, either due to longer hours or more stressful working conditions. The latter kind of basis, however, only counts as a coherent basis for a desert claim to higher income if compensation can coherently be deserved. I hope the account can be usefully applied to debates such as these and will provide greater precision for those offering justifications for compensation claims in cases of past injustice.

NOTES

I wish to thank Julian Lamont, Gerald Gaus, Thomas Christiano, Geoffrey Cupit, Holly Smith, and David Miller for comments on the paper upon which the chapter is based, and I continue to acknowledge the influence of my mentor, the late Joel Feinberg, and his own mentor, Josiah Carberry.
    1. Joel Feinberg, "Justice and Personal Desert," *Doing and Deserving* (Princeton, N.J.: Prince-

ton University Press, 1970), 55–94; Brian M. Barry, *Political Argument* (London: Routledge and Keagan Paul, 1965), 111, 165–66; Alistair Macleod, "Economic Inequality: Justice and Incentives," in *Economic Justice*, ed. Kenneth Kipnis (Totowa, N.J.: Rowman and Allenheld, 1985), 176–89; Joseph Carens, "Compensatory Justice and Social Institutions," *Economics and Philosophy*, 1 (1985): 39–67; Heather Milne, "Desert, Effort and Equality," *Journal of Applied Philosophy*, 3 (1986): 235–43; Richard Norman, *Free and Equal* (Oxford: Oxford University Press, 1987); George Sher, *Desert* (Princeton: Princeton University Press, 1987), 99–108; Arthur DiQuattro, "Rawls and Left Criticism," *Political Theory*, 11 (1983): 53–78.

2. James Dick, "How to Justify a Distribution of Earnings," *Philosophy and Public Affairs*, 4 (1975): 248–72; Wojciech Sadurski, *Giving Desert Its Due* (Dordrecht, Holland: D.Reidel, 1985), 144–46; Julian Lamont, "Incentive Income, Deserved Income, and Economic Rents," *Journal of Political Philosophy*, 5 (1997): 26–46.

3. Joel Feinberg, "Justice and Personal Desert"; David Miller, *Social Justice* (New York: Oxford University Press, 1976), 83–121; William Galston, *Justice and the Human Good* (Chicago: University of Chicago Press, 1980), 174.

4. David Miller, *Social Justice*, 69, 103–14; William Galston, *Justice and the Human Good*, 174.

5. Geoffrey Cupit, *Justice as Fittingness* (Oxford: Clarendon Press, 1996), 61; Fred Feldman, "Desert: Reconsideration of Some Received Wisdom," *Mind*, 104, no.413 (January 1995): 63–77.

6. Feldman, "Desert: Reconsideration of Some Received Wisdom," 63–77.

7. Cupit, *Justice as Fittingness*, 27.

8. Miller, *Social Justice*, 63.

9. David Cummiskey, "Desert and Entitlement: A Rawlsian Consequentialist Account," *Analysis*, 47 (1987): 15–19.

10. Feinberg, "Justice and Personal Desert," 61.

11. Samuel Scheffler, "Individual Responsibility in a Global Age," *Social Philosophy and Policy*, 12 (1995): 219–236; David Miller, "Review Article: Recent Theories of Social Justice," *British Journal of Political Science*, 21 (1991): 371–391.

12. Raymond Evans, "Steal Away: The Fundamentals of Aboriginal Removal in Queensland," *Journal of Australian Studies*, 62 (1999): 83–97; C. Edwards and P. Read, *The Lost Children* (Moorebank, NSW: Doubleday/Bantam, 1989).

13. Cupit, *Justice as Fittingness*, 41–42.

14. Ibid., 42, 12n.

15. One might object that "respect that prohibits forcible removable of children from their parents" is more like a basic right all people share equally, rather than a desert basis, so that rather than "aboriginals deserved not to suffer the harm of removal from their family members," they would have had a moral and legal right not to suffer such harm, in which case they would be entitled to compensation, and the failure to compensate them might express inappropriate evaluations of them, but this would not imply that the compensation is, strictly speaking, deserved. This objection would raise larger questions about the relationship between rights claims, equality claims, and desert claims, so I'm afraid I must leave that to a more extensive discussion of such matters elsewhere. I hope here, at any rate, I have managed to clarify how some causes of loss, compensation for loss, or withholding compensation can express evaluations of people, and hence can make the language of desert (given its expressive element) comprehensible rather than merely confused.

16. Cupit, *Justice as Fittingness*, 42, 12n.

17. David Miller, *Principles of Social Justice* (Cambridge, Mass: Harvard University Press, 1999), ch. 7.

CHAPTER 5

PRODUCTIVITY, COMPENSATION, AND VOLUNTARINESS

Julian Lamont

1. INTRODUCTION

Every society has a multitude of institutional systems interacting to determine the earnings that individuals gain from productive work. These include the taxation, education, and business regulation systems; the unions; the industrial legislation systems; and the licensing and registration systems. These systems are constantly changed by government legislation. Individuals, professional associations, unions, employer organizations, charities, educational institutions, and many others argue each year about these changes, as do the politicians representing the populace. One of the most common appeals made by these parties, when arguing about earnings, is to what people deserve: Workers deserve better conditions; small businesses deserve a fair deal; nurses and teachers deserve better pay; people from poorer backgrounds deserve better access to higher education; CEOs deserve considerably less pay. David Miller, in an evaluation of the empirical survey and experimental literature on people's attitudes toward income justice, notes the relative lack of discussion regarding desert in the philosophical literature compared to how commonly the general population appeals to considerations of desert when assessing the justice of distributive systems. He argues ". . . if notions of desert are as deeply embedded in popular notions of justice as I believe, then it may be difficult to win support for policies whose justification depends on the assumption that desert is an . . . irrelevant idea."[1] While economists have a role to play in this area, philosophers have a crucial responsibility to help in the articulation and critical development of conceptions of justice—a task vital to the rational reform of the distribution system.

In this chapter, I examine two of the most common desert-based principles of income justice: the productivity principle and the compensation principle. Their basic form and rationale are given in Sections 2 and 3. In Section 4, the voluntariness requirements that come from a conceptual analysis of desert are considered. I also outline the structure of the debate about the best basis for claims to deserve income, in order to avoid confusion about the role voluntariness plays in such debates. In Section 5, the values underlying both the productivity and compensation principles are made explicit. In Section 6, I explore how the two principles deal with the "problem of natural talents," arguing that the compensation principle is morally superior because it realizes the value of voluntary control to a greater degree than the productivity principle.

2. THE PRODUCTIVITY PRINCIPLE

While compensation and productivity principles come in many different versions, for ease of reference, "the compensation principle" will be used to refer to the version of the principle I favor here, and "the productivity principle" will be used to refer to the class of productivity principles developed by David Miller and Jonathan Riley.

The productivity (or contribution) principle expresses the view that:
(After morally prior claims of basic welfare and equality of opportunity have been met) income from productive work should be distributed in proportion to the value of one's contribution to the social product.

This principle of distribution is justified by Miller and Riley in terms of desert, with the desert-basis being a person's productivity or contribution.

The basic rationale for the productivity principle will be familiar to many. John Locke presented it in several forms, and it has undergone innumerable reformulations by writers since. Locke's rationale is that people deserve those things (or the value thereof) that their toil and industry have produced because they are a fitting reward for the work performed. The idea is to guarantee to individuals the fruits of their own labor and abstinence. The Lockean formulation of the principle is a common starting point for many writers, including Miller who begins his justification with Locke's familiar appeal to the state of nature. After some discussion and reconstruction of Locke's argument Miller says,

[Locke] also points out repeatedly that it is labor that adds almost all the value to produced items. The justification of appropriation is then that a person deserves to have those items which his toil and industry have produced, the products being a fitting reward for the effort expended and a compensation for the costs incurred.[2]

Riley's argument relies not on Locke but on Mill. He quotes Mill approvingly:

Private property . . . is supposed to mean, the guarantee to individuals of the fruits of their own labor and abstinence. . . . The institution . . . when limited to its essential elements, consists in the recognition, in each person, of a right to the exclusive disposal of what he or she have produced by their exertions, or received either by gift or by fair agreement, without force or fraud, from those who produced it. The foundation of the whole is the right of producers to what they themselves have produced.[3]

Riley continues,

Justice under capitalism stipulates that individuals deserve rewards that are proportional to their productive labor. Mill goes on to argue that this principle of desert does not justify the actual economic inequality in any modern economy. In this view, "the principle of private property has never yet had a fair trial in any country."[4] If the principle were given a fair trial through suitable reform of property, he suggests, then any remaining inequality of results "could not justly give umbrage" in societies whose members are capable of work . . .[5]

Riley further claims that, according to the principle of desert, any person's remuneration should be proportional to his work or effort.[6] For the purposes of the later discussion, it is worth noting that both Riley and Miller, in the specification and justification of their principles, use notions such as "work" and "effort" that, we will see, are ambiguous between the productivity and compensation principles. Miller, for instance, says that the ownership of the product is "a fitting reward for the effort expended and compensation for the costs incurred." The emphasis on effort and compensation looks more like a justification for a compensation principle than a productivity principle, though this is not the justification Miller finally emphasizes, namely that products (or the value thereof) are a fitting reward for the contribution the person has made to society. I will argue that these slippages have moral significance because the reasons driving a person to embrace the productivity principle should drive that person beyond it to the compensation principle. But more about this later in the chapter. It is also worth noting that although I emphasize the differences between the principles, I should not understate the similarities. The productivity principle is the closest and most plausible alternative to the compensation principle. Many of the arguments for it, and defenses of it, are similarly arguments for, and defenses of, a compensation principle. For the first-time visitor to the literature on deserving income, re-iterating those arguments and defenses would make the argument here more complete; however, since this defensive task has largely been done,[7] my plan is to emphasize a significant moral advantage the compensation principle has over the productivity principle.

3. THE COMPENSATION PRINCIPLE

The compensation principle, in its basic form, says that:

given people should be free to choose their occupations, the variations around the average income rate for the different occupations should be proportional to the net relative burdens and benefits in the jobs. Those jobs with higher net relative burdens should be paid more; those with less should be paid less.

In a sense, the compensation principle is the normative version of the positive economic Theory of Compensating Differentials. As Sherwin Rosen says of the economic theory: "On the conceptual level it can make legitimate claim to be the fundamental (long-run) market equilibrium construct in labor economics. Its empirical importance lies in contributing useful understanding to the determinants of the structure of wages in the economy and for making inferences about preferences and technology from observed wage data."[8] The central claim of the positive (not normative) theory is that the main determinants of differential wages in market economies *are* the differentials in net nonmonetary burdens and benefits between jobs. These nonmonetary burdens/benefits include: security of employment; length of training/education required; risk to life or health that a job involves; clean or dirty working conditions; flexibility of working conditions; desirability of the location of the job; and social status of the job. The idea is that the more nonmonetary benefits there are associated with particular jobs the less monetary benefits will need to be paid in order to attract people to those jobs and the opposite for nonmonetary burdens. While the theory may be the best positive theory available, many wage differentials are not a pure reflection of the nonmonetary differentials. The normative principle says that they should be.

The positive Theory of Compensating Differentials does not say anything about how average after-tax income is determined for a society. The normative principle is similarly silent on this issue; so the compensation principle proposed is not a complete theory of income justice. It shares this feature with most forms of the productivity principle that similarly say that differential earnings should be proportional to people's different levels of productivity. Taxation for public goods, income from nonwage sources, welfare payments justified on grounds other than desert, and so on are all external to the two principles' scopes but may be an important part of an overall theory of income justice. But both principles do address one of the most substantial issues of income justice: the relative wage differentials competent adults receive from work. The relative moral merit of how they deal with these differentials is the focus here.

4. THE "EXTERNAL VALUES" OF THE PRODUCTIVITY AND COMPENSATION PRINCIPLES

My intention is to give an argument for the claim that compensation is a morally preferable desert-basis to productivity. I have argued elsewhere that disagreements about what should constitute the basis of deserving income

cannot be resolved by appeals to the concept of desert itself; such disagreements are not about the concept of desert, but are about values; that is, they
are disagreements about what should be valued more.[9] I have also argued
that values and goals external to desert play an important role in the determination of desert-bases. Moreover, the concept of desert itself does not fully
supply the appropriate desert-basis—desert is not a completely "internally
defined" concept. This has the consequence that proponents of any desert
principle need to identify and argue for what I have called the "external values" underlying their choice of desert-bases. Specifying the external values
for compensation and productivity principles is the task of this section, with
a view to arguing for the moral superiority of compensation in the concluding section.

4.1 The Primary Values

Both principles are motivated by two "primary" (or "fundamental") values
that are realized through the principles' operation in a society. The first is the
value of increasing "the social product." Under both principles, people only
come to deserve income through activity directed toward increasing the social product. This value is held independently by society and does not come
from an internal consideration of the concept of desert. Desert principles,
in using as their desert-bases such grounds as compensation or productivity (that is, bases tied to socially productive activity), do not do so because
the concept of desert requires this. They do so because societies value higher
standards of living and therefore have increasing the social product as a primary value relevant to desert-based distribution of economic goods in the
society.[10] This means that proponents of either principle will need to specify
(and defend) those activities counting as socially productive and, hence, as
deserving of remuneration.

The second fundamental value for both principles is that of giving people
control over the factors determining the economic benefits they earn. The
idea is that the earning of economic benefits should not be tied to factors
over which people have little or no control. Miller calls this value "the voluntary control principle," and for continuity of reference I use this expression
even though, in the conceptual framework used here, it is one of the two
fundamental values shared by both distributive principles.

Having specified these shared values, I can now better address a common confusion about the relationship between voluntariness and desert. For a person to be deserving because of their actions, their actions must satisfy some minimum voluntariness conditions. That they meet basic voluntariness conditions is conceptually required by the notion of desert—a person whose action is not voluntary cannot deserve something on the basis of that action. While it is beyond the scope of this chapter to explore these minimum voluntariness requirements in detail, it seems clear that the actions must at least be free and intentional for them to be deserving. There is no doubt that under all the productivity and compensation principles proposed, these minimum requirements are met. The systems proposed are always ones where there is no forced labor and the productive actions of the individuals in the systems are intentional. Having noted that productivity and compensation principles satisfy these minimal conceptual requirements, the focus for the rest of this chapter is not on the concept of desert itself but on the external values to be realized via the distributive principles. As I have already noted, these values are not derived from the concept of desert itself, but they nevertheless help provide the normative force of the compensation and productivity principles.

So the two primary values provide two criteria for judging between the principles:

1. The degree to which an economic system operating under each principle increases the social product.

2. The degree to which an economic system operating under each principle realizes the value of increasing the control people have over the factors determining the economic benefits they earn.

There is no doubt that both the productivity and compensation principles substantially realize these values, so there is not a question of whether either of the principles fails to realize one of the values. The question is one of degree. If one principle performs better on both criteria, or better on one and the same on the other, then it is dominantly superior. If one performs better on the first criterion and the other better on the second, then a weighing of the relative importance of the criteria is required. My view is that the compensation principle is dominantly superior. However, the argument for the conclusion that a system operating under the compensation principle will do at least as well as a productivity-based system in terms of increasing the social product must be left to another time. The focus here is on the value of voluntary control. In the final section, I will argue that under a compensation principle people have greater control over what economic benefits they gain than they do under the productivity principle; hence, the compensation principle realizes this value to a greater degree. But before that argument can be fully made, a brief specification of the "secondary" (or "derived" values) needs to be given.

4.2 The Secondary Values of the Productivity and Compensation Principle

Although the primary value for both principles is increasing "the social product," what distinguishes them further are their secondary defining values or goals. For the productivity theorist the secondary value is that of having people receive the marginal value society places on the goods and services they provide. For the compensation principle the secondary value is that of having people receive compensation in proportion to the net costs and benefits they incur in contributing to the social product. In Section 2, a brief characterization (with further references) was given of why productivity theorists value people receiving the marginal value of their produced goods and services. Let me explain why compensation theorists value compensation for net costs incurred in productive activity.

Under a compensation principle people are viewed as freely putting their abilities and talents to use in whatever manner they see fit. They apply themselves, in differing degrees, to doing socially productive work. Given that we live in free societies, this is seen as each person's prerogative. We generally do not think poorly of people who apply themselves less (unless they fall below some sort of socially acceptable minimum). All this is shared with productivity theorists. The compensation principle claims that in so far as producers (interpreted broadly) take on greater burdens (or disutility) in performing work that others want done, they should receive greater economic benefits in return, on the grounds that they deserve such pay. The basis for this claim is that the producer's actions have helped others in the ways they have desired, and that the producer has taken on a cost in performing those actions. As for the amount of pay, the compensation principle says people deserve the amount reflecting the net costs and benefits of the work they have chosen relative to the net costs and benefits of other work. The compensation principle says that the differences in earnings between occupations should be those required to compensate for the differences in the nonmonetary costs and benefits between occupations.[11] It has as its rationale that those who take on greater burdens in performing work making others better off should not thereby be left relatively worse off themselves. Society in a way becomes "indebted" to such people and the pay rates should reflect the differences in this indebtedness. The greater the costs of work, the greater the remuneration for that work should be.

It can be seen that the compensation principle, in a strong sense, provides for reciprocity among members of society and lays the groundwork for the members to see their society as a mutually beneficial and cooperative enterprise. The more people choose, at a cost to themselves, to cooperate with members of society by providing them with the goods and services they desire, the more goods and services the providers should receive in return. Similarly, people who give less of themselves in the provision of goods and services for others should receive fewer goods and services in return. To say this is not to imply a moral criticism of such people (with the proviso that a basic minimum is met). In a free society this is seen as a legitimate choice.

5. NATURAL TALENTS AND THE VOLUNTARY CONTROL PRINCIPLE

5.1 Miller on Desert, Markets, and Voluntary Control

With the above characterization of the values underlying the choice of the two desert-bases, let us consider how well the principles realize these values.

Miller anticipates an objection from the value of voluntary control to his productivity principle:

The fifth objection raises the much-discussed question whether desert may be based on involuntary capacities, or whether its basis is properly limited to features such as effort, which are potentially subject to the conscious control of the agent in question. The case for the latter view is sometimes put in a misleading way, for instance by Rawls, who claims that "no one deserves his place in the distribution of native endowments" and then takes this as a reason for holding that he does not deserve the material advantages achieved through having those endowments.[12] But against this it has been argued, convincingly I think, that the basis for a judgement of desert need not be a personal feature that is itself deserved. So any case against basing desert on involuntary capacities must rest on other grounds. The key consideration, I believe, is our wish to link personal desert to personal responsibility. We want to see people as deserving on the basis of features for which they can be held responsible. Where some capacities are innate, or at least brought into being by external forces beyond our control (I shall subsequently use the term "native abilities" to cover both these possibilities), we cannot be held fully responsible for the results of their exercise. . . .

This appears to generate a major objection to the thesis that markets can be socially just. For market receipts clearly depend on native abilities as well as on other features of our behaviour. I shall not attempt to rebut this objection directly but instead try to weaken its force in a more roundabout way.

Observe to begin with that the voluntary control principle doesn't draw a line between capacity and effort, as is sometimes suggested, but between voluntary and involuntary personal characteristics of whatever sort. . . . [I]t will be impossible in practice to separate the results of voluntary and involuntary characteristics in the way that the principle demands. Given someone's existing set of capacities, there is no feasible means of deciding which are the results of previous voluntary efforts and choices. Abilities do not divide themselves neatly into those that are always native and those that can only be acquired by conscious effort.

A further implication is that there is no realistic possibility of bringing market allocations into line with the voluntary control. . . . It may therefore turn out that even someone who is wedded to the voluntary control principle will come to see the first solution [the productivity principle], which measures desert by value created, as the better means of realizing distributive justice in practice.[13]

Miller claims, correctly, that his productivity principle gives considerable weight to the voluntary control principle. He is also right that a well-designed productivity principle may track voluntary control better than an effort-based principle using some other objective criterion, such as time, to measure effort apart from productivity.[14] But, as I will argue, a compensation-based principle is better still at tracking voluntariness.

One of the ways distributive principles deviate from the voluntary control principle is through giving economic premiums to natural talents, the acquisition of which people cannot control. In his reply to the objection that his productivity principle provides large premiums to natural talents, Miller appeals to practical considerations, not normative ones. The only partially normative claim he makes is that if we try to track the voluntary control principle to a greater degree then it will be done badly and thereby violate equity, but he does not argue for this. His main argument relies on impracticality. He leaves open the question of whether it would be a good idea for a distributive principle to track voluntary control to a greater degree if it were practical to do so. I think it is practical, but arguments about practicalities are best left to another discussion; the main focus here is on the normative issue of whether compensation is, in principle, morally preferable to productivity as the desert basis. The question we need to look at is whether it is valuable for people to have greater control over the economic benefits they receive.

5.2 Virtue and the History of Moral Thinking about Desert-Bases

Desert-bases do not have to be moral bases, and moral bases make up only a small percentage of desert claims made in everyday speech—there are many nonmoral personal actions/qualities that are also valued. This fact is consistent with all desert claims being normative.[15] Still, the moral ones make up an interesting class. For instance, the most common counterexamples against desert-based distributive principles employ desert claims with moral bases. Philosophers, arguing against desert-based distributive principles, typically begin with an example and then examine what judgment the principle will make about the income distribution in that example. Then it is usually claimed, "Surely the person does not deserve that." Almost inevitably in these purported counterexamples the implicit desert-basis is a moral one. As Miller explains, one of the reasons for this is that many make the common mistake of thinking that a desert claim has to have a moral basis.[16] But an alternative explanation exists for why the appeal is so common to moral desert-bases: People have a strong desire to tie a person's treatment to the "quality of will" the person displays.[17] They believe in the importance of tying our fortunes to factors within our control and are confident that we have control over acting rightly or wrongly. The productivity and compensation principles are vulnerable to the argument that most people's actions are not under their control in the requisite sense, and that people cannot take credit for, or be blamed for, their actions. Some have argued that all ability, and also the willingness to use that ability, are products of factors over which the individual has little or no control,[18] such as genetics, family background, social class, and so on.[19] In the strongest form of this argument, people are no longer seen as agents at all. If this is correct, all desert claims are undermined along with many, perhaps all, other moral claims. But this is an issue that has been well-discussed elsewhere.[20] For our purposes people are assumed to be responsible for most of their actions.

Let us briefly review the history of moral thinking about desert-bases. Aristotle proposed that income should be distributed on the basis of personal virtue: The most virtuous receive the most economic benefits, the least virtuous receive the least. John Locke proposed that each should receive "the full product of his labor." This was the inspiration for later, more refined productivity proposals. It should be noted though, given that hard work in Locke's day was such a large determinant of productivity, and Locke highlighted hard work as a basis for his claims, the system he proposed would not be particularly different, in terms of the distribution recommended, from a compensation-based system. For instance, Locke tended to illustrate and motivate his distributive claims with agricultural examples, or examples from the "state of nature." The difference between a distribution based on compensation instead of productivity often would not have been substantial in Locke's time. Whether the intuitions Locke relies upon support distributions according to labor, compensation, or productivity is unclear. Also unclear is whether Locke thought that the intuitions supporting a right to the product of one's labor in a state of nature support such a right once the transition to civil society is made, or whether, in civil society, such intuitions only support a right to the value of the contribution, not the product itself.[21] Setting these interpretative questions aside, Locke clearly saw his productivity proposal as a moral advance over the distributive systems of his day. Locke used it to argue against the landed classes receiving most of their income from land rent. There are several reasons why Locke was right that such productivity-based systems are an improvement over the distributive systems of his day. For instance, income depended on what social position one had, what opportunities one had (as these were commonly determined by birth), what wealth one had access to, and so on. With factors like these determining a person's income, it was clear that people's economic benefits depended greatly on factors over which they had little control. The same problem arises when race and sex are determining factors in people's economic benefits. People have much greater control over their productivity than they do over their circumstances of birth, their sex, or their race. As a consequence, using productivity as a basis for distributing economic benefits realizes, to a higher degree than systems based on the contingencies of birth, the (democratic) ideal of people having greater control over their destiny.

Although Locke's principle does not approximate Aristotle's proposal to tie economic benefits to virtue, it does yield a pale, modern shadow of it. People value increasing the social product and also believe those contributing to this increase should benefit in return. Just as being virtuous is valued, so is being productive. This idea that people should benefit in proportion to how much they contribute to raising the social product shares a similar normative structure to Aristotle's proposal. But productivity seems a poor substitute for virtue as a basis for community-wide deserving, so why have people given up on Aristotle's virtue proposal for this substitute? Some popular writers have argued that modern societies simply no longer value good people and deeds as highly and instead mainly value the satisfaction of wants, whatever form they take. If this were true, it would provide one explanation. An alternative (though not wholly contrary) explanation is that, in a large, complex, and pluralistic society, institutionalizing a system of recognizing and rewarding goodness on a society-wide basis is practically impossible. The idea of having the good prosper and the bad wither may still have strong theoretical appeal to many people, including myself, but unfortunately, the practicality of Aristotle's proposal was dubious even in the small, well-knit communities of ancient Greece, let alone in modern nation-states. Information on how virtuous individuals are and to what degree cannot, practically, be publicly collected. Many modern states attempt, in a modest way, to institute Aristotle's idea, partly by rewarding moral desert through a public honors system. The difficulty of making the required judgments and designing institutions to implement them can be seen from the experience of trying to institute even this modest form of the idea—many of the nationwide systems are open to corruption and, in any case, are rarely seen as rewarding virtue in anyone other than public figures. While people can achieve recognition of good and bad people and deeds in their personal relationships, institutionalizing such recognition is beyond our capabilities. Institutionalizing a system of tying benefits to productivity instead of goodness is possible. When people are productive in a society they are doing something that most judge as valuable, and this judgment is institutionalized into a productivity principle. As a society we may not know whether a person is being mean to the neighbors, or whether this productive person is neglecting the children's emotional development. But, to some extent, we can institutionalize a system of recognizing and rewarding productivity. The productivity principle thereby embodies a value important to many people. In addition to its merits, we need to recognize its limitations. This distributive principle certainly does not achieve the Aristotelian objective of distributing according to people's overall moral worth.

A distributive system based on the productivity principle is a substantial improvement over a distributive system where economic benefits are tied so tightly to the contingencies of birth, social position, sex, race, and so on. A productivity-based system, in tying the distribution of economic benefits more to valuable personal acts and less to the contingencies, ties them to something that people have much more control over. In doing so it better realizes the ideal that people are agents who can make choices for themselves, who can deliberately act to influence others' treatment of them, and who can choose, or not, to act in ways that bring into the world goods and services that others find valuable.

5.3 The Superiority of the Compensation Principle

We are now in a position to build on this understanding of the productivity principle in arguing for the compensation principle. Let us return to the issue that prompted Miller to consider the objection to his productivity principle in the first place—the problem of premiums to natural talents that are not under the voluntary control of people. Several empirical features about natural talents and the earning of premiums need to be clarified before the final normative comparison of productivity and compensation can be completed.

The first empirical point is that the acquisition of natural talents does not impose any cost on those who have them. Generally, people do not require any extra compensation to employ their natural abilities. This is constantly overlooked in discussions of the subject. The situation changes if people are engaged in a strategic game where they can misrepresent their preferences by artificially withholding their labor. But writers commonly fail to recognize that strategic behavior has to be present for extra pay to be needed. Even then, reasonably effective strategies often exist for strategic game-playing to be prevented or minimized. In general, two persons, one with a high level of natural abilities and one with a lower level, with the same attitude to work, will only require the same level of pay to perform jobs having the same level of net nonmonetary burdens/benefits, even if one is more productive than the other. Confusing these premiums to natural abilities with compensation has been a stumbling block in previous discussions of this issue.[22]

The other empirical point to note is that people normally only receive ongoing premiums for their natural abilities when they are employed in occupations having an absolute and ongoing shortage of skills; that is, in occupations where an absolute and permanent constraint exists on the number of people who are able to perform the job. So from the point of view of the compensation principle, many natural abilities are irrelevant because they are not employed in situations where such absolute shortages exist. If occupations exist with such absolute shortages then people may earn premiums in virtue of the fact that they are lucky enough to have some natural talent in permanently short supply.

Having highlighted the normative advantages of the productivity principle over distributive systems that tie economic benefits so tightly to contingencies of birth, and having clarified these final empirical points, the normative advantage of the compensation principle is relatively straightforward to explain. It simply does a better job of advancing the values that motivate the adoption of the productivity principle in the first place. In particular, it better realizes the voluntariness values of the productivity principle by recognizing the limits of control people have over their productivity. For instance, as we have noted, natural talents, not under the control of people, play a larger role in determining people's economic benefits under the productivity principle than under the compensation principle. The acquisition of higher natural levels of abilities does not impose any additional cost or burden on those who have them, so extra compensation payments are not justified. The

premium payments allowed under the productivity principle undermine the
goal of making it so that society treats people, as far as is practical, on the
basis of actions for which they can be held responsible. A person can legitimately complain that the productivity principle makes it so that economic
benefits depend significantly on factors, such as the level of native abilities, a
person cannot, as an agent, influence. The compensation principle responds
to this complaint. A system operating under the compensation principle will
allow people to have greater control over the factors determining their level
of economic benefits in the world. For instance, natural talents will have
less influence on people's economic benefits. A compensation-based system
will not eliminate the influence of these nonvoluntary factors, but it will
reduce them. This constitutes a significant moral improvement and provides
a strong reason for preferring the compensation principle instead of the productivity principle. Consideration of whether a compensation-based system
will also increase productivity compared to the productivity principle is the
next task.

NOTES

1. David Miller, *Principles of Social Justice* (Cambridge, MA.: Harvard University Press,
1999), 131.

2. David Miller, *Market, State and Community* (Oxford: Clarendon Press, 1989), 55.

3. John Stuart Mill, *Principles of Political Economy*, in *Collected Works of John Stuart Mill*, ed.
J. M. Robson (London: Routledge and Keagan Paul, 1965), 208, 215.

4. Ibid., 207.

5. Jonathan Riley, "Justice Under Capitalism," in *Markets and Justice*, eds. John W. Chapman
and Roland Pennock (New York: New York University Press, 1989), 134.

6. Ibid., 137

7. David Miller, *Social Justice* (Oxford: Clarendon Press, 1976); Miller, *Market, State and Community*; Miller, *Principles of Social Justice*; Riley, "Justice Under Capitalism"; Wojciech Sadurski,
Giving Desert Its Due (Dordrecht, Holland: Reidel, 1985); George Sher, *Desert* (Princeton: Princeton University Press, 1987).

8. Sherwin Rosen, "The Theory of Equalizing Differences," *Handbook of Labor Economics: Volume 1*, eds. Orley Ashenfelter and Richard Layard (New York: North Holland, 1986), 641–92, 641.

9. Julian Lamont, "The Concept of Desert in Distributive Justice," *The Philosophical Quarterly*, 44 (1994): 45–64.

10. Lamont, "The Concept of Desert in Distributive Justice"; Lamont, "Problems for Effort-
Based Distribution Principles," *Journal of Applied Philosophy*, 12, (1995): 215–29.

11. Julian Lamont, "Incentive Income, Deserved Income, and Economic Rents," *Journal of
Political Philosophy*, 5 (1997): 26–46.

12. John Rawls, *A Theory of Justice* (Cambridge, MA.: Harvard University Press, 1971), 103–104.

13. Miller, *Market, State and Community*, 167–70.

14. I have developed an argument for this conclusion in "Problems for Effort-Based Distribution Principles."

15. Miller, *Social Justice*; Miller, *Market, State and Community*, 158.

16. Miller, *Social Justice*; Miller, *Market, State and Community*, 158–59.

17. Miller, *Social Justice*, 97.

18. See George Sher, "Effort, Ability, and Personal Desert," *Philosophy and Public Affairs*, 8 (1979): 361–76; George Sher, *Desert*.

19. Bruce Waller, "Just and Nonjust Deserts," *Southern Journal of Philosophy*, 25 (1987): 229–38.

20. For one of the seminal discussions see Miller, *Social Justice*, 95–102.

21. Gerald G. Gaus, *Value and Justification* (Cambridge, England: Cambridge University Press, 1990), 410–16, 485–89.

22. I have argued this in "Incentive Income, Deserved Income, and Economic Rents."

CHAPTER 6

DISCRIMINATORY PRIVILEGES, COMPENSATORY PRIVILEGES, AND AFFIRMATIVE ACTION

Robert A. Kocis

1. INTRODUCTION: THE PROBLEM

Preferential treatment for the underprivileged, commonly called affirmative action, is not yet, but should become, a part of the very structure of modern pluralistic societies concerned with economic and distributive justice. Created in response to the perceived economic injustices of racial segregation and discrimination, these programs sought to incorporate disadvantaged minorities into the mainstream of American life by first taking "affirmative" steps to identify disadvantaged applicants and then by granting them preferential treatment in selection processes. Such preferential treatment—clearly unearned—would be wrong were it not deserved on other grounds. Called into being as a temporary policy aimed at dealing with a temporary problem, affirmative action (AA)—or its functional equivalent—should now become an integral component of liberal societies.

1.1 A Fundamental Distinction

To clarify the nature of the justificatory task, it is essential that we exclude the things that do not require justification in this context. AA is *not* to be confused, for instance, with judicial efforts to redress grievances, which can be justified only in fundamentally different ways. Even though these judicially mandated programs have frequently been confused with, and caused more rancor than, true affirmative action programs, their justification is not extraordinarily difficult. In these cases, a person or group of persons has alleged, in a court of law, that a right (typically but not necessarily federal) has been violated by an identified defendant or class of defendants. Typically, after a jury has heard the case and determined that such a right had been violated, courts ordered that this wrong be rectified. These judicial mandates are presumptively (but not definitively) justified by the judicial authority to rectify wrongs and are a different topic from this one.

The voluntary, executive programs that have largely constituted affirmative action are distinct from their judicial cousins in several ways: The wrong, like the victim and the perpetrator, is not particularized; the remedy cannot be a simple mandate but must be a policy of granting preferential treatment to the disadvantaged; and, despite appearances to the contrary, these programs have remained largely voluntary—as a matter of fact, though not of necessity. Granting preferential treatment to the disadvantaged in the absence of judicial findings of specific, wrongful actions requires a different type of justification. The type of program in question, typically created by executive action during the Kennedy/Johnson/Nixon years (1960–1972), came to provide preferential treatment for disadvantaged minorities, including women. Initially, they required only that a federal agent/agency take affirmative steps to identify minority applicants and then to assure them of equality of opportunity in the selection process; that is, those offering opportunities were not to be content to passively accept applications from the traditionally disadvantaged but were to actively seek them out. The purpose was to end discrimination by first enabling minorities to find their way into the pool of applicants and then empowering them to find their way into productive positions in society. (It should be noted that rigid quotas are constitutionally prohibited in affirmative action programs.[1])

1.2 The Nature of the Task of Justifying Preferential Treatment

It might seem easy, at first glance, simply to extend to affirmative action programs the reasoning that Chief Justice Burger employed to justify minority
set-aside programs: "to cure the effects of prior discrimination," he argued,
we needed to create "limited and properly tailored" remedies to bring disadvantaged minorities into the mainstream.[2]

Alternatively, one might argue that contemporary inequalities justify
a redistribution of opportunities: Given that some have wealth, privilege,
and nearly universal access to opportunities for advancement while others
do not, that monopoly should be broken by granting similar access to the
disadvantaged.[3]

But while the first functions well in the particularized context where a
judicial wrong has been identified and the second may be persuasive to egalitarians, both attempts founder when taken out of the contexts in which they
are effective. In the first case, past injustices do not justify actions that appear to punish or harm persons who are not responsible for the sins of the
past. We cannot, as a matter of policy or of institutional arrangement, punish those with privileges because others have acted badly in the past.

In the case of the purely egalitarian argument, even contemporary inequalities fail to justify institutional arrangements or policies to favor the disadvantaged. Inequalities, after all, are not all equivalent. Some may be just
and so require no redress; others, perhaps better called inequities, may be the
products of wrongs. But if we were to take this approach, then we would have
to prove that the inequalities are rooted in identifiable wrongs by identifiable
wrongdoers—and concerns of economic justice would shade into concerns
of judicial redress. At the level of policies or institutional arrangements, the
mere existence of inequalities does not justify preferential treatment for the
disadvantaged. (To clarify: affirmative action may become, as a matter of
practice, necessary in the light of such inequalities; but the mere existence of
inequalities cannot justify it.) What further complicates arguments from inequalities is that some believe that the inequalities and racial discrimination
of yore have already disappeared, since most minorities now have equal legal
rights.[4] Given that both of the major national parties in the United States
have now selected men as different as Barack Obama (the Democratic party's

newly elected president) and Michael Steele (the Republican National Committee chairman) for positions of prominent national leadership, who needs affirmative action? But the mere fact that this appearance is deceiving does not make the moral argument any easier.

2. PREMISES

The premises of our argument should be as minimal as possible, to remove as much bias as possible from our conclusions. For instance, if we were to assume a robust theory of human moral motivation, a simple appeal to moral primitives (like compassion or a sense of justice) might permit us to appeal to moral intuitions as a way of justifying AA. But that would beg the question of why we should be moral in this way.

2.1 Assumptions about Society and the World

Keeping our assumptions about the nature of the world minimal requires that we not surreptitiously smuggle in any premises that predispose our conclusion in some way. In this sense, it is innocuous to assume that our deliberations about affirmative action will apply to a world populated with multicultural and even multinational societies aspiring to a liberal notion of justice without having achieved it perfectly.[5] Perfectly homogeneous societies would have no more need for affirmative action than would perfectly just societies. But neither exists in our world.

Similarly, we make no metaphysical assumptions about a world teleologically inclined to virtue or the good. Nor would our deliberations be cogent if we lived in a world fully determined by higher powers or beings. Rather, ours is the humanist (open-ended) world of most modern political thought. In the spirit of Sir Isaiah Berlin, we may posit that if the world were different, or were to become different, or were to prove to be actually different, our usual moral notions would not be applicable to human action.[6]

2.2 Minimal Assumptions about Human Motivation

It seems almost a truism to suggest that humans are complex beings who, in various contexts, are motivated in various ways. At times, a dark view of human nature as inherently evil (the Augustinian notion of original sin) manifests itself, and we do well to remember the Machiavellian advice to writers of constitutions that they must proceed as if humans were inclined to evil—for the sake of creating a system of laws to neutralize that proclivity. At other times and in other contexts, one might entertain the dream of human perfectibility derived from the more optimistic followers of Jean-Jacques Rousseau.

Neither approach is minimal enough for our purposes. Instead, we follow theories of political economy that assume simply that humans are rational calculators of self-interest who would not want to live in a society that would be structured in a way inimical to those interests. In ascending order of realism, we may add Herbert Simon's recognition of our limited or "bounded rationality" (that humans do not always know all they need to know to pursue their self-interests)[7] and, drawing from that inspiration, Oliver Williamson's recognition that humans can be frequently devious in the pursuit of their self-interest.[8] Finally we may note that our notions of interest may be construed rather narrowly (egotistically/selfishly) or broadly (in terms of family, ethnicity, nationality, or race). In sum, humans may not always know what is right or just, but they are much more likely to recognize when others "do them wrong." I will call this our "sense of injustice," a minimal moral sense that permits us to know when we or someone we like/love has been the victim of a wrong.

2.3 A Maximally Minimal Assumption

Finally, since we assumed a world composed of multinational and multicultural states, we must explore human motivation with regard to that diversity in a way that is neither excessively optimistic (that humans are so saintly that the desirability of AA becomes immediately obvious) nor excessively pessimistic (that humans are so intrinsically evil that it becomes easy to demonstrate the need for AA). As we posit that humans are cultured beings, we move beyond a professional consensus on minimal assumptions. However, this assumption is justified as a minimal assumption because, for the sake of this argument, it is more minimal than the alternatives.

It is a truism among critics of the liberal tradition that liberal thinkers are far too individualistic and easily fail to recognize the importance of our communal side. The validity of this criticism leads us to posit that we are "cultured beings," beings who begin our existences in families and who first experience intense emotional ties in that context.[9] This understanding implies that we are beings who individuate, creating our personalities through the mediation of a culture or cultural group. Assuming that we are cultured permits us to recognize the deep psychological reality that human identities are forged, in a process fraught with deep and conflicting emotions, within groups like families and cultural communities, and that cultural values are—somewhat selectively—internalized and taken as the individual's values. To become acculturated is not simply to be imprinted but is rather a dialectical and creative interaction between the individual and the community.

The cultural diversity of the twenty-first century poses many difficulties for justifying political authority. Not only do most polities contain a plurality of competing cultural, religious, ethnic, and racial groupings—many of which do not even share a worldview, let alone moral and political values—[10] but we observe a plurality of human responses to acquiring a culture. Few of the countries of the world today can claim to be without any ethnic or racial mixing, whether that diversity is celebrated or bemoaned.[11] And those that aspire to ethnic purity, like the Serbian confederation before it abandoned policies of ethnic cleansing, are earning a decidedly bad reputation for the notion. Whether we are born into Serbian ethnicity, Italian Catholicism, German Jewishness, or an African American family in Harlem, as human beings we are sensitive to our origins and to the interests of those with whom we identify.

A corollary implies that the interests of the group can become, by extension, the interests of the individual. (We do well to differentiate this assumption that we individuate within groups and learn to take the groups' interests as ours, from the assumption found in some theories of sociobiology, that altruism is a recognition of the primacy of the interests of a small collective group and so is a form of genetic selfishness. By contrast, Robert Axelrod articulates and James Q. Wilson echoes an argument that morality has survival value and that natural selection "selected for" morality in the evolution of species.[12] [13]) But it is neither necessary nor desirable to construe this to require any kind of strict collectivism, for the importance of culture does not require elevating the importance of the group over that of the individual. We can still continue to see individual persons as the primary repositories of value and worth, even though they are cultured beings.

Insofar as humans mature within a group and frequently come to need to belong to a group, they are somewhat—but far from perfectly—social beings. Subscribing to this account of human motivation neither unfairly burdens this demonstration with unwanted ideological baggage nor seems implausible. Rather, it is the most minimal assumption available.

3. A CONTRACTARIAN CASE FOR COMPENSATORY PRIVILEGE

3.1 Overview

The type of rational, self-interested, and cultured beings that we are, living in a multi-lingual, -cultural, and -religious word like ours, would not agree to live in a pluralistic society without affirmative action (or something functionally similar). In a contractarian demonstration, we can imagine ourselves as rational agents in a presocial condition, like the Pilgrims on the Mayflower, deliberating about the structure or constitution of our society. In a thought experiment like this, we can imagine ourselves in a hypothetical condition before creating a "social contract" to call authority into being. Calculating our self-interest, we are positioned to demonstrate the rationality of creating social structures and institutions, along with the moral obligations and duties embedded in them.[14] In general, contract theorists prohibit violence—along with threats of violence—against other agents, so that right, rather than might, may prevail. We are to remain ignorant of our places in society so that we are not inclined to favor the places we happen to occupy; this keeps the process fair by counting only reasons that are objective. We begin with assumptions, frequently about human motivation; in most variants, we assume the agents reach universal agreement via rational deliberation or bargaining.

3.2 The Conventions of Social Contract Theory

By contractarian convention, we have at our disposal the basic and objective facts from the social sciences about the workings of society and other relevant data, but we may not bring information of our personal situations to the deliberations. For example, we would know that preindustrial societies leave their inhabitants relatively unprotected against diseases, but we would not know how prone to disease we are as individuals. We would know that poverty increases the risks of disease, but we would not know if we as individuals were rich or poor. We would know that skills, talents, and dedication increase a person's chances at economic success, but not the degree to which we possess any of these desired characteristics, nor could we be influenced by knowledge of how wealthy or poor our parents were. Our deliberations are to be rooted in reality, but they are not to be merely selfish or egomaniacal.

It is commonly presumed by contract theorists, from Thomas Hobbes in the seventeenth century to John Rawls in the last, that rational and self-interested agents would consent to a social system if and only if that system were to maximize or optimize the benefits of social cooperation for the members of that society by recognizing and enforcing a set of moral requirements; disagreement centers on the content of those moral requirements. To illustrate, let us consider a few basic issues and the presumptions for which social contract theory has become famous. Would each person deliberating in this presocial space agree to a dictatorship, given the extremely slim chance that he or she would be the dictator? Would they agree to a society that would not accord them full equality of rights? Would they agree to a society with unjustified inequalities? Would they agree to a society without full equality of opportunity? Presumably, the answer to all of these questions is "no." Given the strong reasons for negatives to each of those questions, we now ask what our obligations should be with respect to the distribution of privileges in a pluralistic and multicultural society.[15]

This concept leaves open several other considerations related to justice, and some of them must remain unresolved here. We must resist twin temptations: either to tie this demonstration too closely to a particular theory of justice or to see it as totally independent of any background theory of justice. If we were to make this discussion only a rehashing of Rawls's "fair equality of opportunity" as provided in his second principle, then a danger exists that this demonstration would appeal only to Rawlsian liberals. We need to cast our nets a bit more broadly; this demonstration would be consistent with the Rawlsian notion of justice, but it should also be compatible with several other prominent notions of justice, including Ronald Dworkin's notion of "equal concern and respect."[16] Hence this demonstration is not totally independent of background notions of justice, but neither is it tightly tied to one notion or conception.

3.3 The Moral Problem

We have posited that we are deliberating in the context of a multicultural society aspiring to a liberal notion of justice without having achieved it perfectly. Presumably, we would not agree to live in a society if there were inequities in it. But would according equal rights to ethnic and other minorities remove all inequities? Not if our assumptions about human nature are correct.

We have assumed that humans are cultured beings with group loyalties. This human propensity precludes the possibility that all persons will receive the same (or even equivalent) sets of privileges or preferential treatment. Rather, those whose actions, beliefs, and values we share (whether or not they resemble us) are more likely to elicit from us more cooperation than others; we will be partial to them without any desire to do anything evil. In short, we are inclined to be partial to "our own." Given this partiality, we would not consent to live in a society where some groups experience systematic grants of preference while others do not—especially since, for all we know, we could be one of those not treated so well. If inequities could arise even in situations where basic respect for equal rights and fair equality of opportunity obtained, some (nonjuridical) redress is needed to elicit consent from the persons deliberating in the precontractual situation.

It is our human desire to pursue our interests with guile that causes us to pause in our deliberations and proceed with the utmost of caution. Societies confer many privileges in both legitimate and illegitimate ways; by definition, such privileges advance the life prospects of those who enjoy them. Many are earned or deserved in other ways, as when a war hero wins acclaim for saving the lives of others. Others, while not earned or deserved, are legitimate in other ways, as when parents seek, out of love, to advance the interests of their children.

A series of hypothetical cases illustrates our worries about this aspect of a cultured humanity. These hypothetical cases serve our purposes well as we deliberate in the absence of knowledge of our place in society.

First, a faculty member has a student from another culture who has, for the first time, missed an important examination by oversleeping; the syllabus for the course permits no make-ups—although this faculty member generally permits one unless faced with repeated abuses. Should a make-up be granted in this case? Note that it is not necessarily wrong or iniquitous for a teacher to decide this case either way; yet if cases like this proliferate, the members of the "out" group do suffer an inequity. In the light of such behaviors, equality of opportunity is but a myth. We would not consent to live in a society that condones such discriminatory privilege. But we are not likely to find one without it.

In a second case, a college affiliated with a religious denomination might grant preferential treatment to children of alumni and to graduates of high schools of that denomination for many noble reasons. For example, officials may feel a loyalty to alumni who contribute to the annual fund or they may have developed a commitment to high schools with which they have strong relationships. Yet unless their alumni and the enrollment in those high schools are reasonably diverse, the granting of such preferential treatment is limited to those who are culturally similar.

In a third hypothetical situation, some groups of children could have their aptitude—and some adults have their qualifications—measured in their native variant of a dominant language while others are measured in a language or variant other than their own. Many critics of these evaluative devices see them as shaping the life-prospects of the upwardly mobile: "But competence in standard English may also determine what opportunities students have before they leave school."[17] If so, the second or disadvantaged group is wrongfully denied a privilege routinely afforded others. If we were uncertain of whether we belonged to the dominant language group, we would not consent to live in such a society unless institutional mechanisms eliminated or minimized the effects of this grant of discriminatory privilege.

Similarly, some groups of children in a hypothetical society could receive higher quality educations than do other children because they live in particular neighborhoods.[18] But the privilege of living in such neighborhoods could also be denied to members of some groups. If this happens, the uneven distribution of privilege has discriminatory impact. If we were not certain of our group membership (and our deliberations prevent our knowing this), we would not consent to living in a society that condones such discriminatory privilege.

In another hypothetical case, some kinds of life experiences, such as internships, could become qualifications for a job or an educational opportunity, such as law school; but some group or groups of people could generally enjoy these life experiences while persons from less advantaged groups are denied them. If so, the impact again would be discriminatory. If a person's parent is the owner or high official of a company, that person's life prospects would be quite predictably different from those of competitors for positions in that company, yet owners and officials are disproportionately white males from the upper and upper middle classes, and denying other children such privileges has discriminatory impact.[19] Again, without assurances of membership in the privileged group, no rational agent would consent to live in such a society without measures to prevent discriminatory privilege—or to compensate those deprived of it.

In a final case, reforms might prevent a once-racist system of criminal justice from violating minorities' rights or depriving minorities of their rights. However, if majority defendants have a series of privileges operating in their advantage that minorities lack, inequality as well as inequity may result. There need not be any violation of rights to bring about this discriminatory impact: If nonminority defendants get all of the discretionary breaks while minorities get none of them—even if they have the same moral and legal status—the impact is discriminatory. *Time* magazine recently reported that "minority youths are more likely to face trial as adults" where the system is less forgiving and the penalties are higher. In their hypothetical example, authorities catch two youths dealing drugs in their high schools. One is white in a suburban high school; the other is Latino in an inner city school. "Both are first time offenders. The white kid walks into juvenile court with his parents, his priest, a good lawyer—and medical coverage. The Latino kid walks into court with his mom, no legal resources and no insurance. The judge lets the white kid go with his family, placing him in a private treatment program. The minority kid has no such option. He is detained." While their case might be hypothetical, these privileges have a profound discriminatory impact: "Over the past six years, 43 states have passed laws that make it easier to try juveniles as adults. In Texas and Connecticut in 1996, the latest year for which figures are available, all the juveniles in jails were minorities."[20]

Generalizing from these hypothetical cases is not difficult for rational agents in our presocial situation. Even if none of the actors enjoying a privileged position has come to have it through their malicious personal actions, even if persons enjoying these unearned privileges, as well as the persons granting them, may have committed no wrong and hence merit no punishment, still no rational agent would consent to live in a society in which the scales of justice have been so disturbingly tipped. Our deliberations have been concerned with identifying the relevant moral dimension of privileges attached to group membership that have discriminatory impact. We have seen that, without efforts to prevent such discriminatory privilege or to redress its effects, rational agents would not consent to live in a particular society. We would do well to end this stage of our deliberations by framing a hypothetical moral imperative: If we live in a society where membership in groups invites discriminatory privilege, then our institutions should respond to the inequitably distributed beneficial effects.

3.4 The Reasoning for Compensatory Preferences as a Solution to the Problem

Now our concern turns from identifying the problem of discriminatory privilege to examining solutions. Our question is: If such privilege exists and attaches discriminatorily to group membership, what does justice demand of us in response? Should we prohibit it? Permit it but require compensation? Or just permit it without any effort to compensate those deprived?

To structure the moral dialogue about the solution, let us consider the alternatives: (1) in the authoritarian alternative, eliminate all groups; (2) in the ideal egalitarian alternative, eliminate all privilege, both the discriminatory and the nondiscriminatory; (3) in the libertarian alternative, choose to ignore inequitable preferences, out of respect for more fundamental rights like property and contract; and (4) in the affirmative action alternative, create compensatory privileges to counterbalance the other privileges whose impact is discriminatory.

Deliberators would reject the first alternative, to eliminate the groups upon which discriminatory privileges rest, even if this option is attractive in the abstract. Eliminating the groupings and the ways of life that go with them would require either a transformation of human nature to eliminate our cultured propensities, massive violations of rights, or both. Even if, contrary to our assumptions, it were possible to eliminate groups from our lives, the steps necessary to do so would involve so many violations of liberty that they would not be tolerated by persons deliberating about first principles in the state of nature. Consequently, this alternative would be rejected in the precontractual deliberations.

Deliberators would also reject the second alternative, to remove all privilege. While again preferable in the abstract, this option runs contrary to our assumptions about human motivation. If we are cultured beings who attach importance to belonging to culturally defined groups, we can expect that members of a group would seek to protect and advance one another. Even more seriously, we see arenas within which it is appropriate and legitimate to do so, where morally significant differences exist between persons, as when parents advance the interests of their children or when religious denominations seek to preserve the religious identity of their colleges by granting preferences to members of that denomination. Normally speaking, those who confer privileges are acting from the highest of moral motivations; that someone is from my family is a morally relevant condition for my treating them differently and better. To remove all conferrals of privilege from society would punish these legitimate uses of privilege. We would then reject attempts to remove all privilege as both imprudent and immoral.

The third, libertarian, alternative is an invitation to consider the reasons for doing nothing about unearned privilege. Presumably, such reasons are rooted in rights seen as more fundamental, such as property and contract. As such, it will be enough if we have reasons to set aside each invitation and then have reasons for believing the series of invitations to violate our assumptions about human behavior. Initially, this alternative rests on an assumption that one critical reason for acquiring property is to use it to advance the life-prospects of loved ones, to win privileges for them. Presumably, to coerce a person not to so use personal property is to violate both the fundamental right of property and the sanctity of the family. Similarly, to require an employer to hire an unqualified applicant because of the applicant's group membership appears to be a violation of freedom of contract. These would be powerful reasons to consider.

But, if we are deliberating as specified by contractarian convention, we will decline both invitations. First, although granting preferences to those close to you is not inherently wrong, it is not the case that one can expect to win consent from all participants in the precontractual deliberations if the consequences of doing so are not examined and placed under some restriction. The situation parallels that of property: There are good reasons to consent to the institution of property, but no rational agent would give consent if only a few were to enjoy those rights in a fashion unrestricted by concern for the remainder of humanity. Like property rights, grants of preference must be exercised responsibly.

The second libertarian objection is to the hiring (or promoting, or admitting, etc) of unqualified individuals. But there is no reason to presume that the underprivileged are unqualified or less qualified than their more privileged competitors. Indeed, one standard explanation for the economic success of so many children of immigrants in the United States is that they acquire, from dealing with the everyday challenges of being different, a strong work ethic.

We conclude that those who would deliberate under the prescribed circumstances would reject the libertarian temptation.

The fourth and final alternative is to create compensatory privileges to counterbalance the others (in other words, to create affirmative action). It first recommends itself to us in our deliberations because it does not suffer from the defects of the prior alternatives. More positively, this alternative accords best with our minimal assumptions. To address the plight of the underprivileged is the only way to assure those deliberating in the precontractual situation that they and their children will not be hopelessly captured in a prison within society that they do not deserve. Similarly, it is the least coercive way, as already argued, to address the concern.

All things considered, then, rational deliberation prior to the social compact would lead those deliberating to prefer a social arrangement that grants off-setting preferential treatment to the underprivileged to the other social variants that we considered.

3.5 Potential Objections

At this point, let me anticipate and answer four objections; the first two are methodological and the others are substantive. First, one might say that the issue of discriminatory privilege does not concern matters of fundamental justice; hence, we should be concerned with a temporary policy instead of with institutional arrangements. Similarly, second, we have erred in employing the sophisticated moral decision-making procedures of the social contract, which may be far more sophisticated than is needed. One might believe that concerns with fairness between groups have arisen only in the last few decades and may disappear in another few. Following this line of reasoning, our concern is merely a policy concern and the normal tools of analysis for policy studies, such as cost-benefit analysis, would be called for.

But the question of what economic justice demands of us in multiethnic states is a fundamental moral question exactly *because* our societies are no longer cultural monoliths—and that reality is not likely to become more homogeneous in the foreseeable future. The concern is not a passing concern because the problem is structural and arises from our nature as cultured beings. Indeed, we may not confront a more significant moral issue in the next century. The gravity of the issues merits the sophistication of the methods.

Further, it is not unusual to employ such moral devices for issues of this sort; Rawls, for instance, employs it to decide questions about "democratic equality" and "fair equality of opportunity" that are under consideration in the original position. In this quite narrow sense, we merely extend his discussion of what "fair equality of opportunity" requires, given our different assumptions about human motivation. Our concerns with economic justice, while distinct from Rawls's, are no less significant and no less a moral concern than are the issues he raised.

3.6 Substantive Objections

We still have two substantive objections to anticipate and answer: 1) that affirmative action constitutes a type of reverse discrimination and 2) that it punishes innocents.

A straightforward reply to the reverse discrimination objection can be found by examining the nature of reverse discrimination. Consider a society in which a once-privileged group now shares that privilege equitably. We might say that the original discrimination had been halted—but not reversed. For the situation to become "reversed," the once-privileged group would have to become the underprivileged group. But any time that a compensatory program has transformed an underprivileged group into an overprivileged group, that group is no longer entitled to compensation. If that group, now privileged, were to continue to enjoy additional privileges, they would no longer be compensatory privileges but would become the opposite, discriminatory privileges. If affirmative action transforms a minority, who had been the victims of discriminatory privileges at one time, into a dominant group, they would no longer be institutionally entitled to affirmative action.

For instance, if it were to occur that minorities and women began to earn more than the typical white male, then white males would be entitled to compensatory privileges. Consequently, a just institution would phase out affirmative action for the old disadvantaged groups as the discriminatory impact of old privilege narrows. Whenever a disadvantaged group actually becomes a privileged group, any preferences accorded them are no longer compensatory and so not affirmative action but rather the inequity against which AA is directed.

The last objection, tightly related to the reverse discrimination objection, is that qualified persons, who ostensibly have earned a right to an opportunity, are being punished by being deprived of that opportunity. For example, an applicant for a job or for admission to a university, who would otherwise have had a right to that good, has now been denied that right in favor of a minority applicant. The claim in this example rests importantly on two presumptions: (1) that nonminorities have a "right" to preferential treatment in the selection process while minorities do not and (2) that being required to share that privilege is a type of punishment.

But neither claim is valid. Again, trying to deliberate in a precontractual situation is useful. No one would consent to a social arrangement in which one group has a right to all of the preferential treatment; rather, whatever privilege is to exist must be shared equally to earn the consent of participants in our thought experiment.

Similarly, since there is no wrong, there can be no punishment in designing a society where privilege must be shared. Nevertheless, outside of our deliberations and in the context of a society with a history, it must be conceded that the privileged *would be harmed* by giving up their exclusive privileges. In any case where a society decides to dismantle an unjust system of privilege or preference, those who enjoyed that privileged position will, in a comparative sense, be harmed by the removal of the privilege. When suffrage was extended, white male property holders, who had been the only persons to enjoy the privilege of voting, were harmed in that they could no longer exclusively decide the outcomes of elections. Similarly, today, as nonminority applicants lose the privilege of being the only group to receive preferential treatment, they are harmed—but only relative to their old position of exclusive privilege. Nevertheless, while they are comparatively less well-off than they were before, they still retain a relatively privileged position in society. Their old privileges are not even denied; they are merely made to share these privileges with others. This hardly qualifies as punishment. In employing affirmative action programs to extend preferential treatment to those usually denied it, a society is no more punishing its white male citizens than it punished its white male property holders when it extended the vote to others less well-positioned.

With these objections dismissed, we may now conclude that rational agents, calculating their self interests, would not consent to live in a society without some system of preferences to compensate for harm done by privileges with discriminatory impact. In a world of perfect justice and perfect humans, this would not be true; but in a world populated by imperfect humans, it would be the minimal condition for consent.

4. CONCLUSION

Despite appearances to the contrary, considerations of economic justice require preferential treatment for the underprivileged. Rationally self-interested persons, employing a minimal but realistic series of assumptions about human motivation, would not give rational consent to a system that did not compensate for the invisible and discriminatory privileges enjoyed by some almost-permanent and identifiable groups. While a society with no privileges or even without sub-national loyalties would seem morally preferable in the abstract, our assumptions about human motivation suggested that it would be most unlikely that such societies exist. Given that humans create privileges for members of their groups, no prudent agent could give rational consent to living in a society unless that society compensated its underprivileged in some offsetting way.

If liberal-democratic societies are to remain a beacon for humanity, inspiring us to seek freedoms and to grow into unique individuals within cul-

156 ROBERT A. KOCIS

tured communities, it must grow to meet new challenges. Our greatest challenge now is to deal with the multicultural realities of our societies. One place to begin is with the human sense of injustice that permits us to understand the plight of the underprivileged and instills in us a desire to avoid it for ourselves and our loved ones.

NOTES

1. Swann vs Charlotte-Mecklenburg Board of Education, 402 U.S. 1; 1971.
2. *Fullilove vs Klutznick*, 448 U.S. 448; 1980.
3. Barbara Bergmann, *In Defense of Affirmative Action* (New York: Basic Books, 1996).
4. Dinesh D'Souza, *The End of Racism* (New York: The Free Press, 1995).
5. Will Kymlicka, *Liberalism, Community, and Culture* (Oxford: Clarendon Press, 1989), esp. ch. 7, "Liberalism and Cultural Pluralism."
6. Sir Isaiah Berlin, "History and Theory: The Concept of Scientific History," *History and Theory* 1 (1960).
7. Herbert Simon, *Models of Man*: Social and Rational. (New York: John Wiley and Sons, Inc., 1957).
8. Oliver Williamson, *The Economic Institutions of Capitalism* (New York: The Free Press, Macmillan, 1985).
9. Charles Taylor, *Multiculturalism: Examining the Politics of Recognition*. (Princeton: Princeton University Press, 1994) and Alisdair MacIntyre, *Whose Justice? Which Rationality?* (Notre Dame: Notre Dame University Press, 1988).
10. John Rawls, *Political Liberalism* (New York: Columbia University Press, 1993).
11. Kymlicka, *Liberalism, Community, and Culture*; especially the beginning of ch. 7.
12. Robert Axelrod, *The Evolution of Cooperation* (New York: Basic Books, 1984).
13. James Q. Wilson, *The Moral Sense* (New York: The Free Press, 1995).
14. John Rawls, *A Theory of Justice* (Boston: Harvard University Press, 1971), esp. ch. 4, "The Original Position," and ch. 24, "The Veil of Ignorance."
15. The later Rawls addressed similar concerns in *Political Liberalism*, albeit at a higher level of generality. It is important to differentiate this effort from him. Most simply, Rawls makes stronger and more optimistic assumptions about human nature. His belief that humans can rise above mere rationality to become "reasonable" is a very optimistic extension of his belief in our "sense of justice" or capacity for moral reasoning.
16. Ronald Dworkin, *Taking Rights Seriously*. (Cambridge, Mass: Harvard University Press, 1978).
17. Nancy Faires Conklin and Margaret A. Lourie, *A Host of Tongues* (New York: Free Press, 1983), 253. See chapter 10 in particular, "Policy and Education in a Multilingual Society."
18. Andrew Hacker, *Two Nations: Black and White, Separate, Hostile, Unequal* (New York: Ballantine Books, 1993).
19. Bergmann, *In Defense of Affirmative Action*, 140, quite effectively employs a photograph of a proud banker and his four sons to illustrate how family connections provide preferential treatment.
20. Anamaria Wilson, "Lock 'em up!" , *Time* (February 14, 2000): 68.

PART III

ETHICS AND EFFICIENCY

CHAPTER 7

DEONTIC EFFICIENCY
AND EQUALITY
T. M. Wilkinson

1.

The allegation that economic equality is wasteful has been nearly the most damaging of all the objections to equality. It is a large part of the reason why egalitarianism has retreated politically in the last few decades. The idea that equality is economically bad for people is not confined to political polemic. Academic writings in economics and subjects influenced by economics discuss trade-offs between equality—or equity—and efficiency, sometimes giving a lot of weight to equality, sometimes none, but rarely concluding that equality should not be compromised at all for the sake of efficiency. Favoring an equal distribution at whatever cost in efficiency seems like a peculiar dogmatism. But the objection that equality is inefficient is not straightforward. Many possible versions exist based on different conceptions of both equality and efficiency. My interest here is in one particular conception of efficiency and whether it conflicts with equality.

The version of efficiency I develop expresses two intuitions. One intuition treats people as individuals whose welfare is not fungible. It is expressed as a constraint, ruling out actions that worsen other people's positions. The other intuition is a constraint on what the state may do. The state should not prohibit people from bettering their positions when they would harm nobody by doing so. On the face of it, both intuitions conflict with equality when it requires redistribution that does worsen the position of some or where preserving equality requires stopping people from harmlessly improving their lives.

These intuitive objections to equality can be expressed in terms of Pareto efficiency. Here are the relevant definitions:

> A state of affairs is Pareto efficient when it is not possible to make someone better off without making someone else worse off.

> A state of affairs is Pareto inferior to another when it is possible to make someone better off without making anyone else worse off.

> A state of affairs is Pareto superior to another when at least one person is better off and no one is worse off.

> A state of affairs is Pareto incomparable to another when at least one person is better off and at least one person is worse off than in the other.

Under the usual interpretations of Pareto efficiency and its associated terms, "better" and "worse off" refer to welfare. Some believe that welfare is not the appropriate currency for justice and prefer resources or primary goods or capabilities or other alternatives, but we can avoid that debate if we let "better off," "worse off," and people's "shares" be taken in whatever is the right currency.[1] To keep things simpler, I will continue to write of Pareto efficiency, superiority, and so forth, but the welfarist connotations are dispensable.[2]

Pareto efficiency, as commonly employed in economics, is taken in consequentialist terms. In those terms, Pareto efficiency forms part of an evaluation of outcomes where superior outcomes should outrank those inferior to them.[3] It is by no means clear what follows for our actions and omissions from taking Pareto superiority as a constraint on ranking outcomes, not least because, it is no simple task to work out what ought to be done from a ranking of outcomes.

The Paretianism I will discuss offers more direct instruction of a deontological kind.[4] This version of Pareto is not the standard kind, but I believe it is a quite common response to the intuitions that make Pareto efficiency normatively attractive to some. To restate, the intuitions are that people are individuals whose interests are not fungible and they should not be prohibited from advancing their interests when they would not harm others by doing so. Both can be put in terms of constraints, which I shall call deontic efficiency constraints ("deontic" being short for "deontological"). The constraints are not supposed to be inferences from the definitions I gave of Pareto efficiency and its associated terms. They are instead an attempt to make more precise certain underlying intuitions.

2.

The first intuition, about people as individuals, can often be found in writings objecting to utilitarianism on the grounds that it ignores the separateness of persons.[5] As is well known, utilitarians ultimately care about the maximization of utility and not its distribution. Even those sympathetic to utilitarianism think that its insensitivity to distribution has its faults if it involves overriding rights or requiring improvements to the welfare of the better off at the expense of those worse off. On the other hand, most of us do find something attractive in the imperative to improve people's welfare, so long as this is not at some unjustifiable cost to others. What would count as unjustifiable cost? The kind of Paretianism that is the subject of this section gives one answer. Anthony Kronman writes that "the Principle of Paretianism ultimately rests on the notion that one person should be permitted to make himself better off at another's expense only if it is to the benefit of both that he be allowed to do so."[6] Kronman's concern in this instance is contract law, but it is natural to take his remarks as having broader scope: Generally we should not worsen the position of others whether or not for our gain. The basic idea is that actions are only legitimate if they do not harm anyone. This amounts, in Paretian terminology, to a constraint prohibiting both inferior and incomparable actions. Only superior actions, and ones affecting no one's interests, would satisfy the constraint of harming no one. Here is a more formal statement of the constraint:

> DEC 1: An action is permissible only if it is superior to or has no effect on people's shares. (Necessary condition.)

This constraint would allow no inferior or incomparable actions. Because it merely states a necessary condition, DEC 1 leaves open, as I do, whether superior or non-affecting actions are always permissible. We can bypass the difficult issue of what count as harms if we take harm to occur whenever an action causes someone to have less welfare, resources, or whatever is the right account of nonmoral interests for efficiency.

The apparent effect of DEC 1 is to preclude redistribution—making someone worse off for the sake of benefits to others—as well, of course, as waste—making someone worse off for no benefit to others. Those, like Robert Nozick and David Gauthier, who believe that justice is a matter of respecting rights or mutual advantage, often think the anti-redistributive implication attractive.[7] But is it really never acceptable to worsen the position of some for the sake of others, as DEC 1 would have it?

Suppose the only way you can save a baby from falling over a cliff is to knock someone out of the way in the process. To forestall unhelpful objections, suppose your victim does not know the reason why you pushed him down and wanders away disgruntled, believing it to be the act of a hooligan. You never see the person again, so you cannot compensate him. Moreover, to forestall another unhelpful objection, suppose the, rather unpleasant, victim would not have consented to your pushing him even if he knew why you had done it. In our terms, you have produced an outcome that benefits one person, the baby, at the expense of another, the one you knocked down, and that is creating a change that is not superior, but incomparable. The constraint prohibits incomparable moves.

If the deontic efficiency constraint does prohibit saving the baby, then I cannot see any reason to accept it, and it would not matter if equality were in conflict with such a strange constraint. Moreover, defenders of real-world free markets would have to reject the constraint, too. Real markets have externalities that, uncorrected, worsen the position of third parties. Even if we ignore externalities, the results of trading in a real market may be that one party does worse, as when he buys defective goods by mistake, or they turn out not to be quite what he wanted.

I want to defend the constraint rather than dismiss it out of hand.[8] A first suggestion is to weaken its force, allowing other considerations to outweigh it. But this move to greater plausibility would leave the constraint less

DEONTIC EFFICIENCY AND EQUALITY

able to rule out equalizing redistribution because it leaves open whether the benefits of redistribution could be one of those outweighing considerations. How some redistribution, such as that which saves lives, could still be ruled out by such a weakened constraint, is hard to see.

Another way to defend the constraint against the counterexamples is to claim that it applies only to particularly serious kinds of damage to interests. It is more plausible to think it impermissible to impose big losses on some for the sake of others, as opposed to minor losses for the sake of big gains to others. But, whatever its merits, this response gives up DEC 1, since it allows a weighing up of harms to some against gains to others and DEC 1 does not. As we saw earlier, what counts as a harm will depend on what view one takes about the currency of justice. But any properly developed view would count shoving someone out of the way as a harm. The shoved person has a reasonable complaint. The problem for the deontic efficiency constraint is that it would say it is not permissible to shove, whereas intuitively we want to say that it can be permissible to shove when, for instance, doing so is necessary to save babies from cliffs.

So the first defense made the constraint more plausible but at the cost of reducing its anti-egalitarian force; the second defended something other than the constraint. Perhaps we should reinterpret the lessons we are to draw from the counterexamples. We might best think of the sacrifices demanded of some in saving the baby or in market transactions as part of mutually beneficial practices.[9] *Ex ante* the sacrifices are in the interests of even those who make them. So we might characterize the baby example as saving a life at a minor cost to someone and hence as part of a requirement of mutual aid. We could construct a similar defense of the free market. Just how much ex post facto redistribution that DEC 1 can allow in the name of ex ante mutual advantage is an interesting question, but I think it must allow some if it is not to be dismissed.[10]

3.

No amount of ex ante finesse to the deontic efficiency constraint would allow the redistribution that equality would require. Unlike the devices of mutual aid, to aim for equality is not going to count as in the ex ante interests of the better off. To achieve equality in existing societies would require taking from the rich to give to the poor and the constraint seems, straightforwardly, to rule that out. But again, matters are not so straightforward. Suppose we can abolish slavery, a gross injustice, only at the expense of the slaveholders. If the deontic efficiency constraint prohibits the abolition of slavery in such circumstances, again, I can think of no reason to accept it. Once more, the constraint needs qualification.

The obvious qualification is to apply the constraint only to some baseline that is just. Once the starting point is morally acceptable, only superior and non-affecting moves are permissible. On this suggestion, though, efficiency, as expressed by DEC 1, cannot tell us which baselines are legitimate, since it applies only once the baseline is determined. This silence opens the way to reconcile efficiency and equality. DEC 1 needs supplementing with other moral principles and why could equality not be such a principle? The morally acceptable starting point could be an equal one; the constraint would apply to moves from that equal baseline. Far from equality conflicting with DEC 1, equality could be the supplementary principle the constraint needs.[11]

The conjunction of equality as the baseline and efficiency as the constraint on moves may not satisfy some egalitarians. As anti-egalitarians often claim, even if equality were the starting point, it would not last long. As David Hume wrote, "Render possessions ever so equal, men's different degrees of art, care, and industry will immediately break that equality."[12] A return to equality would require the redistribution prohibited by the constraint. As the anti-egalitarians would have it, after the initial point, we can either have inequality or, in this special sense, inefficiency. But the anti-egalitarian conclusion is too quick. Whether or not equality could be preserved from the baseline depends on the nature of the baseline, the conception of equality, and the moves allowed.

It is a theorem of welfare economics that the result of free trading from a set of endowments—any set—in a perfectly competitive market will be a Pareto optimal equilibrium.[13] If we take the idea of a baseline as a literal starting point, we could redistribute endowments equally and allow people to trade or otherwise use them as they wish. Anti-egalitarians believe that free economic activity would produce inequality before long. But the egalitarian who favors this method could reply that the causes of inequality, such as diverse preferences for risk or labor and leisure, are morally acceptable, in which case the inequality would not be objectionable.[14] Unacceptable causes, such as differences in ability, can be handled by compensating those of lesser ability at the outset.[15] The idea here is that some causes of an unequal outcome are justified. But even those who aim for equality of outcome could embrace the method by distributing endowments—including abilities or, more accurately, rights in the labor of others—in such a way that the predicted result of free trading would be a Pareto optimal equal outcome.[16]

This literal interpretation of the idea of the baseline as a starting point includes no requirement to redistribute (or worsen any positions) after the starting point in order to preserve equality, so it does not conflict with DEC 1. Some redistribution will be required to equalize the baseline for succeeding generations, but that is a matter of getting the baseline right again and, as we saw, the deontic efficiency constraint cannot conflict with that.

The theorem of welfare economics is not as comforting to egalitarians as might be hoped. Egalitarians might well hesitate to adopt a strategy that achieves equality and efficiency at the price of giving some ownership rights to others. Moreover, attempts to equalize starting points involve large costs—working out the right endowments, finding and implementing a sabotage-proof redistributive strategy, upsetting expectations, coping with generational overlap, and so forth. But these are not the sorts of costs DEC 1 notices. They are problems with getting the right baseline, but DEC 1 only applies after that. They do, however, suggest that the idea of a baseline might be taken less literally and more as an analytic idea.

If we imagined an equal starting point, we might regard distributions as acceptably egalitarian if they come within the class of distributions that could have been generated from the starting point.[17] Or we could use the starting point as a thought experiment to test causes of inequality against our intuitions about fairness and conclude that some causes are justified and some not. We could then design institutions so as to nullify as far as possible the inequalities caused in unjustified ways, like brute luck.[18] In Ronald Dworkin's scheme, for instance, income taxes are justified as the best feasible approximation to a hypothetical insurance scheme designed to deal with inequalities in handicaps and abilities.[19] But many claim that income taxes are inefficient. If this is correct, is this an efficiency that DEC 1 could object to?

Let us first see the standard objection. Suppose income is taxed at thirty percent. Some people will decide to put in fewer hours if their final wage is reduced by thirty percent, and they would be better off if the tax were lower and they worked harder. So would their employers; they think it is worth paying the wage to the workers for those hours, and now the workers are not working those hours. But the tax authorities are no better off for the tax because they are getting no tax on those extra hours because the workers are not putting them in. So the income tax at thirty percent causes a Pareto inferior state of affairs because it would be possible, by reducing the tax, to make some better off and none worse off. This example is can be generalized across any level of income tax. The response of some to the tax will be a cause of inefficiency.

This standard efficiency objection to income tax may point out an important drawback, but it is not one relevant to DEC 1.[20] The income tax is necessary to approximate to the baseline, and we have already seen that DEC 1 has nothing to say about that. Its plausibility depends on that baseline.

A different strategy aims to prevent inequalities by limiting the market.[21] We might try to stop people from being in a position to cause inequalities, for instance by banning private ownership of the means of production. Or we may aim for equality in some important areas, such as basic needs. One part of this strategy might be to keep some things out of the marketplace, like kidneys or places in the military. Another is to supply goods equally to all, as in a state health system, or to put maximum prices on important goods and services, as with rent control.[22] Let us rehearse a typical efficiency objection to one of these proposals.

Consider an attempt to improve the lot of low-income earners by controlling housing rents. If rents are kept below a free market price then, it is claimed, some potential landlords will not rent out their property. Those potential landlords would be willing to rent their property at a higher price, one that some people would be willing to pay. But the rent controls prevent these mutually beneficial transactions that would have no bad effects on others. They produce a state of affairs that is Pareto inferior. We could generalize this example to all attempts to interfere with market prices, externalities aside, or to limit the scope of the market. Again, though, any inefficiency here is not of a sort that DEC 1 can notice because it is the result of measures that aim to approximate its baseline.

In the case of taxing to achieve the right baseline, the constraint was too incomplete to have anything to say, so it could not conflict with one chosen on the grounds that it is equal or that it would predictably produce an equal outcome. Nor does the constraint have anything to say about the various moves one ought to allow from the baseline, and so it cannot conflict with market limitations either. The constraint expresses a necessary condition: Moves would be wrong only if they worsen people's positions. That constraint does not say anything about which moves are allowable as opposed to which ones are not. Whether or not the constraint is plausible in its own right, its silence about the choice of baseline and permissible moves means that no apparent conflict exists between equality and efficiency in this sense.

5.

The second intuition was that people should not be prohibited from bettering their positions when doing so would harm no one else. That intuition can also be put in terms of a constraint. Here are two versions.

> DEC 2: It is permissible to prohibit the actions of others only if those actions are inferior or incomparable (that is, worse for at least one). (Necessary condition.)

> DEC 2': It is permissible to prohibit the actions of others if and only if those actions are inferior or incomparable. (Necessary and sufficient condition.)

Only the necessary condition is worth consideration. It cannot plausibly be a sufficient condition of prohibiting people's actions that they will make some worse off. That would license the prohibition of rude or inconsiderate behavior and bad marriages or job choices. The state should not prohibit everything that has bad effects on people. On the other hand, it is quite plausible to suppose that we should not prohibit actions that have no bad effects on anyone, especially if, as with Pareto superior actions, they also have some good effects.

DEC 2 refers to prohibiting actions rather than preventing them. If we prohibit something, then, if we are sincere about it, we hope that it will not happen and generally we do something to prevent it. In prohibiting something there is usually an implication of disapproval of the forbidden acts.

What DEC 2 says is that we should not disapprove and try to prevent the actions of others if they have no bad effects on anyone. The constraint does not say that we should not prevent harmless actions. It may be that my deal with you prevents your making a harmless deal with her but that does not mean that I fall foul of DEC 2. I am not prohibiting your deal, merely preventing it in the sense that you take my deal in preference to hers.

DEC 2 has a good deal of intuitive plausibility, particularly in ruling out prohibitions of Pareto superior actions. What could be wrong with actions that harm no one and benefit some? And, if nothing could be wrong, how could it be legitimate to prohibit them? Liberals, including egalitarian ones, certainly feel the force of these questions when they reject the enforcement of morals. They deny that it is acceptable to criminalize actions (minority religions, consensual homosexual sex, etc.) that harm no one and have good effects on some precisely because they harm no one and have good effects on some. In this sphere they seem to side with the constraint. Can they then reject its application to economics? Compare the intuitive force in Nozick's Wilt Chamberlain example. Chamberlain is much better off than others because some have paid to watch him play:

Can anyone else complain on grounds of justice? Each other person already has his legitimate share under D1 [the initial distribution]. Under D1 there is nothing that anyone else has a claim of justice against. After someone transfers something to Wilt Chamberlain, third parties still have their legitimate shares; their shares are not changed.[23]

Nozick's example is supposed to support his general claim that we cannot preserve equality without interfering with people's liberty, but we could also draw the different lesson, as in DEC 2, that we cannot preserve equality without prohibiting efficient actions. Is this lesson the right one?

The first constraint failed to conflict with equality largely because it needed a baseline, and egalitarian strategies could be defended as ways of securing it. The silence of DEC 1 about the baseline kept it quiet about equality as well. But DEC 2 need not be similarly silent. DEC 2 is quite plausible even in the absence of a just baseline. It is hard to justify, even if an unjust baseline exists, stopping people from doing things that do not make anyone else worse off. Egalitarian liberals think that the state should not criminalize even genuinely immoral actions if they are harmless, and their view does not depend on there being a just baseline. So why think that economically Pareto superior actions should be prohibited even in unjust circumstances? Even if there are some cases, for instance involving mutually advantageous exploitation of the badly off, these probably will not generalize to all cases that produce inequality, as when Chamberlain trades with his equally and reasonably well-endowed fans.

The intuition underlying DEC 2 is that there is not much wrong with people trying to get along by striking mutually beneficial deals and, even if there is, it is not the business of the state to stop them from making these deals when that will leave both worse off. (It is another matter when it comes to stopping some deals when the result would be alternative, still mutually beneficial deals with a different distribution.) This intuition has an apparent anti-egalitarian force that is not vulnerable to the criticisms of Nozick's Wilt Chamberlain example. Nozick's critics have rejected his assumption that, if Chamberlain owns his labor power, he has the right to sell it for its full market value and they have rejected his view that self-ownership would justify that right.[24] These criticisms are probably sound, but anti-egalitarians might say that Chamberlain should not be prohibited from selling his labor power for its full value even if he does not have a right to it, if paying him the full value is needed as an incentive to supply that labor and benefit others. It is DEC 2 and the intuition that people should not be prohibited from improving their lot that makes the Chamberlain example a problem here, not claims about Chamberlain's just acquisition of his labor power.

DEC 2 states that it is only permissible to prohibit the actions of people if they would worsen the position of others. Assuming income taxes and market limitations produce Pareto inferior states of affairs, do they involve the prohibition of actions that do not worsen the position of others? On a reasonably standard construal of the term, income taxes do not count as prohibiting and so do not conflict with the constraint. Market limitations, on the other hand, both prohibit and appear to conflict.[25]

Income taxes do not prohibit actions; they merely put the price up. (I ignore the complication that they prevent performing the actions without paying the tax.) You are free to work the extra hours, even if you decide that, given the tax, it is not worth it. Moreover, the attitude of the taxing authority is

not one of disapproval. On the contrary, the taxing authority is delighted if
you produce more taxable income. They do not hope you will not engage
in the taxed activity. But market limitations are subjects of prohibition and
often involve the criminal law. The market might be limited by, for instance,
making it illegal to buy and sell kidneys or to set up private enterprises employing more than a few people. The involvement of the criminal law would
mean that people were prohibited from engaging in mutually beneficial
transactions and, if they would harm no one, prohibiting would violate the
constraint. (The refusal of courts to enforce unconscionable contracts is of a
rather unclear status. These refusals do not prohibit and do not involve the
criminal law, so they do not conflict with DEC 2 as stated here.)[26]

What if egalitarians deny that any harmless market activities exist? As
G. A. Cohen points out in his criticism of Nozick's use of the Chamberlain
example, third parties might be badly affected, if Chamberlain, or people
with a similar unequally large share, can exercise political power over them.[27]
My interest here is in the structure of Cohen's claim. He does not say that
Chamberlain's and the fans' actions will, taken on their own, worsen the
position of third parties. Instead, the practice of paying Chamberlain-sized
incentives will generate the bad effects. We can run a similar claim on behalf of any proposed market limitation. Rent control and minimum wage
legislation would have good effects on some, so ending these practices would
be bad for some. It is true that a minimum wage law, for instance, might
prohibit a Pareto superior transaction between an employer and a potential
employee that would have no bad effects on others. But ending minimum
wage laws would be bad for those whose wages fell and who would have kept
their jobs at the minimum wage rates and, conversely, imposing a minimum
wage would be better for those whose wages go up and hold their jobs.

DEC 2 does not rule out the prohibition of actions that have bad effects on others, if "having bad effects" includes those of the social practices
of which actions are a part and not merely the discrete actions. If someone
would be worse off if a market limitation were ended or better off if one were
imposed, then DEC 2 would not even conflict with the market limitation
strategy to achieve equality. Like DEC 1, DEC 2 would have no anti-egalitarian force. This would be part of a bigger problem; on the broad construal
of actions as part of practices, there are few harmless actions and so DEC 2
would have virtually no force.

My aim is not to defend DEC 2 but to avoid objections to equality, so I am not worried if the constraint lacks force. If it does, I conclude that it does not conflict with equality. If, on the other hand, some good way exists to resist an account of actions that makes it inevitable that they would have bad effects on some, then DEC 2 would conflict with market limitation methods of achieving equality. But that would leave redistributive taxation, something about which DEC 2 is silent. Egalitarians would have to look to the tax mechanism rather than, for example, interfering with freedom of contract, to achieve their goals.

6.

This chapter has worked up efficiency constraints on actions on the basis of two intuitions: that people's interests are not fungible because they are individuals and that people should not be prohibited from bettering their state in life if they do not harm someone else. Both the intuitions are plausible. Both appear to conflict with equality. But, I have argued, if the constraints are to be made normatively attractive, they turn out not to conflict with equality after all. People may not be fungible, but the idea that their welfare should not be reduced is sensible only relative to a baseline and the baseline could be an equal one. It may be that people should not be prohibited from bettering their position at no one else's expense, but taxation does not prohibit and the transactions that market limitations would block may turn out not to be harmless. If efficiency is the basis for deontological constraints on the permissibility of actions, then there is little to worry egalitarians. If the constraints are to be plausible, then they simply fail to conflict with the various methods of achieving equality except, maybe, limiting the market. Equality just need not be deontically inefficient.

NOTES

1. G. A. Cohen, "On the Currency of Egalitarian Justice," *Ethics*, 99, no.4 (1989): 906–44.
2. T. M. Wilkinson, *Freedom, Efficiency, and Equality* (New York: St. Martin's Press, 2000), ch. 4.
3. T. M. Wilkinson, *Freedom, Efficiency, and Equality*, 54–57.
4. Jules Coleman, *Markets, Morals, and the Law* (Cambridge, England: Cambridge University Press, 1988), 72.

5. Examples include P. Vallentyne, "Rights Based Paretianism," *Canadian Journal of Philosophy*, 18, no.3 (1988): 527–44; and A. Kronman, "Contract Law and Distributive Justice," *Yale Law Review*, 89 (1980). David Brink criticizes the Pareto interpretation of the separateness of persons in "The Separateness of Persons, Distributive Norms, and Moral Theory," *Value, Welfare, and Morality*, eds. R. Frey and C. Morris (Cambridge, England: Cambridge University Press, 1993), 252–89. Michele Goodwin argues for paying for organs from dead people in Pareto terms. See *Black Markets* (Cambridge: Cambridge University Press, 2006).

6. Kronman, "Contract Law," 488.

7. Robert Nozick, *Anarchy, State, and Utopia*; and David Gauthier, *Morals by Agreement* (Oxford: Clarendon Press, 1986).

8. Brink, "Separateness," 256–58.

9. Kronman, "Contract Law," sect. D.

10. Ronald Dworkin, *A Matter of Principle* (Oxford: Clarendon Press, 1985), 283ff.

11. Julian Lamont, "Pareto Efficiency, Egalitarianism, and Difference Principles," *Social Theory and Practice*, 20, no.3 (1994): 311–25.

12. David Hume, *An Enquiry Concerning the Principles of Morals* (Oxford: Clarendon Press, 1975), 194. See also Nozick, *Anarchy*, 160–64.

13. A. Sen, "The Moral Standing of the Market," *Social Philosophy and Policy*, 2, no.2 (1985): 9–10.

14. Ronald Dworkin, "What is Equality? Part Two: Equality of Resources," *Philosophy and Public Affairs*, 10, no.4 (1981): sect. IV.

15. J. S. Mill, *Principles of Political Economy in Collected Works* (Toronto: University of Toronto Press, 1965), 201–202.

16. P. Dasgupta, "Utilitarianism, Information, and Rights," *Utilitarianism and Beyond*, eds. A. Sen and B. Williams (Cambridge, England: Cambridge University Press, 1982): sect. 2.

17. Dworkin, "Equality of Resources," 291.

18. Ibid., sect. III.

19. Ibid., esp. sect. VI. See also "The Place of Liberty," Iowa Law Review, 1 (1987), sect. VI.

20. T. M. Wilkinson, *Freedom, Efficiency, and Equality*, ch. 10.

21. See Thomas Nagel's response to Nozick in "Libertarianism Without Foundations," *Reading Nozick*, ed. J. Paul (Oxford: Blackwell, 1981), 201–202.

22. J. Tobin, "On Limiting the Domain of Inequality," *Economic Justice,* ed. E.S. Phelps (Harmondsworth, England: Penguin, 1973), 447–63; T. Scitovsky, "Equity," *Human Desire and Economic Satisfaction* (Brighton, England: Wheatsheaf, 1986); and Michael Walzer, *Spheres of Justice* (Oxford: Martin Robertson, 1983).

23. Nozick, *Anarchy*, 161.

24. Nagel, "Libertarianism Without Foundations"; Barbara Fried, "Wilt Chamberlain Revisited: Nozick's 'Justice in Transfer' and the Problem of Market-Based Distribution," *Philosophy and Public Affairs*, 24, no.3 (Summer 1995): 226–45; and Michael Otsuka, "Self-Ownership and Equality: A Lockean Reconciliation," *Philosophy and Public Affairs*, 27, no.1 (Winter 1998): 65–92.

25. Nozick, *Anarchy, State, and Utopia*, 57.

26. Seana Shiffrin, "Paternalism, Unconscionability Doctrine, and Accommodation," *Philosophy and Public Affairs*, 29, no.3 (Summer 2000): 205–50.

27. G. A. Cohen, *Self-Ownership, Freedom, and Equality* (Cambridge, England: Cambridge University Press, 1995), 24–28.

CHAPTER 8

COHEN ON INCENTIVES, INEQUALITY, AND EGALITARIANISM

Thomas Christiano

1. INTRODUCTION

Many egalitarians agree that social and economic inequalities can be just if they constitute Pareto improvements over equality or if they work to the advantage of the worst off. John Rawls and Brian Barry have argued that these Pareto superior inequalities can be just even if they are achieved by offering special incentives to some in the form of higher incomes for their work. G. A. Cohen has recently given a powerful argument against this approach.[1] The crucial idea in his critique is that arguments for the principle of equality or the difference principle are incompatible with the incentive-based argument that inequalities are sometimes just. What motivates the concern for equality, on his account, should undermine the legitimacy of the kinds of incentives that make inequalities necessary as a condition of Pareto improvement.

To see the problem, let us think of a talented person as someone who makes a contribution of greater value than others merely on account of his or her innate capacities. Hence, if a talented person and an untalented person work the same amount of time and put in the same amount of effort, the talented person will produce more value. The fact that the work of the talented is an exercise of talent is not a cost above the costs involved in time and effort. The extra product of the talented is, so to speak, gravy; it does not result from greater sacrifice. Hence, if talented persons get more income than others because they produce more merely on account of their talents, the extra income they earn cannot be compensation for any extra effort or time put into their work. Incentives that promise larger than average incomes for the more talented in return for their contribution to the common good are disturbing to egalitarians, because they appear to appeal to the talented people's desires to have more than others. Their effectiveness depends on degrees of avarice or mere indifference to others that seem incompatible with the kind of ethos of mutual concern and respect that egalitarians espouse. After all, by hypothesis, if talented persons were to work for the same wages as the others, they could enhance the position of the worst off without being worse off themselves than the others are. If we understand the difference principle to say that inequalities cannot be justified unless they work to the advantage of the worst off, then any special incentive payments seem to come directly from the pockets of the worst off. The need to appeal to the greed of the talented, or to accommodate their indifference, actually sets back the welfare of the worst off. The talented get more merely because they want more and because they can get away with it. Incentive payments seem to be at odds with equality and the difference principle.

2. A BRIEF NOTE ON WHAT IS AT ISSUE

The whole of Cohen's discussion concerns the proper understanding of the difference principle alone, not the proper understanding of social justice in general. Cohen claims that self-interested incentives are contrary to the basic idea behind the difference principle to the extent to which they produce inequality or do not work to the advantage of the worst off. Self-interested incentives can never be a legitimate defense of the inequalities supported by the difference principle. He says: "On my view of what it means for a society to institute the [difference] principle, people would mention norms of equality when asked to explain why they and those like them are willing to work for the pay they get."[2] Here he is saying that the difference principle cannot justify inequalities generated by self-interested incentives.

Cohen claims in addition that Rawls believes that the difference principle requires an interpretation that is inconsistent with this. He says that Rawls adheres to the lax version of the difference principle. The lax difference principle countenances inequalities that are only necessary to making the worst off better off because some people's motivations are self-interested motives. "It is satisfied when everyone gets what he can through self-seeking behavior in a market whose rewards are so structured by taxation and other regulation that the worst off are as well off as any scheme of taxed and regulated market rewards can make them."[3] The strict difference principle, by contrast, counts inequalities as necessary only when they are necessary apart from people's chosen intentions. It is fully satisfied only when each person defends his economic decisions in terms of the norm of the difference principle. On Cohen's view the above intuitive reasoning, and the reasoning I will lay out in more detail in the section on Cohen's argument (§4), support the strict reading of the difference principle.

Some have worried that this reasoning raises a question about the demandingness of justice. They wonder to what extent this account of justice is compatible with the idea that individuals ought to be able to live their own lives on their own terms. It appears to demand that persons constantly devote themselves to the well being of the worst off. Such a demand seems to wipe out any chance for citizens simply to devote themselves to their own projects. This consequence would count against the account of justice that generates it. I think we can see that Cohen's approach, properly construed, does not generate this extreme conclusion.

The concern is not legitimate as it stands because Cohen's account of the difference principle is quite compatible with "the integrity of a conception of justice which allows the agent a self-regarding prerogative."[4] He strongly resists embracing a moral rigorism that implies all of one's decisions be guided by considerations of equality.[5] But he says that even if some role exists for self-interested incentives in justice, this implies that justice is a compromise between concern for the difference principle and self-interest.[6] "The compromise idea is different from the idea that inequalities are justified if they are

necessary to benefit the badly off, given that agents are self-regarding maximizers on the market."[7] The self-interested prerogatives do not enter into the
characterization of the difference principle; they arise as separate considerations that compete in some way with the considerations generated by the
difference principle, itself interpreted in the strict sense specified above. I will
not discuss this possible worry any further in this chapter.[8]

Instead, I want to bring out a different difficulty in Cohen's discussion. It
begins with his insistence that between the lax version of the difference principle that allows persons to be completely self-regarding maximizers and the
strict version that expects considerations of the difference principle to motivate persons in all their economic decisions, we can find no third way.[9] This
two-choice approach is problematic, because, first, the distinction between lax
and strict versions of the difference principle does not seem to line up neatly
with the distinction between the difference principle as taking for granted
fully self-regarding maximizers and that principle as requiring fully egalitarian motives. The lax version of the difference principle is compatible with a
mix of egalitarian, self-interested, and other-regarding motives. The definition
of the lax version is that it takes motives as they are, whatever they may be.

Second, the stark contrast presented is not true to the complexity of motives individuals often have and ought to have. Sometimes we think that in
order better to satisfy one aim, we should act on the basis of a different motive. We often establish hierarchies of motives in our practical reasoning. In
these cases a higher order motive makes room for and regulates a lower order
motive. We do this especially in the case of complex institutions that make
use of divisions of labor to achieve the basic aims of the institution. For example, in criminal courts that make use of the adversarial system, we expect
lawyers to be motivated to defend their clients and prosecutors to go after
the defendants though the overall aim of the institution is to ensure that we
punish the guilty and let the innocent go free. We would regard the lawyers
as being remiss if they guided their actions solely in terms of the ultimate
aim. This is because we think that we best achieve the ultimate aim when the
prosecutors and defenders single-mindedly pursue their respective, more narrow tasks. A conscientious lawyer can see the higher-order motive of justice
as making room for and regulating the lower-order motive of defending the
client. The overall aim of the institution justifies the hierarchical organization of motives. These kinds of hierarchical relations between motives are

important in social life generally. In my view, this observation will help us show how self-interested incentives can play an important role in implementing the difference principle.

In what follows, I lay out the case for inequality and Cohen's critique. I show that Cohen's understanding of the role of incentives in generating inequality from equality is too narrow. His conception of the way incentives work is not the only or even the most important way in which they can work. And I show that once we see beyond this conception, the worries that he raises regarding incentive-based inequality are less pressing. I offer an informational account of how self-interested incentives can generate a productive society. Self-interested incentives are necessary to generating information about the interests of citizens. They can play a role in a cognitive division of labor that makes each person largely responsible for understanding his or her interests. These incentives and the institutions that create them can give rise to inequalities that are by-products of the institutions. But their usefulness does not imply that the talented are greedy or indifferent. Individuals can be justified in acting on these motives on the grounds that the information only such actions can generate is required to realize the aims of the difference principle. They are compatible with an egalitarian conception of justice because they are essentially informational and because the inequalities they give rise to are necessary concomitants of the productive power of the society. Or so I argue.

3. RAWLS'S AND BARRY'S ARGUMENTS FOR INEQUALITY

The argument for inequality begins with a premise usually regarded as a formal principle of justice:

1. A distribution of benefits is just only if individuals receive more than others only on the grounds of differences that are morally relevant.

By contraposition, we get the principle Rawls uses in his attacks on liberal equality of opportunity and natural liberty.

2. A distribution of benefits is unjust if individuals receive more than others on the grounds of differences that are arbitrary from a moral point of view.

3. Differences in social background and differences in natural endowment are arbitrary from a moral point of view. Therefore,

4. It is unjust if individuals receive more than others in the distribution of benefits on the grounds of differences in social environment or natural endowment.

From this conclusion, it follows by contraposition that:

Justice in the distribution of benefits occurs only if differences in what people receive in the distribution of benefits are not grounded in differences of social environment or natural endowment. (Principle 1)

The premise that argues for inequality as a just alternative to equality says:

If an institutional arrangement produces an unequal distribution of goods that makes everyone better off than one that produces equality, then these inequalities are just, even if it does this by means of incentives to the most talented to work harder. (Principle 2)

In Principle 2, the common good is specified as the ground of the inequality. Differences in natural talent or social background are not themselves the ground. The justification for this claim is this: If individuals are at a baseline position of equality and they realize that they could bring about a state wherein everyone would be better off, they would be irrational not to bring about the inequality even though some receive more benefits than others. Hence, the inequality is just. And this is so even if the inegalitarian improvement comes about as a result of providing special incentives to the talented.[10]

Notice that there may be many ways in which inequality may arise from a baseline of equality that are consistent with this principle. For instance, if the goods to be distributed are lumpy goods in the economic sense, then some will get more than others unless none of the goods are distributed. In the latter case, everyone would be worse off. The Cohen objection does not target these kinds of cases. It targets only those cases of inequality that arise because some refuse to produce more unless they get a greater share of the product than others.

Contrary to what Cohen sometimes suggests, no logical inconsistency of principle 2 (with the inclusion of the incentives-based inequalities) with principle 1 exists. The idea expressed in principle 2 is that the inequality is justified by reference to the Pareto improvement. It may be the case that the cause of the Pareto improvement is that some people receive more pay than others to use their superior talents. What makes the inequality consistent with principle 1 is that the difference in talent is not what grounds or justifies the inequality. What justifies the inequality is that this is a way of making everyone better off. Differences in talent do not themselves ground a just inequality; but they may, not unjustly, bring about inequality if their bringing it about is necessary to producing Pareto improvements. But reasons exist for seeing a tension between the desire to use incentives to the most talented for the purpose of generating Pareto improvements and the ideal of equality. And this tension is the real source of Cohen's worries.

4. COHEN'S ARGUMENT

In this section, I will discuss Cohen's formal argument against the legitimacy of the use of incentive payments to secure Pareto improvements. The basic structure of the argument directs us to compare different cooperative arrangements that have distinct distributive consequences. It shows us how individuals from an initial state of equality might choose a cooperative arrangement with incentive payments to secure the common good. Cohen argues that the choice conditions are unsuitable for the justification of inequality. Cohen thereby asserts a deep tension between the principles 1 and 2.

Imagine two individuals in the choice situation, a talented person and an untalented person, and three cooperative arrangements: D_1, D_2, and D_3. These comprise the intensity or cost of work expected from each person and the relations of work to wages for each individual. We have four different possible wage packages for each individual: W_t, W_e, W_u, and W. These are total packages in the sense that they include benefits and burdens. They include the amount each person is paid minus the amount each person must sacrifice by working. The basic metric is well-being. (Note the difference between Cohen's discussion and Rawls's. In Rawls, the difference principle is about the distribution of income and wealth, while Cohen's discussion uses a kind of welfarist metric wherein benefits and burdens are included.) The individuals find themselves in the initial arrangement D1 and they are now deciding whether to move onto D2 or D3 or stay where they are.[11] What is crucial here is that the two individuals must reach agreement on any change they make; otherwise they will remain in D1. (I have slightly altered the argument's structure here by making explicit the idea that the higher wages are supposed to stimulate harder work from the talented.)

D1. Equality—Talented gets wage W for working (not very hard), Untalented gets wage W for also working (not very hard).

D2. Pareto improving inequality—Talented gets Wt for working hard, Untalented gets Wu for working hard.

D3. Pareto improving equality—Talented gets We for hard work, Untalented gets We for working hard.

The values of these wages (including both benefits and burdens) are Wt > We > Wu > W. We are assuming that both workers have the same utility functions and that the functions are cardinally comparable. The reference to work and hard work is merely an idealizing assumption for purposes of intuitive illustration. We might just as well say that in D2 and D3 they had to do something they preferred less than what they do in D1. What is important is that the extra burdens assumed by the talented person in D2 or D3 are no greater than the burdens assumed by the untalented person.

D1 is like the Rawlsian baseline. D2 and D3 bring about a larger product than D1 because both Talented and Untalented work harder in D2 and D3 than in D1. The difference between how hard people work in D1 and D2 or D3 is merely comparative; the issue for us is what condition will persuade the individuals in D1 to work harder than they already are working. In D2 the product is distributed unequally and in D3 it is distributed equally. Cohen argues D3 would be feasible were the talented willing to work for wage We as opposed to Wt. D2 is justified, if at all, only because it gives incentives for the talented to work hard. Only Wt is able to provide the incentive for the talented to be productive in the way that is necessary for D2 or D3.

Cohen considers three different ways to justify the move to D2 as opposed to D3, given the difference principle. Each depends on the choices of the talented. In the first way, the talented may hold out for a higher wage, exploiting their superior bargaining advantage. They can hold out for Wt because they know that the untalented will not give up the gains acquired in D2 and the talented can threaten to give up the gains of D3 and settle for D1 if they do not get D2. The way that the talented person holds out is by claiming that under a regime of equality of wages, he or she will not work hard, because he or she has no incentive to work hard. The talented person will simply say that a higher rate of remuneration is required for there to be any incentive to work harder.

The claim made by the talented amounts to a kind of bargaining strategy because they are not merely predicting that they will not work hard; whether they work hard or not under the regime of equality is still up to them to a large extent. Or this is a plausible hypothesis to maintain. If instead they are determined, for example by some law of psychology, not to work hard without the inequality generating incentive, then their argument for the incentive is not a bargaining strategy, but a mere prediction and counsel of prudence. But such an interpretation seems to be quite implausible.

We can see that this is very much the kind of argument many people give when faced with a potential tax increase. They claim that they will not work as hard because they have not as much incentive to work hard since the marginal benefit of working is diminished by the higher tax rate. We can imagine the original state D1 as a kind of tax scheme that restores full equality by redistributing the product of each person's labor. The talented in effect are arguing that they will not work any harder than they currently do because they have no incentive to work harder under the equality generating tax scheme. They argue that only if the tax scheme will ensure they end up with a greater net benefit will they work harder than under the equality generating tax. Cohen argues that the talented can in effect bargain for a lower, inequality generating, tax rate on these grounds. So after bargaining, the talented and the untalented persons will agree on the Pareto Superior inequality of D2.

In the second way of justifying inequality, a talented person may simply claim to be working harder than the untalented, or claim that the costs of developing talents are high and require compensation. In effect, the higher income is simply compensation for greater sacrifice. The result of this argument is the conclusion that the talented may not be better off than the untalented after all. The claim is in effect that only D2 can compensate the talented for harder work and that D3 fails to compensate the talented for the greater burdens imposed on them. If we put the matter in terms of our equality- or inequality-generating tax schemes, the talented argue that the equality-generating tax scheme makes them worse off than the others by failing to give them tax credits for the special burdens imposed on them. So the apparent inequality is justified by appeal to a deeper equality.

In a third way that Cohen discusses only briefly, the talented person may invoke another standard of justice according to which it is right for the more talented to get more because they have contributed more.[12] This could come in two different versions. On one version, the talented may insist on receiving more on the grounds that they deserve more. They uphold quite consciously a distinct conception of justice that endorses inequalities grounded on considerations of desert. Ex hypothesi, that conception is false. But they believe in it and insist that they receive more as a consequence. On another version, the talented believe, as a result of socialization, that receiving less after-tax income is a sign of an inferior estimate of them. Perhaps the origin of this belief comes from a now defunct conception of justice as desert, but now it is an automatic response, and with the response comes a kind of debilitating demoralization. They feel demoralized if they are not treated as special and so they work less hard. Only if they receive the inegalitarian wage of D2, will they have the morale to work hard.

These are the main reasons offered for how the incentive of Wt could justify bringing about D2. Cohen rejects the first way of justifying the inequality. It appears to be merely a case of the talented bargaining from a superior position. The inequality would be justified merely because the talented can hold out for more. This seems an implausible justification for an inequality. If differences in natural endowment and social environment are arbitrary bases for distribution then so will differences in bargaining power be arbitrary. Call this constraint on producing inequalities the No Bargaining Constraint.

There appears to be a conflict between the egalitarian desire that individuals act in ways that express equal concern for one another and the bargaining strategy for bringing about inequality. The talented bargainer is acting on a motive of greed or at most indifference to the well-being of his fellow producers. Unless we make the implausible assumption that the talented are somehow forced or compelled to pursue their own interests regardless of the interests of others, we are allowing the talented to voluntarily determine the distribution of benefits on the basis of their desire to have more than others.

The second way of defending the inequality is self-undermining. It does not entail a departure from equality if the more talented person's higher wage is in fact compensation for harder work. Cohen is supposing here that the difference principle concerns the distribution of benefits and burdens and that the extra labor burden on the talented may cancel out the difference in benefits between the talented and the untalented.

In effect the second way violates the hypothesis with which we started. In D2 we assumed that both the talented and the untalented were working harder, while the second way assumes implicitly that the talented has increased work intensity while the untalented has not or at least not as much. Nevertheless, the second way is an instructive one precisely because of the differences between it and the first.

The third way, wherein the talented simply invoke a different standard of justice, seems to involve a violation of the premises of the first argument as well, because the talented person is making a claim to Wt on the basis of a false conception of justice. A just society cannot honor such a claim, nor can it honor the expectations of those influenced by a false conception of justice. Let us call the constraint on producing inequalities here the No False Conception of Justice Constraint.

In the second way, no inequality exists, and so no problem. In the first and third ways, D2 happens in a way that is generally in tension with saying that it is just. Cohen compares the incentives the talented have to try to get more than an equal share out of the arrangement to the incentives a kidnapper has to try to get a large ransom from the aggrieved family. The talented seems to be extorting the money from the untalented if equality or even the difference principle is the correct principle of justice. The egalitarian should just say that justice requires D3, and by doing so may compromise with the talented in order to make everyone better off. But this compromise does not bring about justice any more than giving ransom money to a kidnapper does. The function of such incentives is to appease a greedy appetite that intends to be satisfied by hook or by crook. This function is incompatible with justice. Hence, the difference principle does not justify inequality between the talented and the untalented though the inequalities give incentives to the talented to work harder.

The idea for Cohen is that only D3 is a Pareto improvement over D1 mandated by the difference principle. The talented are capable of working harder for the wages gained in D3. They would not be undertaking any greater burden than the untalented and they would not be getting any less than the untalented. And all would be better off. If they were to hold out for D2 they would in effect be holding up the Pareto improvement for ransom because they can get more. So how could their refusal to work for an equal share be justified? Cohen argues that the incentive argument cannot provide a basis for justifying inequality to proponents of the difference principle. Hence Cohen concludes that only the strict reading of the difference principle is defensible.

In what follows, I will show first how Cohen's conception of the way self-interest might generate inequality is faulty. Then I will show that, contrary to his claim, some self-interested incentives play an essential role in the application of the difference principle, which is much easier to see once we understand some different functions of self-interested incentives.

5. DIFFICULTIES WITH COHEN'S ARGUMENT

Cohen's claim that the talented could get D2 by means of bargaining is undefended. Why should we think that the talented have any more bargaining power than the untalented in this context? The non-agreement position for the two is equality, by hypothesis. The talented are trying to get Wt for themselves, while the untalented are trying to get We for themselves (actually they should try to get Wt for themselves if they bargain rationally). Cohen says that the talented could refuse to work hard for We and be willing to fall back on W. This is a threat that the talented might use to motivate the untalented to accept a deal wherein they simply get Wu while the talented get Wt. But Cohen has not considered that the untalented can bargain as well. The untalented can also refuse to agree to D3. They can say that they are willing to fall back on W if they do not get Wt (for themselves) for working harder. Do we have reason to believe that the untalented stands to lose more by failing to get Wt and only getting W than the talented stands to lose by failing to get Wt and falling back on W? By hypothesis, they do not have less to lose.

If the talented and the untalented bargain by making claims to Wt each for themselves, the bargaining situation is entirely symmetrical.

Do the untalented have more to lose by being unwilling to accept Wu than the talented have by being unwilling to accept We? Here it appears that the talented have more to lose. By hypothesis, the distance between Wu and W is smaller than the distance between We and W. Since strength of bargaining position is inversely proportional to how much you have to lose if you have no agreement, it appears that the untalented have the superior bargaining position. It should be easier for them to get what they want. They should hold out for We. It is not clear why the outcome even among self-interested bargainers would be what Cohen claims it will be once we assume that the baseline is equality. In this case, self-interested incentives should produce equality at the higher level specified by D3.

Perhaps Cohen is assuming that only the talented can unilaterally affect whether the outcome is D3 or D1. So if the untalented insist on equality, then the talented can simply refuse to do well what they do in order to pro-duce enough for D2 or D3. But again, the talented lose as much as the untal-ented by failing to use talent to the full extent under equality. They cannot keep any more of the extra product if they do produce more. The assumption is that both have to agree to the regime of distribution of work and income; the talented cannot just go off and do what they want.

Someone might say that the talented do not lose as much since they somehow work harder to produce D2 or D3, so they lose less. Cohen has ruled this out; he is assuming that in each of these different states, the time and level of work given by both is the same, only the talent is different.[13] So it looks like the talented person cannot have more bargaining power than the untalented.

Nor will it do to say that the untalented want the money more than the talented. By hypothesis, they both start with the same amount and thus any assumptions about how utility functions vary with money will apply to each. Finally, perhaps Cohen is imagining a situation where the talented are more talented at bargaining. So they bluff and bluster until they get what they want. This is probably one way in which the wealthy do end up better off in capitalist economies; they have better educations; they can afford better lawyers and advertising and so on. But in our idealized framework, we are assuming that only differences in productive talent are at issue. We have no reason to expect the talented to be better at bargaining than the untalented. And if this is what is doing the work, then it is not clear that any general solution ought to be expected or that this has anything to do with Rawls's difference principle or Barry's argument for Pareto improvements over equality.

As long as the situation remains as Cohen has described it, it is not clear how the talented can get D2 rather than D3 just by bargaining. But this should help cast doubt on Cohen's third way in which D2 might result instead of D3, in which the talented hold out for more on the grounds that they deserve more. For why should the untalented assent to the phony justice claims of the talented that Cohen has specified? If they are at all self-interested then they will say to the talented that if they are willing to give up We and just get W on the basis of his peculiar ideas about justice then so be it. An equal distribution will seem like a much more salient agreement point than the odd claim that the talented person is making, especially when the baseline is egalitarian.

The diagnosis of the problem so far is clear. Cohen has confused two possible bargaining situations. In one situation, the talented can withdraw from the scheme of cooperation entirely and produce independently or with some third party. In this situation the untalented may end up worse off than under equality and may have more to lose from failing to agree than the talented. Inequality will come about here. But this is not the situation envisioned by the Rawls-Barry argument for Pareto improving inequalities. The situation they describe assumes a baseline of equality wherein all have the same to lose. In brief, it is not clear how Cohen has shown that inequality can come about even if the talented and untalented act on self-interested incentives. He has not grasped the incentive-based argument for inequality from a baseline of equality.

The reasoning I have given here is a variant on Cohen's own discussion of the example of the bargaining between Able and Infirm. There he argues that if Able and Infirm must agree on the distribution of work and benefits, their agreement will be egalitarian.[14]

6. ANOTHER WAY OF THINKING ABOUT INCENTIVES AND INEQUALITY

Brian Barry has suggested one way in which the talented might be able to secure greater benefits as a result of their greater talent.[15] Suppose we have

freedom of occupation and an initial equality in which the talented and untalented people do jobs that make them reasonably happy. This initial state
is D1* and the wage level is equal at W* (remember we are including total
benefits and burdens in the wage packages). Suppose two effects would result from the placement of individuals in jobs for which their talents suit
them. First, the whole arrangement would be more productive. Second,
many would be in jobs that they did not like very much. So garbage col-
lectors would prefer to be poets and great tycoons of industry would prefer
to be selling food on the beach. But suppose that the arrangement would
be so productive as to be able to increase everyone's well-being because of
the greater leisure afforded to everyone. Let us say that everyone will end up
with wage We* in this situation D3*. If we assume freedom of occupation,
we will see that the talented have more options in choice of occupation than
the untalented. Some of the tycoons and professionals might prefer to go
back to their simpler lives than work at their jobs for an egalitarian wage. If
they do go back to their old jobs the total product will decline to near W* for
everyone. The only way we can stop them from going back to their old jobs
is by offering them an incentive payment. So in order to get them to keep
their highly productive jobs, they will have the level of well-being everyone
else has plus the incentive payment to stop them from going to the other job.
Now they have more than equal benefits Wt* and the rest get the less than
equal benefits Wu*. Or so the argument goes.

Despite appearances, the situation above is no more likely to generate
inequality than the one in the previous section. Either the talented are better
off in their old jobs and the lower wage, in which case equality is not brought
about in D3*; or they are worse off in their old jobs with wage W* than in
their new jobs with wage We*. If their working in the right jobs really makes
a difference to the total product, then their choice is between We* at the
unpleasant but productive job, or W* at the pleasant but unproductive job. If
they are better off with We*, then We* provides sufficient incentive to work
at the productive job. If they are better off with W*, then the incentive payment Wt* to get them to do the productive job is real, but it may merely be
a kind of compensation that restores equality to the person who is doing an
especially onerous job. Hence, inequality is unnecessary as an incentive in
this case. The difference principle would require equality even among self-
interested persons.

We might think that the talented persons' preferences do not track their interests because they do not know what their interests are or because they do not care about their interests. Both of these points require fuller treatment. The assumption under which my discussion and Cohen's is operating so far is that individuals know what their interests are. This involves two different claims: first, that their interests are objectively real things (in the sense that beliefs about them can be correct or incorrect), and second, that the individuals involved know these interests. So benefits and burdens are measured along a single metric of well-being. Well-being and the interests that make it up are not defined in terms of preferences, although preferences do usually track well-being, because individuals know their interests and pursue them. For the moment I offer four reasons for accepting this presumption in this context. First, to assume the ignorance of the talented about their own interests does not seem like a reasonable presumption, since the distributive agency supposedly does know what their interests are and the untalented know their own interests. Second, if we assume the talented do not know what their interests are, then it is not clear that incentive payments will have the systematic effect that we desire. Third, if we suspend the idea that people know their interests and that the agency doing the distributive work knows everyone's interests, then we will have a hard time figuring out what will happen in the above cases. Finally, if people are not pursuing their own interests, then we are to some degree outside the terms of the debate. Suffice it to say here, we will presume a low incidence of this kind of effect for the moment.

We will suspend the assumption regarding the knowability of interests in the later part of the discussion. The suspension of this assumption will help us rethink the role of incentives in generating equality.

7. THE INCENTIVE PROBLEM WITH EQUALITY

The incentive arguments Cohen discusses do not justify inequality, but they also do not imply inequality. A proper understanding of the relation between incentives and inequality will clarify matters. The trouble with Cohen's and the alternate characterization of the problem is that he views it as if it were a bargaining problem between two people or between two small groups of people. In fact, self-interested incentives raise problems for equality in large groups of persons wherein each one gains very little by working hard if the entire product is divided equally and loses very little by not working hard. Since each person has little impact on the overall product, each has little incentive to work hard under equality since each will get more or less the same regardless. So the incentive problem for equality is a large-scale collective action problem. And it is not a problem that exists merely between the rich and the poor or between the talented and the untalented. The problem would occur if everyone were equally talented. No one has a self-interested incentive to contribute.

The odd thing about this is that the super talented may have more reason to contribute to an egalitarian scheme than the untalented. They may, if they are really talented, have an impact on the average product that actually increases their well-being even if the product of their labor is equally distributed. If anyone does have a self-interested incentive to produce under equality, it is the talented and not the untalented.

Would the situation improve if we paid the talented more to work harder? The higher pay would in effect compensate them for the greater effort they put into the collective effort; they would still have an overall equality of benefits and burdens. Or perhaps we could simply ask the talented to work more time at the same wage rate; then they would end up the same to the extent that their leisure-labor trade-offs remained the same. But the situation would not improve. In principle we are presupposing that only higher pay will compensate for harder work or greater amount of time expended. Since the total benefit would remain the same and the contribution to the total would be quite small on the average, we must suppose that the person will not have a self-interested incentive to contribute.

8. HOW SOME INCENTIVE-GENERATED INEQUALITIES CAN SATISFY THE DIFFERENCE PRINCIPLE

In order to bring about equality at the same time as high productivity in large number groups, individuals will have to be completely devoted to the realization of justice for all at the highest productive level and inclined to work despite the small effects on their own well-being. I find nothing incoherent about this idea, but in my view it cannot be at the foundation of a just society, and I will try to show why in what follows.

Cohen focuses on the narrow case of a small group of persons who will have no trouble figuring out how to divide up the goods in a productive and egalitarian way and in which everyone's (or at least the talented's) contribution makes an appreciable difference for each. This is not the case in large-scale societies where the contribution of any person or small group of persons makes little or no appreciable difference to the average. More important, a severe deficit of information obtains in large societies about how well off people are, how equal people are, and how to achieve a more productive allocation of goods. This notion provides the key to why egalitarians should permit the inequalities that result by taking advantage of self-interested incentives. Here is the argument.

Suppose, counterfactually, that we live in a world with only three possible economic systems: a central planning system, a market system that redistributes the profits in accordance with the principle of equality, and a market system that distributes profits in a decentralized market way. Although these are not the only or the best alternatives, the point of thinking in terms of these three alternatives is to illustrate the institutional component of the reasoning that undergirds incentive-generated inequality. The considerations in this chapter should be perfectly generalizable to any finite list of alternative institutional arrangements.

Central planning systems determine all the allocations of factors of production such as labor and capital, and they determine all prices for producers and consumers. The net return that results from the operation of such a system is distributed in accordance with a principle of equality. The trouble with these systems has been that they do not allocate factors of production efficiently: They fail to produce things that people want at the prices that people want. The other trouble is that these systems are not capable of much innovation. They can produce a lot of what they produce, but they cannot find ways of developing technology or even new consumer products. The essential difficulty here has been that the central planner simply cannot have the enormous amount of information that is necessary to make these decisions well. With the best will in the world, the central planner cannot figure out how to satisfy demand because it does not know what the demand is. Nor can it develop new technology to meet that demand.

Now consider a market system. Suppose that we have a market in a variety of different goods with competition and where supply and demand determine prices of technology and consumable goods. Thus the knowledge that each person has of needs and well-being is what determines demand for consumable goods. The knowledge that individuals have through trial and error of the demand of others determines what they supply and the allocation of factors of production. This knowledge is not centralized; it cannot be. Prices are set so as to maximize profits and so they are set in a way that reflects the cost to the producer and the interests of the consumer. This makes everyone better off in many contexts.

We may think that we ought to redistribute the profits or that the profits ought to go into a pot and be distributed by a central agent. This would make the profit-maximizing motive a motive for justice.[16] The egalitarian scheme is that everyone is to receive income as compensation for the labor put in, measured in terms of time and intensity of effort, pleasantness of work, and so on. In many cases, the most talented may not get very much on such a principle since they may not work very much or their work may be really interesting. But here we have an effort to bring about equality.

To bring about equality by means of the market plus a redistribution scheme, a central distributing agent will have to know a lot of things: How much effort persons have put into their work, each person's labor-leisure trade-offs, and what kinds of jobs people like to perform and how much they like to perform them. And the agent will have to compare the well-being of each of the participants in order to ensure that they all end up equally well off. The complexity of this scheme and the immensity of the information necessary to make it work in a large society are likely to result in enormous numbers of mistakes. The information needed to make such a system work well is beyond the grasp of humans as we know them.

These facts are likely to contribute to a dampening of everyone's enthusiasm for working in the scheme. The return each gets will probably not correspond well with the work done and each is likely to see that the benefits to others are not often commensurate with their work. So they will not believe that the fruits of their labor have been justly distributed. Hence, even those motivated only by a sense of justice will be discouraged. This will inevitably disincline persons from working hard because their sense of justice is a primary source of their motivation to work. That is, they see that the scheme to which they contribute does not distribute goods equally and thus they no longer have confidence that their labor really is for justice.

Compare the above market plus redistribution scheme with a market system wherein the profits fall into the hands of the people who make them. It is decentralized and it is highly likely to result in inequalities as a result of the different talents people have and a good deal of luck. Because people's incomes depend more on their own activities, they will have to make assessments of what the optimal trade-offs of labor and leisure are for themselves, and no one will have to live with the assessments that others make of their trade-offs. This is much like the fact that only a system of decentralized production can determine what the appropriate allocations of factors of production are and what the proper supply of goods is. Only when consumers determine for themselves what they think is in their interest and what is not, and act on these assessments, can this information get anywhere close to being accurate. Only when producers can experiment with different ways of producing will technological development occur and will people reveal themselves as talented or not. Only when producers can determine how much work in which job is worth what return from their labor, can information about labor-leisure trade-offs and the desirability of jobs be anywhere near accurate. Hence markets supply crucial information that a central planner or a central distributor cannot possess, about the interests of consumers and producers. That crucial information can only come about when people act in their self-interest to some extent. Individuals will only be able to acquire information about these matters if they focus on their interests and ignore the interests of others, and then act on those interests. Otherwise each will be lost in a maze of unmanageable considerations like those that face the central planner. Only in this case, it will be more complex, because he is not coordinated with other individuals. I will explain this more in the next section.

Again, suppose for the sake of illustration that the three schemes are the only three available to us and that the facts I have described are correct. And suppose that everyone is in fact better off under the third highly unequal scheme than under the second or first. Would egalitarians, and proponents of the difference principle in particular, have much reason to prefer the second or first to the third? Would it not make sense to prefer the third on the grounds that it is Pareto superior? The distributions of talent and environmental conditions are playing roles in this scheme in distributing benefits and burdens, but they are not the grounds for the distribution. The reason for allowing the unequal distribution is that it is a necessary concomitant of the scheme that makes everyone better off.

Notice also that no one in the market scheme is bargaining for a higher wage and no one is demanding wages in accordance with a false conception of justice. Individuals act in accordance with their self-interest primarily because this is the means to uncovering and properly using the kind of personal information each, and no one else, is good at uncovering and using. They need not be trying to get more than others; inequality is a by-product of a scheme that is the only one capable of producing and using the kind of information that makes society work well. All of them may be deeply committed to the difference principle but realize that the only way to make everyone better off is for all to concern themselves, regarding some issues, with their interests instead of with everyone else's interests.

9. THE INFORMATION-PRODUCING
FUNCTION OF INCENTIVES

Let us explore this informational account of the importance of incentives and the justification of inequality that attends a bit more closely. The basic argument for self-interest and incentives requires a few premises. First, I argue that human beings have very little knowledge of what their own interests are. Second, I argue that human beings have little knowledge of how to compare their interests with those of others. Third, these two claims imply that we generally have only a small capacity to determine when we reach equality or when we advance the common good. Fourth, I argue that self-interested incentives are often (though not always) necessary to increase the amount of information we have about what interests people have and how to compare them. Therefore, fifth, I argue that self-interested incentives are, partly, necessary to help us bring about equality and the common good. But since, sixth, self-interested incentives also tend to bring about some inequalities (or so we must assume), we must sometimes have to live with the inequalities that self-interest brings about in order to help advance the common good.

So let us take each step in turn. First, it is common sense to acknowledge that we spend each day of our lives learning about and revising our ideas about what is the best way for us to live. We find that we understand little of what our interests are and are constantly trying to improve our understanding of those interests. We must make many difficult decisions regarding what careers we wish to follow, what friends we wish to spend time with, what we wish to do in our spare time, and so on. And we often make mistakes in these decisions and have to start over or modify our plans. In addition, we sometimes find ourselves in circumstances where we must determine how much we ought to work and for how much money. Some kinds of hard work are not worth the money; other kinds of work are worth a lot even if we do not get as much money in return. Each of us is different in many of these respects, so we cannot simply follow others and expect to receive the same well being as they do from the same actions.

Second, it is very hard for us to compare how well off we are in comparison to how well off others are. Obviously, this is in part due to the fact that we do not know very much about our own interests. It is also due to the fact that we often know even less about others' interests. Some enjoy very hard work, others do not and can only do it willingly if they receive significant compensation. We have different views about how to compare the interests of individuals, and we are clearly capable of making mistakes about these. Overall it is very hard to determine when two people are equally well off or not.

Third, information about these kinds of facts regarding our interests and how they compare with those of others promotes equality and the common good and our assessment of when and to what degree we reach these. The measure of equality and the common good is in terms of benefits and burdens to people, which in turn are partly defined in terms of people's interests. As a result, the advancement of equality and the common good requires this information and is more likely to occur when more information about the interests of the individuals involved is available.

Fourth, self-interested incentives are often necessary to get information about our interests. How do we learn more about our interests in life? We learn partly through education and reading, and through hearing about the experiences of others. But we also must learn through our own process of discovery. In large part this kind of learning takes place through trial and error. We try different kinds of activities and we find that they are not as desirable as we had thought they might be. So we try other kinds of activities. Much of this must take place through our own self-interested behavior. That is, if we are to learn about our own interests, we must often pursue courses of action that we think are in our self-interest. And we must pursue them because we think that they are in our self-interest. If others try to figure out what my interests are, or must decide whether something is in my interest or not, quite often they will be mistaken and will do a worse job than I do.

Why is this? Mainly it is because I have a closer acquaintance with myself than others do, so I am able to determine with greater reliability what is good for me than they are able to do. Also, by having the power to learn about my own interests and being able to experiment with different activities, I am more likely to acquire an ability to learn about my interests through practice. These two reasons arise purely from the cognitive limitations of persons and have nothing to do with whether they are ultimately self-interested. In addition, since the interests involved are mine, I have a much greater interest in getting them right than others have, so I am likely to make greater efforts to understand my interests and needs than others are likely to do.[17]

None of this implies that I will always, or even usually, be completely right about what my interests are, but in many contexts it seems clear that I will have a much greater chance of learning about my interests than others will. I am likely to be the best judge of my interests, given the chance to discover them. And given the chance to discover my interests, I will most likely be able to improve my ability to grasp my interests through practice.

I must have the opportunity to discover my interests through action and choice; I cannot simply discover them by reading or listening to others. I must find my own way by trying different ways. But in order to do this, I must pursue my own interests, and I must have the opportunities to do so. But this is what self-interested incentives are. They are merely opportunities for me to pursue my own interests. For example, wage incentives are opportunities for me to discover whether and to what extent a job is desirable to me and whether the wage incentive adequately compensates the burden undertaken. I often cannot know this in advance. Hence, self-interested incentives are necessary to collect information about my own interests. And in general, self-interested incentives are necessary for the society to collect information about the interests of its members.

But if these claims are true it follows that, fifth, self-interested incentives are important in the promotion of equality and the common good. These latter principles are partly defined in terms of the interests of the individuals involved. So advancing equality and the common good requires knowledge of them. Hence, an increase in that knowledge can increase our chances of bringing about equality and the common good. From these claims, it follows that self-interested incentives are necessary for us to get a firmer grasp on how to promote the common good.

In some cases, markets and capitalism will be necessary to enable people to engage in these pursuits. They are among the institutions that enable individuals to learn about their interests, not only with regard to what they consume but also in the process of production. Under these circumstances, individuals are able to try out different forms of productive activity coupled with different wage packages. Only then can they learn what it is that enhances their well-being. It is the freedom individuals have in markets and the fact that they must bear responsibility for their decisions about their own well-being that enables them to try out different forms of life and discover their interests in the process.

Markets and capitalism generate inequality, especially since the supply and demand for human capital such as talent and knowledge will bring a higher wage to the more talented. But if we were to eliminate the process that brings about these inequalities, we would also undermine our capacity to yield information about the interests of the participants. It is not the case that every inequality that is observed or believed to exist can be rectified without undermining the whole point of the institution. If, on the one hand, we decide to redistribute income every time someone earns more income than someone else does, we run the danger of ruling out the possibility that different trade-offs of wages and labor may be desirable for different individuals. And surely we ought not rule out this possibility. We would foreclose options that may enhance the well-being of some. If, on the other hand, we redistribute income every time we think we see some net inequality of benefits and burdens, we are likely to make many mistakes because of our ignorance of these matters and foreclose possibilities of learning about the value of different trade-offs to different people. Hence, we cannot attempt to bring about complete equality without undermining some of the important virtues of these institutions. These virtues are precisely those that help us understand ours and other people's interests and thus help us advance the common good and even equality.

10. INSTITUTIONS AND MOTIVES

We can see that some of the inequality that results from self-interested behavior is a by-product of a process that is necessary to the pursuit of equality and the common good. This helps us establish two conclusions. First, we can see that institutions that divide cognitive labor overcome cognitive limitations best, and that self-interested behavior and the incentives that elicit it may be necessary components of such a division of labor. Since these institutions may be necessary to advancing the common good, they may also be necessary to the difference principle. Second, we can also see that those who act on these self-interested motives need not be acting in opposition to an underlying commitment to equality and the common good. They may see their self-interested behavior as playing a role in advancing equality and the common good.

In our world the structure of social institutions must take into account the fact of ignorance. It is one of the main reasons that we need institutions in the first place. Institutions provide for a division of cognitive labor wherein the limited cognitive abilities of individuals combine in ways that enhance social life. In a world where we know so little about ourselves and others, it is useful to have institutions positioning individuals with the task of figuring out what is good for themselves and those close to them. This too involves a cognitive division of labor. Self-interested incentives are necessary to discerning this information, and so part of the way the cognitive division of labor is organized is by permitting individuals to pursue their own interests in given contexts. Not to have such institutional provision for individuals is likely to make everyone worse off.

I am not arguing that individuals ought always or even usually to pursue their own interests in the economic sphere. I am only arguing that it is useful for the whole society that individuals be able to pursue their own interests in some economic contexts. I cannot say which contexts now; that is something that we can only learn through long and hard experience.

My second point is that individuals, seeing the importance of the cognitive division of labor, can see their pursuit of their self-interest as essential to the overarching aims of equality and the improvement of the conditions of the worst off. We need not think of these as necessarily opposed to each other. Individuals' might well organize their motives into a hierarchy placing concerns of justice at the highest order while making subordinate room for self-interest as a kind of lower-order aim justified and controlled by the higher-order aim. It does not seem to me that egalitarian motives and self-interested motives have to conflict, even though they often do. This may be just one instance of the widespread ability of individuals to reason practically on different, hierarchically organized, levels.

This kind of reasoning is not especially unusual. In the case of friendship, we often think that it is important for friends to act in accordance with their self-interest for the better health of the friendship itself. It is important for the participants in the friendship to know what they like and do not like, and what aspects of the relationship appeal to them. But this is often possible only if the friends come to learn what their interests are, which they often discover only when they pursue their interests without regard to the interests of the other. Here, they may be deciding to act in their individual interests on the basis of higher order motives to preserve and expand the friendship, justifying the pursuit of self-interest.

11. CONCLUSION

Once we take into account the facts of cognitive limitations on individuals, we see that a cognitive division of labor is the most productive way to deal with these limitations. Self-interested incentives play an important role in the cognitive division of labor that advances the common good. Once we see these facts we can see that the difference principle can take into account self-interested incentives without assuming that people are greedy or indifferent to each other. Their primary motives may be their concerns of justice, but such concerns lead them to act in some contexts on the basis of self-interest. I think that we can see then how self-interested incentives can be compatible with an egalitarian ethos in a society where individuals do not attempt to acquire more than others do. These incentives will produce inequality, but only as a kind of by-product. I conclude that the strict interpretation of the difference principle is unwarranted, because self-interested incentives can contribute to enhancing the position of the worst off in some important but innocent ways.

I do not endorse the laissez faire economics suggested in the comparison above, nor do I endorse all the kinds of inequalities that arise in modern market societies. Many more alternatives exist than the ones I list, and some mixtures of different institutional arrangements are superior to the ones I have described here. But markets and decentralized decision making and knowledge acquisition will play some fundamental role in a productive society, even for egalitarians, and these will generate inequalities even when they play a confined role. What is clear is that some self-interested incentives and the inequalities they generate are necessary for egalitarian justice in our complex world.

NOTES

I thank Andrew Williams, Jerry Cohen, David Schmidtz, Richard Arneson, Jerry Gaus, and Christi Favor for discussing previous drafts of the paper on which this chapter is based with me and giving helpful comments.

1. G. A. Cohen, "The Pareto Argument for Inequality," *Contemporary Political and Social Philosophy*, eds. Ellen Frankel Paul, Fred Miller, Jr., and Jeffrey Paul (Cambridge, England: Cambridge University Press, 1995), 160–85; G. A. Cohen, "Where the Action Is: The Site of Distributive Justice," *Philosophy and Public Affairs* (Winter 1997): 3–30; and Cohen, "Incentives, Inequality and Community," *Tanner Lectures on Human Values*, 13 (Salt Lake City: University of Utah Press, 1992), 263–329. This paper was written prior to G. A. Cohens' book *Rescuing Justice and Equality* (Cambridge, MA: Harvard University Press, 2008) and the papers referenced remain substantially the same in the book as they were in their original form so I have retained the pagination of the original papers.

2. Cohen, "Incentives, Inequality and Community," 317.

3. Ibid.

4. Ibid., 314.

5. Ibid., 302.

6. Ibid., 314.

7. Ibid., 315.

8. For an illuminating discussion of prerogatives and the difference principle, see David Estlund, "Liberalism, Equality and Fraternity in Cohen's Critique of Rawls," *Journal of Political Philosophy*, 4 (1996): 68–78.

9. Cohen, "Incentives, Inequality and Community," 315, fn. 33.

10. John Rawls, *A Theory of Justice* (Cambridge, Mass: Harvard University Press, 1971), 75; and Brian Barry, *Theories of Justice* (Berkeley, Cal: University of California Press, 1989) 217–34.

11. In Cohen, "The Pareto Argument for Inequality."

12. Cohen, "Incentives, Inequality and Community," 290.

13. Cohen, "Incentives, Inequality and Community," 296; and Cohen, "The Pareto Argument for Inequality," 173.

14. G. A. Cohen, *Self-Ownership, Freedom and Equality* (Cambridge, England: Cambridge University Press, 1995), 94–96.

15. Brian Barry, *Theories of Justice*, 399.

16. Joseph Carens, *Equality, Moral Incentives and the Market* (Chicago: University of Chicago Press, 1981).

17. John Stuart Mill, *On Liberty* (New York: W. W. Norton & Co., 1975), ch. 3.

PART IV

CHOICE, CONSENT, AND MORALITY

CHAPTER 9

BEHAVIORAL LAW AND ECONOMICS

The Assault on Consent, Will, and Dignity

Mark D. White

The field of *behavioral law and economics* (BLE) resulted from the merger of two successful interdisciplinary ventures in economics. One is *behavioral economics*, itself a combination of psychology and economics, which is exemplified by veterans such as Nobel laureate Daniel Kahneman and Amos Tversky, as well as relative newcomers such as Richard Thaler and Matthew Rabin. The other is *law and economics*, which has produced its own Nobel laureate in Ronald Coase (and Gary Becker, to some extent), as well as prominent advocates such as Richard Posner. Behavioral economics strives to examine how persons actually behave, versus how mainstream economic models predict they will (or should) act. Law and economics seeks to use economic theory to predict the effects of laws (its positive side) and to recommend reform to law based on this theory (its normative side). BLE, therefore, uses behavioral insights to improve our understanding of how persons react to laws and to recommend reforms based on this improved understanding.

One of the more successful developments of behavioral economists is the description and exploration of various cognitive biases and dysfunctions, anomalies in the way that human agents weigh and choose amongst options that vary in some respect: immediate versus later rewards (or costs), resources owned or not, and risks that differ in magnitude and are regularly or rarely experienced, just to name a few. Not only do these biases cause actual choice to differ from the predictions of utility theory, but perhaps more important, they often deviate from what persons would like to choose if they could correct for or otherwise avoid the biases (as evidenced by persistent efforts to lose weight, reduce spending, increase savings, stop procrastinating, and so on).[1]

Based on these findings of suboptimal choice, BLE advocates—most notably Richard Thaler and Cass Sunstein, authors of the bestseller *Nudge* and much academic work on the topic[2]—have endorsed what they term "libertarian paternalism" (also called "light" or "soft" paternalism by other authors[3]). Mainstream economics has long endorsed utilitarian social policy and regulation in the name of optimizing externalities in the interest of the "greater good," but this has usually been tempered by a qualified respect for individual choices in the name of "consumer sovereignty," which helped to restrain any paternalistic impulses. However, behavioral economics has questioned this respect based on cognitive biases and the resulting observations that agents do not always make the choices they would have liked to make. From this observation, behavioral economists conclude that paternalistic laws are justified, which is where behavioral law and economics comes in. BLE scholars use insights from behavioral economics not just to analyze the effects of laws on human behavior, but also to design laws to manipulate that behavior, ostensibly in persons' own interests.

This approach seems to preserve mainstream economists' respect for consumer sovereignty, in that ideally a person's own goals and ends are retained; the behavioral law and economics expert is merely helping her achieve them by correcting for her cognitive failures. Furthermore, the recommendations of BLE seem fairly benign: rearranging the order and presentation of options to help people make the best choices (such as organizing a cafeteria to steer people toward healthy options) and setting default rules and options (with the possibility of opting out) to what people would "really" want (such as with automatic enrollment in 401(k) plans).[4] BLE advocates argue that their libertarian paternalism is less intrusive and more choice-endowing than old-fashioned paternalist measures such as banning or taxing disapproved behavior; for instance, Sunstein and Thaler argue that "libertarian paternalism is a relatively weak and nonintrusive type of paternalism, because choices are not blocked or fenced off."[5] By subtly rearranging the choice environment, policy makers portend to "nudge" people to make the choices that they would make if they had complete information, perfect rationality, and no self-control problems.

But this thinking betrays a profound lack of respect for the dignity and autonomy of persons by refusing to acknowledge their ability to determine their own true interests, which are unknowable to policy makers unless revealed through choice or consent—two ways in which dignity can be respected. As BLE advocates emphasize, preferences are imperfect reflections of true interests, but even the most stable, coherent, and "rational" preferences do not capture agents' complete and true interests, which can also include principles that can override preferences. Because of this complexity, often ignored by both behavioral and mainstream economists as well as economics-oriented legal scholars, the best way (understood prudentially and morally) to ascertain an agent's true interests is to obtain consent or observe choice over the decisions that affect her. Although these choices may not always be best from the agent's own point of view, the policy maker has no way—or right—to judge this for himself. Neglecting persons' dignity is a crucial step toward justifying paternalism and other legal manifestations of utilitarianism in social engineering.[6]

Implicitly, BLE considers a person as a thing to be manipulated, a machine that needs to be fixed, even if only for its own good. In the case of cognitive bias, the processing mechanism (the brain) is not working properly, so the inputs must be manipulated to achieve the desired ends. The source of the problem lies in BLE's understanding of human behavior and action, which lacks the concept of autonomy, specifically as described by philosopher Immanuel Kant. Ironically, BLE's conception of choice is no more advanced or sophisticated than mainstream economists' in this way. To both, choice is wholly determined by a person's preferences and constraints (to which BLE would add her limited cognitive capacities). So there is no true choice involved, in the sense that the person can never do anything but what is determined for her by factors over which she has no control. To a Kantian, however, autonomy is the ability of persons to resist external *and* internal factors when making choices, rendering one's choice a true act of will. In ethical choice situations, autonomy manifests itself in following the moral law that each agent legislates to herself, and it allows her to choose her own ends and interests in accordance with this moral law. It is autonomy, the capacity for truly free choice, that separates human beings from the beasts and grants each person an incomparable dignity, the observation of which requires that each person be treated always as an end and never simply as a means.

Of course, to go from observing cognitive biases to endorsing paternalistic laws takes both an epistemological and an ethical leap, neither of them unfamiliar to economists and legal scholars, but troubling nonetheless. Both tend to start with "I don't think people make choices in their best interests," and from this conclude "I *can* and *should* help them make better choices to further those interests." But there are deep, interrelated problems with both the positive and normative claims in the second statement. In the pages that follow, I will argue first that regulators do not, and indeed *can* not, have enough information to engage in these plans; and second, that there is no way for regulators to know that people are making suboptimal choices without verification from the choosers themselves. Then I will introduce Kant's concepts of autonomy and dignity to show that such manipulation of choice is morally questionable, failing to respect the dignity owed to autonomous persons. Finally, I will discuss the claimed "inevitability" of paternalism in circumstances of cognitive failures and offer alternatives that respect the dignity of agents.

1. WELL-BEING AND JUDGMENT SUBSTITUTION

Typically, BLE advocates talk of well-being or welfare when discussing what is important to (or for) agents: "We argue for self-conscious efforts, by private and public institutions, to steer people's choices in directions that will improve the choosers' own welfare."[7] Mainstream economics (including law-and-economics) often takes preference-satisfaction to be the appropriate measure of an agent's welfare.[8] On a basic level, preference-satisfaction respects the heterogeneity of valuations across persons and imposes no substantive constraints on preferences themselves, imposing only structural constraints such as transitivity. But it is difficult to imagine that preferences completely describe well-being, given the widely recognized existence of other-regarding preferences, self-harming preferences, and other preferences that substantively contradict common-sense ideas of well-being.

BLE does not hold preference-satisfaction to be equivalent to welfare, as it regards preferences—at least, immediate preferences that upon which choices are made—as unstable, transitory, and manipulable.[9] However, if we rule out preference-satisfaction as a measure of personal well-being, regulators must find another measure, and two possibilities immediately come to mind. The first is an objective measure of well-being, such as wealth, health, security, capabilities, or some combinations thereof, that both defines and avoids the problem of self-destructive preferences.[10] This makes measurement significantly easier, but we lose the subjectivity and respect for individual differences that preferences give us (even those we may judge to be imprudent, foolish, or reckless). The second is to use an idea of "real," "rational," or "informed" preferences, commonly understood as what an agent *would* want *if* she were fully informed and not under the influence of any cognitive biases.[11] The two theories of personal well-being can be collapsed into one if we assume—as is commonly done—that when of "sound mind," agents would make choices in pursuit of their long-term well-being, comprising wealth, health, security, and so forth.[12]

But this theory is problematic—how is the policy maker to know what a person's informed or rational preferences or choices would be under ideal conditions? J. D. Trout writes that paternalistic intervention designed to counter the effect of cognitive biases "promotes the agent's autonomy by intervening when the agent's decision is not one that, if fully informed and cognitively unbiased, the agent would have made."[13] But Robert Sugden asks:

How, without making normative judgements, do we determine what counts as complete information, unlimited cognition, or complete willpower? Even if we can specify what it would mean to have these supernatural powers, how do we discover how some ordinary human being would act if he were somehow to acquire them? And what reason do we have to suppose that this behaviour would reveal coherent preferences?[14]

Whether we call them rational, informed, or real, these "preferences," and the measure of well-being derived from them, are artificially and arbitrarily constructed by someone other than the agent herself and cannot be held to represent the agent's true interests. Furthermore, any policy maker's judgment about what should comprise an agent's well-being necessarily involves the preferences of the policy maker himself. Dan Brock sums up the general problem in his review of several theories of paternalism:

... paternalistic interference involves the claim of one person to know better what is good for another person than that other person him- or herself does. It involves the substitution by the paternalistic interferer of his or her conception of what is good for another for that other's own conception of his or her good. If this involves a claim to know the objectively correct conception of another's good—what ultimate values and aims define another competent individual's good, independent of whether that other accepts them—then it is ethically problematic.[15]

This problem is by no means unique to behavioral law and economics. For instance, unconscionability doctrine in contract law allows judges to refuse to enforce contract terms as written if they deem the terms to be unfair to one party or the other. While the presumption is normally that the contracting parties would not have agreed to the contract had it not been in their best interests (at the time the contract was agreed upon), unconscionability doctrine allows the judges to substitute their own judgment of the parties' best interests for the parties' own interests as expressed when they consented to the contract terms. Disputing unconscionability doctrine does not require that we hold all decisions of contracting parties to be flawless, but absent information regarding the parties' true interests, judges have no basis on which to substitute their own judgments when invalidating contract terms based on consent in the absence of coercion or deceit.[16]

Such judgment substitutions are also made when policies are evaluated according to the Pareto criterion, which approves of changes that make at least one person better off and no person worse off. The problem here is with determining when a person is "better off," and without her involvement or consent, this judgment can only be made with an external measure of her well-being. But unless the person's consent is attained, or her choice is observed, there is no way to do this and at the same time respect her autonomy and true interests—other ends are inevitably substituted for her own by the policy maker. This is particularly ironic, as the normative basis for Pareto judgments is normally held to be consent, but consent is only assumed or imputed, not actually secured. But if consent were secured, then the Pareto standard would be redundant, emphasizing the questionable nature of the standard itself.[17]

2. "DUMB" CHOICES

So I agree with BLE proponents when they say that preferences are not stable or coherent, and they are not closely linked to well-being. But neither do preferences or well-being completely explain choice—principles also play an important role, and they may have nothing to do with preferences or well-being, often driving choices in directions opposed by them. People make choices based on principle every day, despite adverse consequences in terms of preferences or well-being. As a result, assuming all choice is made on the basis of preference or well-being is a gross misunderstanding of decision-making and of what agents' true interests actually are.

I will use the term *interests* to refer to whatever matters to an agent and whatever motivates her choices, whether that be preference, principle, or any other reason for choice. As such, interests are broader than economists' standard concepts of preferences, self-interest, or well-being, incorporating any influences on choice that she regards as important. For the purposes of this chapter, I make no assumptions about the "wisdom" of these interests, nor do I make any judgment regarding their morality or prudence. An agent's interests are simply what matters to the agent or what she has the most compelling reasons to care about and devote her time, attention, and resources to attaining.

As BLE proponents never fail to remind us, people make "dumb" choices in terms of being the suboptimal means to further their interests:

Drawing on some well-established findings in behavioral economics and cognitive psychology, we emphasize the possibility that in some cases individuals make inferior decisions in terms of their own welfare—decisions that they would change if they had complete information, unlimited cognitive abilities, and no lack of self-control.[18]

Of course, people do sometimes make dumb choices—*but no one knows they are dumb choices expect the person making them.* This is because no one knows what an agent's true interests are other than that agent, so choices that are optimal from that agent's point of view, given her true interests, may appear dumb to an outsider, who lacks access to information about the agent's ends.

Understanding that an agent makes choices according to her interests, which cannot be narrowed down to simple preference or any objective sense of well-being, the "rationality" of choices becomes impossible for the outside observer to evaluate. A choice that seems counterproductive or "irrational" to the outside observer may not be based on biased or irrational preferences or cognitive processes, but rather on stable, coherent preferences that may seem odd to others. Or the choice may be based on firmly held principles, and as such may be perfectly sound from the agent's point of view, however much it may seem to contradict what the observer takes to be her well-being. For example, economists often question the choices of voters who support candidates who are likely to raise their taxes or lower their benefits. But economic policy is just one element of a candidate's platform—voters may be responding to positions on war, abortion, religion, or any number of non-economic issues that have more in common with principle than payoffs. The observer assumes the voters' only interest is economic, an assumption that has no normative justification and is merely a judgment substitution (as described in the previous section).

J. D. Trout, an advocate of what he terms "bias-harnessing" measures, writes: "Regulation can be permissible even when it runs counter to that person's spontaneous wishes, particularly when the regulation advances the agent's considered judgments or implicit long-term goals."[19] But this assumes too much knowledge on the part of the decision-makers; as Claire A. Hill asks, "What is a better guide than people's choices? Even if people may really want something else, what might that be, and on what grounds can we claim we have access to it that gives us a better claim on what they are going to do than what they otherwise would choose?"[20] The only ways that policy makers can be certain about an agent's interests are indirectly, to observe them through choice, or directly, to obtain consent regarding policies that affect them. If the agent reveals that, in her own judgment, she is making suboptimal choices, she is free to seek help from private or public sources. But a policy maker has no basis on which to assume or infer that her choices are suboptimal and thereby impose "nudges" on her. As Gerald Dworkin writes,

From the fact that in some particular case it would be rational for the agent to have his choice restricted, it does not follow that others may do this for him against his will. Whereas the question of what is in the best interests of the individual is relevant to deciding issues of when coercion is justified, it is by no means conclusive. A decent respect for the autonomy of individuals will lead us to be very wary of limiting choices even when it is in the rational self-interest of the individuals concerned.[21]

The true paternalism in "libertarian paternalism" consists of substituting the policy makers' own ends for those of the agents being "nudged." While ostensibly respecting choice, BLE proponents are structuring the choice environment to manipulate these choices toward furthering what they believe (or want to believe) are the agent's true ends. For instance, regarding decisions about smoking and drinking, Sunstein and Thaler boldly claim that "people's choices cannot reasonably be thought, in all domains, to be the best means of promoting their well-being."[22] But they cannot know the agent's true ends (or interests) without observing them through choice or consent, absent manipulation of the options themselves. Rather, they impose their version of the agent's well-being through the manipulation of the choice environment, and their imposed values are then "confirmed" when the agent makes the "right" choice. Even Richard Posner—who is well-known for recommending that judges "mimic the market" when deciding civil cases, in presumption of knowledge of persons' interests—writes that, under BLE, regulators would be "charged with determining the populace's authentic preferences, which sounds totalitarian to me."[23] As Gregory Mitchell writes, "the proper evaluative view of choice behavior from the libertarian perspective is not an objective consequentialist view, but rather one that examines only the quality of *individual consent*."[24]

Consider the much lauded automatic 401(k) enrollment and "Save More Tomorrow" programs: Policy makers decide that agents should save more, and that they would really like to save more "if they only could." To this end, they manipulate the choice options for 401(k) plans (through the default choice, to be discussed below), such that agents "choose" those plans more often. Then the resultant higher participation rate is given as evidence that this is what the savers *really* wanted to do—as Sunstein and Thaler proclaim, "very few of the employees who join the plan drop out"—not that it is simply what the policy makers manipulated them into doing.[25] Instead, the result tells us only that before the manipulation, employees were too lazy to enroll, and after, they are too lazy to drop out, not that enrolling is what employees *really* want to do. Sunstein and Thaler write, "If employers think (correctly, we believe) that most employees would prefer to join the 401(k) plan if they took the time to think about it . . . then by choosing automatic enrollment, they are acting paternalistically by our definition of the term . . . steer[ing] employees' choices in directions that will, in the view of employers, promote employees' welfare."[26] But as Ronald Dworkin succinctly wrote, "the fact of self-interest in no way constitutes an actual consent"[27]; even if higher savings were important to employees and were in their self-interest (narrowly defined), they may have other reasons not to increase their savings, reasons that should be respected as important to them.

Here is a hypothetical scenario (I hope): Suppose the members of a local election board, who are charged with designing the ballot for an upcoming presidential election, "know" who the local voters should choose, based on what is good for them, and are afraid they might choose the other candidate based on emotional appeals and negative advertising. So they use BLE principles to structure the ballot in such a way that more voters will "choose" the "right" candidate. They are still free to choose the "wrong" candidate, but the ballot was designed to lead the voters to the "right" conclusion—the candidate that represents their "true interests." I hope this "nudge" seems less benign and illustrates the danger of BLE policies when taken beyond the realm of more personal choices like saving (or diet, as we will see below).

There is no need to question the intentions of such policy makers or of the adherents to BLE and "libertarian paternalism." They may indeed be trying to help people better their lives, as the "therapists" in the title to George Loewenstein and Emily Haisley's recent paper.[28] But unlike actual therapists, BLE advocates are "helping" in a way that fails to respect agents' true interests, instead substituting their ideas of what is important for the agents' own. Despite the benevolence of their intentions, their actions still use persons as means to ends that are not necessarily their own and to which they may have active opposition, based on preferences or principles that conflict with the policy maker's definition of well-being. This is the most important objection to paternalism—that it substitutes judgment of others for a person's own—an aspect that is as present in "libertarian paternalism" as in the old-fashioned variety.[29]

The true libertarian choice is clear, and it is the one that respects the essential dignity of persons. As I will describe in the next section, autonomous agents can determine their own ends and interests, independent of their inclinations, preferences, or personal well-being, in accordance with the moral law that they legislate for themselves according their individual judgment. No one else has access to those judgments, and no one else has access to the true interests that each agent chooses for herself. To substitute the policy maker's ends for the agent's own is to fail to recognize her autonomy and to respect her dignity as an autonomous agent.

3. DIGNITY, AUTONOMY, AND CONSENT

According to the moral philosophy of Immanuel Kant, every person has a natural capacity for inner freedom or *autonomy*, the ability to make choices according to the moral law she sets for herself, without interference from any external or internal influences that may counter the pull of duty.[30] Resisting external factors such as social pressure and authority reflects the everyday sense of autonomy as freedom from rule by others, but Kant goes further in requiring that the autonomous agent also resist the influence of internal factors, specifically her own inclinations or preferences. The perfectly autonomous person will always obey the dictates of duty for the sake of duty, regardless of any inclinations to the contrary. Of course, Kant recognized that no person is perfectly autonomous; everyone occasionally lets inclination or preference overwhelm her duty, which Kant terms a failure of virtue or strength, rather than an inclination to immorality. However, a deliberate flouting of one's duty, on the other hand, is definitely immoral, or in Kant's terms, represents *radical evil*.[31]

By virtue of her capacity for autonomy (regardless of the strength of her character), every person possesses *dignity*, an incalculable, incomparable worth.[32] In this way, persons stand in contradiction to mere things, which have prices that enable them to be traded off for other things. As Kant wrote, "whatever has a price can be replaced by something else as its equivalent . . . whatever is above all price, and therefore admits of no equivalent, has a dignity."[33] The dignity of the autonomous agent in turn requires respect from others as well as from the agent herself, based on a person's capacity to hold herself to the moral law despite the pull of inclination or preferences. This is embodied in a popular version of Kant's categorical imperative, the Formula of Respect for Persons: "act in such a way that you treat humanity, whether in your own person or in the person of another, always at the same time as an end and never simply as a means."[34] This formula, which conveys the humanistic tone of Kant's ethics much better than the more familiar universalization formula, generates both negative, perfect duties (such as "do not lie") from the prohibition of using persons merely as means, and positive, imperfect duties (such as duties of beneficence) from the requirement to always treat persons as ends-in-themselves.

Dignity can never be taken from someone, as it is an inherent property of persons derived from their capacity for autonomous choice; but someone can fail to *respect* the dignity of another.[35] The two seminal ways this can be done are deceit and coercion, both of which treat the person simply as means to the violator's own ends. The person who is deceived or coerced cannot rationally assent to the true actions or the ends of the other person, because either she is not aware of them at all (in the case of deception), or she is not given the chance to assent to them (in the case of coercion). In reference to the prohibition on making false promises, Kant writes:

[T]he man whom I want to use for my own purposes by such a promise cannot possibly concur with my way of acting toward him and hence cannot himself hold the end of this action. . . . [A] transgressor of the rights of men intends to make use of the persons of others merely as a means, without taking into consideration that, as rational beings, they should always be esteemed at the same time as ends, i.e., be esteemed only as beings who must themselves be able to hold the very same action as an end.[36]

Note that the agent need only be rationally "*able* to hold the very same action as an end" (emphasis mine), not that they would actually want to. The agent can disagree with the ends of the other person, thinking them inappropriate, ridiculous, or offensive. The important thing is that she can consider them at all, which requires the absence of deceit or coercion. Onora O'Neill states it well: "To treat others as persons, we must allow them the *possibility* of either of consenting to or dissenting from what is proposed. The initiator of action can ensure this possibility; but the consenting cannot be up to him or her. The morally significant aspect of treating others as persons may lie in making their consent or dissent *possible*, rather than in what they actually consent to or would hypothetically consent to if fully rational."[37]

In this sense, manipulation of choice sets or default options uses the agent merely as a means.[38] (The issues of *whose* ends to which she is used will be discussed below.) The person whose options are rearranged is not a participant in this manipulation and was given no chance to assent or dissent to it. Her consent was not sought out; the presumption is that she would consent if asked, because it is being done in her best interests. But "inferred consent . . . is not actual consent that remains unexpressed. It is simply a judgment about what the agent would have agreed to under certain circumstances."[39] Since the agent had no chance to express her position on the "choice architecture," it fails to respect her dignity as an autonomous person and uses her simply as a means.

The BLE advocate may reply that choice is manipulated *for* the agent, not just *to* her. In other words, she is treated as a means, but also at the same time as an end, because her well-being is the end being sought. As Gerald Dworkin writes, "The denial of autonomy is inconsistent with having others share the end of one's actions—for if they would share the end, it would not be necessary to usurp their decision-making powers. At one level, therefore, paternalism seems to treat others as means (with the important difference that it is a means to their ends, not ours)."[40] But we know, from the previous section, that it is not the agent's interests that are being furthered, despite the benevolent intentions of the policy maker, but rather the policy maker's own judgment about what her interests should be. The agent cannot share in the ends of the policy maker, not only because she has no chance to assent to them, but also because she is not aware of them—they are not hers, for only she has access to that private knowledge and reveals it only through choice or consent, neither of which are consulted in cases of choice manipulation.

Why do economists—mainstream and behavioral, "law and" or not—have no consideration for autonomy and dignity? Economists have long clung to a mechanistic conception of the individual, in which her choices are wholly determined by preferences, expectations, and endowments of material resources and time. As such, there is no role for true agency or choice in economic models of decision-making—the person never *makes* a choice or decision, as her choice or decision is predetermined by the factors influencing it. If there is no true choice, the "agent" has no autonomy and therefore no dignity in the sense used herein. She is a machine, or a simple animal, never actually choosing how to act, merely reacting to external and internal influences.[41] Mainstream economists see the decision-makers in their models as machines, and behavioral economists further see these machines as flawed due to various cognitive biases and failures, requiring repair or (at the very least) adjustment, explaining (though not justifying) their impulse to regulate behavior. If, instead, they could see persons as capable of determining their own ends and interests in consideration of both preferences and principles, even if their choices do not always perfectly reflect this, they may understand the dignity persons possess and the respect they are owed due to it, and the drive to manipulate them, even out of benevolent intention, may diminish.[42]

4. THE "INEVITABILITY" OF PATERNALISM

BLE proponents often defend libertarian paternalism by arguing that choices must be made—options have to be arranged, defaults have to be determined—so how else should this be done but paternalistically? Choice cannot fail to be designed somehow, they argue, so why not design it for "good"? As Sunstein and Thaler argue,

The first misconception is that there are viable alternatives to paternalism. In many situations, some organization or agent must make a choice that will affect the behavior of some other people. There is, in those situations, no alternative to a kind of paternalism—at least in the form of an intervention that affects what people choose.[43]

This is correct, of course; defaults and arrangements must be designed somehow, and there are many options available. But BLE advocates are drawn to the paternalistic option too quickly, as a result of their lack of respect for the dignity of autonomous (if imperfectly rational) agents.[44] As we have seen, the problem is with their conception of the "good": Rather than respecting each agent's individual conception of the good as best revealed by her choices, it substitutes the policy maker's own judgment of what that good is.

The two most common policy examples in the BLE/libertarian paternalism literature are manipulation of the choice environment (such as in the cafeteria example) and the determination of default options (such as the automatic 401(k) enrollment). Concerning the arrangement and presentation of options, there is little doubt that these factors play a role in the resulting choices. But this fact does not justify taking advantage of this effect to further an end, even if that end is imagined to be in the interests of the chooser.[45] For instance, sometimes there is a natural ordering, such as alphabetical or numerical; a cafeteria can be ordered by the stages of a meal (soup, salad, entrees, dessert). Is there anything necessarily "better" about these orderings? They certainly do not serve a greater purpose or goal, but as the only "goal" that respects dignity is to allow for choice without manipulation, any unmanipulated ordering will do. At least the chooser will not suspect that the choice set was manipulated for him, unlike under paternalistic ordering, in which he notices that the fruit is well-lit at eye level, while the cake is hidden in the dark where he cannot reach it. Being respected as an individual capable of choice is a goal, but one that is defeated by manipulation.[46]

Concerning default options, there are two separate but related issues: setting the default for the first time a choice is made and also when the choice can or must be renewed. Take the example of a new employee, who must decide on her retirement or health plan options upon starting at her new job, and afterward perhaps face this decision only periodically (such as during open enrollment periods for health insurance). Despite the claims of BLE proponents—"because both plans alter choices, neither one can be said, more than the other, to count as a form of objectionable meddling"[47]—the choice of default rules is not neutral with regard to freedom and dignity in either of these cases.

When an employee starts a new job, she has agreed to provide certain labor services for a package of payment and benefits. She has not signed over control of her life choices to her new employer (unless specified in her contract or in pre-employment negotiations), nor has she agreed to be nudged in the direction her employer finds prudent. It follows that, if dignity is to be respected, the default rule should be chosen as the least disruptive to individual plans and choice. She did not agree to be signed up for a 401(k) plan automatically, and if she does not make an active decision to enroll, she should not be enrolled. Perhaps she forgot, or she was ignorant of the effects of such a plan on her future well-being—either may be true, but there is no way for any other party to be certain of this, and there is no justification to take any positive action based on a supposition to that effect. The default rule for periodic renewals of decisions should be set by the same principle. If the employee made an active choice to enroll or not to enroll in the 401(k) plan, then the rule should affirm (and thereby respect) this choice and continue her chosen status until such time as she makes an active choice to change it.[48]

For the most obvious alternative to paternalistic manipulation, we need look no further than the market. Since markets are based on voluntary transactions, choice, and consent, they ensure respect for the dignity and autonomy of persons. Buyers and sellers in markets act for their own ends, and of course do use each other as means to those ends, but not *merely* as means—they also treat each other as ends by relying on voluntary exchange assured through mutual consent, and avoiding deceit and fraud. Buyers and sellers can also assent to each others' ends, because their goals are clear and apparent: Buyers want goods and services for the money they offer, and sellers want money for the goods and services they provide.

Robert Sugden provides a vigorous defense of the market as an alternative to "inevitable" libertarian paternalism (without claiming that it is superior in every case, which he regards as an empirical question, albeit an unaddressed one).[49] He argues that incoherent preferences do not automatically justify paternalism, but instead actually make the argument for markets stronger, based on their ability to harness and unleash creativity. Using the example of a cafeteria selling cakes, he admits that consumers' preferences over cakes may be vague and undefined before they see the offerings, but this provides an incentive for the cafeteria to experiment with different sizes, colors, and flavors, as well as presentation, to earn the consumer's money. If the consumer likes one of the cafeteria's cakes better than anything else she could spend her money on, she buys it. He writes:

I want it to be the case that they try to offer me products that I want to buy. I want their cakes to look attractive, and to be presented in ways that stimulate my appetite. It is not that I am a paragon of informed desire, acting on complete information with unlimited cognitive abilities and no lack of willpower. It is just that I would rather have my willpower challenged by tempting cakes than license cafeteria managers to compromise on the attractiveness of their products so as to steer me towards the ones that they think best for me.[50]

Ultimately, the market leaves the choice up to the buyer and the seller, ensuring that the dignity of both is respected. Obviously, the state does not share the profit-maximization goal assumed for private firms—nor should it—but the market does provide a powerful counterexample for the "inevitability" of paternalism.

CONCLUSION

If there is evidence that the way options are presented affects choice independent of the options themselves, respect for dignity would require that manipulation be avoided, not embraced. Policy makers only manipulate choice when they disapprove of the choices made, and we have seen that there is no logical or normative basis for doing that, absent the consent of the choosers themselves. In Kant's words, "I cannot do good to anyone in accordance to *my* concepts of happiness (except to young children and the insane), thinking to benefit him by forcing a gift upon him; rather, I can benefit him only in accordance with *his* concepts of happiness."[51] In the minds of BLE advocates, their nudges may be gifts, but unless they are explicitly requested, they are wrongful, presumptive impositions.

NOTES

1. See Christine Jolls, Cass R. Sunstein, and Richard Thaler, "A Behavioral Approach to Law and Economics," *Stanford Law Review* 50 (1998): 1471–1550; and Russell B. Korobkin and Thomas S. Ulen, "Law and Behavioral Science: Removing the Rationality Assumption from Law and Economics," *California Law Review* 88 (2000): 1051–1144. The former essay is included in Cass R. Sunstein, *Behavioral Law & Economics* (Cambridge: Cambridge University Press, 2000), an early collection of literature related to the nascent field. For a more recent collection, see Francesco Parisi and Vernon L. Smith, *The Law and Economics of Irrational Behavior* (Stanford, Cal.: Stanford University Press, 2005).

2. Richard H. Thaler and Cass R. Sunstein, *Nudge: Improving Decisions about Health, Wealth, and Happiness* (New Haven, Conn.: Yale University Press, 2008). Their seminal academic contribution to BLE (besides the paper with Jolls cited in Note 1) is Sunstein and Thaler, "Libertarian Paternalism Is Not an Oxymoron," *University of Chicago Law Review* 70 (2001): 1159–1202. (A condensed version, presumably designed paternalistically to account for irrational impatience on the part of economists, is Thaler and Sunstein, "Libertarian Paternalism," *American Economic Review Papers and Proceedings* 93 (2003): 175–79.) I will cite extensively from the former (henceforth as "Sunstein

and Thaler"), as it is the most complete academic description and defense of libertarian paternal-ism available; much of it appears in *Nudge* as well in a different form, as well as in the *American Economic Review* piece. For another important contribution to the policy ramifications of BLE, a bit more reserved and with more emphasis on distributional concerns, see Colin Camerer et al., "Regulation for Conservatives: Behavioral Economics and the Case for 'Asymmetric Paternalism,'" *University of Pennsylvania Law Review* 151 (2003): 1211–54.

3. It is unclear how consistent BLE's definition of "soft paternalism" is with others in the lit-erature. For instance, Joel Feinberg defines soft paternalism as holding "that the state has the right to prevent self-regarding harmful conduct . . . *when but only when* that conduct is substantially nonvoluntary, or when temporary intervention is necessary to establish whether it is voluntary or not" (*Harm to Self*, Oxford: Oxford University Press, 1986, 12; see also chs. 20 and 21 on voluntari-ness and failures thereof). To be consistent, BLE would have to maintain that choice made in the presence of cognitive biases or failures is nonvoluntary, a claim I have not encountered as such, but may require further discussion.

4. Sunstein and Thaler, 1159–60.

5. Ibid., 1162.

6. For a "slippery slope" argument against "libertarian paternalism," see Douglas Glen Whit-man and Mario J. Rizzo, "Paternalist Slopes," *NYU Journal of Law & Liberty* 2 (2007): 411–43.

7. Sunstein and Thaler, 1162. Some use the term "interests": "To the extent that the errors identified by behavioral research lead people not to behave in their own best interests, paternal-ism may prove useful" (Camerer et al., "Regulation for Conservatives," 1212), though their use of the term is not elaborated, and they fall back on standard "objective" interests such as health and wealth. They do, however, acknowledge the possibility of nonwealth interests, using the example of buying extended warranties that are generally thought to be irrational: "If informed consumers continue to purchase the warranties, then it is quite possible that they have good reason to do so, however *unfathomable* that decision may seem to an economist," 1254 (emphasis mine).

8. See Louis Kaplow and Steven Shavell, *Fairness versus Welfare* (Cambridge, MA: Harvard University Press, 2002); Daniel M. Hausman and Michael S. McPherson, *Economic Analysis, Moral Philosophy, and Public Policy*, 2nd ed (Cambridge: Cambridge University Press, 2006), Section 8.3.

9. "We are emphasizing, then, the possibility that people's preferences, in certain domains and across a certain range, are influenced by the choices made by planners. . . . Across a certain do-main of possibilities, consumers will often lack well-formed preferences, in the sense of preferences that are firmly held and preexist the director's own choices about how to order the relevant items. If the arrangement of the alternatives has a significant effect on the selections the customers make, then their true 'preferences' do not formally exist" (Sunstein and Thaler, 1164).

10. See James Griffin, *Well-Being: Its Meaning, Measurement, and Moral Importance* (Oxford: Clarendon Press, 1986), Ch. III.

11. See Griffin, *Well-Being*, 11–16; Amartya Sen and Bernard Williams, eds., *Utilitarianian and Beyond* (Cambridge: Cambridge University Press, 1982), 9–11; Hausman and McPherson, *Eco-nomic Analysis*, 128–29.

12. On the difficulty of choosing an adequate concept of welfare or well-being on which to base paternalistic policies, see, e.g., George Loewenstein and Emily Haisley, "The Economist as Therapist: Methodological Ramifications of 'Light' Paternalism," in Andrew Caplin and Andrew Schotter, eds., *The Foundations of Positive and Normative Economics: A Handbook* (Oxford: Oxford University Press, 2008), 210–45.

13. J. D. Trout, "Paternalism and Cognitive Bias," *Law and Philosophy* 24 (2005): 393–434, 433.

14. Robert Sugden, "Why Incoherent Preferences Do Not Justify Paternalism," *Constitutional Political Economy* 19 (2008): 226–48, 232.

15. Dan W. Brock, "Paternalism and Autonomy," *Ethics* 98 (1988): 550–65, 559.

16. Philip Bridwell argues that courts should invalidate contracts only when negative freedom is violated (deceit or coercion), rather than positive freedom, violation of which in any given case is open to arbitrary judicial interpretation. See Bridwell, "The Philosophical Dimensions of the Doctrine of Unconscionability," *University of Chicago Law Review* 70 (2003): 1513–31; also Guido Pincione, "Welfare, Autonomy, and Contractual Freedom," in Mark D. White (ed) *Theoretical Foundations of Law and Economics* (Cambridge: Cambridge University Press, 2009), 214–33 (particularly Section II); and Richard A. Epstein, "Unconscionability: A Critical Reappraisal," *Journal of Law and Economics* 18 (1975), 293–315 (particularly Section IV, on substantive unconscionability).

17. See Mark D. White, "Pareto, Consent, and Respect for Dignity: A Kantian Perspective," *Review of Social Economy* 67 (2009): 49–70. For a similar point with respect to capability and happiness approaches to normative analysis, see Robert Sugden, "Capability, Happiness, and Opportunity," in Luigino Bruni et al., eds., *Capabilities and Happiness* (Oxford: Oxford University Press, 2008), 299–322.

18. Sunstein and Thaler, 1162. However, see Gregory Mitchell, "Libertarian Paternalism Is an Oxymoron," *Northwestern University Law Review* 99 (2005): 1245–77, 1247n8 for criticism of the various cognitive biases and failures at the heart of BLE and libertarian paternalism. Richard A. Posner argues that many of BLE's "irrationalities" can be modeled with standard rational choice theory; see his "Rational Choice, Behavioral Economics, and the Law," *Stanford Law Review* 50 (1998): 1551–75 (in response to Jolls, et al., "A Behavioral Approach to Law and Economics"). See also Gregory Mitchell, "Taking Behavioralism Too Seriously? The Unwarranted Pessimism of the New Behavioral Analysis of Law," *William & Mary Law Review* 43 (2002): 1907–2021.

19. Trout, "Paternalism and Cognitive Bias," 394.

20. Claire A. Hill, "Anti-Anti-Anti-Paternalism," *NYU Journal of Law & Liberty* 2 (2007): 444–54, 450.

21. Gerald Dworkin, *The Theory and Practice of Autonomy* (Cambridge: Cambridge University Press, 1988), 77–78.

22. Sunstein and Thaler, 1168.

23. Posner, "Rational Choice, Behavioral Economics, and the Law," 1575. Also, Hill writes that BLE advocates "sometimes speak as though they have access to the knowledge of what people really want apart from what they choose. This position is ultimately untenable. . . . As convenient and tempting as it may be to extrapolate from our own introspection that others want what we do, or should, want, we simply have no access to others' beliefs and desires" ("Anti-Anti-Anti-Paternalism," 448).

24. Mitchell, "Libertarian Paternalism Is an Oxymoron," 1260 (emphasis mine).

25. Sunstein and Thaler, 1185.

26. Ibid., 1172–73.

27. Ronald Dworkin, "Why Efficiency?", reprinted in *A Matter of Principle* (Cambridge, MA: Harvard University Press, 1985), 267–89, 276.

28. Loewenstein and Haisley, "The Economist as Therapist."

29. One could say, even, that libertarian (or "soft") paternalism is worse because of its covert nature. Cigarette taxes are obvious "nudges" too, and are less manipulative for their overt nature. Hiding the cigarette rack in the back of the grocery store is crafty and presumptuous, taking advantage of cognitive dysfunction, and therefore much more insulting. Furthermore, as Edward Glaeser notes, "persuasion lies at the heart of much of soft paternalism, and it is not obvious that we want governments to become more adept at persuading voters or for governments to invest in infrastructure that will support persuasion" ("Paternalism and Psychology," *University of Chicago Law Review* 73: 133–56, 135; see also 155–56).

30. Immanuel Kant, *Grounding for the Metaphysics of Morals*, trans. James W. Ellington (Indianapolis: Hackett Publishing Co., 1785/1993), Ak. 400–402, 440–41. (All citations of Kant's works will give the standard Akadamie pagination, available in all reputable translations.) See also Roger J. Sullivan, *Immanuel Kant's Moral Theory* (Cambridge: Cambridge University Press, 1989), Ch. 5; and Thomas E. Hill, "The Importance of Autonomy," reprinted in *Autonomy and Self-Respect* (Cambridge: Cambridge University Press, 1991), 43–51.

31. See Sullivan, *Immanuel Kant's Moral Theory*, 129–130, and references therein.

32. Kant, *Grounding*, Ak. 428; Immanuel Kant, *The Metaphysics of Morals*, trans. Mary Gregor (Cambridge: Cambridge University Press, 1797/1996), Ak. 434–35.

33. Kant, *Grounding*, Ak. 434.

34. Ibid., Ak. 429.

35. See Kant, *Metaphysics of Morals*, Ak. 462.

36. Kant, *Grounding*, Ak. 429–30 (emphasis mine). For more on Kantian dignity, deceit and coercion, see Onora O'Neill, "Between Consenting Adults," reprinted in *Constructions of Reason: Explorations of Kant's Political Philosophy* (Cambridge: Cambridge University Press, 1989), 105–25, and Christine M. Korsgaard, "The Right to Lie: Kant on Dealing with Evil," reprinted in *Creating the Kingdom of Ends* (Cambridge: Cambridge University Press, 1996), 133–58.

37. O'Neill, "Between Consenting Adults," 110. See also Korsgaard, "Right to Lie," 138: "It is important to see that [Kant does] not mean simply that the other person *does not* or *would not* assent to the transaction or that she does not happen to have the same end I do, but strictly that she *cannot* do so: that something makes it impossible."

38. According to Gerald Dworkin, in instances of paternalism "[t]here must be a usurpation of decision-making, either by preventing people from doing what they have decided or *interfering with the way in which they arrive at their decisions*" (*Theory and Practice of Autonomy*, 123, emphasis mine).

39. Ibid., 88.

40. Ibid., 123–24.

41. Robert Sugden makes a similar argument in "Incoherent Preferences," derived from James Buchanan and Friedrich von Hayek, in relation to the standard mathematical optimization techniques used by economists.

42. Social economists are unique among economists in recognizing and emphasizing the dignity of the economic individual; see, for example, Mark A. Lutz, "Centering Social Economics on Human Dignity," *Review of Social Economy* 53 (1995): 171–94; John B. Davis, "The Normative Significance of the Individual in Economics," in *Ethics and the Market: Insights from Social Economics*, eds. Betsy Jane Clary, et al. (London: Routledge, 2006), 69–83; and Mark D. White, "Social Law and Economics and the Quest for Dignity and Rights," in *The Elgar Companion to Social Economics*, eds. John B. Davis and Wilfred Dolfsma (Cheltenham, UK: Edward Elgar), 575–94.

43. Sunstein and Thaler, 1164.

44. Mitchell adds that, if manipulation were inevitable, it would be so only "so long as individuals remain subject to these irrational influences," which is to say only if these "influences" themselves were inevitable and incurable ("Libertarian Paternalism Is an Oxymoron," 1251, emphasis removed; see 1248–60 in general on the supposed inevitably of paternalistic manipulation). Posner makes a similar point, accusing BLE of "treat[ing] the irrationalities that form the subject matter of behavioral economics as unalterable constituents of human personality. All their suggestions for legal reform are of devices for getting around, rather than dispelling, our irrational tendencies" ("Rational Choice, Behavioral Economics, and the Law," 1575).

45. Indeed, Jonathan Klick and Gregory Mitchell argue that accommodation of cognitive bi-

ases, rather than efforts to combat and lessen them, may make the biases themselves worse ("Government Regulation of Irrationality: Moral and Cognitive Hazards," *Minnesota Law Review* 90 (2006): 1620–63).

46. See Mitchell, "Libertarian Paternalism Is an Oxymoron," 1260–69 on BLE's favoring of welfare over liberty in their paternalism.

47. Sunstein and Thaler, 1173.

48. Ironically, Sunstein and Thaler come to the same conclusion with regard to automatic enrollment in parking plans, but their argument is to save people from their forgetfulness; see Ibid., 1171.

49. Sugden, "Incoherent Preferences," Sections 5 and 6.

50. Ibid., 247.

51. Kant, *Metaphysics of Morals*, Ak. 454.

CHAPTER 10

CONSENT AND THE
PRINCIPLE OF FAIRNESS
Calvin G. Normore

1.

Philosophical anarchists think there is no general obligation to obey law. Philosophical statists disagree. The disagreement is about our obligations with respect to a particular kind of social institution, but it suggests more general questions about how obligations may arise in situations in which they did not previously exist. I want here to consider how consent, in the sense discussed throughout the chapter, interacts with considerations of fairness and whether this interaction might provide a general mechanism for generating even political obligation.

Some obligations, my obligation not to kill innocent you, for example, seem natural in the sense of not requiring for their existence any social arrangement. It does not seem that all obligations are like this. I may have an obligation to reimburse your travel expenses when you speak at a meeting—

or I may not. If I do it may be that the obligation arises from my having promised to do so when I invited you. Promising is one way of creating obligation where none was before.

Some theorists have suggested that we might ground the obligation to obey the law in the obligation to keep promises. One reason for doing so is that the latter seems more primitive than the former. It is possible to conceive of societies that had nothing like law and to ask how such societies could come to have laws (and the obligations to obey them); it is harder to imagine a society without a mechanism for making commitments like promises.

Promising seems to require a social mechanism and seems to require something more. One may make a promise without intending to keep it, but one cannot make a promise without what I shall call undertaking a commitment. For this reason, among others, the strategy of grounding an obligation to obey the law in the obligations that arise from promising seems unlikely to succeed. Although there were and are jurisdictions in which many or most explicitly promise to obey the law, such jurisdictions are rare, and even in them, the cost of not making the explicit promise is usually so high that it is far from clear that one has really committed oneself—and so really promised. These problems suggest few obligations could be justified in such a way. If the obligation to obey the law is to find a ground, it seems it must be in another way.

The relations between incurring obligations and committing to incur them are complex. Promising, and, more generally, making commitments are ways of creating obligations, but there are constraints on the creation of obligations in these ways. There is a long tradition, going back to Plato and Cicero, that holds that a promise to do wrong is not binding. More recently Michael Otsuka has pointed out that even if a group of people explicitly promised to live by a heinous set of institutional practices, they do not thereby create legitimate practices that induce an obligation to accept and obey them.[1] Even explicitly agreeing to abide by an arrangement creates an obligation to abide by that arrangement only if the arrangement is morally acceptable. Some, Robert Paul Wolff, for example, have thought that a promise to abide by rules whose content one did not know in advance would be intrinsically immoral.[2] If they are right, the power of promises to create obligation is limited indeed.

2.

If morality can constrain the power of commitments to induce obligations can it also induce obligations without commitments? I have moral obligations that did not require my commitment—obligations that I previously called *natural*. Could it also be that morality interacts with the creation of social institutions, so that I may come to have new obligations to which I did not at all commit?

There are at least two distinct issues here: Could morality obligate the creation of social institutions and could it require me to participate in and share the costs of social institutions that are in place? These are distinct because it seems that obligations to share the burdens of institutions may be more demanding than obligations to create them. What seems true of states, trade unions, grading schemes, and many other arrangements is that they may give rise to obligations once they are in place whether or not there are any obligations to put those arrangements in place. It is far from obvious that if we lived without a state we would have any moral obligation to create one. Could morality itself require me to play a role in a scheme of institutional arrangements, whether or not I agree to do so, while not requiring me or anyone else to set up such institutional arrangements in the first place?[3]

Promising is one kind of institution, the positive law another, language a third. They are all (more or less) plausibly conceived as normative, and all plausibly give rise to obligations that could not exist without them. Politicians, criminals, and Mrs. Malaprop all do something wrong that they could not do wrong without a normative institutional frame. How does it come about that an institution gets a normative grip so strong that we do some kind of wrong by not governing our behavior by its rules?

This question lies at the heart of debate about whether and how to justify the obligation to obey the law. Because law seems so clearly a product of social arrangement, it seems unlikely that an obligation to obey it could be natural. Again, it seems very unlikely that if most of us have such an obligation, it could have arisen through our promising or explicitly undertaking a commitment. It seems very likely that if there are obligations to obey the law, they arise out of the matrix of social arrangements themselves. What then are the prospects for social arrangements creating obligations in persons who do not commit to them?

3.

One plausible proposal is that such obligations can arise through a Principle of Fairness. The history of formulations of Principles of Fairness is instructive. The first formulation with any impact on current debate seems to have been H. L. A. Hart's. In his paper "Are There Any Natural Rights?" Hart suggests:

When any number of persons conduct any enterprise according to rules and thus restrict their liberty, those who have submitted to these restrictions when required have a right to similar submission from those who have benefited by their submission.[4]

As Hart formulates this idea, it is very far-reaching. Robert Nozick points out that it would serve as a counterexample to the view that individuals in combination cannot create new rights that are not simply the sum of preexisting rights.[5] We find even stronger consequences. Suppose, for example, that we understand "benefited" in Hart's last clause to mean "made better off than they were before the enterprise came into being." Then not only could the Principle be used to generate obligations to obey the law—provided everyone is better off if everyone submits to the law than if there were no law—but it can also be used as a foundation for morality itself. Suppose that morality is a system of rules such that everyone benefits more from the submission of others to the rules than they lose by their own submission. Then all those who are moral have a right that those others who benefit from their submission also be moral. If there were no other "natural" moral obligation than the obligation to obey the Principle of Fairness, we could, using it, bootstrap ourselves into a full-blown morality.[6]

Hart's formulation of the Principle of Fairness (as John Rawls later called it) is not hard to criticize. First, it runs afoul of the Cicero/Otsuka constraint. If we set up an unjust system of rules that benefits you (such as apartheid), we do not thereby create in you an obligation to play along. Second, as Nozick famously complained, it is far from obvious that we can create obligations in you by providing you against your will with even genuine goods that you acknowledge as such.[7] Nozick advances several complaints: (1) The goods provided may not be worth the costs to you. (2) How, even in principle, could we assess the costs to you—do they include all the opportunity costs? (3) What if the benefits are unequally distributed? (4) What if you preferred that all cooperated in another venture instead of this one?

There have been two basic lines of response to Nozick's critique of Hart. Rawls presented one of them, anticipating Nozick, in 1964:

Suppose there is a mutually beneficial and just scheme of social cooperation and that the advantages it yields can be obtained if everyone, or nearly everyone, cooperates. Suppose further that cooperation requires a certain sacrifice from each person, or at least involves a certain restriction of his liberty. Suppose finally that the benefits produced by cooperation are, up to a certain point, free: that is, the scheme of cooperation is unstable in the sense that if any one person knows that all (or nearly all) of the others will continue to do their part, he will still be able to share a gain from the scheme even if he does not do his part. Under these conditions a person who has accepted the benefits of the scheme is bound by a duty of fair play to do his part and not to take advantage of the free benefits by not cooperating.[8]

Rawls's formulation has several requirements. First the scheme of social cooperation must be just. That takes care of the Cicero/Otsuka constraint. Second, the scheme is a public good. Third, a party must have accepted benefits under the scheme. If all three requirements are met, Rawls seems to have thought, the party is bound by a duty of fair play to pay a share of the costs of the scheme.

Rawls's third requirement is not transparent. It could be interpreted to mean that a party accepts benefits under the scheme if the party actually receives them and keeps (does not refuse) them. In this sense we can accept a benefit involuntarily. It is in this way, I think, that Nozick understands Rawls. In a more natural sense, I accept a benefit only if I consent to receive it. It is in this way, I think, that Rawls intended his formulation. So understood, Rawls's formulation incorporates consent into the Principle of Fairness. I have a duty in fairness only if I consented to the benefit under the scheme. I shall return to this in the following sections.

Many writers have tried to take another route past Nozick's objections. Eschewing making consent part of fairness, they have tried to characterize a type of benefit the reception of which brings a duty in fairness to bear a share of the costs of supplying it. For example, George Klosko suggests that for there to be an obligation to bear a share of the costs of a scheme to be incurred the goods supplied must: (i) be worth the recipient's effort in providing them, (ii) be "presumptively beneficial", and (iii) have benefits and burdens that are fairly distributed.[9]

Klosko intends his second condition to identify a range of goods so basic that we would presume that someone who protested that he or she did not want those goods was either lying or irrational. In short, the presumptively beneficial goods are those that any rational agent could be presumed to want. If we understand Klosko this way, then the intuitive force of his formulation is that if I benefit from a fair scheme that supplies me with goods I cannot rationally fail to want, then I am obligated in fairness to bear my fair share of the costs of the scheme.

Klosko's formulation evades Nozick's counterexamples (which concern goods rational individuals might not want) but misses Nozick's point: That even if I agree that the goods are worth having and am glad to have them, it does not follow that I am glad to get those instead of other goods, or glad to get these goods in this way instead of in some other way. And if I am not glad to get just them instead of others and in this way instead of in some other way, I may still have a complaint against the scheme that would intuitively undermine any hold of obligation it may have on me.

Let me articulate this idea with a scenario that I think has a pretty wide application. Suppose we start in the state of nature. As yet, no rule-governed enterprises exist that are relevant to my example: no property, private or communal. Suppose that a group of us get together and devise and agree to abide by a system of rules for the private appropriation of property out of the common. We agree that if someone comes upon a patch of ground that has no fence inside it, and that person fences it, then the ground inside the fence becomes that person's property. We recognize that this arrangement is permissible only if this person thereby makes others no worse off than they were, and we agree that he or she can satisfy this proviso by hiring the others at wages that enable them to live better than they would have in the state of nature.

Such a scenario satisfies Klosko's conditions, but the economy thus set up also has an opportunity cost. Because the land is now private property, we cannot set up a system for working the land in common. While we agree that we are all better off than we were in the state of nature, some of us think that we are worse off than we would have been if the private economy had not been established. We think that if the private economy had not been established, it is very likely that a better public economy would have been created. Given the choice between the private economy and the state of nature we prefer the private economy, but given the choice between the private economy and the state of nature together with the chance to transform it, we prefer the possibility of transformation. Suppose that we are right that if the private economy had not arisen to fill the space a more beneficial public economy would have. Does fairness now require us to support the private economy?

I think that if we look at Klosko's Principle of Fairness in this way and in this light it loses much of its appeal. If a group of us can create obligations in others by setting up an institution marginally better than the status quo and that thereby preempt much better ones that the others might well have set up had we not preempted them, then the Principle of Fairness becomes not a way of avoiding unfairness but a powerfully conservative principle. If we focus on the kind of goods provided or on the gap between our situation after the setup of the enterprise and before, it is hard to avoid these consequences. What we need is, at a minimum, a principle that is sensitive to the alternatives to the enterprise in question.

One proposal sensitive to the alternatives—though perhaps not designed with such sensitivity in mind—is Garrett Cullity's.[10] Cullity's explicit interest is in the question of what is free-riding and what is wrong with it, but in the course of discussing that problem he recommends a variant of the Principle of Fairness. It reads:

If a person receives benefits from a scheme that satisfies the following conditions, it is unfair for her not to meet the requirements it makes of her in respect of her enjoyment of those benefits.

(1) The practice of participation in the scheme represents a net benefit for her.

(2) It is not the case that practically everyone would be made worse off by the practice of participation in the recognition as obligatory of those further requirements that must in fairness be regarded as obligatory if the requirements in question are regarded as obligatory.

(3) She is not raising a legitimate moral objection to the scheme.[11]

Condition 2 of Cullity's proposal is opaque, but we can see its consequences by considering how Cullity thinks it deals with the case of the Enterprising Elves.

The Enterprising Elves go about at night looking for and repairing things people have left outside their houses. Having completed the repairs the elves return the objects and demand a reasonable price for their labors. Cullity claims that we have no obligation to pay the Elves because their scheme does not meet the second condition. As he puts it:

> Consider what would be entailed if we were to recognize as obligatory all the further demands that would in fairness have to be so regarded if the demands of the Enterprising Elves were regarded as obligatory. (I shall call this fairly generalizing the demands made by the Enterprising Elves.) It would mean holding everyone liable to pay for all unsolicited benefits that are worth their cost. A commercial system that recognized this sort of liability would be so cripplingly inefficient that it would impoverish us.[12]

We can understand the scheme Cullity thinks would impoverish us in various ways. One way of understanding it (perhaps the way Cullity does understand it) is as setting the price of each good at the maximum a rational buyer would pay if there were no other demands of that kind on her purse. Another, I think more plausible, way to understand it is as setting all prices at the maximum a rational buyer would pay given the other demands on her purse. Since the value to me of having my shoes repaired is sensitive to what else I might do with the money, these are not equivalent. On the second understanding of the scheme it might be hard to defend the fairness of such a price, but I know of no reason to think an economy that set prices in this way would thereby collapse. For a scheme to obligate in Cullity's frame, it must not only benefit us, but it must be the case that almost all of us would not be made worse off if we were obligated by it and by anything that it would be unfair to distinguish from it.

This condition does take account of alternatives. If almost all of us would be better off in an alternative scheme, then we might well be worse off if we were to be obligated to participate in this one. In that case, we would not meet Cullity's second requirement, and so the existing scheme would not obligate.

Although it is a step in the right direction, Cullity's proposal does not go far enough. One way it fails is that condition 2 requires that almost all of us be better off in the alternative scheme. Suppose that only half of us would be better off in the alternative scheme but the other half no worse off. Then Cullity's condition 2 is satisfied, and we are obligated by the existing scheme. We can imagine a continuum of forms of condition 2: that supposing the obligation and its generalization would make at least one of us worse off, a few of us worse off, and so on. These forms differ in the degree to which they privilege the status quo. Cullity's is a very extreme privileging.

I think this a symptom of a deeper problem. Suppose we have two practices, A and B, such that practice B would be in place were practice A not in place and all would be better off were practice B in place than they are, given that practice A is in place. It is quite counterintuitive to suppose that A is obligatory. Surely if a practice A is strictly dominated by a practice B that it preempts, then we have no obligation to support A. According to Cullity's condition an existing practice gets to obligate us if imposing and generalizing the obligation does not make almost all of us worse off. It does not matter if the mere existence of the practice itself makes us worse off than we would otherwise be (though better off than we were) unless the practice will remain only if it is morally obligatory to support it. This conclusion seems quite odd.

We cannot safely assume that if a given practice were not in place we would be back in the situation that existed before the practice emerged, nor can we safely assume that even if there were a practice that would have emerged had this one not arisen, that the practice would now emerge if this one were to cease. Many of the counterfactuals we need to evaluate to determine the background against which we apply Cullity's Principle of Fairness to a practice are very difficult to evaluate. My suspicion is that most of the relevant "would" counterfactuals are false: That if a given practice were not in place, any one of several situations might arise, and it is simply false that any *one* undoubtedly would arise.

But if this is true then proposals like Cullity's condition 2 will be far too easily satisfied. Whenever we find no fact about what would happen if a practice were to wither, there we will find no fact about whether we make almost everyone worse off by creating obligations that prevent its withering.

In such a case Cullity's condition 2 is satisfied, and on his formulation we have an obligation to support a morally acceptable goods-supplying practice simply because it exists.

I suggest that proposals like Cullity's and Klosko's point in the wrong direction. Such proposals presuppose that we can find objective features of a practice sufficient to ensure that a person will have a moral obligation in fairness to support it regardless of the attitude that person has toward the practice. As Rawls may already have understood, the intuitions that underlie the Principle of Fairness point in a different direction. These intuitions support the thought that people have an obligation not to take unfair advantage of others. But whether or not people take unfair advantage of others is not simply a matter of what goods the parties give or receive but also of the spirit in which they give and receive them. If you insist on paying the bill at all our joint dinners and would get very angry if prevented from doing so, then I do not take unfair advantage of you by allowing you to pay more than your share. But if I hang back so that you, to avoid the embarrassment of suggesting that it is my turn, pay more than your share, then I may be taking unfair advantage of you. If this is right, then two parties could be in objectively the same situation but one could be taking advantage of someone and the other not. I suggest that we cannot determine whether a person is taking unfair advantage of someone apart from the attitudes of the parties concerned.

Understanding the Principle of Fairness as ruling out taking unfair advantage does not mean that fairness is entirely a matter of the attitudes of those concerned. Under some interpretations, the Principle of Fairness rules out free-riding, but free-riding in the sense of benefiting from a practice without contributing to its costs is not always wrong. As Richard Arneson stresses, we have no obligation to support cooperatively organized fashionable dressers even if we enjoy watching them stroll by, and we have no obligation to support the railroad just because we enjoy watching the freight train roll by.[13] In general, if a group of people organize a practice for their own purposes, and that practice happens to benefit us, they do not thereby create obligations for us.

Arneson thinks that free-riding is only wrong when certain objective conditions hold. Some of these we have already canvassed—the practice must not require immoral action, the participants must benefit from it, the practice must be fair and must also be perceived as such. Arneson suggests that we also need other conditions—that the benefits provided be genuine public goods that could not be easily converted into private goods worth their cost to each participant and which it would not be worth the costs for an individual or small coalition to supply by themselves, and that the choice whether to contribute is for each person independent of the choices of the others. When these conditions are satisfied, Arneson suggests, they make sound dominance reasoning of the following sort: "Either other persons will contribute sufficient amounts to assure continued provision of B [the benefits of the practice] or they will not. In either case I will be better off if I do not contribute."

Reasoning of this kind in situations characterized by the satisfaction of the objective conditions just mentioned is labeled "free-rider reasoning" by Arneson. He contrasts free-rider reasoning with two other kinds of reasoning that he does not think blameworthy: "nervous cooperation" and "reluctant cooperation." Nervous cooperators decline to contribute because they fear that not enough others will contribute to keep the practice afloat and do not want to waste resources on a lost cause. Reluctant cooperators decline to contribute because they expect that enough others will decline to create a serious free-rider problem and they do not want to support free-riders. Arneson proposes that where the objective conditions are satisfied and free-rider conduct is possible, "their obligations arise, under the principle of fairness, prohibiting such conduct."[14] Arneson's suggestion that it is the grounds on which the free-rider declines to contribute instead of the mere fact that he declines to contribute that determines whether his failure to contribute is wrong seems to me to hit the mark.

I suggested in the discussion of Cullity's proposal that what is relevant for fixing obligations is not whether a practice confers a net benefit on its participants relative to the previous situation or relative to the situation in which no practice is in effect, but how a practice fares when compared with what would or might well be the case if that practice were not in place. Determining what would or would likely be the case if things were different from the way they actually are is notoriously difficult, so the introduction of this counterfactual element into the determination of the baseline for evaluating the benefits conferred by a practice makes it highly likely that reasonable people will disagree in many cases about whether a practice does yield net benefits relative to the baseline. Such disagreement may well be intractable.

I suggest that this reasonable disagreement will affect whether one has an obligation to support the existing practice. It is plausible that for me to have an obligation it must be the case that if I am rational, fully informed of all the facts, and accepting of all the relevant moral principles, I will think that I have reason to fulfill the obligation. But if the facts make it reasonable for someone to think that the existing practice, perhaps because it appears likely that it preempts a better one, does not confer a real net benefit, then they leave it reasonable for someone who accepts the facts, and accepts an obligation to be fair, to reject any obligation to support the existing practice. Such a person would have no reason in fairness to support the existing practice. We could put this point differently by insisting that a person in the situation just described who was forced to support the existing practice would have a legitimate complaint—such a person would be being made to do something that, in his or her considered judgment, would be better not done. Matters are otherwise for the person who thinks that the existing practice confers a real net benefit, even taking into account what it preempts. Such a person does not think that it would be better if the existing practice were not in place, and so has no grounds for complaint with it.

Still, we are not done. Even someone who had no complaint with the existing practice might protest against the idea that the goodness of the practice made support of it obligatory. Commonsense morality does not ordinarily require us to support every good thing that comes along, even if it is good for us. It is hard to see why fairness should require us to support practices we admit are good to have if we are adamant that, good or not, we do not want them. The value of autonomy grounds a presumption that we need not endorse even a morally acceptable practice just because we may benefit from it. The core of Nozick's complaint with Hart was that Hart's Principle of Fairness would make it necessary that people take steps to reject a good if they were not to be obligated in fairness to help provide it. But this seems unfair— why is it that you can say simply by showing up with a benefit for me that I must incur, willy-nilly, the burden of explicitly rejecting or returning it?

These considerations find a natural place when we return to Arneson's suggestion that it is the grounds on which someone declines to support a practice that determine the obligations in fairness to its other participants. Arneson puts his point in terms of the reasoning that moves the person who declines to contribute, but this is too narrow. Someone may decline to contribute without reasoning about it, and someone may take advantage of others without even being aware of the dominance reasoning that characterizes Arneson's free-rider. What we need to capture a prohibition against taking unfair advantage is not an appeal to the noncontributor's reasoning but to his dispositions. We can capture this with a principle like the following:

Principle N: Where there exists a just and mutually beneficial scheme of social cooperation that provides a public good, and a party receives benefits under the scheme and would pay a share of the costs of the scheme were the party to be excluded from the scheme otherwise, then that party has a obligation in fairness to pay up to that share of the costs of the scheme consistent with others bearing costs in a similar fashion.[15]

This principle specifically forbids failing to contribute on the basis of free-rider reasoning. But the principle is stronger than that. It also cuts against those of Arneson's reluctant cooperators who would rather receive the good at the expense of tolerating free-riders than not receive it at all. Moreover, it confronts Arneson's nervous co-cooperators with a choice of foregoing the benefits of the practice or taking a chance that they contribute fruitlessly.

The Principle of Fairness, as just formulated, does not require that, in order to have an obligation in fairness, we actually perform any act of accepting the benefits of the practice. But it is plausible that some ways of receiving those benefits provide very strong evidence that the counterfactual is satisfied. If I find myself eagerly awaiting the weekly pickup by the Enterprising Elves and saving my repairs for them, I have some explaining to do if I then insist I would rather do without their services than pay their fees. The counterfactual may be satisfied without any such strong evidence. I may simply receive goods and not bear a share of the costs of providing them in a thoughtless way, and it would still be true that if there were a threat to cut them off I would scurry to pay up. Still, the Principle exempts from obligation those who receive benefit under the existing scheme and agree the benefits are worth the costs of the scheme but who would, given the choice of contributing or doing without, forego the benefits.

Principle N, I claim, carves at the joints the issue of when fairness requires that one support a practice. It gets the cases right. But it also draws support from another direction. Peter Abelard claimed that in action what was blameworthy or praiseworthy was not the act itself, which often lies outside our control, but what he called consent (consensum) to action—which he described as an inward readiness to act should the circumstances arise.[16] It was Abelard's view that someone who was ready to perform an act in given circumstances, but for whom the circumstances never arose, had consented to the act in the same sense as, and was morally on all fours with, someone for whom the circumstances did arise and who then performed it. Principle N exploits this intuition. Someone who is inwardly ready to support a practice in the circumstances in which that is necessary to obtain its benefit has as much consented to supporting the practice as has the person who openly gives the practice support. If such persons were forced to support the practice, they could not claim that they were supporting it against their will. (Though they could insist that it was against their will that they be forced to support it). In whatever sense consent is required to ground the obligation to support the practice, consent is here present. Principle N has it that it is consent—the inward readiness to pay should it be necessary to obtain the good—plus the refusal to pay, that combine to make one's behavior in the context of a practice of supplying goods unfair. Merely accepting a good that one would not have been willing to pay for is in no way unfair.

4.

I suggested at the beginning of the chapter that consent to a practice such as the legal system of a state was not always sufficient to generate obligations with respect to it. Other conditions, notably moral conditions, had to be met as well. The road followed since suggests, I think, that considerations of fairness, without a leavening of consent, will not yield obligations to a legal system either (though they might if it were clear that states were the best possible environments for us). But the Principle of Fairness does rule out free-riding in one sense—we have obligations to support practices we would support if such support were necessary to obtain the benefits of the practice. Free-riders in this sense have consented to the practice. This is as it should be. Practices that obligate us provide us with reasons for action. But reasons for action should be reasons that could get a grip on the actor. Consent is the most transparent mechanism through which a practice might get such a grip.

Do I then have an obligation to obey the laws of the societies in which I live because they are those laws? Nothing herein suggests that I do unless I consent to the practices that make up the legal systems of those societies. But I can consent without realizing it. Whether I have consented may be a matter of what is true about what I would do in situations that do not obtain. A morally consistent philosophical anarchism is possible, I maintain, though it is not as common as one might think.

5.

Let me return to John Rawls's discussion of the role of the Principle of Fairness in our moral and political life. Rawls explicitly built into his formulation that it applied to those who "accepted" goods under the practice. It is somewhat unclear what this "acceptance" comes to but it is plausible to construe it as consent to receiving the goods. If we understand it in this way then Rawls's formulation does not provide a Principle that will bind all who benefit from a society, and this no doubt is part of the motivation for his abandoning, in *A Theory of Justice*, his earlier view that politics could be founded on the Principle of Fairness in favor of positing a natural duty of justice. Rawls formulates the natural duty this way:

From the standpoint of the theory of justice, the most important natural duty is that to support and to further just institutions. This duty has two parts: first, we are to comply with and to do our share in just institutions when they exist and apply to us; and second, we are to assist in the establishment of just arrangements when they do not exist, at least when this can be done with little cost to ourselves.[17]

In *A Theory of Justice* Rawls distinguishes obligations, which he conceives as always arising through voluntary acts, always having their content specified by an institution or practice, and always being owed to the individuals who cooperate in those institutions and practices, from duties that lack these features.[18] He argues that all obligations in his sense can be grounded in the Principle of Fairness, and he understands this Principle as requiring the voluntary acceptance of benefits by those whom it binds. He concludes that ordinary citizens have no general political obligations. But, Rawls insists, natural duties of justice exist that ground political duties—that is, duties to support and further just political institutions—and he argues that in the original positions, if they were up for choice, citizens would choose these duties.[19] For Rawls, that these duties (and not, say, a duty to accept only what the Principle of Fairness required of us) would be chosen in the original position explains, in some sense, why these natural political duties (and not others) exist. But it is these duties that ground our normative political life. Thus Rawls is not a hypothetical consent theorist. For him the duty to obey just law is a natural duty. We would be unjust not to fulfill it, but we would not be acting unfairly in the sense of fairness captured by the Principle of Fairness.

The explanatory distance between simply assuming that political duties exist and assuming a natural duty of justice in Rawls's sense is so small that recourse to such a natural duty amounts to putting aside the project of grounding political duties in anything more basic. That Rawls has taken this approach should give pause to those who think that an acceptable form of the Principle of Fairness will yield universal political obligations. It should also give pause to those in the Social Contract tradition broadly conceived. If supposing that universal political obligations exist drives one either to unacceptably strong forms of a Principle of Fairness or to natural duties that are hardly more than reformulations of those political obligations, perhaps it is time to consider again the consequences of doing without that supposition.

NOTES

Earlier versions of the paper on which this chapter is based were read to the Programme in Ethics at the Queensland University of Technology and to the Southern California Law and Philosophy Reading Group, and a closely related paper was read to the Philosophy Department at the Université de Montréal. I would like to thank the participants in each of these meetings for many helpful comments. I would also like to thank Christi Favor, Jerry Gaus, and Julian Lamont for their help and patience and two anonymous referees for very helpful comments.

1. See Michael Otsuka, "Political Society as a Voluntary Association" drafted in Sept. 1997.

2. R. P. Wolff, *In Defense of Anarchism* (New York: Harper and Row, 1970). I am not clear whether Wolff thought that it would not be a promise or thought that it would be a promise one should not keep, but in either case it appears that he thought it would not generate an obligation to obey the law. So we have constraints on the creation of obligations through promising.

3. *Cf.* A. John Simmons, *On the Edge of Anarchy* (Princeton, N.J.: Princeton University Press, 1993), ch. 8.

4. H. L. A. Hart, "Are There Any Natural Rights," *Philosophical Review*, 64 (1955): 175–91, 185.

5. Nozick, *Anarchy, State and Utopia* (New York: Basic Books, 1970), 80.

6. There are moral phenomena that suggest that this is just how moral obligations have been generated. Gilbert Harman has emphasized that we tend to evaluate the actions of others according to the common morality of their surroundings and not according to our common morality. For example, we do not blame Cicero for keeping slaves in anything like the way we would blame each other, even though Cicero had studied with teachers who put forward the very same arguments against slavery that we would put forward if required to argue the case. An ancient Roman who freed slaves is praiseworthy while a twentieth century Roman who inherited slaves (say from a relative dealing in slaves in the Horn of Africa) would be expected to free them as a matter of course and hardly be considered praiseworthy for doing so. This is what we would expect if the moral demands on each Roman reflected the moral practices of his community. *Cf.*, Gilbert Harman, "Moral Relativism Defended," *Philosophical Review*, 84 (1975): 3–22; and *The Nature of Morality* (Oxford: Oxford University Press, 1977), 106–108.

7. Nozick, *Anarchy, State and Utopia*, 90

8. John Rawls, "Legal Obligation and the Duty of Fair Play," *Law and Philosophy*, ed. Sidney Hook (New York: New York University Press, 1964), 9–10.

9. George Klosko, *Principle of Fairness and Political Obligation* (Lanham, Md.: Rowman and Littlefield, 1992), 39.

10. Garrett Cullity, "Moral Free Riding," *Philosophy and Public Affairs*, 24:1 (Winter 1995): 3–34.

11. Ibid., 18–19.

12. Ibid., 14.

13. Richard J. Arneson, "The Principle of and Free Rider Problems," *Ethics* 92 (1982): 616–35.

14. Ibid., 623.

15. *Cf.* Simmons, *On the Edge of Anarchy*, 256.

16. Peter Abelard, *Ethics*, in the collection *Peter Abelard: Ethical Writings*, trans. P. V. Spade (Indianapolis: Hackett Publishing Company, 1995).

17. *Cf.*, John Rawls, *A Theory of Justice* (Cambridge, Mass: Harvard University Press, 1971), 33

18. *Cf.*, Ibid., ch. 2, sect. 18 and 19, 108 ff.

19. *Cf.*, Ibid., ch. 6, sect. 51, 333 ff.

PART V

THE FUTURE—
EQUALITY AND FAIRNESS

CHAPTER 11

THE COSTS AND BENEFITS
OF FUTURE GENERATIONS

Russell Hardin

How do we bring future generations under the coverage of moral and political theory? This is arguably the most difficult question currently facing all of such theory. Some moral and political theories seem ill suited to handling future generations at all. Others may be able to handle them, but they will apparently require substantial rethinking and revision before they do so. The question of how to approach future generations is another of those major moral and policy issues that catch us with our theories in the lurch in this era of the great and increasing impact of technology on our lives, our capabilities, and our limits. The first glimmerings of how pervasive such issues would be came perhaps in the rise of modern, high-tech warfare, which went stratospheric after World War II, and in the massively expensive delivery of high-tech medical care, which now threatens to consume our entire gross domestic product.

Despite the recent rise of environmental concern for the well-being of future generations, analogs of the problem have long plagued moral and political theory. At its beginnings, contractarian political philosophy, for example, was troubled by the question of how to bring future people under the putative agreement that supposedly justifies a coercive political order. Early utilitarians debated the different appeals of average and total utilitarianism, with advocates of average utilitarianism pointing out that the total utility criterion could be satisfied by the creation of large numbers of destitute people, so long as their lives are still barely worth living.

The more general problem moral and political theorists face is how to extend their arguments to cover additional groups—not only future people, but also different nations or communities, and maybe also other entities besides people. The problem of whom or what to include is central to much of medical ethics. Is a human zygote, a newborn who is anencephalic, or someone in a persistent vegetative state a person? Through his vicar on earth, god has recently asserted that the zygote is a person, and therefore an object of full moral concern. Many of those who accept this authority therefore say the zygote is a person. Many other people say it obviously is not. Despite thousands of pages in print on this issue, resolution of the disagreement is not likely to turn on the quality of argument within moral theories. The issue is, instead, about the boundaries of moral theory. The implicit, not explicit, boundaries of many contemporary moral and political theories exclude concern with future generations. We may be able to gain some purchase on the problem of future generations by drawing insights from other extensions of the covered community. The central, distinguishing difficulty of future generations is that they are not well defined. The "class" of future individuals cannot be members of the class of people to whom any theory applies, at least under traditional conceptions. Bringing future generations into the present class of those covered by a theory may at first glance seem to be a straightforward task, and many claims by moral theorists have treated resolutions of problems of future generations as almost trivially obvious. Such claims are naive. Quick intuitions in this field sound pompous and foolish. Increasingly we must face up to the apparent fact that our theories are wanting.

1. COSTS AND BENEFITS:
ENVIRONMENTAL AND RELATED ISSUES

We may break our actions into two classes according to their effects on future generations: positive effects and negative effects. Typically, these are not independent but are interrelated. We cannot reduce negative effects without affecting positive effects. We should look at the package, not the individual elements, of what we hand on to future generations. All our negative actions might eventually have the effect of reducing future numbers of people, perhaps only in some generations, perhaps in toto. Among actions with negative effects are using fixed, exhaustible resources, causing harmful pollution, and damaging the gene pool. Among those with positive effects are capital investments and beneficial intellectual and technological advances.

Although the harms we do to future generations may be hard to assess, recent concern with them makes it unnecessary to characterize them here. Not long ago, we had much more interest in the benefits we bestow on future generations than in the harms we inflict on them. This generation bequeaths many benefits to future generations in the form of capital and capabilities that enable the future generations to be productive, perhaps even to be more productive than we are. We may analytically distinguish two ways in which we do this. We do things that have great opportunity costs in the sense that we deliberately invest in those activities in lieu of other activities. For example, we invent things, which may benefit future generations but whose price we cannot fully extract from future generations. Instead of inventing these things, we might simply have spent our time with the pleasures of leisure or other consumptions. In such cases, the benefits of our inventions may be largely a gift to future generations.

Apart from activities that have substantial opportunity costs that we choose to suffer, we also do things that create what is sometimes loosely called cultural or social capital. We create language and we use it here and now, but we leave it behind for future generations. We create social organizations that directly benefit us now but that may also be useful to those who follow.[1] That these things benefit future generations is merely an unintended by-product of our motivated activities. We do not forego other activities of interest to ourselves in order to make these investments for the benefit of future generations.

In this century, several diseases have been completely or nearly eliminated through the application of hygienic principles or through vaccination. The governments and others who paid for the eradication of small pox or who are now paying for the eradication of polio and other wild diseases give up other benefits.

The case of disease control suggests an unanticipated and perhaps still widely unnoticed harm that we may be doing to future generations. And that unanticipated harm suggests why we must look at the whole package of costs and benefits instead of at any single one. We should weigh against the good of disease control the harm of diseases we spawn. Joshua Lederberg has noted that the contest in evolutionary history between humans and microbes is still being waged, and he sees no clear sign of which will finally prevail.[2] Diseases may seem new, in the sense that we had no prior history of them, but they may actually be quite old, and they have only recently been able to gain an epidemic hold on human populations. Why the change? Because we have changed the ways we treat the world around us, the ways we aggregate in compact areas, and the ways we travel. We have radically altered some ecological systems, giving some microbes better odds of conquest. (Consider one example: Argentine hemorrhagic fever came out of obscurity after farmers began to clear the Argentine pampas to grow corn. Clearing benefits the corn-eating mouse *Calomys musculinus*, which harbors the Junin virus that causes the fever.[3]) We have also used antibiotics extensively enough to stimulate widespread resistance among diseases.[4]

If we are to make sensible claims about the effects of our actions on future generations, we must weigh together the costs and the benefits we impose on or offer to them. And if we are to assess the morality of what we do, we must also consider the costs and the benefits to us of our actions. We need not simply sum costs and benefits to all to reach a simple utilitarian judgment. But we cannot expect to achieve compelling piecemeal assessments of actions or policies without simultaneously taking into account related, sometimes even causally related, actions and policies in other areas.

2. CONTEMPORARY THEORIES: THEIR FAILINGS

The number of contemporary moral and political theories is quite large, and the theories are often strikingly different. It is instructive to survey many of them to assess their capacity to address the conflict between present and future generations. Among the most articulate theories of the day are autonomy, communitarianism, egalitarianism, libertarianism, utilitarianism, and theories of rights, respect for persons, and distributive justice.

My remarks here will be too cursory to carry much force, but I think they are basically correct. If they are, they imply a strong and discouraging message for us: Most of moral and political theory has little to say to us about the rightness or wrongness of our environmental actions and their impact on future generations.

Theories fail to address the problem of conflict between present and future generations for different reasons. Some theories apparently have a problem even in principle—virtually by definition they cannot handle future generations. Some are, to date, simply under-articulated—they are in need of further development before they can give us competent advice on our policies. Some run aground because the class of those in future generations is not well defined.

Why should it matter that the class of persons in future generations is ill defined? It matters conceptually for many theories, which gain their force from arousing our sympathies for people or from having particular people do something that creates a moral consideration, as reaching an agreement or signing a contract might. If we cannot fill in the identities of real people, then under these theories we may be able to reach no conclusions.

Let us quickly survey some currently widely discussed theories.

2.1 Libertarianism

Let us begin with libertarianism. Because it has a long history of articulate concern with problems of inclusion of new people or groups, it can exemplify many of the problems all theories will face. It also has much in common with contemporary microeconomic concern with efficiency, and, for present purposes, it can stand proxy for market economics and the Pareto criteria, the central principle being that we should (or will) end at an allocation of goods in which no one of us can be made better off without harming the lot of any other. Vilfredo Pareto proposed the Pareto criteria as morally neutral principles that anyone could accept. Often libertarians write and speak as though their principles of consensual, mostly dyadic exchange and the protection of property in the status quo were morally neutral principles or, more presumptuously, as though they were moral principles that everyone must accept.

Libertarianism also shares with utilitarianism and with economics the central concern with welfare. This concern is sometimes hard to read be-

tween the lines in libertarian writings because libertarian theorists often start
at the level of rights somehow posited, often deontologically assumed. But
the rights are worth protecting only if they contribute to the right holder's
welfare. If the rights of property and dyadic exchange were typically harmful
to the right holders, they would not be a fit concern for libertarians.

Rights of property and exchange can only be moralized if they are beneficial to those who have them and if they do not involve wronging others. It is on this latter concern that libertarianism depends on a grounding
principle, the Lockean proviso, which is at the core of the problem of justice
toward future generations. This proviso stipulates that it is within my right
to appropriate what I find in nature so long as I leave "enough, and as good
left" for others.[5] Locke raises this concern after discussing the rightness of an
individual's appropriating acorns. This is an odd constraint for Locke's larger
purpose, which is to justify an individual's appropriating and coming to
own a particular piece of property. Despite the breathtaking ease with which
Locke generalizes from acorns that will soon spoil to land that is forever, his
constraint could not plausibly be met for the ownership of land, which is in
more or less fixed supply.

Robert Nozick discusses how the constraint of the Lockean proviso
might complicate the libertarian story that runs from justice in historical appropriation of natural resources through to the justice of present ownership
of them. He peremptorily concludes a nuanced and complex discussion by
stating his belief, a seeming non sequitur in its context, "that the free operation of a market system will not actually run afoul of the Lockean proviso."[6]
Unfortunately, if we do run afoul of the Lockean proviso, for whatever
reason, Nozickian libertarians have virtually nothing to say. In a footnote
Nozick gives away the enterprise by saying that when the proviso has been
historically violated and we now struggle to restore everyone to a position of
right, we may have to resort to other moral theories, such as utilitarianism
or distributive justice, to ground a new status quo, from which we may then
proceed on our libertarian way as though this had been merely a "subsidiary"
sidestep.[7]

Hillel Steiner, who is sympathetic to libertarianism, thinks the very concept of a right disallows any putative right of a future generation against a
present generation. A right, he says, "entails the presence of an obligation in

COSTS AND BENEFITS OF FUTURE GENERATIONS 251

someone other than the right-holder. One exercise of that right consists in the right-holder's invoking that obligation, in his choosing that the obligatory performance or forbearance will occur."[8] But, when the future right-holder comes into being, the earlier generation of those whose performance or for-bearance would be obligatory if demanded by the right-holder may no longer be alive to perform or forbear. Hence there can be no such moral right as that of the future generation against depredations by the present generation.

Against Steiner's conclusion is that it is typically possible in the law to empower a right holder through an agent even when the right holder is un-able or legally incompetent to act on his or her behalf. To some extent, at least to the extent to which we can foresee future consequences of present ac-tions, we could therefore appoint agents of future generations to act for them now in securing their rights. But appointing agents to act for future genera-tions recursively raises a variant of Steiner's complaint: The future genera-tion cannot hold its present agent accountable. To this we may respond with institutionalized agents, instead of individuals as agents. The institutional agent can well survive until the time of the future generation whose interests it has represented. But its response must necessarily be in compensation for violation of rights, not achieving performance. We have this time asymmetry no matter how we institutionalize agents. Unfortunately, if all that future generations can get is compensation instead of performance, their rights be-gin to look like positive legal rights and they take on a utilitarian cast that must make libertarians bridle.

Appointing agents to act for future generations would be an extraordinary move in a libertarian theory in still another sense. It suggests that concern for future generations is inherently paternalistic. We generally have strongly and purely paternalistic policies toward only the young and the rationally im-paired. Future generations join these groups by virtue of their helplessness be-fore our choices. Russell Grice and many others presumably would reject the use of rights talk here altogether, as they would in the discussion of children and incompetents. Perhaps we ought to give these groups consideration, but they do not have a right to it.[9] This is a conceptual, not merely a moral claim.

But the conceptual problem of a future generation in a rights theory is even worse than this. The future generation faces a perverse difficulty in ar-guing for its right to actions by a prior generation. On the best biological

understanding, the people of that generation would not exist but for the actions of all prior generations. If nineteenth century industrialists had acted
to secure our supposed right that the planet not be so massively denatured by
their development policies, they would also have secured that we would not
come into existence to have such a right. Their policies are part of the cause
of the births of exactly you and me instead of other people altogether. In a
compelling sense, no future generation can claim rights to our acting differently and no agent of a future generation can make any claim on behalf of
any definable group of people.[10]

In legal decisions this distinction may be blurred, and people who would
not exist if actions had not been taken may have tort claims against those
who created them. In the Johnson Controls case recently argued before the
Supreme Court of the United States, the justices were not required to act
on the interests of some future person born of a genetically damaged ovum
or who suffered genetic harm in utero. But they delivered the opinion that,
given what they had decided about the requirement of the law that Johnson
Controls not discriminate on the job against women who might eventually
bear children, it would be implausible for a future court to rule in favor of a
tort claim against Johnson Controls from a damaged person. Nothing of the
sort would be implausible in the sense that it could not happen. One might
think it likely would happen. But the tort claim itself would be logically
odd unless it were a claim that being brought to life in that condition was
worse than not being brought to life at all and that living was worse than
not living. In that case, the most apparent remedy might seem to be court-
permitted euthanasia.[11]

2.2 Nonlibertarian Rights Theories

Rights may be asserted from direct intuition, as they commonly are in libertarian theories, or they can be derived from other considerations. Typically,
we may derive rights in two ways. We may derive them from the bottom
up, by reference to individuals and their interests in welfare, autonomy, or
whatever. Or we may derive them from the top down, as they must be in a
holistic view of what makes society or the lives in it good and that can therefore yield prescriptions for rights as an institutional device to secure those
goods. Joseph Raz offers a rights theory grounded only in interests and not
in such moral constraints as the Lockean proviso. Raz employs the bottom-

up version, deriving rights directly from individuals, who have prima facie rights implied by their interests. The larger society only imposes a constraint on these prima facie rights in that it balances rights of one person or group against conflicting prima facie rights of another person or group. For example, Raz supposes Palestinians have an interest, and therefore a prima facie right, in a homeland under their rule. They may not have a right if the conflicting prima facie rights of other groups would override it.[12]

Some core of this view is correct: We cannot credibly defend a set of rights that do not somehow serve the interests of the protected right holders. But, unfortunately for our purposes, such a rights theory fails as libertarianism itself does. It fails even if we can invoke some overriding principle of equality or utility to resolve conflicts and trade-offs between present and future generations. The failure is conceptual: A future generation that becomes the present generation cannot make any rights claims against past generations whose actions have determined who the future generation is.

This criticism may also apply to Brian Barry's narrow focus on productive resources under a variant of the Lockean proviso if he is using the Lockean argument to motivate a notion of obligation independently of some more abstractly grounded duty of, say, beneficence.[13] When we adjust our policies based on what resources we leave to the future, we also adjust who the future people will be. If we are willing to suppose that trade-offs among individuals are straightforwardly acceptable, as in a beneficence theory, it need not matter who the people in the future generation are. All that matters is how well off they are. Most utilitarians suppose such trade-offs are morally acceptable, but autonomy and rights theorists generally reject such trade-offs. The term "respect for persons" has become the vogue battle cry for rejecting the morality of such trade-offs.

2.3 Autonomy

Theories of autonomy are varied and complex, as one might expect from their dual parentage in Immanuel Kant and John Stuart Mill. Despite the long history of concern with autonomy, there has been relatively little effort to construct a substantial moral and political theory from it. Much of the writing on autonomy is still at the level of debating foundational intuitions instead of at the level of applying a principle or drawing practical inferences from it. In one of the best recent accounts of autonomy, Gerald Dworkin concludes that applications of the autonomy principle to practical questions, such as policy questions, will not usually involve a mere deduction from theory to policy recommendation. (He thinks this is true more generally of all moral theories.) The autonomy principle will only help us know which actions best express the ideal of autonomy. Dworkin's final words for us are, "What to do may be theory guided, but not theory determined."[14] Autonomy theory may be ad hominem in the sense that only someone within the fold can be trusted to tell us what autonomy has to say about a problem such as the environmental conflict between present and future generations.

2.4 Respect for Persons

Again, a difficult problem with future generations is that our policies will determine who populates those generations. It is hard to see how the vague notion of respect for persons can say much about what policy choices we should make. Should we create persons of kind A or kind Z? How does our respect for each particular person yield an answer to such a question? We suspect that many bold, possibly novel intuitions stand between us and answers to major policy issues if the answers are to turn on respect for persons, a notion that is nowhere clearly enough articulated to permit critical evaluation. H. L. A. Hart's discussion of this issue in the context of criticizing Ronald Dworkin's theory of rights is still more generally valid today.[15]

Usually, respect for persons is asserted as a criticism of utilitarianism because utilitarianism allows trading my interests for another's. In allowing that trade-off, the theory supposedly violates respect for me by taking from me on behalf of the welfare of another. But suppose a theory based on respect for persons yields a recommendation on our environmental policy toward future generations. That theory must do what utilitarianism does, or something quite similar. It must implicitly recommend creating one set of better off or less damaged people instead of other sets of less well off or more damaged people. This does not merely detract from my welfare to enhance that of someone else; it rules me out of existence in order for a somehow preferred person to exist. Concern for future generations is inherently about trade-offs.

2.5 Contractarianism

Traditional contract theory, in which actual consent or a credible form of tacit consent is required, fell on the problem of bringing future generations under the contract. Even someone who thought the consent basis of a real contract was an overwhelming moral consideration could not easily suppose there was any basis to the so-called social contract. As Hume artfully noted, the theory might be compelling if, like butterflies, we entered on and then left the stage a generation at a time.[16] For more than a century, contract theory was therefore more an object of inquiry in the history of thought than it was a living part of moral and political theory.[17]

In lieu of anything resembling actual contract, some theorists have turned to hypothetical contract. Hypothetical reasoning carries great practical weight in the common law. Unforeseen contingencies in contract relations are often handled by judges according to what they think the parties would have agreed to if they had thought of the contingency at the stage of contracting. Still, recent versions of hypothetical contract in moral and political theory, such as that commonly attributed to John Rawls, are not usefully characterized as contractarian because they are rationalist.[18] [19] Rawls's argument from the choice made by one representative person behind the veil of ignorance appears necessarily to be an argument from truth or objective rightness of the choice. There exists a right choice and any conscientious person focusing only on relevant considerations will select it and it only. We ask, what form of government or of economic distribution would a reasonable person consent to under given morally relevant constraints? We somehow find an answer. And we declare that form of government or distribution to be just. It is demoralizing that the answer one philosopher finds to the apparently factual question is different from the answer any other finds—similar degrees of disagreement among intuitionist moral theorists about the facts of "our" intuitions seriously discredited such theory.

Thomas Scanlon, a hypothetical contractarian, argues that the core of this vision is "reasonable agreement."[20] That does seem to be the necessary core. But the contractualist vision is hollow at its core, because we have no way to determine what would be reasonable agreement. Much of modern philosophy suggests it is utterly unreasonable to expect agreement here. In any case, if "reasonable" has content in this context it appears likely that the content must be something that can be rationally deduced or directly intuited.

Consider a standard move in hypothetical contractarianism since Rawls. We suppose ourselves behind some version of the veil of ignorance. Before Rawls, John Harsanyi used this device for doing a clean utilitarian account.[21]

Let us apply the device not to a fixed society of those now living and choosing a constitution for their society but to a multigenerational society. Behind the veil I do not know which generation I am in. But if that is true, I do not know whether I will ever exist if I choose a particular social order. Hence, while behind the veil I am a rather odd sort of person. Odds are, I am an ideal observer, not an eventual participant in the system I am choosing. The element of choice in the usual sense of choosing according to my interest in entering a contract virtually vanishes. My task is simply to deduce what would be the best social arrangement.

2.6 Distributive Justice

More than is true of any other general moral theory, distributive justice is associated with the theory (or theories) of one person: John Rawls. Rawls explicitly deals with the problem of future generations by substituting his "just savings rate" for the difference principle. An enormous literature on these issues exists, and we have no need to add to it here. The chief problem with the just savings rate is that it appears not to flow directly from Rawls's theory of justice. Part of the justification of that theory is that society and its rewards are a joint product of all our actions. Unfortunately, I find no useful sense in which the present structure of society and its rewards is partly the product of actions of future generations. But the argument from mutual advantage turns on there being some reciprocal advantage to all parties from all others in the system we erect.

We cannot generally expect future generations to reciprocate for advantages we offer them. We might couple the advantages we offer with grievous debt or other costs, but we cannot really get reciprocation from future people. The moral force of the mutual advantage argument is emptied for future generations. Rawls's mutual advantage argument for justice cannot produce intergenerational concern, which can only result from beneficent concern by the present generation for future generations.[22]

2.7 Communitarianism

An oddity of the current wave of communitarian thought is that environmentalists have actually invoked it. They note that economically less advanced cultures, in which values seem, as a descriptive matter of fact, to be communitarian, often protect their environment through individual, spontaneous commitments. These cultures do not seem to need the institution-alized protections currently used by industrial states to force industry and individuals to be less environmentally destructive. The claim that native or primitive peoples are environmentally more acute may be exaggerated, as we have substantial evidence that many native cultures have destroyed their environments enough to destroy themselves. But even if the claim is basically accurate, it is still odd to suppose that local community values are primarily what are at stake in current environmental problems. Many of these problems transcend local communities; they even transcend nations and continents. They are almost inherently universalistic in their nature, not community specific. The brunt of communitarian theorizing has been to attack universalistic concerns and principles, to reduce justifications to the local level. Such theorizing is beside the point for major environmental concerns and especially beside the point for any concern with future generations.

Among the forerunners of contemporary communitarian thinkers are those humanists who have often pushed for the maintenance of a particular economic regime, as Jefferson and Tolstoy both argued for the goodness of keeping people on the land. Although land holdings were the source of the relatively great wealth of both Jefferson and Tolstoy, the life of those who work the land must be harsh and even miserable if their proportion is large in a modern economy. If more than half the work force is agrarian, while they can produce only a small fraction of their nation's income, those on the land must live in relative poverty, as historically they have done. Hence, whatever the merits of beliefs about the values of living on the land, those values are apt to be swamped by concomitant disvalues. It might even be impossible for a nation to opt out of standard economic growth (while others continue with aggressive economic growth) without falling into real decline. For example, in a world with only socialist nations of the Soviet type, the eastern nations might not have capitulated to the blandishments of capital-ism and markets.[23]

2.8 Utilitarianism

Utilitarianism and egalitarianism might both be able, at least in principle, to handle trade-offs between present and future generations, although to do so they would require much better scientific understanding from the social, biological, and physical sciences than is now available. There exist two common foundationalist complaints against utilitarianism today. First is that it wrongly requires trade-offs between people and second is that it wrongly requires maximization. The first of these complaints is sometimes grounded in a claim that trade-offs violate "respect for persons," which, as already discussed, is a woefully imprecise notion. The complaint is also often grounded in a claim that utilitarianism may require trade-offs that violate distributive justice. Although we have no good showings of this claim, it may well be true in principle with respect to any given theory of distributive justice. That leaves open whether we should conclude in favor of a theory of distributive justice or of utilitarianism in some variant.

The complaint against maximization is odder. Gerald Dworkin and Michael Slote propose many examples of choices that they suppose call our desire for individual choice maximization into doubt. Unfortunately, in virtually all of these examples, the core problem is a causal relation between maximization of one thing, such as money or the menu of choice, and other considerations. The other considerations include the kinds of thing one might want money for, so that the choice to have less than the maximum possible amount of money is, or is similar to, a choice to use money to consume or own things instead of to own more money.[24] This is not a failure of maximization. Or the other considerations include new social relations that may be coercive as a concomitant of something that is being maximized. For example, if we keep open the option to choose to duel for our honor, we simultaneously keep open the opportunity for others to use that custom to manipulate us through the threat of invoking the duel.[25] Again, this is not a failure of maximization overall, it is rather a logical or causal constraint on what we can independently maximize without affecting other concerns.

If precise measurement of interpersonally comparable welfare is not possible, the debate between average and total utilitarianisms, mentioned in the introduction, loses its interest. At the same time, the theory may be less powerful in the face of problems to be resolved: It may not be able to recommend a resolution at all for many imprecisely measured comparisons.

3. A PARTIAL ANALOG: ENVIRONMENT BEYOND BORDERS

Although occasional policy debate takes place over our environmental impacts on future generations, far greater debate and even negotiation at present over international environmental impacts on other peoples is more common. The problems appear partially analogous. Perhaps we can learn something for the intergenerational problem from consideration of the international problem. The governments and peoples of Brazil and China are willing to pollute more and to contribute more to greenhouse warming than are many in the North Atlantic community. A colleague of mine says the Brazilians and the Chinese are morally wrong insofar as they pollute in ways that harm others than themselves. Let us stipulate that they do pollute more. Must we agree that they are wrong?

It is plausible that the Brazilians and Chinese would think it in their interest to have generally higher levels of pollution than North Americans and Scandinavians would want. But much of the current pollution problem and of the problem of greenhouse warming is that it is inherently collective. If we reduce pollution of many kinds over the North Atlantic, we reduce it elsewhere as well. If we slow greenhouse effects here, we slow them everywhere. Conversely, if the Chinese and Brazilians pollute more, we suffer more. But the Brazilians and Chinese may genuinely prefer the trade-off of more pollution for more economic growth for the current generation. They therefore may simply place a different value on the collective bad of pollution than people in the North Atlantic do.

Given that the bad of international pollution is a collective bad, we can adopt a policy to set its supply at some level, but that level will be de facto the same for all. As with other collective goods and bads, some may want a lower level at the given costs of supply and some may want a higher level.[26] This is a matter of different interests, not of prima facie morality. The Brazilians and Chinese are not immoral to think their interests are better served by economic development than by reduced pollution. They pollute because less-polluting technology is more expensive. We might devise the lowest possible Pareto efficient level of pollution if the high demanders pay disproportionately large shares of the cost of reducing pollution while low demanders pay small shares.

The industries of the Industrial Revolution in England and of many other nations soon thereafter were polluting massively. To some extent, they may have polluted within the carrying capacity of the environment, so that their effects were not as cumulative as many environmental degradations today seem to be, as, for example, destruction of the ozone layer is. Still, they

surely have entailed real costs for subsequent generations. They have also entailed real benefits for subsequent generations by putting capital—material
and human—into place. Reputedly, the largest dune in North America in
the nineteenth century, on Lake Michigan near the Michigan-Indiana bor-
der, is now distributed in concrete throughout the Midwest. The dune is lost
but much of the capital it went into still benefits people.

We might suppose something is inherently wrong in the Brazilian and
Chinese actions. What is wrong is that they are inflicting harms on others.
But this is not an especially powerful moral principle that sweeps the field
of other concerns. In ordinary individual ethics, the effects of my actions on
you matter for deciding how I should act, but they do not generally matter in
a simply lexicographic fashion. It is not tout court wrong for me to do something that entails costs for you. If I get a law passed that stops your pollution,
it may be a harm to you, but one that may be justified. If I just happen to
do harm to your business while leading mine to great success, it may not be
wrong at all. We could go on multiplying cases. Virtually all significant actions, especially actions by nations or large corporations, have negative external effects. Positive effects might directly offset some of these negative effects
for the same people. But many of them will not be offset. A moral and political theory that says such actions are therefore wrong is itself likely wrong.

Harms do not have a prior status that trumps other considerations. We
might suppose some harms do trump other considerations, but we reach this
conclusion from attention to the significance of the harms in comparison
to the significance of the other considerations. On a simple utilitarian account, we might conclude that the harms from using chlorofluorocarbons
in air-conditioning massively outweigh the benefits in comfort and energy
efficiency from such air-conditioning.

Suppose it is true that Brazilians are contributing massively to greenhouse warming by clearing vast tracts of natural forest. Their effect on global
warming comes largely from their following the previously massive clearing
of European and North American forests. If the North Atlantic community
benefited economically from clearing its forests, perhaps it should share that
benefit with others who now face restrictions on the effort to catch up economically. On the theories that require some variant of the Lockean proviso,
the North Atlantic nations owe some of their gain to the rest of the world for

having exhausted the capacity of the planet to carry our economic activity. The Brazilians do not contribute more to greenhouse warming than other nations have done. Instead, their contribution comes at a point at which it may help tip the scales past the carrying capacity.

The correct moral conclusion from the conflicting values of developing and developed nations on these issues may be the simple one that developed nations, who more dearly want pollution reduced now, should pay more dearly for it now. If we want the rain forests to be protected, perhaps we should buy them and develop them in other ways. If we want the Chinese to burn coal in cleaner ways, we should provide them with the relevant technology. If we can reasonably think of a national interest in a particular level of pollution at a particular price, we can think of Edgeworth boxes in which to locate national contract curves over which to negotiate. In this case, the correct moral conclusion is none other than the correct neoclassical economic conclusion: The governments of the North Atlantic should make relevant deals with the governments of developing nations for mutual advantage.

Indeed, one might even note that the strictly moral concern those in the developed nations feel toward actions of the less developed nations is itself a kind of luxury consumption good. One who is not yet well off may be little motivated by abstract beneficence—especially beneficence directed at persons unknown, even future persons. We in the North Atlantic may want to weigh future generations more heavily in our consideration than the Brazilians and Chinese do. But even we are not likely to weigh them heavily. If protection of future generations to the level required by some moral theory entailed the investment of twenty or forty percent of our current gross domestic product, we would surely expect our government to invest considerably less.

4. ONE ENVIRONMENT: MANY GENERATIONS

Present and future generations share some of the problems of differently situated national peoples. What we now do to the environment may affect future generations. The environmental harms we wreak often have something inherently collective about them. We share them with others, now and in the future. But there exist also important, arguably overwhelming, differences.

First, we have the problem that already bothered Locke: present and future generations cannot get together to cut deals, so that the present generation's deliberate policies of protecting future generations are paternalistic. Second, a future generation's constitution is affected by our activities as much as or more than is its welfare.

High levels of risk aversion have been given moral status by Rawls in his very risk-averse attitude from behind the veil of ignorance. They have also perhaps been reinforced by the perception—surely correct—that the experts whose careers depend on risky technologies often underrate their riskiness. (The dishonesty of tobacco company officials and scientists is merely an extreme version of what is a widely perceived phenomenon.) Unfortunately, the level of risk that a society sets from some activities is, as greenhouse warming and some kinds of pollution are, a collective good that cannot be provided at individually selected levels. We all get risk-averse policies or we all get risk-neutral policies. (We may disagree about when the policy moves from risk neutrality to aversion.) Economists, engineers, and physical scientists may be more risk neutral than other social scientists and humanists. They may then quarrel about the rightness or wrongness of a policy when they have conflicting interests, just as the developed and the developing worlds may have conflicting interests. Recognition that the issue in conflict is the level of risk acceptance might make politics clearer and more readily resolvable.

5. FROM INDIVIDUAL TO SOCIETY: INSTITUTIONS

The solutions to large-scale social problems such as intergenerational transfers are almost all institutional. Messianic leadership by self-selected, morally committed individuals might have some effect. But even then, the main effect must finally be at an institutional level instead of merely at the level of voluntary self-denial by vast numbers of individuals concerned about future generations.

This is not surprising. The union of moral and political theory often depends on an institutional connection or understanding. We politically achieve the outcome a moral theory would require through the good functioning of some institutional structure. The relevant institution or institutions must somehow bring the affected interests into account. Alas, if some of the relevant interests are the interests of future generations, we face all the core problems above. I have argued elsewhere for an institutional utilitarian account of moral and political philosophy.[27] In that account, among other things, we set up rights—positive legal rights—to protect individuals and groups. We do this in part because we can expect more utilitarian outcomes from a system in which individuals have the incentive to look after their interests under the regime of relevant rights. As powerful as this device might be, it may falter before the problem of future generations. There may be no one extant who has incentive to look after the interests and welfare of future generations.

Consider an example of the institutional burden. Barry and others have argued for a variant of the Lockean proviso to govern our responsibility to future generations. We cannot possibly have as much and as good left over for others who follow us. Who will leave undeveloped acres of central Manhattan or London to whoever is still to come or as much petroleum underground as was there before us? Instead of such a proviso on our appropriations, Barry supposes we leave merely as good "productive opportunities" in general as we have had.[28] We can accomplish this in many ways, among the least attractive of which would be to use none of the world's natural resources ourselves. But we could de facto leave as much titanium to future generations as we have ourselves. And we could leave about as much iron, merely that the process for its recovery would be different from the process of mining and smelting that we have used. The real problem is fossil fuels, especially petroleum, which cannot be recycled as iron and other minerals and resources can. We could exhaust the supplies of plentiful petroleum in a few generations. If we are to leave comparable productive opportunities to future generations, we will have to develop new forms of energy and productive technologies that use less energy. We may have a better chance of doing so if we use petroleum more conservatively in the meantime.

But the difficult task before us is to create an institutional structure that can embody and enforce the relevant incentives for accomplishing our policy toward future generations. For example, right now we might expect a simple beginning would be to price energy use at a level more nearly approaching its full cost, including associated external costs. In the case of coal, this might radically change the appeal of using it in massively polluting ways if the users have to compensate owners of forests, bronze and marble statuary, and painted houses for the costs their coal use causes. (This might be handled as a Coasean reallocation of rights assignments. Or it might be handled by administrative agency. In general, arguments for handling it through decentralized rights assignments have strong incentive effects on their side.) In the case of petroleum from the Middle East, prices might double or quadruple if the full costs of military protection were charged to users.[29]

The more fitting comparison between intergenerational and international actions here is not to pollution in developing nations such as Brazil and China, but to third world suffering in the Sahel, Bangladesh, and Kenya. What is required is straightforward paternalism, which is a form of beneficence. The paternalism might be directed at welfare, resources, autonomy, or whatever, but still it is paternalism. Historical arguments against beneficence (or charity) in one's society and time do not fit the problem of future generations. One might claim with some force that aid to the peoples of the Sahel, Bangladesh, and Kenya would tend to encourage natal and agricultural policies and practices that lead to the requirement for further aid, so that aid may not accomplish the paternal goals intended. (This issue has been debated since the time of the Elizabethan poor laws.[30]) But the analog of this for the future generations suffering from our environmental assaults would be implausible. The latter may be the unusual case of untarnished paternalism, without concomitant perverse incentive effects.

Paternalism may be hard to motivate if it has real costs. (Paternalism of the simple form that tells people what to do may be easy to motivate, as those who have had or who have been parents must know.) You and I may be paternalistic toward our children at great cost even if we are otherwise generally niggardly toward others. The upper middle-class professional couple who contributes less than 1 percent of income to charity may pay upwards of $40,000 a year (and rising) for the university educations of each of their children, and if the children go to graduate school, significant contributions may continue some years longer. And these otherwise niggardly people may pay well over 1 percent of income to care for their feeble parents or even for a ne'er-do-well sibling.

With much of traditional moral theory, we can contrive to bring moral injunctions in line with self-interest. We cannot do that with the problem of environmental degradation that especially harms future generations—such as fossil energy depletion and greenhouse warming. Albeit as a side benefit of our present benefit from our actions, we benefit future generations when we clean up the deadly air of late 1940s Donora near Pittsburgh and early 1950s London, or when we reduce pollution in most large cities today. But greenhouse warming may not have great harmful effects on us, our children, or even our grandchildren. If we are to invest now in reducing it, we must act from benevolence. That is a slender reed on which to build a policy.

It is not impossible for us to take an interest in future generations. For example, there have even been laws to protect the future interests of some families, as for example with restrictive alienation and inheritance laws for land. Perhaps the principle of inheritance is not so morally bad as many critics (myself included) think if it broadens our concerns beyond our immediate kin and ourselves and leads us to take an interest well beyond our generation.

6. OTHER WORLDS: OTHER THEORIES?

Is there a bottom line on the relevance of moral theory to environmental problems and future generations? I think that at the moment only two plausible theories among those currently in vogue can seriously address the problem. One of these is utilitarianism, which, as one of the great criticisms of it takes fully to heart, appears to have no moral problem with trading the welfare of one person for that of another. The other is a consequentialist variant of autonomy in which we would judge our policies by their causal effects on autonomy. A unifying element in these two theories is, obviously, their consequentialism. I do not think autonomy is a compelling moral principle, but many philosophers do. Many of those who do would be unsatisfied by a consequentialist theory of autonomy.[31] [32] But these theorists would have great difficulty giving us any assessment of such complicated problems as environmental impacts on future generations.

One reason both these theories have a chance of yielding results is that they could both be conceived in ways that escape the problem of the ill-defined nature of future generations. They might both sensibly be cast with indifference to who the future people are likely to be. Moreover, if we who live now act contrary to such a theory, it would not be a matter of moral inconsistency for a future person to say we had acted wrongly under the theory. These two theories would not escape problems of causal difficulties in accounting effects on future generations, but that is not a distinctively moral issue. And they might both relive the old utilitarian problem of the conflict between average and total utility (or autonomy).

Rights theories, including deontological libertarianism, are in need of more reconstruction than they might be able to bear if they are to apply to future generations. Possibly a top-down derivative rights theory that makes rights a function of general welfare might be made applicable in principle, but such a theory might be a close cousin of utilitarianism or neoclassical economics.

The charade of contractarianism should be abandoned in any case for all of moral and political theory beyond literal contracts between reasonably well informed near equals. Its hypothetical variants should be replaced by more straightforwardly rationalist theories, such as those of Alan Gewirth, Kant, and Plato.

Communitarian theory has yet to begin in any serious way—most communitarian writers spend virtually all their time criticizing the alternatives, especially Rawls's theory of justice and liberal utilitarianism. We can assess communitarian theories only once the theorists tell us enough to give us something to debate. Theories of respect for persons are even less theories than are communitarian theories, and they are wide open to each theorist's idiosyncratic reading. They do not bind anyone's reading enough to get serious discussion underway.

Kantian theories of nonconsequentialist autonomy must be developed in political, and not merely in single-individual, terms before we can see how they will apply. Kantian theory at the individual moral level is sufficiently sophisticated, not to say brilliant, that one should expect a Kantian theory that focused on institutions to be formidable. Such theory may be a major growth industry in the near future. Aristotelian and other virtue theories, which I have not discussed, have little to say about such issues as environmental trade-offs between present and future generations. I suspect the failing is fundamental, but I would be pleased to discover a compelling argument to the contrary.

Until the theorists, including economic and harder scientific theorists, do a good deal more, moral theorists will have little to say to yield firm policy instructions on environmental trade-offs and future generations.

NOTES

1. Russell Hardin, "Social Capital," *Competition and Cooperation: Conversations with Nobelists about Economics and Political Science*, ed. James Alt, Margaret Levi, and Elinor Ostrom (New York: Russell Sage Foundation, 1999), 170–89.

2. Barbara J. Culliton, "Emerging Viruses, Emerging Threat," *Science*, 247 (January 19, 1990): 279–80.

3. Ibid., 280.

4. Karen Wright, "Bad News Bacteria," *Science*, 249 (July 6, 1990): 22–24.

5. John Locke, *Two Treatises of Government*, ed. Peter Laslett (Cambridge, England: Cambridge University Press, 1988, originally published 1690), bk. 2, sec. 33, 291.

6. Robert Nozick, *Anarchy, State, and Utopia* (New York: Basic, 1974), 174–82.

7. Ibid., 153n.

8. Hillel Steiner, "The Rights of Future Generations," *Energy and the Future*, eds. Douglas MacLean and Peter G. Brown (Totowa, N.J.: Rowman and Littlefield, 1983), 151–65, 154.

9. Geoffrey Russell Grice, *The Grounds of Moral Judgement* (Cambridge, England: Cambridge University Press, 1967), 147–50.

10. See, *inter alia*, Derek Parfit, "On Doing the Best for Our Children," *Ethics and Population*, ed. Michael D. Bayles (Cambridge, Mass: 1975); Parfit, *Reasons and Persons* (Oxford: Oxford University Press, 1984), ch. 16, 351–79; Michael D. Bayles, "Harm to the Unconceived," *Philosophy and Public Affairs*, 5 (1976): 292–304.

11. "International Union, United Automobile, Aerospace and Agricultural Implement Workers of America, UAW, et al, Petitioners v. Johnson Controls, Inc.," *The United States Law Week* (March 20, 1991): 59 LW 4209–4215, at 4214. For related cases, see Bayles, "Harm to the Unconceived."

12. Joseph Raz, *The Morality of Freedom* (Oxford: Oxford University Press, 1986), 207–209.

13. Brian Barry, "Intergenerational Justice in Energy Policy," *Energy and the Future*, eds. Douglas MacLean and Peter G. Brown (Totowa, N.J.: Rowman and Littlefield, 1983), 15–30.

14. Gerald Dworkin, *The Theory and Practice of Autonomy* (Cambridge, England: Cambridge University Press, 1988), 166.

15. H. L. A. Hart, "Between Utility and Rights," in Hart, *Essays in Jurisprudence and Philosophy* (Oxford: Oxford University Press, 1983), 198–222, esp. 219n.

16. David Hume, "Of the Original Contract," *Essays Moral, Political, and Literary*, ed. Eugene Miller (Indianapolis: Liberty Press, 1985; essay originally published 1748), 463–87, at 476.

17. J. W. Gough, *The Social Contract: A Critical Study of Its Development* (Oxford: Oxford University Press, 2nd ed., 1957), esp. ch. 12, "The Contract Theory in Decline," 186–206.

18. John Rawls, *A Theory of Justice* (Cambridge, Mass: Harvard University Press, 1971).

19. Jean Hampton, "Contracts and Choices: Does Rawls Have a Social Contract Theory?" *Journal of Philosophy*, 77 (1980), 315–38.

20. Thomas Scanlon, "Contractualism and Utilitarianism," *Utilitarianism and Beyond*, eds. Amartya Sen and Bernard Williams (Cambridge, England: Cambridge University Press, 1977), 101–28, at 115n, 128; Scanlon, *What We Owe to Each Other* (Cambridge, Mass: Harvard University

Press, 1998); Russell Hardin, *Liberalism, Constitutionalism, and Democracy* (Oxford: Oxford University Press, 1999), 145–52; Hardin, "Contractarianism: Wistful Thinking," *Constitutional Political Economy,* 1 (1990), 35–52; and Hardin, "Constitutional Political Economy: Agreement on Rules," *British Journal of Political Science,* 18 (October 1988): 513–30.

21. John Harsanyi, "Cardinal Utility in Welfare Economics and the Theory of Risk-Taking," *Journal of Political Economy,* 61 (1953): 434–35.

22. Brian Barry, *Theories of Justice* (Berkeley: University of California Press, 1989), 189–203.

23. Russell Hardin, "Equity Versus Efficiency and the Demise of Socialism," *Canadian Journal of Philosophy,* 22 (June 1992): 149–61.

24. Michael Slote, *Beyond Optimizing: A Study of Rational Choice* (Cambridge, Mass: Harvard University Press, 1989).

25. Russell Hardin, *One for All: The Logic of Group Conflict* (Princeton, N.J.: Princeton University Press, 1995), 91–100; Dworkin, *The Theory and Practice of Autonomy* (Cambridge, England: Cambridge University Press, 1988), 62–81.

26. Russell Hardin, "Asymmetries in Collective Action," *Collective Action* (Baltimore: Johns Hopkins University Press for Resources for the Future, 1982), ch. 5, 67–89.

27. Russell Hardin, *Morality within the Limits of Reason* (Chicago: University of Chicago Press, 1988), chs. 3, 4.

28. Barry, "Intergenerational Justice in Energy Policy," 17.

29. Harold M. Hubbard, "The Real Cost of Energy," *Scientific American,* 264 (April 1991): 36–42.

30. For brief discussion, see Russell Hardin, "Incentives and Beneficence," *Social Justice Research,* 4 (June 1990): 87–104.

31. For elaboration, see Russell Hardin, "Autonomy, Identity, and Welfare," *The Inner Citadel: Essays on Individual Autonomy,* ed. John Christman (New York: Oxford University Press, 1989), 189–99.

32. Dworkin, *Theory and Practice of Autonomy,* 165.

CHAPTER 12

INTERGENERATIONAL JUSTICE AND SAVING

Clark Wolf

If current and proximate generations were to destroy the resources of the earth, then later generations would be much worse off. Would such destruction violate any requirements of justice? Many people have recently argued that the answer to this question is not obvious. First, current destruction might change the identities of the people who exist in future generations: Different people will exist if we adopt more destructive policies than would have existed otherwise. Members of the deprived generations, then, could not complain that they had been made worse off by our destructive treatment of the earth's resources since they would not have been better off—they would not be at all—had we behaved differently. Many people regard this so-called non-identity problem as surprisingly important.[1] But a second reason why some people regard it as unclear whether current destruction of the earth's resources would be unjust to future generations is that we have no widely accepted account of intergenerational justice, and most of the literature on the problem of intergenerational justice has been negative. Not only does no widely accepted theory exist, we do not even have a substantial set of contender theories, and no agreement about what an account of intergenerational justice would look like. While this chapter will not remedy all of these gaps, it will examine a promising way to look at the problem of intergenerational justice.

I will assume that one crucial part of any theory of intergenerational justice is an account of whether and how much the present generation ought to save resources for the future rather than destroying or consuming them. The problem of just saving is not the only problem that would be treated in a full theory of intergenerational justice. But within the broader subject of intergenerational justice, the saving problem is crucial and has received scant treatment from philosophers. The problem is not just a philosophical exercise: Practical proposals to mitigate pollution, to preserve wild lands, to protect biodiversity, and to conserve resources are often framed in terms of intergenerational justice, and of our current obligations to save resources for future generations. The thought is that we have an obligation to leave later generations an earth capable of supporting their needs, and that we would violate this obligation if we were to use too much of our exhaustible resources, or if we were to destroy the earth's great ecosystems.

By "save," I do not necessarily mean consciously setting aside goods or funds for later use by future persons, or using less oil or coal so that later generations will have it. In the sense relevant here, "saving" applies to whatever resources come to be at the disposal of future persons, whether we consciously set them aside for them or not. We might save in this sense because we are unable to consume resources quickly enough to use them all up, and not because we have any concern for the welfare of future persons. The problem of saving is to some extent independent of an analysis of the institutions used to accomplish it. It might turn out, as some have argued, that free markets will adequately save for future generations, and that we need not concern ourselves with their predicament.[2] Or it might turn out that markets will do this badly or unreliably. If so, then we may find it appropriate to protect resources or ecosystems or institutions from the market. Such protection may be necessary to insure that future persons will have adequate resources to live autonomous lives, or to exercise fundamental human capacities, or whatever it is that justice is understood to require.

I will ignore many important issues that have occupied recent discussions of intergenerational justice, including the non-identity problem, problems of population choice, the paradoxes of intertemporal harm, and questions about the moral standing of future persons and groups. My reason for ignoring these issues is not that I regard them as trivial; I have focused on them in other recent works.[3] But in recent literature on intergenerational justice, an almost exclusive focus on these other problems combined with recent disaffection for distributive justice in general has led to an inexcusable neglect of the problem of just saving. It was not always so: The savings problem attracted the attention of many important economists and philosophers shortly after the publication of John Rawls's *Theory of Justice* in 1971. Three years after the appearance of *Theory*, Kenneth Arrow, Robert Solow, and Partha Dasgupta each published seminal papers on the problem of intergenerational distributive justice and the problem of just saving.[4] But their conclusions were mostly negative, and work on the issue has hardly moved forward since they abandoned it.

This chapter will revive a decades-old discussion of the problem of just saving. I will argue that Arrow, Solow, Dasgupta, and Rawls himself were all led astray by a serious fault in the models they employed in thinking about the problem of intergenerational distributive justice and savings, and that work on this problem has been held back by a simple mistake. One of my aims is to explain where earlier treatments of the savings problem went wrong. But my aims are not primarily critical and my conclusions are not negative: Once we have an understanding of the central problem with the model that has been used to frame the issue of intergenerational distribution, it becomes clear that the model can be improved. The improved model, incorporating the fact of generational overlap, provides a convenient framework for understanding and evaluating alternative conceptions of intergenerational justice. Once it becomes clear that work on the problem has been hampered by faulty modeling and that it is not inherently intractable, the problem of intergenerational justice should take a prominent place in the theory of justice.

1. A SIMPLE MODEL OF INTERGENERATIONAL SAVING AND PRESENT CONSUMPTION

I begin with a simple economic model of intergenerational production, distribution, and saving. With only small variations, this model is the same as the one used by Kenneth Arrow and Robert Solow, but it is most clearly discussed by Partha Dasgupta, whose presentation I will follow here.[5] The model is simple, but it is tremendously useful for framing an understanding of the problem of just savings and intergenerational distribution. As I will argue in Section 4, this useful model is also deceptive. Its implicit and explicit use has led to a persistent and thorough misunderstanding of the problem of intergenerational justice and just savings.

Dasgupta asks that we consider a society that possesses a single, non-deteriorating, homogeneous commodity K, the stock of which at time t is K_t. Assume that time is discrete, and takes on the non-negative integer values. Assume that population is constant from one generation to the next. Each generation lives for only one period, and a new equinumerous generation arrives as soon as they die. With these assumptions in place, we can normalize to one individual per period and consider the consumption and savings rates for each generation separately. We can also describe the stream of consumption and savings from one generation to the next. For example, suppose that generation t consumes C_t of the commodity, where $K_t \le C_t \le 0$. Then $(K_t - C_t)$ is carried on to the next period, where it becomes $\lambda(K_t - C_t)$. Here λ represents the rate at which the saved portion appreciates as it is carried over to the next generation. This gives us a basic accumulation equation:[6]

$$K_{t+1} = \lambda(K_t - C_t)$$
$$K_t \le C_t \le 0 \qquad \text{for } t = 0,1,2,3,\dots \qquad (1)$$
$$K_0 \text{ given.}$$

An intergenerational allocation or consumption stream is series of allocations $(C_t) = (C_0, C_1, C_2,\dots C_n\dots)$, with C_n being the amount consumed by generation n. We can refer to the set F of all sequences (C_t) that satisfy Equation 1. This set contains all *feasible* intertemporal allocation sequences. If we assume, as does Dasgupta, that $\lambda > 1$, then whatever is saved by one generation grows for the benefit of the following generation. But of course there are cases for which this assumption is not justified. If $\lambda = 1$, then the amount of K left over for the next generation does not grow. In this case, the rate at which the resource is depleted is exactly the rate at which it is consumed by the early generations, so in this special case, $K_{t+1} = (K_t - C_t)$ and (C_t) will be a decreasing sequence as long as there is some consumption at all. And in the

worst case, if $\lambda < 1$, then the resource decays over time and the first generation may need to consume it quickly before it spoils. In what follows, I will
accept Dasgupta's assumption that saved resources appreciate in value—that
$\lambda > 1$.

We can represent the savings rate S_t—the rate at which any generation
t saves for the future—as follows:

$$S_t = (K_t - C_t)/K_t \qquad \text{for } t = 0,1,2... \qquad (2)$$

In this model, each generation chooses how much to save for the benefit
of later generations. If they save more, later generations will have more to
consume. If they save less, then future generations will be poorer. But in this
model, any saving by a generation implies that there is less to consume now.
If consumption is an indicator or a partial measure of well-being, then any
saving at all is worse for those who save. This feature of the model will be
important in what follows.

Is there a minimum saving rate required by justice, such that saving less
would violate obligations to future generations? If the first generation gra-
tuitously consumes all of the available resource, the following generations
will be left with nothing at all. On the other hand, if earlier generations save
too much, they might needlessly impoverish themselves for the sake of the
future. A theory of intergenerational justice would, among other things, provide a principled method for choosing an appropriate rate of saving.

2. SAVING FOR THE FUTURE AND
INTERGENERATIONAL JUSTICE: SUSTAINABILITY

When is an intergenerational distribution unjust? We might begin by weed-
ing out those intergenerational patterns of consumption and savings that
seem most undesirable. Dasgupta himself suggests that we should eliminate
those schemes that tend toward zero consumption, and that it would "not be
very just" for early generations to leave nothing for later ones.[7] He suggests
that justice requires that intergenerational consumption and savings should
at least be sustainable over time. But the possibility of sustainable production
and consumption will obviously depend on the sizes of λ and K_t. Suppose we
define "sustainability" as the condition that $K_{t+1} = K_t$. This means that the
amount of K available to later generations is exactly the same as the amount

available to earlier generations. In order to obtain this condition, we must have $K_t = \lambda(K_t - C_t)$. Solving for C_t we get:

$$C_t = (K_t - K_t/\lambda) \qquad \text{(For } \lambda > 0\text{)} \qquad (3)$$

So $(K_{t+1} - K_t/\lambda)$ is the steady state consumption package for any period. As long as each generation's consumption meets the formally weaker condition that

$$C_t \le (K_t - K_t/\lambda) \qquad (4)$$

the consumption stream (C_t) will be nondecreasing. If we put this in terms of necessary savings instead of permissible consumption, we find that the steady state savings ratio for the economy is given by $S = 1/\lambda$. Savings plans that consistently consume more than the sustainable rate and consistently save at a rate lower than $1/\lambda$ will tend toward zero consumption in the long run.

Sustainability in the sense described above might seem reasonable as a minimal requirement of intergenerational justice. We find something similar to it in Sir John Hicks's discussion of income in *Value and Capital*:

The purpose of income calculations in practical affairs is to give people an indication of the amount they can consume without impoverishing themselves. Following out this idea, it would seem that we ought to define a man's income as the maximum value that he can consume during a week, and still be expected to be as well off at the end of the week as he was at the beginning. Thus when a person saves, he plans to be better off in the future, when he lives beyond his income, he plans to be worse off. Remembering that the practical purpose of income is to serve as a guide for prudent conduct, I think it is fairly clear that this is what the central meaning must be.[8]

Hicks's aim was to describe income in terms of prudent individual saving, but one could think of an account of intergenerational justice as a prescription for understanding generational income in terms of prudent saving and investment for future generations. In extreme circumstances, it may be necessary for an individual to consume more than income can sustain over time, but such overconsumption comes at the price of future poverty. In the individual case, this price is paid by the same person who consumed too much too early, but in the intergenerational case the cost of early overconsumption may be passed on to later generations. Although self-interest may dictate prudent consumption over a lifetime, it will not always dictate inter-generationally prudent consumption.

3. RAWLS ON SAVING AND INTERGENERATIONAL JUSTICE

Sustainability in the sense described may be a minimal requirement. But per-haps justice requires more, in some circumstances. Another way to approach the problem of intergenerational justice and savings would be to consider which feasible intertemporal distribution—which allocation sequence (C_n), member of the set F of feasible intertemporal allocations—persons would chose from an original position from which they were uncertain to which generation they will belong. According to Rawls's well-known theory, the principles of justice are those that free and rational persons would choose, under appropriate circumstances, those identified in the description of an "original position," as principles to govern the basic social and political insti-tutions of society. The choice is rendered impartial by a veil of ignorance that blinds them to any knowledge of themselves that would make it possible for them to tailor the choice of principles arbitrarily to favor themselves. Parties to this original position choice will not know their race, position in society, religious commitments, abilities, or anything else that could introduce par-tial bias into the choice of principles. The restrictions of this original position choice force parties to be impartial between their interests and the interests of others.

Rawls argues that parties to the original position would choose two prin-ciples to govern the basic institutions of society. The first asserts that each person is to have an equal right to the most extensive total system of basic liberties compatible with a similar system for all. The second principle speci-fies which kinds of inequality are tolerable, and is in two parts: social and economic inequalities are to be arranged so that they are both (1) attached to offices and positions open to all under conditions of fair equality of op-portunity, and (2) tolerable only when they work to the greatest benefit of the least advantaged members of society. This last requirement, the Difference Principle, is surely the most controversial element of Rawls's theory, and has attracted wide critical discussion. Rawls calls the conception of justice em-bodied in these two principles the "conception of justice as fairness," and his earlier work was devoted to the defense of this conception of justice against perfectionist, utilitarian, and libertarian alternatives.[9]

But what does justice require in the intergenerational case? Rawls is much less specific in what he says about intergenerational justice, and what he does say is confusing. Rawls's veil of ignorance does extend to generational membership, so the parties to the original position do not know in which generation, or at what stage of social and economic development they will live. This ignorance ensures that their choice will not be partial in favor of earlier generations over later ones or vice versa. In the first edition of *Theory*, Rawls wrote:

The parties do not know to which generation they belong or, what comes to the same thing, the stage of civilization of their society. They have no way of telling whether it is poor or relatively wealthy, largely agricultural or already industrialized, and so on. The veil of ignorance is complete in these respects. Thus the persons in the original position are to ask themselves how much they would be willing to save at each stage on the assumption that all other generations are to save at the same rates. That is, they are to consider their willingness to save at any given phase of civilization with the understanding that the rates they propose are to regulate the whole span of accumulation. In effect, then, they must choose a just savings principle that assigns an appropriate rate of accumulation to each level of advance.[10]

In 1971 Rawls stipulated that the motive to save was that parties to the original position choice were assumed to care for their descendants. This was unsatisfactory for many reasons that I can only mention and briefly identify here. First, it is otherwise unmotivated and ad hoc. In the original position, the choice of principles is supposed to be based on self-interest and mutual disinterest, not altruistic concern for others. And Rawls specifies that parties to the original position choice are "mutually disinterested." The interests of contemporaries are represented in the original position by the extended self-interest of the parties to the choice behind the veil of ignorance, but Rawls's ad hoc assumption implies that the interests of future generations are represented in quite a different way. Second, different people have different degrees of concern for their descendants, and there may be no uniquely appropriate level of concern. Because of this, Rawls's ad hoc stipulation renders it difficult and perhaps impossible to specify what principle of savings free rational agents in the original position would choose. Third, some free and rational people will have no descendants. It would seem to follow that parties to the original position should understand themselves to represent some individuals who have an interest in saving for future generations and others who have no such interest. This plurality of interests will lead parties to incompletely represent the interests of later generations. Finally, Rawls uses questionable language to describe the motivational assumption of concern for descendants. He wrote that parties to the original position choice should understand themselves as representing "heads of households," and that they should imagine themselves to be "fathers" deciding "how much they should set aside for their sons and grandsons by noting what they would believe themselves entitled to claim of their fathers and grandfathers.[11] As critics have pointed out, this formulation is sexist and begs many questions about the structure of families. Given ample evidence that the interests of different family members diverge, the assumption that the interests of the "head of the household" accurately represent the interests of families is clearly unacceptable. Since it is usually assumed that the head of a household is a man, it has been argued that Rawls's model might lead to the systematic neglect of the interests of women, the elderly, and children.[12]

In more recent work, Rawls has revised his account of the choice of principles for intergenerational savings. While he still regards the appropriate principle of savings as the one that would be chosen from the original position, he has recently argued that parties to the choice should understand themselves to be choosing that principle they would want earlier generations to have adopted:

[S]ince society is a system of cooperation between generations over time, a principle for savings is required. Rather than imagine a (hypothetical and nonhistorical) direct agreement between all generations, the parties can be required to agree to a savings principle subject to the further condition that they must want all previous generations to have followed it. Thus the correct principle is that which the members of any generation (and so all generations) would adopt as the one their generation is to follow and as the principle they would want preceding generations to have followed (and later generations to follow), no matter how far back (or forward) in time.[13]

This change is an improvement since, appropriately interpreted, it can avoid all of the problems listed above. Most important, it recovers concern for future generations as a function of the extended self-interest of parties to the original position choice.

But what principles would such parties choose? Rawls says very little to identify what a just intertemporal distribution would look like. He does say that he regards the difference principle as inappropriate for the intergenerational case. He adds that the purpose of saving is not just to make future generations more affluent, but to secure justice. Thus savings "may stop once just (or decent) basic institutions have been established. At this point real saving (net additions to real capital of all kinds) may fall to zero; and existing stock only needs to be maintained, or replaced, and nonrenewable resources carefully husbanded for future use as appropriate."[14] According to Rawls, parties to the original position will choose a principle of intergenerational justice that requires savings at stages when too little wealth exists to secure just basic institutions, but maintains existing resources once justice is secure.

Although the changes since the first edition of *A Theory of Justice* are improvements, Rawls's more recent comments about intergenerational justice raise new problems. His remarks are vague; the new account does not raise the issue of changing population size. Perplexingly, Rawls says nothing specific about the rate at which earlier generations should save for the benefit of later ones. Most seriously, such saving appears contrary to other Rawlsian commitments: Rawls argues that it is only poorer generations that have an obligation to save—generations that are too poor to secure just institutions for themselves, but whose members hope that their saving will enable their descendants to be better off. But on Rawls's view their saving implies a sacrifice on their part, and the beneficiaries of this sacrifice will be future generations who will be better off as a result. In other contexts, Rawls insists that it is inappropriate for those who are worse off to make sacrifices for the benefit of those who are better off. Here he recommends such sacrifice as a requirement of intergenerational justice. This is inconsistent with Rawls's insistence that parties to the original position choice would employ maximin reasoning in the choice of principles of justice.

In what follows I will consider a super-Rawlsian theory of intergenerational justice: the intertemporal application of the difference principle. This theory is, as one commentator put it, *"plus Rawlsien que le Rawls."*[15] But as I will argue, it has been discarded for the wrong reasons.

4. HOW TO BE MORE RAWLSIAN THAN RAWLS

Rawls's suggestion is that we should choose that savings principle that we would wish the preceding generation to have adopted if we were ignorant of our own generational membership. One might worry that this guideline would promote too much saving: If we are only concerned with the saving rate of our predecessors, we would naturally prefer that they save as much as possible. The more that earlier generations have saved, the better off our own generation will be, since the alternative to saving, in this model, is consumption. Higher savings rates imply costs for those who save, but those costs are not obviously counted on Rawls's scheme. They might be implicit in the concern that descendants have for the welfare of their predecessors—the concern of children for their parents, for example. From a generation-blind original position, it is not difficult to imagine that parties choosing principles of justice would take such concern into account even between generations that are remote. But a move such as this would re-introduce many of the problems that plagued Rawls's earlier (1971) account of the motivation to save.

We should instead, then, compare savings schemes that cover the "entire span of accumulation," taking into account the interests of individuals in each generation. We should choose the savings scheme that we would want our predecessors to have adopted regardless of our generational membership. But does a unique saving scheme exist that satisfies this vague condition? Sustainability might be considered a minimal requirement for intergenerational justice, and it is plausible to think that parties to the original position choice might begin by restricting themselves to savings schemes that are sustainable. Surely we would wish previous generations to have saved at least at the sustainable rate. But if so, then they would be left with a choice among sustainable schemes: some of the remaining schemes would be more demanding than others. How would a free rational agent choose among more and less demanding principles of intergenerational saving without knowing which generation would be the agent's?

One might expect that such an agent would begin by comparing the problem of intergenerational justice to the problem of intragenerational justice. If, as Rawls suggests, such agents would find the difference principle attractive in the intragenerational case, then they would consider the Inter-generational Difference Principle (IDP) as a solution to the problem of just savings. The IDP holds that just saving should maximize benefits to those who are worst off, regardless of their generational membership.

Most commentators have discarded the difference principle as a requirement on intergenerational distribution, and Rawls rejects the intergenerational application of the difference principle. But we might wonder why he does so: If we accept the argument for the difference principle as a requirement of justice, uniquely acceptable to free and equal contractors choosing from behind a veil of ignorance, then it might be natural to suppose that such contractors would choose the difference principle as an intergenerational requirement as well. And given the general argument for the difference principle and given Rawls's account of "reasonableness" and "fairness," it may be difficult to see what other principle would do as a requirement of intergenerational distributive justice, especially if we accept these other features of Rawls's account. Such saving is inconsistent with Rawls's (dubious) claim that parties to the original position must use maximin reasoning in their choice of principles. Reasonable persons, says Rawls, will be willing to comply only if the terms of the savings scheme are fair. Rawls has insisted elsewhere that fairness requires, among other things, that a system of cooperation must not improve the situation of those who are better off at cost to those who are worst off. It is difficult to see why this should not apply intergenerationally if it is accepted in the intragenerational case. Rawls should either explain why this conception of fairness does not apply in the intergenerational case, or he should accept it as a general principle for distributive justice. I will refer to the view that the difference principle should apply intergenerationally as the "super-Rawlsian" view.

Rawls explains his own reasons for rejecting the difference principle as a requirement in the intergenerational case: He argues that the IDP would inappropriately prohibit saving, since earlier generations would necessarily be worse off than the later generations who would benefit from savings. The model described in Section 1 makes it easy to see why one might come to this conclusion: Given an initial stock K_t, the first generation would have an obligation to save at least K_t/λ. This is the amount of saving required at the sustainable rate, since saving less would increase their consumption at cost to generation t+1, which would then be worse off than generation t. But if any generation t saves at a rate greater than the steady-state replacement rate, then the following generations will be better off at the expense of generation t. Such savings will involve sacrifices for the first generation that saves, and this first generation will not benefit from savings of any earlier generation. Their uncompensated sacrifice will then benefit those who are better off— clearly prohibited by the difference principle. So such saving is prohibited as unjust to the first generation and savings can never get started.

So it has seemed to most of those who have considered the problem. Most are in agreement that an intergenerational difference principle would allow no positive saving to benefit the future. Robert Solow writes:

. . . the max-min criterion is . . . at the mercy of the initial conditions. If the initial capital stock is very small, no more will be accumulated and the standard of living will remain low forever. This result follows from the principle itself. Capital could be accumulated and consumption increased subsequently, but only at the cost of a lower standard of living for earlier generations. It is part of Rawls' general argument for the max-min criterion that we should regard earlier and later generations as facing each other contemporaneously when the social contract is being drawn up. But then it is hardly surprising that the preferred strategy refuses to make some people poorer than others in order to make the others richer, just because the first group can be given the essentially arbitrary label of "earlier."[16]

Kenneth Arrow concurs:

It is pretty obvious that [a straightforward transposition of the Rawls' maximin criterion to the intertemporal context] would lead to zero savings in every generation, for there is no way to compensate the first generation for any savings they might do, and they would be worse off than any of their successors.[17]

And in a (1994) article, Dasgupta writes:

We may conclude that an economy that was poor to begin with would remain in poverty if it were at the mercy of the intergenerational maxi-min principle.[18]

And Rawls makes the same claim in both editions of *Theory*. In the second (1999) edition, he writes:

[W]hen the difference principle is applied to the question of savings over generations, it entails either no savings at all or not enough savings to improve social circumstances sufficiently so that all the equal liberties can be effectively exercised.[19]

As I will show in the next section, Solow, Arrow, Dasgupta, and Rawls are all wrong about this. They were led to a false conclusion by the limitations of the model described in Section 1 above, or, in Rawls's case, by assumptions that mirror those limitations. It may, as Arrow puts it, seem "pretty obvious" that an intergenerational difference principle would imply no savings, but it is not true.

5. INTERGENERATIONAL SAVINGS: FROM A REPEATED GAME TO A MULTISTAGE GAME

The model described in Section 1 is employed, with some small variations, by all of the economists quoted above at the end of Section 4. I have argued that a similar model is implicit in Rawls's remarks about intergenerational justice and savings and is associated with his rejection of the difference principle in the intergenerational case. But the model is flawed: It incorporates an implicit assumption that generations do not interact or overlap. Like mayflies and paulo verde beetles, all members of the Rawlsian population disappear after consuming their share, and the next generation comes on stage all at once. In his earlier papers, Dasgupta claimed that this assumption introduces no special problems, but he was wrong: When the model is adjusted to accommodate generational overlap, it becomes clear that saving can indeed benefit the first generations to engage in it, and that self-interested motives to save can promote positive intergenerational saving. It can even be shown that intergenerational saving is sometimes achievable as a strategic equilibrium among narrowly rational self-interested agents: The adoption of an appropriate intergenerational saving plan may be strongly Pareto superior to sustainability and beneficial to literally everyone involved. It follows that the IDP will permit or even require positive savings rates in a wide variety of circumstances, and that it has been rejected for the wrong reasons. In refining the model described above, we transform it from a repeated game in which each stage is independent from any other, to a "stage game" in which each "play" reflects the choices of different individuals whose ages and interests are different. [20]

Consider a revision on the model described in Section 1. Suppose that we begin with a population of one-hundred people, and suppose that each player "lives" for 10 periods of the game. In periods 1–2 they are "children," in periods 3–8 they are "adults," and in periods 9–10 they are "seniors." After period 10, players leave the game and do not come back. No longer can we normalize to one person per period as in Section 1, since people of different ages have different interests and motives. For now, suppose that population is constant over time, with equal numbers of people at each period, and an equal-sized new population of "children" appearing in each period as the stage 10 "seniors" die off and leave the game for good. In this assumption of constant population, the enriched model still diverges from our own situation in one respect. It will be important to investigate the behavior of the model when this assumption is relaxed.

In one version of the game, each individual must make a decision to "cooperate" in a joint savings plan, or to "defect" by not saving at all. In this version, saving for the future will be effective only if enough people choose to cooperate in each stage. In another version, saving is a group decision and the choice of a saving scheme involves the choice of a level at which each individual's consumption will be "taxed." In either case, saving for the future is a public good: Whatever is saved for the next period will go into a public "pot," where it grows and becomes available for the subsequent generation. As in the earlier model, the saved resources for period t ($K_t - C_t$), will grow at the given appreciation rate, λ, to become $\lambda(K_t - C_t)$ in the next period. Savings are divided into equal shares and distributed to participants at the beginning of each period. If nothing at all is saved, then no resources will be left for consumption in subsequent periods. Call this unfortunate baseline the "state of nature."

First consider whether the IDP permits or requires sustainable savings, or whether it dooms us to the "state of nature"—the outcome in which no one saves at all. The "state of nature" would leave later generations—those who arrive at age one after the first play—worse off than they would have been if previous generations had saved at a sustainable rate. Eventually, unsustainable saving rates will leave nothing at all for later generations. These later generations, the "worst off group," would have been better off if earlier generations had saved at the sustainable rate. Sustainable savings would benefit almost everyone—everyone except the age 10 seniors who leave the game after the first play. These seniors may not have a legitimate "complaint," however, since at the sustainable rate their share, during the period in which they enjoy it, is not less than the share of others, even though their lifetime share might be slightly less than it would otherwise have been. Since the worst-off group is better off under a sustainable savings plan than it would be in the "state of nature," it follows that the IDP requires at least sustainable savings.

But if each individual has a choice to cooperate in the savings scheme or not, and if we imagine participants to be mutually disinterested, then it is quite plausible to think that period 10 seniors will not save. They have nothing to gain and will be unable to consume whatever they save for the enjoyment of others in the future. They might save if, as Rawls first stipulated, they care about the welfare of members of the following next generations. But such concern for the welfare of future generations is not universal, and is not ordinarily thought to be a requirement of rationality.

Given the choice to cooperate or not, is it rational for others (those ages 1–9) to cooperate in sustainable saving? Compare sustainable savings to the state of nature: If all "children and adults" were to save at the sustainable rate, all would be better off over all. But in the case described, saving is a public good. It will be rational to cooperate in the production of such a good only if participants can coordinate their choices, only if those who save can be assured that a sufficient number of others will also save, and only if free-riding can be prevented. Each individual saves in "isolation," but saving is effective only if a sufficient number of others cooperate in saving as well. So younger members might rationally choose not to save even when cooperation in a saving scheme would be mutually advantageous. Amartya Sen calls this the "isolation paradox," but it is really just a special case of the more general problem of public goods.[21] In such circumstances, saving might be achieved only by coercive taxation or through voluntary agreement that solves the public goods problem. For example, it would be rational for all children and adults to sign a conditionally binding agreement to save if and only if all other children and adults will save as well.[22] In this way, saving might be chosen as the object of a voluntary agreement, even if contractors were not in a Rawlsian original position. This should not lead us to conclude that saving for the future, in the sense of the problem described here, will be adequately accomplished by voluntary contract and market exchange. But if such voluntary exchanges can sometimes achieve sustainable saving for the future, this is a hopeful result.

Is the Super-Rawlsian theory trapped by the initial circumstances so that "an economy that was poor to begin with would remain in poverty" if it were governed by the IDP?[23] Or does the IDP sometimes permit or even require saving at a rate greater than the sustainable rate? It can be shown that under appropriate circumstances, the IDP does require positive saving and accumulation and is not "at the mercy of initial conditions" as Solow claims.[24] Suppose that the "saved resource" is a crop like wheat, and that the rate of saving is measured as the proportion of this crop that is planted (in a commons) rather than consumed. The single period payoff for this game is an individual's portion of the resources available at that stage. The difference principle will prohibit savings by the first generation only if such saving makes the worst-off individuals worse off than they would otherwise have been. The first generation to save will consume less during that period than they would have if they had instead consumed everything and saved nothing. It does not follow that they will be worse off tout court.

To see that this is so, we can make the example more specific: Suppose that the initial community includes one-hundred people [$N_1 = 100$], with ten people of each age.[25] The initial stock given this community is 5000 bushels of wheat [$K_1 = 5000$]. Each bushel of wheat planted generates 50 harvestable bushels for the next period, so the next-period return on savings is fifty times what was saved [so the growth rate, $\lambda = 50$]. If each person saves one bushel, then total savings will be 100 bushels [$K_1 - C_1 = 100$]. In the first period, they will have 4900 [$C_1 = 4900$] to distribute, or 49 bushels for consumption each. This is the steady state savings ratio, since planting 100 bushels will yield the same 5000 bushel stock in period two.

But perhaps this savings scheme would violate the difference principle: As noted earlier, the ten people of age 10 would be made worse off without compensation. They would consume one fewer bushel of wheat, but would gain no benefits from savings. These age-10 seniors would be the "worst off" group, and they would be disadvantaged for the benefit of younger generations who would be better off. According to the difference principle, a savings scheme must not come at cost to those who are worst off. This problem is easily solved by relieving the oldest participants, all seniors, of the obligation to save. Only individuals of ages 1–8 are required to contribute to the savings plan. For sustainable consumption, these younger participants will still need to save only a little more than one bushel per period if their aim is intergenerationally sustainable consumption and production.

The younger generations might find it advantageous to save much more than this. If they save at 4 percent per period, then those of ages 1–8 will save two bushels in the first period. Under such a savings plan, those who are age 8 at the inception of the plan (and who therefore contribute only in the first year) would increase their income for the next two periods by over 100 bushels at a cost of two bushels in period 8. Those who are age 1 at the plan's inception would increase their lifetime income by more than 350,000 bushels. Such a savings scheme would be Pareto superior as compared to the sustainable level, since these benefits would be achieved at overall cost to no one.

The older generations would be least advantaged by the savings scheme, since they will enjoy its benefits for the fewest number of periods. But it does not immediately follow from this that such savings violates the difference principle. For even those who are age 9 when the savings scheme is put in place may still benefit quite a lot: Their final period consumption would be eighty bushels instead of forty-nine (their allocation at steady state savings) even though they never contribute a thing. The only generation that would not benefit overall would be the eldest—those who leave the game at age 10 after the first play. In such a case, the IDP would require a first-period tax to benefit these period-10 seniors. After the first period of play, the problem does not arise again, since those who are age-10 seniors in the second period of play (and who were age-9 seniors in the first period) will already enjoy the benefits of cooperative saving. With side payments to the eldest seniors in the first period, saving could be made strongly Pareto superior to sustainability— literally beneficial to everyone involved.

Where positive savings is strongly Pareto superior to sustainability, saving benefits everyone. So it benefits those who are worst off and is favored over sustainability by the IDP. It follows that the IDP is consistent with, and sometimes even requires, positive saving. And it is easy to see why we would choose such an intergenerational savings scheme from an original position like the one Rawls describes. Even if we reject Rawls's questionable argument for maximin reasoning and for the difference principle, mutually beneficial positive saving would be preferable, in some circumstances, to the "state of nature" at which no saving occurs and often preferable to merely sustainable saving. It is worthwhile to make explicit some of the assumptions that make this result possible: First, the possibility of productive saving depends, in part, on the rate of intergenerational appreciation, λ in the model above. Where λ is relatively large, saving will be more advantageous than when it is smaller. But as long as $\lambda > 1$, it will still be possible to describe mutually advantageous saving. Second, in the model described here, positive saving is mutually beneficial in part because population is constant. Where population size grows from period to period, more must be saved if later generations are to enjoy per capita benefits comparable to earlier ones. But where λ is larger than the rate of population growth, positive per capita accumulation over time will still be possible.

Positive rates of savings will not always disadvantage the first generation to adopt a savings scheme. It is also clear that the IDP can permit and will sometimes even require substantial intergenerational savings. The difference principle may be an inappropriate principle for intergenerational distributive justice, but not for the reasons given by Solow, Arrow, Dasgupta, and Rawls.

6. JUST SAVINGS IN THE REAL WORLD

I do not intend the above argument as a general defense of the IDP, the "Super-Rawlsian Theory" of intergenerational justice and saving. From the fact that the adoption of the IDP is consistent with increasing affluence and positive savings over time, it does not follow that it is superior to relevant alternative principles, since there exists a wide variety of other principles that are also consistent with positive savings. It is not clear, for example, that agents in an intergenerational original position would choose the IDP over an intergenerational "sufficiency" principle that minimized the number of persons (or generations) who would fall below a threshold of consumption, or capability, or primary goods provision. And the IDP is susceptible to many of the serious objections that have been raised against Rawls's use of the difference principle in other contexts. Perhaps most important is the so-called "black hole problem": If some persons (or generations) are horribly disadvantaged, the IDP would recommend that all resources be devoted to them, even if the benefits to the worst-offs would be minimal, and resources could alternatively be employed in ways that would provide extravagant benefits for those who are only slightly less disadvantaged. This objection is much more troubling than the standard utilitarian concern that the difference principle would sometimes forbid trade-offs that would, on balance, maximize well-being.

The models employed here are still remote from practical choices we face, and it is difficult to draw from them any simple moral about how we should structure our own saving for the future. We do not choose a savings rate from an original position from which we are ignorant of our own generational membership. In our case, saving for the future does not involve investing a given resource in order to allow it to grow, and we do not redistribute the proceeds of savings at the beginning of each new period. The models described above do not include any accounting of the costs of such redistribution or the nature of redistributive institutions, and they will not tell us whether market institutions are likely to accomplish adequate saving for the future. Future generations are sure to be much more numerous than the present generation: Even if population growth slows and stabilizes in the next century, as some predict, we have good reason to predict that population size will more than double before it finally becomes stable. In all of these respects, our choices are quite different from the choices faced by those in the hypothetical models discussed above.

But even if we do not accept the IDP, we can glean benefits from this discussion. First, savings can benefit those generations that engage in it even while it provides benefits for the future. Since saving is appropriately modeled as a multi-stage game and not as a repeated one, saving for the future can be rational and universally beneficial. Parties to an original position choice like the one Rawls describes would surely choose to save at least at a sustainable rate, but might rationally choose a much higher rate of saving. And under appropriate circumstances, where saving is mutually advantageous, positive saving for future generations can be the object of a voluntary agreement among those who save. A second benefit is equally important: Portions of the model described in Section 1 can still be used to evaluate intergenerational principles. It is still useful to compare principles of intergenerational justice according to the intertemporal allocation streams they imply. And while intergenerational saving is more complex than the original version of the model allows, the analytic strategy implicit in that model can still provide a crucial context for discussions of intergenerational justice.

NOTES

1. Derek Parfit, *Reasons and Persons* (Oxford: Oxford University Press, 1982), 351–79. See Clark Wolf, "Do Future Persons Presently Have Alternate Possible Identities?" in *The Non-Identity Problem,* eds. Melinda Roberts and David Wasserman (New York: Springer, 2009), 93–114.

2. David Gauthier, *Morals By Agreement* (Oxford: Clarendon Press, 1986) 268–305; Robert Nozick, *Anarchy, State, and Utopia* (New York: Basic Books, 1974), 182; and Clark Wolf, "Markets, Justice, and the Interests of Future Generations" *Ethics and the Environment,* 1(1996): 153–75.

3. Clark Wolf, "Property Rights, Lockean Provisos, and the Interests of Future Generations," *Ethics,* 105 (1995): 791–818, "Social Choice and Normative Population Theory," *Philosophical Studies,* 81 (1996): 263–82, "Markets, Justice, and the Interests of Future Generations," *Ethics and the Environment,* 1 (1996): 153–75; "Person-Affecting Utilitarianism and Population Policy, or, Sissy Jupe's Theory of Social Choice," in *Contingent Future Persons,* eds. N. Fotion and J. Heller (Dordrecht, Holland: Kluwer, 1997); "Population," in *The Blackwell Companion to Environmental Philosophy,* ed. Dale Jamieson (Cambridge: Blackwell Publishers, 2000); K. Wellman and R. Frey, "Intergenerational Justice," in *The Blackwell Companion to Practical Ethics* (Cambridge: Blackwell Publishers, 2001); "Intergenerational Justice, Human Needs, and Climate Policy," in *Intergenerational Justice,* eds. Axel Gosseries and Lukas Meyer (New York: Oxford University Press, 2009), 349–78.

4. John Rawls, *A Theory of Justice* (Cambridge, Mass: Harvard University Press, 1971); Kenneth Arrow, "Rawls' Principle of Just Savings," *Swedish Journal of Economics,* 75 (1973): 232–35; Robert Solow, "Intergenerational Equity and Exhaustible Resources," *Review of Economic Studies,* Symposium Issue (1974): 29–45; Partha Dasgupta, "On Some Alternative Criteria for Justice Between Generations," *Journal of Public Economics,* 3 (1974): 405–23; Partha Dasgupta, "On Some Problems Arising from Professor Rawls' Conception of Distributive Justice," *Theory and Decision,* 4 (1974): 325–44; and Partha Dasgupta, "Savings and Fertility: Ethical Issues," *Philosophy and Public Affairs,* 23 (1994): 99–127.

5. Partha Dasgupta, "On Some Alternative Criteria for Justice Between Generations," 407–409.

6. Partha Dasgupta, "On some Alternative Criteria for Justice Between Generations, p. 415.

7. Partha Dasgupta, "On some Alternative Criteria for Justice Between Generations, p. 415.

8. John Hicks, *Value and Capital* (Oxford: Clarendon Press, 1946), 172.

9. John Rawls, *A Theory of Justice,* Section I.

10. Ibid., 287.

11. Ibid., 289.

12. Susan Moller Okin, *Justice, Gender, and the Family* (New York: Basic Books, 1989).

13. John Rawls, *Political Liberalism* (New York: Columbia University Press, 1992), 274.

14. John Rawls, *The Law of Peoples* (Cambridge, England: Harvard University Press, 1999), 107; and *A Theory of Justice,* 1st ed., 287.

15. Solow, "Intergenerational Equity and Exhaustible Resources," 30.

16. Ibid., 33–34.

17. Arrow, "Rawls' Principle of Just Savings," 325.

18. Dasgupta, "Savings and Fertility: Ethical Issues," 105.

19. John Rawls, *A Theory of Justice: Second Edition* (Cambridge, Mass: Harvard University Press, 1999), 254.

20. See Joseph Heath, "Intergenerational Cooperation and Distributive Justice," *Canadian Journal of Philosophy*, 27 (1997): 361–76 for a similar model.

21. Amartya Sen, "Isolation, Assurance, and the Social Rate of Discount," *Resources, Values, and Development* (Cambridge: Harvard University Press, 1997), 135–46.

22. David Schmidtz, *The Limits of Government* (Boulder, Colo,: .: Westview Press, 1991).

23. Dasgupta, "Savings and Fertility: Ethical Issues," 105.

24. Solow, "Intergenerational Equity and Exhaustible Resources," 33.

25. My model here owes much to Heath (1997), though Heath's model is more detailed.

PART VI

POLICY, ETHICS, AND ECONOMICS

CHAPTER 13

COMMUNITARIANISM AND SOCIAL SECURITY
Daniel Shapiro

1. INTRODUCTION

In 1981 Chile replaced its Social Security system with a compulsory private system; many countries have, in varying degrees, followed suit. Philosophical discussion of Social Security alternatives lags behind political realities. This topic should be important for political philosophers concerned with institutional questions, for the heart of the welfare state, in a budgetary sense, is social insurance programs such as Social Security and national health insurance. In *Is the Welfare State Justified?*[1] I tried to remedy the relative philosophical silence about retirement pensions. I argued that egalitarians, positive rights theorists, communitarians, and liberals should join libertarians in preferring compulsory private pensions (henceforth CPP) to Social Security (henceforth SS) and similar old-age insurance programs in other welfare states.[2]

In this chapter, I discuss some objections that have been raised since the book's publication. To make the topic more manageable, I focus just on one

nonlibertarian perspective, communitarianism, devoting most of my attention to whether the financial crisis undermines the case I made in my book
that communitarians should favor CPP. So let us turn to that case.

2. WHY COMMUNITARIANS SHOULD SUPPORT CPP

The term "communitarian" gained currency in political philosophy around
thirty years ago. Earlier communitarian writings tended to argue that liberalism ignored the importance of community for our personal identity and
social well-being, but it generally did not recommend specific policies. More
recent communitarian writings are less philosophically abstract, more policy
oriented, and rather than opposing liberalism explicitly, instead emphasize
that liberalism's concern with individual liberty should be balanced with
needs of communities. Weaving the more philosophically abstract ideas with
the more policy-oriented writings, we obtain this central communitarian
claim: Our relationship to various communities is so important for our individual and social well-being that some degree of individual liberty may need
to be sacrificed to sustain that relationship.[3]

Two ideas are central to communitarians' analysis of community. First,
a community is an association of individuals who share common values, especially a sense of what is public and private, or phrased somewhat differently, a shared sense of the common good. Second, a community has a
shared sense of "we-ness" or solidarity, which is a sense that one's identity
is at least partially constituted by membership in this association. Since a
political community consists of some shared values, and to some extent constitutes a person's identity, communitarians should favor that pension system
that has a comparative advantage in sustaining common values and feelings
of solidarity among citizens. What specific criteria do communitarians use
to determine which system has that comparative advantage? An examination
of communitarian writings on SS as well some inferences from main lines of
communitarian thought suggest the following.

1. **Universality**. A pension system that does not cover all citizens tends to
   create divisions in the community, thus weakening solidarity.[4]

2. **Shared responsibility.** A pension system should express a commitment
   that all members of the community are obligated to one another.[5] Indi-

viduals should take responsibility for both their own welfare and that of
other members of the community, especially those unable to adequately
provide for their old age. Thus communitarians oppose purely individualistic notions of responsibility whereby persons take responsibility only
for their retirement or that of their families.

3. **Reciprocity or Equity.**[6] Shared responsibility must also be equitable.
   Communitarians favor an equitable division of responsibility because
   this is essential for justice and/or because inequities create social division
   and instability.

4. **Fidelity.** Amitai Etzioni and Laura Brodbeck, communitarians who discuss the United States Social Security system, state that the "commitments ought to be honored, because it is the ethically appropriate thing
   to do, because if one violates such commitments the social and moral
   order of a society is diminished."[7] Their reasoning is that a public pension system that breaks its (explicit or implicit) promises creates distrust
   between the government and its citizens and between generations. If later
   generations sense that they are not getting promised benefits and what
   earlier generations received, intergenerational hostility becomes a serious
   possibility. A communitarian who prizes solidarity between citizens will
   want to avoid this.

Given these four desiderata, which system should communitarians favor?
Both systems are universal. SS provides pensions to all citizens, while CPP
compels all citizens to contribute a percentage of their salary or income to an
individual pension savings account and also provides a minimum pension
for those with inadequate or nonexistent retirement pensions.[8] It appears,
however, that SS expresses a deeper sense of shared responsibility. CPP is
basically a system of individual responsibility, with a residual safety net for
the indigent. Individuals in a private pension system have a property right to
their pensions. They decide, within limits, how to invest their contributions:
These contributions plus the interest or capital gains fund their pension. In
SS, by contrast, only traces of a notion of individual responsibility exist—
earning history helps to determine benefits. Individuals lack property rights
to their pension, and pay-as-you-go financing funds the system. Rather than
individuals choosing how to invest their contributions that fund their retirement, retirees' pensions are provided primarily by taxes on present work-

ers.[9] (The existence of a "trust fund" in the United States and in some other SS systems does not alter this fact, since the "fund" consists of government IOUs, not invested assets.[10] I will return to this point later). It is primarily others (in our generation and younger generations) that assume responsibility for our retirement. As the United States Social Security Advisory Commission report put it, "Social Security is based on the premise that *we're all in this together*, with everyone sharing responsibility not only for contributing to their own and their family's security, but also the security of everyone else, present and future."[11]

This more collectivized sense of responsibility has a huge cost, namely extremely large intergenerational inequity. A pay-as-you-go system (henceforth PAYGO) was a great deal in its early stage.[12] Payroll taxes were relatively low, and retirees (who did not pay into the system their whole lives) got an excellent "rate of return" on their taxes, way above a normal market investment. The support ratio—the ratio of workers to retirees—was high (ranging from fifteen to one to eight to one), thanks to vigorous population growth that supplied a steady stream of new taxpayers and a relatively low life expectancy of retirees, which moderated growth in the implicit public pension debt or the liability for expected future benefits. But today's retirees have paid SS taxes their whole lives, life expectancy has increased, and population growth has slowed. The system's maturation and a decrease in the support ratio (less than four to one, and in some countries less than two to one) has produced high payroll taxes, a poor "rate of return" for young workers, and a huge implicit public pension debt.[13] These inequities are absent in private pension systems, which avoid PAYGO's life cycle, since individuals own their individual retirement accounts funded by investing their contributions.

Defending SS because it embodies a deeper sense of shared responsibility than a privatized system comes at the price of admitting that SS is worse than a private system at minimizing intergenerational inequities. SS also compares quite unfavorably to CPP on the criterion of fidelity. SS is steeped with deceptive rhetoric and misleading terminology. Calling IOUs *trust funds*, payroll taxes *contributions*, even calling SS social *insurance* (as if it was akin to a private plan, which one owns) all give the distinct impression that SS is a funded pension plan, rather than a PAYGO system. In the United States, the illusion that SS was akin to funded pensions may have been crucial for obtaining the high level of support that it has enjoyed [14] (or has enjoyed until very recently). Even if citizens realize that SS cannot promise a market rate of return, PAYGO systems make it quite difficult for citizens to understand the system and determine what is being promised. The relationship between taxes paid and benefits received is opaque: Taxation and benefit levels frequently change, SS's actuarial status heavily depends upon population trends and growth in wages, and it is affected by frequent political maneuvering. Such opaqueness is unsurprising, since the absence of individual property rights in a PAYGO system means little incentive exists to provide this information and that enforcing an obligation to provide it is more difficult. In the United States it was not until 1999 that every person with an address began receiving earnings and benefit estimates and other countries are even worse in this regard.[15]

Compared to SS, CPP is pellucid, and its promises are not difficult to keep. CPP, except for the minimum pension guarantee, is a defined contribution system, meaning that the value of the pension at retirement depends upon one's investments and returns on the investment. (After retirement, one's earnings are converted into an annuity and/or taken as phased withdrawals). It is relatively easy to understand the relationship between premiums and benefits: What you receive depends upon what you contributed, plus capital gains and interest from your investments, minus administrative costs. Private pension plans have both the incentive and the obligation to provide reasonably accurate information about their actuarial status and expected rates of return, so the investor has a fairly good basis for understanding the system.[16] Except for the definition of the minimum contribution and minimum retirement pension, CPP is not inherently subject to political manipulation, and participants have genuine property rights to their pension, which adds further incentive to follow and monitor the progress of one's investments.

Thus communitarians should favor CPP, not SS. CPP avoids creating intergenerational inequity, keeps its promises, and expresses a sense of shared responsibility via its safety net for the elderly poor. Admittedly, the kind of shared responsibility involved in CPP is more individualistic than communitarians would like. But the more collectivized sense of shared responsibility in SS is achieved at the price of creating enormous intergenerational inequities and making misleading promises that it cannot keep. This is too high a price for communitarians to pay, since such inequities and failure to keep promises threaten to create social division and undermine solidarity between the old and the young.

3. FIDELITY, EQUITY, AND THE FINANCIAL CRISIS

My argument that CPP beats SS on the criterion of fidelity is open to two objections. First, my contrast is overstated. Deception and opaqueness occur in private pension systems. Commissions or other administrative costs may obscure the real rate of return, salespeople can pressure participants into making investments contrary to their interests, and fund administrators may line their pockets. A survey that showed that only half of the Chilean pension system participants understood what percentage of their income was going toward their contributions[17] and the destruction of numerous individuals' and institutions' investment plans and dreams by the crook Bernie Madoff illustrate the problems.

Granted that we should exercise caution in exaggerating the advantages of CPP regarding fidelity, it is still clearly superior to SS. Even if the Chilean pension system's opaqueness regarding one's income/contribution ratio would generally occur if other countries adopt CPP, accurate information would still be far more accessible than in SS—since even in an opaque private system workers would still know that it is their money that is being invested, unlike a PAYGO system that makes it very difficult to obtain accurate information about the system's actual workings. As for crooks and charlatans, they exist in any system, private or public, but fraud and deception are not a systemic or central problem in private pension systems. Competition between funds and legal penalties for fraud keep the problem at a manageable level, whereas the problems with deception in a PAYGO system are more central or systematic: The remedies of competition and legal penalties for misleading people into thinking that a PAYGO system is like a private pension are virtually absent.

A deeper objection is that the current financial crisis swamps CPP's advantages regarding fidelity. This is because the promise of a defined contribution system to deliver market rates of return becomes empty when the market

COMMUNITARIANISM AND SOCIAL SECURITY   299

ruins people's retirement hopes. After all, while a defined contribution system does not promise a *specific* benefit—the contributions are specified, but
not the benefit—the *appeal* of CPP is that given the long-run performance
of the capital market, its promise of a market rate of return is a promise that
returns will be greater than most other investments (government securities,
CDs, etc.), a promise that SS in its final stages cannot make or keep. But
this appeal of CPP is illusory when that promise of a long-run performance
can no longer be credibly made. Furthermore, the financial crisis also undermines CPP's advantages in avoiding PAYGO's life cycle that produces
intergenerational inequities. While *that* life cycle is still avoided, since the
crash of markets does not mean they become PAYGO systems, now a *different* life cycle emerges, namely that the rate of return varies significantly
across generations depending on whether one was unlucky enough to retire
when markets' long-run performance turned dismal. Since in CPP people
are forced to participate,[18] these inequities and the mockery of promises of a
market rate of return greater than other investments would threaten to create
social division and undermine solidarity. And so the financial crisis seems to
undermine CPP's advantages (more equitable, better at keeping promises),
leaving SS a clear winner—since the latter will at least be superior in sustaining a more collectivist sense of responsibility between the generations.

4. WHY THE OBJECTION FAILS

The second objection looks more powerful than it is. To see why, let's ask:
What sort of a financial crisis are we facing? Two possibilities seem salient.
First, the crash or bear market abates within a year or so, with a return to
the long-run historical norm. The second possibility is something like the
American Great Depression, which lasted from 1929 to 1939.[19] (In what fol-
lows, I focus on the United States, to simplify matters.)

If the first possibility eventuates, then the objection fails. Relative to
what would have occurred had there been no crisis, the retiree will experience some period of a large decrease in his retirement benefits. However, the
retiree will also have forty or forty-five years of investment in equities or a
mixed portfolio (equities and bonds) prior to the crash, which gives him a
rate of return far higher than he would have received if he was in a late stage

PAYGO system. So a short bear market will not dramatically damage his nest egg. To be more precise, investment in equities or a mixed portfolio would have provided a rate of return of around 5 to 6 percent, while the rate of return for a retiree in a late stage PAYGO system is around 2 percent. Or to put matters slightly differently, prior to the crash, the monthly benefit the investor in CPP could have anticipated is more than double than what he could have anticipated with SS.[20] As long as it is not sustained, a dismal bear market will not alter the comparative advantage of CPP, if rates of return revert to their normal long-run levels prior to what occurred before the crisis.[21] Thus a couple of years of a dismal bear market does not undermine the long-run superiority of capital markets as a provider of better rates of return than the alternatives. Since it was the alleged falsity of that claim that was the linchpin of the argument that CPP is worse on the criteria of equity and fidelity, if the current financial crisis passes in a couple of years, the argument has been refuted.

Suppose, however, the crisis lasts around a decade. That is, suppose a retiree has forty to forty-five years of normal market returns followed by around ten years of retirement in down markets that perform like they did in 1929–1939. What then? I am unaware of any analysis regarding comparative rates of return in this situation. Suppose this situation leaves him with average annual benefits no better than what was promised to a retiree in SS during that period, even if markets then return to their historical norm in the next decade.[22] If so, it seems that CPP is no longer superior to SS on the criterion of fidelity, because it can't fulfill its promise that a market rate of return provides a better long-range rate of return than the alternatives. However, matters are not as clear-cut as they seem, because we need to consider how SS will perform from 2008 to 2018 if there is a long-term financial crisis. Recall my earlier discussion of the way SS misleads its citizens. That problem with fidelity will worsen in the coming years and will worsen still if there is a long-run financial crisis. Here I return to my discussion in Note 10. In less than a decade, SS will face annual deficits, that is, payroll taxes received will be insufficient to fund expected or promised benefits. While SS has a large "trust fund" surplus that supposedly pays for those deficits, that surplus has been spent by other parts of the government, so when these deficits arise, it will have no assets to pay for the shortfall. Thus, there will need to be an increase in payroll taxes and/or *a cut in benefits* in order to make up the shortfalls. If benefits are cut for retirees, then the benefits they expected or thought were promised will not be forthcoming. Thus the failure of SS to keep its promises that is inherent in a late stage PAYGO system will become quite apparent in less than a decade—and could worsen the retiree's rate of return, as the ratio of payroll taxes to benefits received worsens. Furthermore, the financial crisis will exacerbate the problem and possibly shorten the time period when annual deficits begin, because SS's financial health is partly dependent on the state of the economy, and a long-run situation akin to the Great Depression will reduce the amount of payroll taxes received. That in turn could increase the need for benefit cuts to handle the deficits, thus further lessening the retiree's rates of return.

The upshot of the preceding discussion is that while a decade-long financial crisis means CPP can't fulfill its promise that it will provide a better long-run rate of return than other investments, it is unclear how CPP fares compared to SS vis-à-vis the criterion of fidelity, given the looming problem with SS's finances that will be exacerbated by a long-term financial crisis. Those problems make quite visible SS's problems regarding the criterion of fidelity as well as worsen the rate of return for retirees and could make SS worse than CPP vis-à-vis the criterion of fidelity. However, with so much uncertainty, the safest thing to conclude is that the matter is indeterminate.

What about intergenerational equity? Here CPP seems superior, since a decade-long financial crisis is an unusual event, whereas SS faces continuing issues of intergenerational inequity throughout its lifetime, this being a systemic problem with PAYGO systems. It might be argued, however, that since the dramatic differences between PAYGO's rates of return in the early and late stages are now gone, that future problems of intergenerational inequity will be relatively minor. In a note, I explain why it's doubtful that this objection succeeds.[23]

Let us take stock regarding the claim that the financial crisis that began in 2008 undermines the communitarian case for CPP. If that crisis ends in a year or two, then CPP remains superior to SS, because that kind of crisis does not change the basic argument for CPP set out in Section 2: SS is superior on the criterion of shared responsibility, and a short-term crisis does not undermine CPP's superiority regarding fidelity and intergenerational equity.

If the crisis that began in 2008 persists for around a decade, neither system is clearly superior. CPP is no longer clearly superior regarding fidelity, but it remains superior regarding intergenerational equity.

These are significant results. If I am right, not only is the conventional view that communitarians should favor SS incorrect, but even the crisis that began in 2008 does not undermine that case or provide a clear victory for SS. Even so, it doesn't follow that there is a transition to a more just system in a way consonant with communitarian values. In *Is the Welfare State Justified?* I argue that there is a way,[24] but that argument was made prior to the crisis that began in 2008, and whether it holds under present conditions is a matter to investigate another time.

NOTES

1. (New York: Cambridge University Press, 2007).

2. Virtually all modern welfare states have the same structural features of SS. When features of the American SS system play a role in my argument, I will mention them.

3. For guides to communitarian literature, see my "Liberalism and Communitarianism," *Philosophical Books*, 36, no. 3 (July 1995): 145–55; Chandran Kukathas, "Liberalism, Communitarianism, and Political Community," *Social Philosophy and Policy*, 13, no.1 (Winter 1996): 80–90; Daniel Bell, *Communitarianism and Its Critics* (Oxford: Oxford University Press, 1993); and Amitai Etzioni, "Introduction," *The Essential Communitarian Reader*, ed. Amitai Etzioni (Lanham, Md.: Rowman and Littlefield, 1998), ix–xxiv.

4. Robert E. Goodin, *Reasons for Welfare: The Political Theory of the Welfare State* (Princeton, N.J.: Princeton University Press, 1988), 73–74 (on communitarianism's commitment to a "single-status moral community"); and Philip Selznick, "Social Justice: A Communitarian Perspective," *The Essential Communitarian Reader*, 69 (on the "principle of inclusion").

5. Eric Kingson and John Williamson, "Undermining Social Security's Basic Objectives," *Challenge*, 39, no.6 (November/December 1996): 30.

6. "At the heart of the communitarian understanding of social justice is the idea of reciprocity." "The Responsive Communitarian Platform," *The Essential Communitarian Reader*, xxxiv.

7. Amitai Etzioni and Laura Brodbeck, *The Intergenerational Covenant: Rights and Responsibilities* (Washington: The Communitarian Network, 1995), 3, the authors' emphasis.

8. Some proposals for CPP allow opting out of the system when the amount in one's pension savings account is sufficient to purchase an annuity that is a certain percent above the poverty level. Shapiro, *Is the Welfare State Justified?*, 289.

9. *Fleming v. Nestor*, 363 U.S. 603 (1960); and World Bank Policy Research Report, *Averting the Old-Age Crisis: Policies to Protect the Old and Promote Growth* (New York: Oxford University Press, 1994), 113.

10. In the United States, payroll tax revenues not needed to meet current benefits are "invested" in special-issue government bonds. The trust funds are credited with a bond—an IOU from one part of the government to another—and the U.S. Treasury gets the cash, which helps

finance the general operations of the federal government. Currently trust fund records show a large surplus, but that surplus is merely a record of transfers from one part of the government to another. When SS's cash outflow exceeds the cash inflow from taxes (around 2016, if not sooner) the government will not find any money to pay promised benefits, only U.S. Treasury obligations. When the government then calls in the IOUs, it will have to do what it would do were there no trust fund: raise taxes and/or cut benefits and/or borrow money and/or obtain the money from general revenue. June O'Neill, "The Trust Fund, the Surplus, and the Real Social Security Problem," *Cato Project on Social Security Privatization* (April 9, 2002): 2–3.

    11. *Report of the 1994–1996 Advisory Council on Social Security Volume 1: Findings and Recommendations* (Washington: Government Printing Office, 1997) 89, their emphasis.

    12. World Bank Policy Research, *Averting the Old Age Crisis*, 315–17.

    13. In the United States, rates of return for most medium wage earners born in 1985 are less than 2 percent. Orlo Nichols, Michael Clingman, Kyle Burkhalter, Alice Wade, and Chris Chaplain, "Internal Real Rates of Return under the OADSI Program for Hypothetical Workers," Social Security Administration, Office of the Chief Actuary, Actuarial Note no. 2008.5, Social Security Administration April, 2009, table 3, http://www.ssa.gov/OACT/NOTES/ran5/an2008 5.pdf accessed June 2009. (I use their figures for "payable" benefits rather than "present law schedule benefits," because, as I explained in Note 10, and will discuss in Section 4, it is likely promised benefits will not be paid to retirees). The public pension debt in the United States is around 11 to 13 trillion dollars. Shapiro, *Is The Welfare State Justified?*, 296, Notes 9 and 10. Payroll taxes in the United States increased from 2 percent in 1937 (on wages up to $3000) to 12.4 percent in 2009 (on wages up to $106,800): http://www.ssa.gov/OACT/ProgData/taxRates.html and http://www.ssa.gov/OACT/COLA/cbb.html#Series, accessed June 2009.

    14. Carolyn L. Weaver, *The Crisis in Social Security* (Durham, N.C.: Duke University Press, 1982), 80–86, 123–124; Martha Derthick, *Policymaking for Social Security* (Washington: Brookings Institution, 1979), 199–201, 204; and John Attarian, *Social Security: False Consciousness and Crisis* (New Brunswick, N.J.: Transaction Publishers, 2001), chapters 4–10.

    15. Virginia P. Reno and Robert B. Friedland, "Strong Support but Low Confidence: What Explains the Contradiction?," *Social Security in the 21st Century*, eds. Eric R. Kingson and James H. Schulz (New York: Oxford University Press, 1997), 194, Note 8; and Axel Börsch-Supan, "Comments," in *New Ideas about Old Age-Security*, eds. Robert E. Holzman and Joseph E. Stiglitz (Washington, D.C.: World Bank Publications, 2000), 74.

    16. That CPP participants have a good understanding of how the system works and that it is fairly easy to understand the premium-benefit relationship, doesn't mean that the participant knows prior to retirement his retirement benefits. In a defined contribution system, one can only make estimates, since no specific benefit is promised. I discuss this further in the next section.

    17. Christopher Tamborini, *Social Security: The Chilean Approach to Retirement* (Washington D.C: Congressional Research Service, May 17, 2007), 24.

    18. But see Note 8.

    19. Arguably, one could extend this period to 1949, since it took around another ten years for the stock market to decisively recover from the 1929 crash. However, that twenty-year period includes the Depression plus World War II, and it seems more congruent to match the length of the two financial crises, rather than postulating a 21st century crisis that is comparable to a financial crisis and a world wide conflagration. For data on U.S. equities from 1929 to 1949 see *Stocks, Bonds, Bills and Inflation 2006 Yearbook* (Michigan: Ibottson Associates, 2006), 262 and 264.

    20. The Office of the Actuary of the Social Security Administration estimates that the long-term real rate of return of stocks is 6.5 percent and bonds is 3 to 3.5 percent. Their estimates for rates

of return in SS for a recent retiree vary depending on marital status, gender, and earning level. Two percent seems reasonable, since they estimate most medium level earners receive around that rate. These figures from the Social Security Administration are available in Michael Tanner, "A Better Deal at Half the Cost: SSA scoring of the Cato Social Security Reform Plan," *Cato Institute Briefing Papers* (April 26, 2005) 3; and Michael Tanner, "The Better Deals: Estimating Rates of Return Under a System of Individual Accounts," *Cato Institute Project on Social Security Choice*, no 31 (October 22, 2003), 12.

21. I base my argument on William Shipman, "Meltdown Was Perfect Stress Test for Market Based Pension Reform," *Investor's Business Daily*, May 12, 2009; and Andrew G. Biggs, "Social Insecurity: Personal Accounts and the Stock Market Collapse," *American Enterprise Institute for Public Policy Research* (Inaugural Issue No.1, Nov. 2008, http://www.aei.org/outlook/28971). Shipman compares how an average wage earner would have fared had she retired in early 2009 (after the 2008 crash) with how the wage earner would have fared had she invested her Social Security payroll taxes in a mixed portfolio. Despite the market meltdown in 2008, she would fare far better—her annual benefit for twenty years after retirement would be around 20 percent higher than she would have received from Social Security, and this is even with a conservative assumption that her retirement nest egg received a real annual post-retirement rate of return of 2 percent. Biggs compares how someone who retired in 2008 who invested around one-third of their Social Security payroll taxes in a mixed portfolio would have done compared with someone retiring in late 2008 in a pure SS system and concludes that the total benefit at retirement would be 15–20 percent greater. Biggs's comparison is not as direct as Shipman's for our purposes, but that even an investment of some SS taxes would produce a greater total benefit than a pure SS system provides some confirmation of Shipman's analysis.

22. If the retiree annuitizes all of her nest egg, this may not be true, since in that case she could contractually guarantee herself a fixed rate of return. This would insulate her from the market downturn (up to a point—there is a risk the insurance company goes bankrupt).

23. The 2009 Social Security and Medicare Trustee report indicates that funding SS's upcoming deficits over the next fifty to seventy-five years requires significant tax increases and/or benefit cuts. (E.g., they estimate that funding these liabilities by payroll taxes requires raising them from 12.4 percent to 16.6 percent in less than half a century. See Pamela Villarreal, "Social Security and Medicare Projections: 2009," *National Center for Policy Analysis*, Brief Analysis (June 11, 2009), http://www.ncpa.org/pub/ba662, accessed June 2009). Significant tax increases and/or benefit cuts during the next fifty to seventy-five years may drop the 2 percent average rate of return for present retirees toward zero (or possibly below) for later retirees. These retirees may then reasonably complain that while 2009 retirees received *some* positive return, they received *no* return or lost money. It's unlikely to provide much consolation to future retirees that the gap between their return and 2009 retirees is less than the gap between 2009 and, say, 1950s retirees. This suggests that complaints about intergenerational inequity are affected by very low absolute rates of return.

24. See Chapter 8, in particular 295–96.

CHAPTER 14

RIGHTS, POLLUTION, AND PUBLIC POLICY

H. Sterling Burnett

1. INTRODUCTION

Quite often, the discussion of environmental policy quickly moves from the recognition of a problem to the claim that something must be done, usually by government, to fix the problem. Then "liberals" and "conservatives" begin arguing whether the science used to justify action is of a high quality or is politically biased, and whether the costs of proposed regulations and mitigation actions are justified by their benefits to human health and environmental quality. Participants in these debates rarely recognize the illegitimate nature of the move from "is" to "ought." For example, burning fossil fuels produces residue or smoke as a byproduct. This is a fact. Whether people ought to care about that fact, and whether producing such residues is wrong, meriting censure and corrective action, are value questions and cannot be answered solely through reference to the fact that the residues exist.

Questions of right and wrong should precede those usually asked by policymakers and serve as a foundation for the arguments among citizens over the appropriateness of environmental laws. For instance, economists often argue that a particular pollution control policy ought or ought not to be undertaken because it is efficient or inefficient. Such claims seem commonsensical and are rarely challenged. Such claims obscure the fact that arguments that the government should only pursue policies that are efficient, as measured by a cost-benefit analysis or because they minimize social costs, are underpinned by a controversial moral theory: utilitarianism. Because such claims are normative, they must be underpinned by a sound argument, not accepted as descriptive of facts about human behavior. That is the task of ethics.

This chapter examines how and the extent to which a strong theory of property rights, as developed within the Lockean tradition of natural rights, might be used to protect people from pollution. This approach differs from much of the contemporary philosophical discussion concerned with humanity's ethical obligations in relation to the nonhuman environment, so before proceeding, the nature of this enterprise should be briefly addressed.

Gregory Cooper argues that environmental ethics has developed quite differently from other fields of applied ethics.[1] Medical ethics attempts to draw out the ethical (and, if relevant, political) implications of traditional moral theories for decision-making or policy formation in the practice of medicine. Business ethics does likewise in the field of business practice. Cooper points out that environmental ethics is a much more theoretically ambitious endeavor. Instead of applying extant moral theories to environmental problems, environmental ethicists are attempting to change our understanding of ethics per se by expanding the class of beings or objects that have moral standing or are deserving of moral consideration. Three trends dominate the extensionist movement in environmental ethics: the extension of direct moral considerability to all sentient beings;[2] the extension of direct moral considerability to all living things;[3] and the extension of direct moral considerability to ecosystems.[4]

Whereas ethics in general and applied ethics in particular have been concerned with appropriate relations among people, environmental ethics since its inception has argued for an extension of the class of morally considerable objects. Though I would argue that extentionist arguments in environmental ethics fail, that topic will not be part of this discussion. Instead, this is a study of traditional applied ethics. I apply a version of an established moral theory to the problem of environmental pollution, although I am not the first to chart this course.[5] For example, John Passmore rejected the argument that a new kind of ethic, which granted rights or direct moral standing to nature in general or species or individual animals in particular, was needed to ground concern for a healthy environment.[6] Rather, he argued that sufficient grounds for environmental protection can be found in both Jewish tradition and in a proper scientific understanding of the interconnections in nature and how environmental damage often harms human health or welfare. From his point of view, concern for the environment flows from the concern for human well-being and flourishing that is at the core of traditional ethics.

I examine how a variant of classical liberal rights theory would handle pollution problems. Such a theory is enshrined in the U.S. Constitution, and the Constitution serves as a starting point and framework within which U.S. environmental policy occurs. Even if one rejects rights theory in general or the strong theory of property rights used here in particular as a proper ethical basis for addressing pollution problems, or even if we accept one of the number of extensionist's environmental ethics, it should be instructive to examine the strengths and weaknesses of property rights as a tool to address the ethical and political conundrums resulting from pollution problems.

After presenting what I mean by property rights, I will provide a fairly standard definition of pollution and analyze two different policy approaches to pollution problems. The current command-and-control model of pollution control has been well criticized elsewhere, and I will not examine it here.[7] The policy options discussed in more detail are often suggested as alternatives to the current approach, but each of them has problems that will be examined.

2. CLASSICAL LIBERAL RIGHTS THEORY

Most classical liberal rights theories are variants of natural rights theories. Natural rights are rights that humans have by their nature as reasoning, purposive beings. To say that a person has a right is to say that person [the rights holder] has a claim on an act or forbearance from another person [the duty bearer] such that, should the claim be exercised and the act or forbearance not be done, it would be justifiable, other things being equal, to use coercive measures to extract either the performance required or compensation in lieu of performance—or punishment if performance cannot be obtained and compensation will not suffice.[8]

Rights also include, at a minimum, the existence of liberties, such that we may say the rights holder is at liberty with respect to others to do or not to do a given thing. The others have no claim against the rights holder, either to effect that the thing not be done, or that it be done.

Found in John Locke's *The Second Treatise of Government,* "Life, Liberty, and Property (estate)" is the classic formulation of rights that all discussions of rights theories must contend with, and within which I work.[9] According to Locke, among our rights are rights to life, liberty, and property. Without these rights, life would be left to chance and dependent upon the forbearance of others. Continued survival necessitates the recognition of these rights. These rights, though not presocial, do predate the formation of government. Government is instituted to facilitate the more effective protection or enforcement of these rights and does not have the power to abrogate an individual's natural property rights. Government is a contrivance created by consent; natural rights, including the right to private property, are not grounded in consent.

The foundational right that people have is the right to life. Neither rights to liberty nor property make sense without a prior right to life. Arguments for the right to liberty and property can flow from the equal right of every person to preserve his life in line with the laws of nature. As a rule, natural rights theorists argue that rights in general, and property rights in particular, are necessary for human survival and the existence of a moral order. Ellen Frankel Paul is one theorist who forcefully makes this argument.[10] For Paul, the survival of the individual is the minimal condition without which the pursuit of all other goals, desires, or needs is impossible. Continued existence is necessary for anything else that makes life desirable. Thus, for each individual, pursuing the strategy that will maximize chances of survival—that is, make it the least contingent, the least dependent upon forces beyond his control, and the least reliant upon the actions of other individuals—will provide the foundation from which he can proceed to choose other values and objectives.

All people require food, air, water, shelter, clothing, a spot of earth to stand upon, and a weapon to fend off beasts. However, all of these goods come to exist only after the application of effort or labor of some type. In addition, the natural conditions of scarcity place limits upon the chances of any individual's survival. From these conditions, one can conclude that, at a minimum, in order for any individual to survive he must have a moral right to motility (the right to be free from constraints upon his physical person), and he must be able to act upon material things—to use or mold them into goods useful for his survival.

Establishing that any representative person, X, needs a type of object or condition in order to survive, however, is not the same as establishing the existence of a right to said object or condition. Accordingly, one must ask if anyone else has the right to inhibit X's free movement or her possession and use (acquisition) of material goods for survival's sake. Three choices present themselves: (1) X has no rights to motility and acquisition of matter, and neither does anyone else; (2) X has no rights, but some or all others do have rights; or (3) X has rights and so does everyone else. Option 1 is unacceptable because it amounts to a world bereft of morality: "A world in which the survival of anyone is rendered as radically contingent, fleeting, and precarious as it could possibly be."[11] To deny rights to all is to allow each person's efforts to survive to be canceled out by the whim and power of his fellows.

Option 2 is also unacceptable because there is no morally relevant difference among representative individuals—all share the same goal of survival and project pursuit, all have the same needs, and all face the same environmental conditions of scarcity. Thus to deny rights to some people while affirming them for others is logically inconsistent and morally bankrupt. This leaves us with option 3, wherein X has rights and so does everyone else. These rights include the right to acquire property.

Proponents of alternative ethical theories, utilitarianism for instance, may reject rights theory in general, as an appropriate moral theory within which humans can (best?) flourish. Others theorists, contractarians, for example, might accept rights but reject the Lockean source of those rights as grounded in nature. This chapter, however, is not an attempt to provide a thorough defense of either Lockean rights or natural rights based property rights; rather, it will assume such rights in order to explore how people and society might wield such rights in the defense of their health and nature.

To say that individuals have property rights is not to specify the content of those rights. Property rights can be understood as a complex bundle of related rights, liberties, and powers. The classic description of the full liberal notion of "property rights" comes from A. M. Honore.[11] According to this description, property rights can be understood as a bundle of rights with eleven elements, or "sticks." The elements are: (1) the right to possess—when possible, exclusive physical control of the owned object (if the object is non-corporeal in nature, such as in cases of intellectual property, and it cannot be physically possessed, possession may be understood as the right to exclude others from the use or other benefits of the object in question); (2) the right to use—personal enjoyment and use of the object as distinct from (3) and (4); (3) the right to manage—to decide how and by whom an object shall be used; (4) the right to income—the benefits derived from forgoing personal use of an object and allowing others to use it; (5) the right to capital—the power to alienate the object and to consume, waste, modify, or destroy it; (6) the right to security—immunity from expropriation; (7) the power of transmissibility—the power to devise or bequeath the object; (8) absence of term—ownership rights of indeterminate length; (9) prohibition of harmful use—the duty to forbear from using the object in ways harmful to others; (10) liability to execution—liability to having the object taken away for repayment of a debt (or under some penal regimes as a punishment); and (11) residuary character—the existence of rules governing the reversion of lapsed ownership rights.

The writers and signers of the Declaration of Independence and later of the Constitution of the United States followed Locke in explicitly recognizing the fundamental necessity of individual rights to both human social existence and political liberty.[12] They enshrined such rights in the Declaration of Independence. And when the new government was formed, individual rights implicitly bounded the powers of the central government established when the Constitution was ratified. The Constitution does not grant "rights" to the federal government; instead it enumerates the specific powers that it has. Individual rights were explicitly recognized in the Bill of Rights as amendments to the Constitution. Indeed, the right to both particular forms of private property (Amendment II) and the security of homes and various types of personal private property (Amendments III–V) from government control or seizure except under particular specified conditions are evidence of the high regard the founders of the American Republic had for private property. By contrast, nowhere in the Constitution is the environment mentioned, nor is the power to protect the environment, however broadly construed, (whether species, individual animals, landscapes, or ecosystems) delegated to the federal government. It is against the background of individual rights that pollution policies in the United States are to be judged.

3. HOW GOVERNMENT SHOULD TREAT POLLUTION PROBLEMS

All production or consumption activities produce residuals or byproducts. Pollution problems arise when residuals are dispersed into common locations such as air basins or bodies of water.[13] They are among the most persistent environmental problems confronting society.

Air and water pollution problems stem, in part, from the nature of traditionally treating the atmosphere and waters as common-pool resources. Aristotle was perhaps the first to note the implications of treating goods as commonly held. Among the deficiencies with commonly held property was, "What is common to the greatest number gets the least amount of care. People pay most attention to what is their own: they care less for what is common. . . ."[14]

Commons problems arise when land or other resources have no owners or are "owned" in common. If property rights do not exist or are somehow difficult to establish, enforce, or transfer, then the land or other resource has no owner, and therefore it has no protector or defender. Where resources are common property, self-interested behavior will often lead to environmental degradation.

The atmosphere is an example of a true commons. Everyone uses the atmosphere. We take oxygen from it and every human action or endeavor, even the simple act of breathing, results in atmospheric emissions. No one person, group, state, or country has exclusive rights to the use of the atmosphere. In part, because of this, for most of human history, it has been treated as a free space. When population densities were low and the population dispersed, most of these emissions into the shared atmosphere were not problematic. However, as with every chemical, it is the dose that makes the poison, and as human societies grew and industrial production developed, the concentrations of certain chemicals and compounds proved to be harmful to human health and the environment—the phrase "air pollution" came into being.

Millions of people benefit from energy use each day, thus contributing to the pollution created through the production of energy, but only a relative few suffer noticeable harmful effects. Linking those harms directly to polluting activities, much less the actions of any individual polluter, is difficult, if not impossible. Reducing pollution can be expensive, and each person, business, or institution that pollutes receives the full benefit of its activities but bears only a small portion of the social costs. Thus, each person, business, or institution has an incentive to overpollute, that is, to maximize their use of the resource and thus produce much more pollution than they would if they had to bear the full costs of their actions.

Pollution problems pose a conundrum for market institutions. As the value of land, wildlife, and other natural resources increases, people usually can and do establish property rights in them and market institutions develop around their exchange.[15] For instance, beaver and beaver pelts were valuable commodities among native peoples in precolonial America. When there were few people exploiting the beaver and no territorial competition, beaver streams and trapping areas were treated as commons. This changed when French fur traders came to the area in the early 1600s. The value of beaver pelts rose. In response, the Montagnais Indians of the Labrador Peninsula hunted them more intensively and the beaver became increasingly scarce. Recognizing the decline of the beaver population and the possibility of its extinction, the Montagnais developed private property rights. Each beaver-trapping area on a stream was assigned to a family. This gave each family both the incentive and the ability to adopt conservation practices. A family never trapped the last remaining pair of beavers in its territory, since that would harm the family the following year.

This system worked well until a new influx of European trappers invaded the area and ignored the native Americans' property rights. Unable to enforce or defend their property rights to the beaver or to their beaver stream, overexploitation began again.[16]

Private decisions function reasonably well for managing resource use issues and land use/habitat issues. This is not true for many pollution problems, such as if a paper mill or some other coal-fired power plant emitted pollution that landed on adjoining landholdings. Under traditional common law rules (described later in more detail) the adjoining landowners, let's say they raise cattle, would be able to sue the owners of the mill or power plant for trespass and as a nuisance for any consequent damage caused by the pollution to their grazing land or their cattle's health. By contrast, air sheds are usually treated as commons, with as many "polluters" as there are people, and no one person has the right to enjoin the activities or others based on claims that any particular right of his, for instance, "right to clean air" was violated. In addition, tying either a general or particular environmental problem or human health threat to any individual source of pollution is difficult. Pollution problems offer a broad scope for various forms of collective decision-making, including government action.

3.1 The First Policy Option: The Economic
Utilitarian Response to Pollution Control

In recent times, governments have treated pollution problems as commons problems. In response, they have attempted to limit air and water pollution to levels at which the social benefits of the activity producing the pollution exceed the social costs. These levels are based on politically determined decisions about what levels of harm to individuals and society are consistent with a goal of continued economic growth. These levels have changed over time as both technology and our ability to measure harms have improved.

A. N. Pigou produced a contemporary classic economic treatment of pollution problems.[17] According to Pigou's analysis, the reason that businesses act in ways that impose harm upon others is a divergence between the private and social costs of business activities. For example, a factory belches smoke onto a neighboring property because it does not face the full cost of its production activities. Pigou concluded that because the factory owner caused the problem, he ought to be held liable for damages to any injured parties; or the government ought to tax the factory owner until the amount of smoke produced is socially optimal (the amount at which the benefits of reducing smoke further are outweighed by the costs.

R. H. Coase, in a widely cited article, rejected Pigou's analysis.[18] According to Coase, the problem of polluter and pollutee is one of a reciprocal nature. To avoid harming the property owners, the government would have to harm the factory owner. In such cases, the government's job is to decide who should be harmed. This is determined by the assignment of rights in a manner that maximizes the value of production.[19] Coase uses other examples to reinforce his case; for example, a fire-causing railroad and adjoining property owners. On this analysis, absent transaction costs, it would not matter which party, polluter or pollutee, rancher or farmer, and so on, is assigned liability or the right to act, because market transactions would occur to bring about a long-run equilibrium position at the point where social costs and social benefits are equal at the margin. Coase recognizes that transaction costs are always positive. Therefore, the initial assignment of rights is critical. For Coase, jurists ought to perceive cases where the problem of harmful externalities is at issue in the way that an enlightened economist would, assigning the right to act to the party who would buy them if transaction costs were zero.

For rights theorists, neither Pigou's nor Coase's treatment of pollution problems is satisfactory. Whether pollution policy is aimed at pursuing maximum value of production, minimized social cost, wealth maximization, the greatest amount of net social benefits, or the Pareto frontier, the analysis is guided by utilitarian principles, and utility is not a solid foundation for individual rights.

Coase's analysis is flawed at several points. First, his argument about the reciprocal nature of harm plays havoc with common sense notions of causation and fault, and it is in direct contradiction to the classical liberal notion of property rights. To hold that a polluter who is forced to stop causing illness and property damage to surrounding landowners is on equal moral footing with those who suffer the harm is akin to holding a rape victim on equal footing with a knife-wielding rapist. After all, had the rape victim not been present at a particular place at a particular time, the rapist would not have been able to rape her (at that time). Does the rape harm her? Certainly. Are we to conclude that the rapist is harmed if he is not allowed to rape her? Not if the common notions of harm, causation, and personal responsibility that underlie the common law tradition of criminal and tort law carry any weight. On this point, Pigou's analysis appears closer to the mark. Property rights are held under a prohibition on harmful use (see the ninth element under the description of classical liberal property rights in Section 2). Classical liberal rights theory provides a foundation for the criminal law and the common law tradition, including tort law.

Classical liberals will also object to Coase's analysis insofar as it provides no principled defense against property confiscation or redistribution. If maximization of production is the objective of law in cases of conflicting claims of harm, why should the law not seek to redistribute property holdings whenever doing so would benefit overall production? If an economic analysis indicates that the best available use of a piece of property that is currently occupied by a private dwelling is as a luxury hotel, even though the current owner does not agree, then why not condemn the property and give it to a developer who will build on the space? Why wait until a conflict occurs to reduce transaction costs and other barriers to productive activity? In practice, redistributing property and the rights commonly understood to attach to owning property may have problematic production implications, but there is nothing in Coase's theory that would prohibit such redistributions in principle.

While Coase intended his view to be supportive of property rights and individualism, he misunderstands both the nature of property rights themselves and the proper (and in the U.S., Constitutional) function of government. Fundamental to almost every conception of private property rights is the right to possess, including the right to exclusive use. Coase's position eviscerates what may be the most important stick in the bundle of property rights. Following natural rights theory, governments are not instituted to assign or rearrange rights, but to protect rights that individuals already have.[20] Accordingly, that a farmer has the right to have his property free of fire caused by a passing train is determined not by the courts but is part and parcel of what it is for him to have the right of exclusive use in his property—and the court's job is to protect and enforce this right. Trains may cause fires on the train owners' properties but not on the property of surrounding landowners.

Instead of misunderstanding the nature of property rights and the legitimate functions of government, Coase may be presenting an alternative conception of property rights and the legitimate function of government. But if so, he must argue for such a position and its utilitarian foundation. That private property rights include as a fundamental element the right of exclusive use and may, on occasion, not maximize the value of production or may not be efficient in the aggregate argues against recognition of that element only if one already accepts a macroeconomic view of promoting efficiency as the guiding principle of government action.

3.2 The Second Policy Option: Relying on the Common Law to Limit Pollution

In general, law can be divided into two broad categories, public law and private or common law. Public laws, created by legislative bodies, encompass statutory-based rules and constitutional strictures. Private law, on the other hand, has traditionally arisen spontaneously as a result of court rulings or judicial determinations in the areas of contract, tort, and property law. At the core of each of these realms of law are private property rights. Contract law governs transactions of private property and personal services. Tort law protects individuals, and their real and personal property, against injury or invasion.

"Common law" is a label used to describe the ancient legal process of discovering and delineating the law on a case-by-case basis. Historically, common law judges did not see themselves as creating law so much as discovering it.[21] As Nobel prize winning economist F. A. Hayek put it, judges subscribed to natural law doctrine whereby "there are natural rules of conduct inherent in humanity itself, most easily discovered by the evolution of customs of dealing. The job of the common law judge was to look to custom in an effort to discern the law that already existed and then render rulings based upon it."[22]

Since what the judges "discovered" was usually reflected in the customs existing at the time that a case, or set of related cases, first arose, there is a large conventional element in divining the rights of property from the laws of nature. Hayek has written extensively concerning how legal rules protecting rights, including property rights, have emerged over time from the spontaneous process of judicial decision-making through common-law cases.[23]

Though not often noted and sometimes missed by analysts such as Hardin, who may have been unaware of the fact, historically the common law was used to "enclose the commons," so to speak. Indeed, until the latter part of the nineteenth century, individuals used three bodies of the common law (trespass, tort, and riparian law) to good effect in defense of themselves and the environment. The common law, for a large range of cases, provides a stronger defense against environmental harm than public law.

First, because common law determinations rely upon the personal initiatives of conflicting parties, (1) the determinations are advised by a careful and equitable consideration of all of the relevant information presented, and that (2) the conflicting parties will present the strongest arguments for their positions. If the judge is unbiased and understands his role correctly, then his legal finding will reflect most accurately the rule that should and does govern the situation.

Second, the common law supports the classical liberal analysis of natural rights to life, liberty, and property. The common law process is conducive to developing law that effectively accommodates the disparate needs and preferences of individuals, and, to the extent that it is respected by legislatures and administrative agencies, limits the power of bureaucratic officials that legislation often creates.

Third, the common law highlights the fundamental importance of private property to the protection and promotion of individual rights. The common law evolved out of a deep and abiding respect for the value of private property and the rights of the property owner to be undisturbed in the possession and use of his possessions. In addition, it possesses powerful tools to delineate or better define property rights, allowing markets for those rights to develop and operate smoothly.

Three realms of the common law are of interest when addressing pollution issues: trespass, nuisance (private and public), and riparian law. Trespass and nuisance are related doctrines that protect interests in the exclusive possession, use, and enjoyment of land. Historically, trespass was regarded primarily as a safeguard against physical intrusion on land, though more recently trespass protections have been extended to other types of material and personal property. By contrast, nuisance actions have a long history of affording protection against obnoxious uses of neighboring land.

Riparian law evolved from nuisance law but has a strong trespass law element. Under the common law, people who own or occupy land beside rivers and lakes (that is, riparians) have rights to the natural flow of water beside, on, or through their property unchanged in quantity or quality.[24] Unlike the law of nuisance, water uses that either alter the quality or quantity of water enjoyed by users do not have to cause identifiable harm to be enjoined or require some kind of compensation. Many early nuisance cases concerned water pollution, and by the 1850s, riparian law had developed into such a finely tuned system of rights and responsibilities that it emerged as a very powerful weapon against the era's severe environmental challenges. Interestingly, riparian law privatizes a common pool resource because its rules and regulations provide a private mechanism whereby a select class of people can protect a commons. In Great Britain, riparian rights are still fiercely defended and routinely upheld. For instance, the Anglers' Cooperative Association fights pollution by defending riparian rights in county courts. The association has won all but two of the cases it has argued since its founding in 1948.

Trespass, nuisance, and riparian law, as historically developed and (until recently) applied, provided a strong bulwark directly against individual rights violations and indirectly against undesirable environmental alterations. The strength of these laws stemmed from the fact that they cut across the boundaries of intentional and unintentional categories of harm. Because of the special importance that the common law traditionally placed upon property, strict liability has been a dominant feature of the law in these areas. In regard to the law of trespass, unauthorized entry by a person or object onto another's land as a result of any voluntary act was subject to liability and future injunction. Even if the entry was unintentional and non-negligent (the person in question thought he was on his land or had permission to be on the land), once it was established that physical entry had occurred, then any technical invasion could serve as a basis of action. In riparian law, under the traditional doctrine of *aqua currit, et debet curerer, ut sloebat es juie naturae* ("water runs, and it should run, as it is used to run naturally"), liability was just as absolute. Riparians did not need to demonstrate harm, it was presumed to have occurred once interference with a riparian right was established.[25]

Two types of nuisance exist: public and private. Nuisance is an action for indirect and consequential interference or injury to the use and enjoyment of land. Initially, nuisance determinations resulted in damages, but courts of equity later provided injunctive relief as well. To prove private nuisance, one had to show harm, but as with trespass and riparian law, once harm was demonstrated, liability was absolute. For example, in William Aldred's case in 1611, the plaintiff brought an action against the defendant's offending hog sty.[26] The defendant asked the court to consider the social value of his operations as a defense to the nuisance action. He argued that since his activities were necessary to sustain humans, the adjacent property owners ought not to have such delicate noses. But the court rejected his argument and ruled instead one should use his property in such a manner as not to injure that of another. In its formulation as an absolute liability concept, the courts found that causing an injury to someone's enjoyment of his property creates a cause for recovery regardless of the legitimacy of the social value or reasonableness or utility of the undertaking.

Polluting industries raise three additional objections to the use of nuisance law to restrain their activities or avoid payment for harm: 1) that their actions are a reasonable use of their property; 2) that they are only responsible for a fraction of a larger harm; and 3) that their operations' long histories justify continued pollution. Historically, the courts routinely rejected these defenses; for example, in a 1952 case arising in Ontario, Canada, the court ruled: "He who causes a nuisance cannot avail himself of the defense that he is merely making a reasonable use of his own property. No use of property is reasonable which causes substantial discomfort to others or is a source of some damage to their property."[27] In another case a defendant tried to excuse the pollution caused by his brick burning by arguing that others had also contributed to local air pollution. In this case, the judge ruled that even if others had polluted, their cases were not before the court, and even if others cause part of the air problem, that is no reason for excusing him for his additional share of the nuisance.[28]

The law of public nuisance has been used to fill gaps left in the protection of legitimate interests by other branches of the common law. Historically, the origins of public nuisance related to minor criminal interferences with the rights of the Crown, which over time became understood as rights of the public (encroachments of commons or roads, etc.). Public nuisance came to cover a wide variety of minor criminal offenses that involved unreasonable interferences with some interest of the general public, such as threats to the public health (through the keeping of diseased animals), threats to the public safety (by storing highly volatile explosives in the midst of a city), or threats to the public comfort (through widely disseminated smoke or dust).

Public nuisance fills in the gaps in private nuisance actions in two ways. First, it is prospective. Harm is prevented in advance, not recompensed after it has occurred. Second, it covers a range of cases for which no individual may have an actionable claim. As currently constituted, no individual person has a right against obstructed highways, or the keeping of diseased animals, or the storage of hazardous waste; but the public as a whole (in order to prevent rights violations in advance) has a legitimate interest in seeing that no one can undertake (or continue in) an action that threatens significant interference with public health, safety, and so on.

We can gauge the strength of common law protections by examining cases. In one case, the defendants engaged in blasting to build a canal.[29] The blasting caused rocks to be tossed onto the plaintiff's land, depriving him of the safe use of his property. The court held that while the defendant's activities constituted a lawful and non-negligent use of his property, they did cause a nuisance, and a nuisance cannot be allowed, even for the purpose of lawful trade. The offending use had to be halted despite the detrimental effects upon industrial development.

Even governments are not immune from common law prohibitions. For instance, in *Roberts v. Gwyrfai District Council* in 1899, the owner of a mill sued a municipal water district over their upstream diversion of water for water and sewage purposes. The mill owner successfully argued that the district council violated his riparian rights to the continued accustomed flow of water that he used to run his mill. In granting the owner an injunction, the majority opinion of the court noted that no duty of the court was more important to observe and enforce than its power of keeping government within its assigned powers.[30] The court stated that the moment governments exceed their authority, they do so to the injury and oppression of private individuals, and those persons are entitled to be protected from government-imposed rights violations. In this case, the court found that the district council had no right to interfere with the accustomed flow of water even though they were doing it for a legitimate public purpose—the social good did not justify the rights violation.

Over time, the common law's usefulness as a guardian of individual rights and the environment was largely subverted during the progressive era in American politics (and this subversion continues to this day). One should not be surprised that the political movement that spawned the first "environmental" ethic (the conservation ethic) is also the movement that, perhaps more than any other, undermined common law property rights. The progressive era and conservation stood for rationally planned industrial development and nationally coordinated natural resource use. Resources were to be used for the greatest good of the greatest number and where adherence to rights would interfere with the pursuit of the "general welfare," rights would be overridden.[31]

For instance, in the case of *McKie, et al v. Kalamazoo Vegetable Parchment Company Ltd (KVP)*, the company's operations committed gross water pollution, creating a noxious odor, robbing the river water of oxygen (killing fish) and interfering with adjoining property owners and recreational and commercial fishers the use of the Spanish River. Farm animals refused to drink from it, and the people who had formerly drawn water from it for drinking, cooking, and washing could not, even after boiling, use it. This could have been avoided had the plant's owners used common methods of treating effluent water at the time—settling basins, for example—but the manager refused, citing the additional costs involved.

The courts found for the plaintiff (a local wildlife organization and six landowners who owned land along the river). The court ruled that KVP had violated the plaintiff's riparian rights by altering the character of the river, and granted the plaintiffs damages and an injunction. When, on appeal, the Court of Appeals affirmed the decision, the provincial government was quick to act, passing the ironically named law "The Lakes and Rivers Improvement Act," which empowered the courts to consider the public interest before restraining a polluting mill. It asked the courts to look to the public interest before awarding damages or issuing an injunction. Using this law, KVP went to the Supreme Court of Canada to challenge the provincial court's decision. The Supreme Court rejected the new law and upheld the verdict for the plaintiffs. The Canadian Government and Parliament was quick to act. The Premier at the time argued that pollution is inevitable in modern society, stating, "We do recognize that in these days of industrialization and . . . increase of population in areas of the province that we are bound to get a certain amount of pollution in our lakes and streams." Continuing, upon introducing "An Act Respecting The KVP Company Limited," the Premier vowed to "take whatever steps may be necessary to bring about the continued operations of this company so that the employment conditions in Espanola shall not be disturbed and that the development of the community will not be retarded."[32]

The act was passed, riparian rights were vitiated, and the pollution continued until the factory itself closed.

Many classical liberals support returning to traditional common law understandings of property rights as protected under the laws of trespass, nuisance, and riparian law.[33] Clearly, such a shift in policy would better protect individual rights than does current law. The question is, how well would it prevent or limit pollution? Arguably better than current legislation. Common law rights are more powerful than might be supposed. With private ownership comes the protection afforded by the common law. Therefore, the common law is a strong tool for defending against the unwanted effects of property uses that travel off site and interfere with human health and exclusive property use. Unwanted pollution (air, water, noise, etc.) could be halted upon the mere finding of trespass or nuisance, and damages could be awarded upon proof of harm. Enforcement of traditional common law protections would internalize some externalities, thus providing industry, agricultural interests, and governments with the incentive to reduce waste and negotiate for allowable levels of productive activities, all the while providing the flexibility of and experimentation with solutions inherent to markets. For example, in a case like *Robert's v. Gwyrfai District Council*, after losing the suit, the municipal water authority could, if technologically and economically feasible install pollution equipment to prevent the harmful pollution. Or it could open negotiations with the mill owner, paying him to allow some level of pollution to recompense for the damage he suffered or they could offer to buy his company out entirely. The point is, once a right to property is established, anyone who wishes to undertake or continue an activity that has a negative impact on others' private property, has to open negotiations with the property owner. The final solution is not known in advance and the resolution negotiated in one case for one problem may be quite different from the resolution involving other property owners fighting similar property violations. One size does not fit all, but in all cases, those undertaking the offending activity are forced to account for or internalize the impact of their actions upon their neighbors' property.

3.3 Criticisms of the Common Law

One might argue that the common law is lacking as an effective tool for environmental protection. When multiple polluters cause a problem, high discovery and transaction costs may make common law litigation unwieldy and inefficient. For example, lead from automobile emissions may contribute to neurological damage in children. If lead was the major source of all types of neurological diseases then lawyers might advise plaintiffs to bring environmental tort suits. But a plaintiff could not possibly sue all drivers of automobiles in a region or urban area. When an extremely high number of defendants exist, aggregation costs may be too high for tort litigation to be a realistic and efficient source of deterrence.

Other criticisms of the common law include that (1) under common law, it is hard to prove causation, and even if proved, it is hard to fairly apportion the costs; (2) the common law is retrospective (cases arise after the harm has already occurred), not prospective; and (3) lawsuits are costly. Among the most interesting criticisms of the common law as an instrument for environmental protection are that (4) the results vary with the individual facts of the case; (5) as traditionally interpreted, the common law does not allow for a weighing of the utility of the activity against the harm caused; and (6) the burden of proving causation falls upon the plaintiffs. The latter point is a problem because it denies relief where the damage is uncertain or speculative.

In response to the last claim, it is true that the common law places the burden of proof upon plaintiffs to demonstrate harm, that demonstrating harm is often difficult, and that the courts deny relief in the absence of such proof. But this as a virtue of the common law, not a vice. Liberties should not be restricted on mere suspicion of harm, founded upon statistical correlation with no strong evidence of causation. Where the remedy to a suit involves a proposed restriction of liberty and the imposition of a harm upon a person, classical liberal theory requires the highest standard of proof with the burden borne by those parties claiming harm because individual liberty is prima facie valuable.[34]

It also seems odd to criticize the common law as a tool for environmental protection on the basis that it does not allow for trade-offs on the basis of social utility. One strength of the common law is that it does not allow individuals to be harmed simply because society benefits from the activities causing the harm. Many criticisms of the common law stem from its modern-day eviscerated appearance. Positive laws promulgated with the goals of enhancing the "general welfare" vitiated common law protections of the environment. The common law is blamed for being too weak to protect the environ-ment, when it was its power to halt pollution caused by industrial expansion that led to its being overridden and weakened by positive legislation.

Finally, it is true that the results of the common law vary from case to case, but once again this is a virtue, not a vice. Environmental harms stem from different sources and have different results. Accordingly, solutions, to be effective, must be tailored to fit the circumstances of the case at hand.

There are two responses to the concern over the high costs associated with bringing a common law suit. First, while common law suits are costly, so is writing, implementing, enforcing, and adjudicating legislation. It is not clear that reliance upon the positive law to protect the environment is any less costly (in either direct, "on the budget" costs or in indirect "off budget," externalized costs) than reliance upon common law prohibitions. Second, the rise of class action suits, public interest law firms, and contingency fee lawsuits have mitigated the cost problem to a large extent.

Criticisms of the common law that focus on its backward-looking nature ignore two points. Although it is not easy, tort suits and riparian suits can be brought to halt a proposed action in advance. Once again, the plaintiff does bear the burden of demonstrating the threatened harm, but this is only fair in light of the fact that significant restrictions of liberty are often at stake (and usually the threatened harm is not permanent or irretrievable). Second, even where private tort actions may not be available, the common law also recognizes actionable public nuisances, and these actions are explicitly for-ward-looking in nature. For any action that threatens the general public with significant harm, public officials have the duty to act to prevent the action from taking place. The courts have the power, upon the reasonable request of a relevant public official, to issue a temporary injunction or restraining order preventing the contested activity until such a time as the case is finally adjudicated.

A final objection that may be raised against using the common law to protect property rights, and thus the environment, is that it is anti-democratic. This is largely true, but the answer is similar to the one given previously concerning social utility. The objection can't be that the common law is unable to prevent pollution to the degree that democratic majorities, or more accurately their representatives, demand, because history shows that, if anything, people have used the common law to stem majoritarian laws that would otherwise allow environmental degradation.

In this regard, one should note that the political process may be viewed as a commons in which everyone—social activists, interest groups, politicians and voters—tries to influence public policy but frequently does not bear the full costs of bad policies or reap the full benefits of good ones. On this analysis, in a typical political system, bad laws tend to be overproduced and good laws tend to be underproduced.

Efforts to produce optimal air quality are undermined because the costs of suboptimal legislation are diffuse—costing very little to any individual (so little that it is not noticed)—whereas the benefits of those undesirable policies are concentrated among the special interests who successfully get their provisions adopted into law.

Modern clean air laws provide an example of the political commons. Federal clean air laws arose in the 1960s and 1970s in response to perceived high and arguably dangerous pollution levels across much of the United States. From an economic perspective, a more efficient and effective policy to reduce emissions from power plants would have been for government to set the level of pollution it felt was protective of public health and, after setting standards and a timetable, simply to direct power plants to meet it.[35] Companies, pursuing profits, would have sought out the most efficient, least costly method or technology to meet the required criteria. For most existing power plants, this would have meant switching from high-sulfur, dirty Eastern coal to low-sulfur, cleaner Western coal.

But this was not the path Congress took. First, under pressure from the power industry, Congress exempted existing power plants from the new clean air standards. Second, under pressure from mining interest in Eastern states, Congress mandated that a particular technology—scrubbers—be used to reduce emissions from new power plants.[36] Using scrubbers, power plants could continue to use dirtier coal from relatively populous Eastern states with strong mining labor unions. This, of course, made the manufacturers of the scrubber technology happy as well. Because Western mining states have smaller populations, they had fewer legislators in the House of Representatives; thus Eastern interests dominated the debate.

Politicians looked good: They were lauded for cleaning the air while saving jobs. The environment and the general public, however, suffered. The costs of installing scrubbers was high, and in the early years the scrubbers were prone to failure—which meant a waste of time, manpower, money and resources used to manufacture the scrubbers. These costs were usually passed on to ratepayers but sometimes on to the general taxpayer as well. Energy costs rose as a result. In addition, air quality improved at a slower pace than it likely would have if Congress had simply set a standard and let industry figure out the best (cheapest and most reliable) way to meet it. Existing power plants were expanded and repaired, keeping them running in many cases decades past their planned useful life in order to avoid building more expensive, but more energy-efficient and cleaner power plants.

One may object to using the common law to protect property rights, however, simply because one believes that democratic majorities should have their way whatever the result. If the majority is for industrialization even with its attendant pollution one day, so be it. By contrast, if the majority favors placing a check on industrialization (to a greater or lesser degree) in defense of the environment the next day, then let it be done. Whatever the result, the majority should rule.

In response, I noted at the outset that this argument is developed within the context of U.S. law, particularly, Constitutional law. It is not just the common law but the Constitution, both grounded in natural rights theories, that limit democratic action. Thus, just like the Constitution protects the rights of the minority, and even property directly, a strength of the common law is that it does not allow individuals to be harmed simply because majorities (or special interest groups who influence the votes of a majority of legislators in a particular instance) benefit from the activities causing the harm.

4. REINSTATING RIGHTS: REESTABLISHING
THE PRIMACY OF COMMON LAW

Rights theorists will, in all likelihood, find the argument for the common law comforting because it reinforces their pre-established ethical view. But many environmentalists may not be rights theorists. There are many other ethical theories competing for people's adherence, some of which conflict with rights theory, including some that have gained a foothold in contemporary

U.S. law. If the common law, a historical guarantor of individual property rights, does protect the environment from pollution as well or better than current legislative regimes and Coasian-style alternatives, then environmentalists would do well to support efforts at reestablishing and/or strengthening the common law. Mark Sagoff, an environmental ethicist who has not shown himself to be enamored of strong property rights, argued in 1992 that "despite every appearance, we environmentalists may find a great deal to support in libertarian political theory"—and most libertarian political theories understand property rights as among the core rights that individuals have.[37]

Assuming that the common law both protects individual rights and the environment better than current efforts, one question remains: What policies are necessary to strengthen or, where they have been almost entirely eroded, reestablish common law protections against pollution? We must recognize that before implementing any policies that would restore the common law to its previous position as prime guarantor of environmental quality, common law advocates would have to overcome a great deal of public and political opposition. Having only had experience with the severely weakened and constrained version of the common law that survived the progressive era assault of the late-nineteenth and early-twentieth centuries, the public has little reason to believe that the common law can effectively protect the environment. Overcoming their fears will not be quick or easy. Even if the general public's fears could be mollified, political opposition to replacing public law environmental protections with common law protections would still be fierce. Many people, including politicians, industries, lobbyists, bureaucrats, and some environmentalists have a stake in preserving the present regime largely intact.

Assuming that public and private opposition to the common law is overcome, strengthening the common law will require both legislative and judicial changes. First, the legislature will have to sunset or end current laws that conflict with or undermine common law protections. These laws could be ended either through the passage of legislation specifically ending law that violates common law protections of property rights or, since many programs are authorized for specified periods of time and are then reauthorized at the end of that time, the legislature could just allow the program's authorization to lapse. Future federal environmental protections would be limited to halting environmentally harmful actions that violated constitutionally protected rights, to regulating the uses of the public lands (most rights theorists would advocate privatizing most public lands), and to adjudicating legitimate inter-state environmental disputes.

The latter point is important because some pollution problems cross state lines and rulings in common law cases from one affected state may conflict with rulings from another. This may open the door to federally established minimal environmental standards. An option more in line with this chapter's argument for strengthening the common law would be to apply federal com-mon law standards of tort and trespass in such cases. When pollution from one state harms citizens in another state, those citizens could bring a suit in federal court to halt the offending activity and/or receive compensation for the damage inflicted. Over time, as historically occurred within states and in other countries with a common law tradition, federal court rulings would become standardized through the judicial practice of stare decicis or "let the decision stand." Like cases would come to be decided alike.

For the common law to be effective in the manner suggested, courts would have to be directed to enforce historical common law standards. Courts would have to use strict liability standards when deciding pollution cases. This would eliminate the "reasonableness" defense now afforded prop-erty owners in nuisance cases. Defendants would no longer be able to de-feat a liability claim and continue polluting by showing that the utility of the action outweighed the harm to the plaintiff and thus the activity was reasonable.

In addition, courts would be required by law (since it would be unlikely to happen otherwise) to move back to a "strict performance" standard in contract and tort law. Courts would no longer be allowed to void contracts that they found onerous. For instance, if a water company signed a munici-pal contract to provide drinking water meeting a standard of cleanliness, the municipality would not be allowed to go into court later to void the contract because it decided it wanted a higher standard of water quality met. If the municipality wanted stricter standards, they would have to negotiate a new contract with the company, presumably with an increased payment to meet the new standards. On the other hand, the water company would not be allowed to go into a court at a later date and either claim that financial hard-ship prevents it from meeting the agreed upon standard or that the standard was unnecessarily high to begin with and that the company should be allowed to provide a lower level of water cleanliness. As long as neither force nor fraud was used to gain contractual agreement, the courts should enforce the letter of the contract. Demanding that parties meet their contractual obligations is not slavery, but an acknowledgment of and sign of respect for the autonomy of contracting agents.

A final point that should be made is that moving to common law protections for the environment means accepting the fact that different states and locales will offer different levels of environmental quality. Californians may make trade-offs in terms of job losses due to lower standards of proof of causation or expanded notions of acceptable risk that Texans would not. Indeed citizens in different locales within states may opt for different balances among wealth creation and other quality of life issues, and one would not be surprised to find the court rulings in different localities reflecting prevailing local rights expectations. Except where basic, constitutionally recognized rights are at issue, there is no reason for expecting, and no justification for enforcing, one-size-fits-all standards of environmental quality and human health protection.

5. CONCLUSION

Ethical concerns lie at the core of all discussions concerning pollution control policy, so it is not simply a matter of moving from recognizing the existence of polluting activity to regulating that activity. There is an intermediate step in which an ethical theory is chosen (even if only implicitly) that frames the permissible range of reactions of policy makers. This chapter developed a particular ethical response to pollution problems: classical liberal rights theory. The chapter then argued that classical liberal theory would support, to the extent feasible, common law solutions to pollution problems—and that the common law, if enforced, would be better protective of the environment than might be expected.

NOTES

1. Gregory Cooper, "Teleology and Environmental Ethics," *American Philosophical Quarterly*, 35, no.2 (April 1998): 195–207.

2. Peter Singer, *Animal Liberation: A New Ethics for Our Treatment of Animals* (New York: A New York Review Book, 1975).

3. Paul Taylor, *Respect for Nature* (Princeton, N.J.: Princeton University Press, 1986).

4. J. Baird Callicott, *In Defense of the Land Ethic* (Albany, N.Y.: State University of New York Press, 1989).

5. John Passmore, *Man's Responsibility for Nature* (New York: Charles Schribner's Sons, 1974); R. G. Frey, *Rights, Killing and Suffering* (Oxford: Basil Blackwell, 1983); Gerald Gaus, "Respect for Persons and Environmental Values," *Autonomy and Community*, eds. Jane Kneller and Sidney Axinn (Albany, N.Y: State University of New York Press, 1998), 239–64.

6. Passmore, "Man's Responsibility for Nature."

7. Richard L. Stroup, "Superfund: The Shortcut that Failed," *PERC Policy Series* (Bozeman, MT.: Political Economy Research Center, May 1996); H. Sterling Burnett, "Superfund: History of Failure," *Brief Analysis*, 198 (Dallas, Tex.: National Center for Policy Analysis, 1996); Bonner Cohen, "The People v. Carol Browner: EPA on Trial," (Washington: National Wilderness Institute, 1998); Bruce A. Ackerman and William Hassler, *Clean Coal, Dirty Air* (New Haven, Conn.: Yale University Press, 1981); and Michael S. Greve and Fred L. Smith, Jr., *Environmental Politics: Public Costs, Private Rewards* (New York: Praeger, 1992).

8. Lawrence C. Becker, *Property Rights, Philosophic Foundations* (Boston: Routledge and Kegan Paul, 1977).

9. John Locke, *The Second Treatise of Government* (Indianapolis: Bobbs-Merrill, 1952).

10. Ellen Frankel Paul, *Property Rights and Eminent Domain* (New Brunswick, N.J.: Transaction Books, 1987).

11. Ibid., p. 226.

12. A. M. Honore, *Essays in Jurisprudence*, ed. A. G. Guest (Oxford: Clarendon Press, 1961), 107–147.

13. A. John Simmons, *The Lockean Theory of Rights* (Princeton, N.J.: Princeton University Press, 1992), 274.

14. Garrett Hardin, "The Tragedy of the Commons," *Science*, 162 (1968): 1243–48.

15. Aristotle, *Politics*, Ernest Baker, R.F. Stalley (translators) (Oxford: Oxford University Press, 1998), 1261^{b}32.

16. Harold Demsetz, "Toward a Theory of Property Rights," *American Economic Review: Papers and Proceedings*, 57 (1967): 347–359; ed. Terry L. Anderson, *Property Rights and Indian Economies* (Lanham, Md.: Rowman and Littlefield, 1992); eds. Terry L. Anderson and Peter J. Hill, *Wildlife in the Marketplace* (Lanham, Md.: Rowman and Littlefield Publishers, Inc., 1995).

17. James D. Gwartney and Richard L. Stroup, "Communal versus Private Property Rights," *The Freeman*, Vol. 38, No. 2 (1988).

18. A. N. Pigou, *The Economics of Welfare*, 4th ed. (London: Macmillan & Co., 1932).

19. R. H. Coase, "The Problem of Social Cost," *The Journal of Law and Economics*, 3 (October 1960): 1–44.

20. Block, Walter, "O.J.'s Defense: A Reductio Ad Absurdum of the Economics of Ronald Coase and Richard Posner," *European Journal of Law and Economics*, Vol. 3, (1996): 265–286; http://141. 164.133.3/faculty/Block/Blockarticles/OJsDefense.htm.

21. Locke, *The Second Treatise of Government*, Chapter 9.

22. Elizabeth Brubaker, *Property Rights in Defense of Nature* (Toronto: Earthscan Publications Limited, 1995); H. Marlow Green, "Common Law, Property Rights & the Environment: Analysis of Historical Developments & a Model for the Future," unpublished manuscript, (Bozeman, Mont.: Political Economy Research Center, 1995).

23. Quoted in Green, "Common Law, Property Rights & the Environment," 3.

24. F. A. Hayek, *The Constitution of Liberty* (London: Routledge & Kegan Paul, 1960), *Law,*

Legislation and Liberty (London: Routledge & Kegan Paul, 1979), *Individualism and Economic Order* (London: Routledge & Kegan Paul, 1948).

25. Mark Sagoff, "Can Libertarians Be Environmentalists?" *PEGS Newsletter,* 2, no.2 (Summer 1992): 7, 19; Garrett Hardin, "The Tragedy of the Commons," *Science,* 162 (1968): 1243–1248.

26. Bellinger v. New York Central Railroad, 23 N.Y. 42 (1861), in Green, "Common Law, Property Rights & the Environment," 13–14.

27. Ibid., 11.

28. Russell Transport Ltd. et. al. v. Ontario Malleable Iron Co. Ltd (1952), 4 D.L.R. 719 at 728 (Ont. H.C.), in Brubaker, *Property Rights in Defense of Nature,* 46.

29. Walter v. Selfe (1851), 4 DE G. & S. 315, 20 L.J. Ch. 433 at 435, in Brubaker, *Property Rights in Defense of Nature,* 47.

30. Hay v. Cohoes Co. 3 Barb. 42, 43; N.Y. App. Div. (1848), aff'd 2 N.Y. 159 (1849), in Brubaker, *Property Rights in Defense of Nature,* 62.

31. Roberts v. Gwyrfai District Council (1899) 2 Ch. D. 608, Ibid., 62.

32. See, for instance, Theodore Roosevelt, *Proceedings of the American Forest Congress* (Washington, D.C., American Forestry Association, 1905) and Gifford Pinchot, *The Fight for Conservation* (New York: Doubleday and Page, 1910).

33. Ibid., 77.

34. See, for instance, Murray Rothbard, "Law, Property Rights, and Air Pollution," *The Cato Journal,* Vol. 2, No. 1 (Spring 1982): 55–99; Roger E. Meiners and Bruce Yandle, "Curbing Pollution–Case-By-Case," *Perc Reports,* 16, no.2 (June 1998): 7–9; and various authors in Roger E. Meiners and Andrew P. Morriss, *The Common Law and the Environment* (Lanham, MD: Rowman & Littlefield Publishers, Inc., 2000).

35. Rothbard, Ibid., 69–72.

36. Robert W. Crandall, "Review: Ackerman and Hassler's Clean Coal/Dirty Air," *The Bell Journal of Economics,* Vol. 12, No. 2 (1981): 677–682; Bruce A. Ackerman and William Hassler, *Clean Coal, Dirty Air* (New Haven, Conn: Yale University Press, 1981).

37. Mark Sagoff, "Takings, Just Compensation and the Environment," Upstream/Downstream, *Issues in Environmental Ethics,* ed. Donald Scherer (Philadelphia: Temple University Press, 1990), 158–79; Sagoff, "Can Libertarians Be Environmentalists?"

CHAPTER 15

PRICE GOUGING AND MARKET FAILURE

Matt Zwolinski

1. INTRODUCTION

By July 2008, at the time of this writing, average gas prices in the United States were approximately 37 percent higher than they were in January of that year.[1] In itself, there is nothing particularly striking about this fact. Gas prices are historically quite variable and the increase was explicable largely in terms of the increased cost of crude oil. What *is* striking is that this increase in gasoline prices, unlike past increases, was not accompanied by any significant calls for a renewal of legal caps on the maximum price of gasoline. Whether this is due to increased economic knowledge on the part of citizens regarding the role of price controls in producing shortages or simply to specific memory of the effects of those controls during the oil crisis of the late 1970s is unclear. Regardless of the explanation, however, Americans appear to be more comfortable with allowing the allocation of gasoline to be determined via the free operation of the price system.

This comfort does not extend to all goods or all circumstances. In periods following disasters or emergencies, especially, Americans are likely to view certain kinds of price increase on certain kinds of goods with great suspicion. Such price increases are often referred to as instances of "price gouging" or "profiteering," and are almost universally the target of moral condemnation and very often legal prohibition.

The reason that price gouging is viewed as morally distinguishable from ordinary price increases, I believe, has to do with the notion of market failure.[2] Under normal conditions, we might think, there are a number of morally significant points to be made in favor of relying on free markets as an allocative mechanism. We might think that markets provide a forum in which agents can exercise their autonomy,[3] that a free market is an institutional system that promotes liberty or reduces coercion,[4] or that markets tend to promote utility or some other form of consequential benefit.[5] However, any plausible theory will recognize that these points in favor of free markets will only hold on the assumption that certain conditions are satisfied. Cases of market failure can be thought of, rather loosely, as cases where these conditions are *not* satisfied. In cases where a seller has monopoly power, for instance, or where a transaction produces negative externalities, the standard justification of markets does not apply and hence gives us no reason to think that such markets will have the morally attractive features they normally have. We might even conclude in such cases that some form of government regulation is called for to correct the market failure. If, then, cases of price gouging are thought to involve some form of market failure, we might thereby conclude that (a) price gouging lacks the morally praiseworthy attributes generally associated with market exchange, and possibly (b) price gouging ought to be regulated or prohibited by law.

This chapter seeks to explore the phenomenon of price gouging, to reconstruct the normative argument underlying its moral condemnation and legal prohibition, and to demonstrate that this argument is seriously flawed. I will begin in Section 2 by defining price gouging in a way that draws on but expands upon the legal understanding of this phenomenon. Section 3 will set out, in skeletal form, the general case for viewing market price increases as morally permissible, while Section 4 will briefly outline the problems of market failure that might undermine this permissibility. The main argument of the chapter will commence in Section 5, where I will make the case that the current legal prohibition of price gouging is morally unjustified and ought to be abolished. Finally, in Section 6, I argue further that price gouging is not only a practice that should be legally tolerated, but one that is often admirable from a purely moral perspective as well.

2. WHAT IS PRICE GOUGING?

The academic literature on price gouging is surprisingly scarce, and as a result there is no definition of the concept that enjoys wide consensus. Nevertheless, most states have enacted laws prohibiting price gouging, and these laws can provide us with a good starting point for understanding the phenomenon. Currently, about thirty-four states have laws against price gouging.[6] And while there is a great deal of variance among these laws regarding matters of detail, there is nevertheless significant overlap regarding three key elements.

1. **Period of Emergency:** Almost all anti-gouging laws specify that they apply only to actions taken during times of disaster or emergency.[7]

2. **Necessary Items:** Most laws further specify that their restrictions apply only to certain classes of items, generally those necessary for survival or for coping with serious problems caused by the disaster. California, for instance, is typical in limiting its scope to items that are "consumer food items or goods, goods or services used for emergency cleanup, emergency supplies, medical supplies, home heating oil, building materials, housing, transportation, freight, and storage services, or gasoline or other motor fuels."[8]

3. **Price Ceilings:** The definitive feature of anti-gouging laws is the limit they set on the maximum price that can be charged for specified goods. Such limits are set either by prohibitions on "unreasonable," "excessive" or "unconscionable" price increases or by specific limits on the percentage increase in price allowed after the onset of the emergency.[9] In the most extreme laws, the maximum allowable percentage increase is set at zero.[10]

These three elements provide us with a good starting point for a definition of price gouging. But still, even in these areas of overlap, there is significant disagreement between states regarding matters of detail. Does a state of emergency require some official proclamation or merely some disastrous event? Which items are to count as necessary items and which are not? And what kind of price increase is too much?

One way of resolving (or side-stepping) some of these difficulties, I will suggest, is to define price gouging partly in terms of broad normative concepts rather than exclusively in terms of natural kinds of actions. Such a move, I think, is supported both by ordinary usage of the term and by the heavy strands of normative language running through the various statutory definitions of price gouging. In terms of ordinary language, "price gouging" is hardly an evaluatively neutral description of a market transaction. "Gouging," in general, is something harmful and nasty that one is typically prohibited from doing to one's opponent's eyes even in combative matches with precious little in the way of restrictive rules.[11] To describe an act as an instance of price gouging is thus to make an evaluative judgment about that act—to view it as *wrong*, in some way. Review of state anti-gouging statutes confirms this hypothesis. The vast majority of state statues define price gouging in terms of normative concepts like "unreasonable" or "unconscionable." And both Arkansas and California claim in the preamble to their laws that their restrictions are necessary in order to prevent merchants from taking "unfair advantage" of consumers.[12]

Hence I propose that we understand price gouging as a moralized concept—part of what we *mean* in calling something an act of price gouging is that it is morally wrong. The only difficulty with such a definition, it seems to me, is that it risks rendering unintelligible what ought to be a legitimate substantive moral question—namely, whether price gouging *really is* immoral. The claim that price gouging seems to be immoral but, on closer examination, turns out not to be, ought to be one that is at least not self-contradictory, even if ultimately false. But if price gouging is immoral by definition, then all substantive moral debate regarding its virtues and vices is rendered otiose. To avoid this difficulty, I will suggest that we understand the wrongness of price gouging in a prima facie sense. Thus, for purposes of this chapter, let us define price gouging in the following way:

Price Gouging: Price gouging occurs when, in the wake of an emergency, the price of some good that is necessary or extremely useful for coping with the emergency is set at what appears to be an unfairly high level.[13]

This definition leaves quite a bit of wiggle room, as I think it ought, for determining what should and should not count as a case of price gouging. Still, it will serve to sharpen the focus of our investigation considerably, for it directs our attention to what is most important in the normative assessment of price gouging—the alleged unfairness of the price charged for the necessary goods.[14] This leaves open the possibility that other wrongs might occur—indeed, they might *often* occur—in conjunction with price gouging. Sellers might deliberately deceive customers regarding the nature of their goods or the availability of cheaper competing goods, force might be used against customers or competing sellers, and so on. But these wrongs are distinct from the wrong of price gouging, and there is probably not much interesting moral debate to be had regarding their wrongfulness. Our question for this chapter is what, if anything, is wrong with price gouging *per se*, and not with these other actions that might be contingently associated with it.

3. THE PRIMA FACIE PERMISSIBILITY OF PRICES

In general, people do not think that there is anything morally problematic about price increases, much less anything that calls for legal intervention. If Nike's executives were to vote to double the price at which they sell their shoes tomorrow, we might perhaps think they were being greedy and short-sighted, but one would be hard-pressed to explain any way in which they were being *immoral*. The same would be true, I suspect, if instead of shoes we considered a good more plausibly considered a necessity—say, milk. What moral violation would a retailer be committing who, under ordinary conditions, raised their price of milk even tenfold?

The reason most of us would not object to such price increases, I suspect, has to do with assumptions we make about the way that markets work under ordinary conditions. In normal circumstances, markets are competitive in the sense that there are multiple sellers of any given good, and competition between these sellers limits the extent to which they can raise prices while still expecting consumers to pay them. Thus, a grocer in a large city who unilaterally doubled the price of her milk would likely find shoppers responding to this move by simply buying their milk somewhere else. As long as there are a sufficient number of other sellers trying to win consumers' dollars by selling the same good, the power of any single seller to extract whatever price she likes from consumers is severely limited. A single grocer might be *trying* to take advantage of consumers, but competitive market pressures render her *unable* to do so. And so, I think, we are inclined to adopt a kind of moral "no harm, no foul" rule with regard to such moves. Because normal market competition prevents most price increases from being harmful or exploitative, there is nothing really immoral about them, and nothing on which to ground any claim for government intervention.

Indeed, there are certain morally significant advantages to using, and legally tolerating the use of, a freely operating price system. One such advantage has to do with the efficiency of prices as an allocative mechanism. In a perfectly competitive market, prices serve to allocate scarce resources toward their highest-valued use.[15] This is important because a resource, like tin for example, can serve many different uses for different people. One potential consumer of tin might want it to use for cans in which to package his tomato puree, another might want it for an object of art she is constructing. For some of these consumers there might be dozens of potential substitute goods, while for others there will not. Aluminum might work just as well for the cans, let's say, but would conflict horribly with the artist's intent. Since, all else being equal, those who would derive more utility from the tin (because of the value they personally would derive from using it, or because of the value they would derive from selling it or some good made from or with it, or because of the unavailability or prohibitively high cost of substitute goods, etc.) will be willing to pay more for it, a system that allows the price of tin to freely adjust in response to changes in supply in demand will ensure that tin goes to where it does the most good.

Moreover, as Friedrich Hayek repeatedly stressed, the market accomplishes this allocation with a remarkable economy of information.[16] No single person, or committee of such persons, could possibly know all the competing uses to which a resource like tin might be applied, let alone the relative values of those uses, the availability of substitute goods, and so on. This knowledge exists in society, but it exists in a radically dispersed form—you know about your need of tin, I know about my need of it, she knows about her portion of the supply of tin, and so on. A market price system responds to this decentralization of information by decentralizing economic decision-making power (each market actor is free to set and respond to prices as she chooses) and by transmitting to market actors just that information about the larger economic context that is needed for them to make their decisions wisely. If the price of tin goes up, this tells market actors that the supply relative to demand has gone down and that they must economize their use of tin as a result. In this way, even if no market actor is aware of the *whole* economic picture, each will nevertheless act in a way that promotes an overall efficient distribution of the resource since on the whole "their limited individual fields of vision sufficiently overlap so that through many intermediaries the relevant information is communicated to all . . . [thus bringing] about the solution which (it is just conceptually possible) might have been arrived at by one single mind possessing all the information which is in fact dispersed among all the people involved in the process."[17]

These considerations, then, establish a kind of prima facie moral case in defense of market price increases. Because normal market competition prevents price increases from being harmful or exploitative, and because a price system that adjusts freely in response to supply and demand serves morally praiseworthy ends, it is prima facie morally permissible for market actors to increase prices, and there is likewise a prima facie case against government regulation of the price system. To the extent that allowing individuals to freely set the price they charge for goods they bring to market fosters autonomy or liberty as well, these considerations must add to that prima facie case.

4. MARKET FAILURE

The extent to which these considerations give us all-things-considered reason to support the use and nonregulation of prices, of course, will depend on how closely actual markets resemble those envisioned in economists' models. And regardless of how closely one might think those models approximate reality in ordinary circumstances, cases of price gouging involve situations where they clearly fall short.

Such situations, in general, are often referred to as cases of market failure. This term is sometimes used loosely to refer to any situation in which markets fail to promote some goal that we think is desirable—whether it is national defense, happiness, or genuinely authentic art. Somewhat more precisely, and more in line with standard economic usage, market failures can be defined as situations where markets fail to produce an efficient outcome. An efficient outcome, in turn, can be thought of as one where the total benefits produced could not be produced at a lower cost.[18] The kinds of market failure that are likely to plague instances of price gouging include the following:

- **Limited Number of Sellers:** Cases of price gouging will be noncompetitive to the extent that sellers enjoy a degree of monopoly power. Without competitive pressures, sellers will be able to charge a price above the competitive level and reap the excess profits for themselves.

- **Limited Information:** Reliable information regarding supply and demand will often be difficult to come by in an emergency situation. Since buyers and sellers can only act on the information they have, limited information means that less than efficient outcomes will be achieved by the market process.

- **Extreme Inequalities of Wealth:** The claim that a free market will allocate resources to those who value them most is only true if all individuals have equal wealth available to pay for those resources. Someone who has no money will not be able to purchase a good no matter how much she values it and, on the assumption that money has a diminishing marginal value, someone who has an extremely large amount of money will be willing to outbid poorer consumers for goods even when those poorer consumers would have derived a greater amount of utility from those goods.

Given these conditions, it is not at all clear that the prima facie permissibility of relying on prices established in the last section should extend to cases of price gouging. Market failures not only undermine the claim that markets are justified because they produce an efficient allocation of resources, but they undermine *any* moral claim that depends on the competitiveness of markets as a prerequisite—such as, perhaps, the claim that markets promote freedom, or that they promote the interests of the poor. More specifically, if the allocation of scarce vital resources is left up to the free market price system, we might worry that the following morally undesirable consequences will result:

1. **Exploitation:** To exploit someone, in the morally significant sense of the term, is to take unfair advantage of their vulnerability.[19] While buyers in normal market conditions are not generally vulnerable, buyers in emer-

gency situations where markets suffer from the above conditions are. Sellers who use their market power to profit from this vulnerability can be said to be acting exploitatively insofar as we think they are acting *wrongly* in doing so. This is true even if the exploitation is *mutually beneficial*, so long as we assume that mutually beneficial transactions can still be unfair.[20]

2. **Inefficient Distribution:** Markets can be guaranteed to generate economically efficient outcomes only to the extent that market failures are not present. To the extent that cases of price gouging involve monopoly power and imperfect information, these outcomes will not necessarily be achieved. Because markets cannot be counted on to produce efficient outcomes, it is possible that some alternative mechanism could produce either the same benefit at a lower cost or perhaps even a greater benefit at an equal or lower cost. For instance, given the assumption of diminishing marginal utility, more utility might be produced by a government-mandated equal distribution of scarce resources than by distribution according to ability-to-pay, since the former policy can prevent hoarding of needed goods by those rich enough to afford it and ensure that goods are distributed to those who need them regardless of their ability to afford them.

3. **Unjust Distribution:** To claim that market outcomes are inefficient is to make a claim about the aggregate level of utility generated by the market. But for most moral theories, claims about aggregate utility do not exhaust the legitimate claims of morality, even if they constitute a part of it.[21] Most moral theories hold that a distribution of resources can be unjust even if it is utility-maximizing if, for instance, it distributes those resources unfairly among separate persons.[22] To the extent that price gouging involves market failures that increase the ability of the economically powerful to advance their interests while increasing the vulnerability of the least well-off, price gouging might be unjust as well as inefficient.

5. THE LEGAL REGULATION OF PRICE GOUGING

If price gouging involves instances of market failure, and if market failure can lead to the sort of morally objectionable consequences described above, then what does this tell us about the permissibility of the governmental regulation of price gouging? Market failure has long been viewed as one of the classic justifications for political authority.[23] So, are the kinds of anti-gouging laws that currently exist in the United States justified on the grounds that they are necessary to correct market failures?

They might be, but we cannot reach this conclusion *just* on the grounds that price gouging involves the existence of a market failure. For we cannot conclude from the mere fact that markets are failing to produce an efficient outcome that government could do any better.[24] In the words of Henry Sidgwick, "It does not follow that wherever laissez faire falls short government interference is expedient; since the inevitable drawbacks of the latter may, in any particular case, be worse than the shortcomings of private enterprise."[25]

Demonstrating that government regulation is the appropriate response to the market failures involved in price gouging will thus require positive argument beyond merely pointing out the defects of markets. In particular, it will require careful examination of the specific form of regulation under consideration, since whether governmental regulation will produce better outcomes than a free market will depend crucially on the *kind* of governmental regulation at issue.

It is obviously beyond the scope of this or any other chapter to consider every conceivable variety of anti-gouging regulation. Because of this, and because they are the rules that actually govern our current practice, I propose to focus my discussion on the kind of anti-gouging regulation that currently exists in the United States. For while these laws vary to some degree from state to state, they share enough in common that a discussion of them as a class will be useful, and will almost certainly have implications for other alternative forms of regulation as well.[26]

Any legal regulation of price gouging must define the activity that it proposes to regulate. Certain aspects of this task can be accomplished without encountering any serious philosophical problems. If, for instance, price gouging is to be defined as a certain kind of price increase that occurs during a period of "emergency," then emergency can (and generally is) either given a stipulated definition elsewhere in the legal rules or is defined as the period following some kind of official government declaration.

Specifying the kinds of goods or services that are to be subject to regulation is somewhat more difficult. The idea is to allow price increases on things that are unimportant and unrelated to the disaster, like high-definition tele-vision sets, while prohibiting them on things that are necessary or disaster-related. Typically, statutes either give a list of items the prices of which may not be increased,[27] or they refer to categories of items by the use of general concepts like "necessary goods"[28] or goods or services "for which consumer demand does, or is likely to, increase as a consequence of the disaster."[29] Certain problems may arise here, as any list of items may be under-inclusive in failing to capture all those items for which price increases would be morally problematic, while general concepts will often have the opposite problem of over-inclusiveness. Even if it were the case, for instance, that demand for beer predictably increases following a disaster—perhaps because people don't have to go to work and are looking for some way to escape thinking about their troubles—it does not follow that price increases on beer are in any way morally problematic. This is because, I suspect, we view beer as a kind of luxury item—and a potentially harmful one, at that. In raising the price of beer, sellers thus do not deprive individuals of a vital necessity. At the same time, though, restricting the scope of anti-gouging laws to "necessary" goods is not terribly helpful either. For goods are only necessary with reference to some end. Sandbags might be necessary in order to protect your *home* from flooding damage, but are usually not necessary to save your *life*. If we define necessity too strictly, we are likely to exempt from regulation a whole host of goods that seem intuitively that they ought to be subject to regulation, whereas if we define it too loosely then our regulation will extend further than its moral justification warrants.

The most serious philosophical problems, however, arise in the attempt to characterize the kind of price increases that are to be prohibited. As noted in Section 2 above, currently laws go about this task in one of two ways. Either the prohibited price increases are defined in a moralized sense, so that price gouging is understood to be involve an "unconscionable"[30] or "unrea-sonably excessive"[31] increase in prices, or it is defined in terms of an allow-able percentage increase over the pre-emergency price, with most states al-lowing a 10 percent increase plus whatever other increases can be attributed to increased costs faced by the seller, while other states are either more[32] or less[33] restrictive.

Both of these approaches have serious problems. Defining price gouging in terms of "unconscionable" or "unreasonable" price increases, for instance, raises serious issues of legal predictability given the difficulty that exists in arriving at clear and shared meanings for these terms. What constitutes an unconscionable exchange, for instance, is matter about which even those who are experts in the law disagree considerably.[34] But if those whose full-time occupation is interpreting, applying, and working with the law cannot get clear on which exchanges are unconscionable and which are not, how can we hope that ordinary merchants will be able to do so—let alone regular citizens who begin selling goods for the first time in the wake of a disaster? Unless individuals can understand which particular kinds of activity the unconscionability provision prohibits, they will be unable to predict how the law will respond to their behavior, and thus unable to plan their economic activity accordingly. This is bad on grounds of economic efficiency since it means that sellers will refrain from engaging in some Pareto-superior exchanges—even when those exchanges would not actually be prohibited by law.[35] And it is also objectionable on grounds of fairness—it seems unfair for merchants to be punished for violating a norm of unconscionability which, even with the exercise of due diligence, they could not hope to adequately understand.[36]

While laws that define price gouging in terms of an abstract standard run into difficulties by being in some sense too flexible, laws that define it in terms of some specific level of permissible of price increase have the opposite problem. The limits they place on permissible price increases are too inflexible to respond to the wide variety of factors that ought to go in to making such a moral determination. This inflexibility is clearest when we consider those anti-gouging laws that make no allowance for whatever increased costs sellers might face as a result of the same disaster that triggered the anti-gouging law in the first place. Such costs might include the increased cost of labor during a period of emergency, as well as the increased costs of raw materials or of transportation. Forcing sellers to absorb these costs by prohibiting them from making up for them with increased prices is morally problematic in several respects. From a fairness-based perspective, it is not clear why merchants should be forced to bear the entire burden of the increase in costs caused by the disaster. The merchants are no more morally responsible for the disaster than were consumers. And indeed, it might be argued that those who amass a stock of disaster-related goods prior to the onset of a disaster have exercised a kind of good judgment and foresight that we as a society should seek to reward, not punish. Besides, it is not as though we are faced with the choice of either letting the cost fall entirely upon merchants or entirely upon consumers. If one believes that it is the responsibility of society to care for its vulnerable members in times of need, then we need not place this burden on the shoulders of merchants alone; the cost can be spread across all citizens by alternative public policies.[37] But not only is forcing sellers to absorb costs unfair, it is likely counterproductive insofar as merchants are the group in society best positioned to improve the position of those made vulnerable by a disaster by selling them the supplies they so desperately need. Stocking resources in anticipation of an emergency and staying open to sell those goods once the emergency has struck are costly activities. The more governmental regulations increase the price (or, equivalently, decrease the profitability) to merchants of engaging in these activities, the less likely they are to be economically worthwhile, and hence the less likely merchants are to stock the goods that would be so very useful in the event of a disaster.[38]

The majority of statutes attempt to avoid these difficulties by allowing price increases above the specified cap if the increased price is directly attributable to increases in cost borne by the seller. But even here, problems persist. Most states that do allow such an exception limit the kinds of costs that can be taken into account due to increased costs imposed by the merchant's supplier and increased costs of labor and material in the merchant's provision of the goods. And this limitation of relevant costs seems arbitrary. Why, for instance, should there be no account made for increased *risk* faced by the merchant in remaining open for business during time of disaster?[39] Surely an increased risk of damage or theft is a factor that merchants ought to be able to consider in deciding whether the benefits of doing business in a post-disaster context outweigh the costs and is a reasonable consideration in favor of raising one's prices. But risk is not the only sort of cost neglected by anti-gouging laws. Such laws also fail to take account the various opportunity costs that the merchant might face in continuing to do business in the area, rather than shifting her capital to other, less dangerous and more profitable, markets. From an economic perspective, opportunity costs and costs imposed by risk can be just as burdensome on the seller as standard monetary costs, so there is no obvious reason why one special category of costs should be privileged above others.[40] But the law is often a clumsy instrument for achieving morally precise outcomes, and here as elsewhere, I suspect, it prefers to look only at those elements of the situation that are easily measurable—costs of products, labor and material. Lawmakers are thus faced with a dilemma. A narrow focus on easily measurable costs might be necessary in order to craft a law that can be enforced and understood, but this clarity can only be accomplished at the cost of failing to take account of all the relevant costs faced by the merchants to whom the restrictions apply. It thus does not seem possible to define for legal purposes the kinds of price increases that are to be prohibited in a nonmorally arbitrary way.

6. PROHIBITING MUTUAL BENEFIT

The difficulties discussed in the last section present a formidable obstacle to any practical method of legally regulating price gouging. Even if this obstacle could be overcome, however, there would still remain a decisive moral objection to current anti-gouging statutes. The most serious problem with such statutes is that they prohibit mutually beneficial exchange in a way that makes those who are already vulnerable even worse off. Even those who have no special fondness for "economic efficiency" should, I think, give serious reconsideration to their support of ant-gouging laws if, as I believe, it can be shown that such laws increase the suffering of those who can least afford it.

In cases of price gouging that do not involve coercion, deception, or some other extraneous factor, consumers are only 'gouged' to the extent that they voluntarily choose to purchase what someone else is selling. To be sure, their choice may not be voluntary in the fullest and most morally significant sense of that term. It might be made in a condition of psychological desperation set on by the emergency and exacerbated by the market failures that accompany it—lack of full and clear information, an absence of reasonable alternatives, and so on. But it would be a mistake to think of voluntariness as something that is either entirely present or entirely absent in an exchange, and even voluntariness in a greatly attenuated sense is sufficient to generate a serious moral problem with legal prohibition. For what a consumer's choice to purchase goods from a price gouger shows us is that *among her severely constrained set of options* she views paying the price as her best alternative.

In other words, the fact that consumers are willing to pay gougers' un-usually high prices shows that they value the good they are purchasing more than the money they are giving up for it. And assuming consumers are not systematically misinformed, deceived, or irrational, there is no reason to think that they are *wrong* in assigning these relative values. The goods that they are purchasing are, after all, genuinely *important*. The reason individuals are willing to pay a higher price for generators in the wake of a disaster that eliminates their normal supply of power is that their *need* for generators is also higher. Their willingness to pay the higher price is a reflection of this increased need and not the product of mistake or irrationality.

Of course, one might insist that consumers are not benefiting *enough* from the exchange. Perhaps merchants have a moral duty of beneficence to sell needed goods to consumers at something less than the market-clearing price. Or perhaps there is some moral notion of a "fair" price that price-gouging merchants are violating. It is possible, in other words, that merchants are unfairly taking advantage of the market failures that plague disaster areas in order to exploit consumers in their vulnerable position. Such exploitation would be wrong and the proper subject of legal regulation, one might argue, in spite of the mutual benefit it produces.[41] Although I am not convinced of the wrongness of consensual, mutually beneficial exploitation in this case, let us put such concerns to the side for the moment. For even those who believe that such exploitation is morally wrong, I will argue, have good reason to reject its legal prohibition.[42] This is because many of the very same concerns that underlie our objection to exploitation also count against any attempt to prohibit mutually beneficial but exploitative exchanges.

For instance, one reason we might be concerned about price gouging is that we wish to protect the interests of those made vulnerable by disaster. Because price gougers charge more than they should for items that disaster victims dearly need, we might worry that they are setting back the interests of those who can least afford to be harmed in this way. Still, even granting all this, it does not follow that price gouging should be legally prohibited. To see this, we need simply to think about how anti-gouging laws work. When such laws have any effect at all, it is because they require merchants to sell goods at below the market-clearing price. The market-clearing price is the price at which the quantity supplied is equal to the quantity demanded. If prices are set above the market-clearing price, there will be insufficient demand for merchants to sell all their goods, and a surplus will result. If, on the other hand, prices are set below the market-clearing price as anti-gouging statutes require, there will be *too much* demand for available supply. There will, in other words, be a shortage of the relevant goods.[43] This point is established both by widely accepted economic theory and by experiences with price caps such as those established during the oil crisis of the late 1970s.[44] The existence of shortages, in turn, means that many consumers who would like to buy goods—even at the illegal market-clearing price—will be unable to do so.[45] Because they are prevented from engaging in the economic exchanges they desire, they are made worse off. And because the goods affected by price gouging laws are *necessary* goods that are especially important for their health and well-being, they are probably made *significantly* worse off. Even if price gouging *is* an exploitative activity that (in some ways) sets back the interests of the vulnerable, the legal prohibition of price gouging sets back their interests even more.

If, on the other hand, one's reasons for objecting to exploitation are of a deontological rather than a consequentialist nature, then a parallel argument can be made regarding the relevant deontological considerations. Exploitation might plausibly be argued to manifest a lack of respect for the personhood of those who are exploited. But laws against price gouging both manifest and encourage similar or greater lack of respect. They manifest a lack of respect for both merchants and customers by preventing them from making the autonomous (even if not fully autonomous) choice to enter into economic exchanges at the market-clearing price. Individuals who buy from price gougers are attempting to use their judgment to make the best decisions they can about how to deal with a horrible situation, and anti-gouging laws prohibit them from making some of those purchases they deem worthwhile. Such laws send the signal, in effect, that *your* decision that this exchange is in your best interest is unimportant, and that the law will decide for you what sorts of transactions you are allowed to enter into. Furthermore, anti-gouging laws encourage a lack of respect for buyers by making it more likely that their needs will be *neglected* by those who are in a position to help them.[46] There are, after all, always many more people who *could* do something to help victims of disaster than who actually *do*. People in unaffected areas have ice, generators, and labor that they could bring to the affected area to help, but most choose not to. Such individuals do not exploit victims of disaster; they simply ignore them. But the number of such persons is not an immutable fact, independent of our public policy. People respond to incentives. So as much as we might wish that people would help out of the goodness of their hearts, the fact remains that the more our policies allow individuals to financially benefit themselves while helping others, the more likely they are to provide that help. Conversely, laws that prohibit the reaping of excessively high profits lead many individuals who would have done something to help to do nothing instead. The neglect such laws encourage may be a less obvious way of failing to value the humanity of such persons, but it is a failure nonetheless, and one that I am sure most disaster victims would be willing to trade for the disrespect involved in mutually beneficial exploitation, if given the choice.

Before moving on, there is one complication regarding the consequentialist case against anti-gouging laws. That case assumes that anti-gouging laws will prohibit some mutually beneficial exchanges, and this seems to be an *a priori* truth. But the argument also assumes that prohibiting those mutually beneficial exchanges will make consumers worse off, and this is more properly seen as an empirical hypothesis than an issue of pure economic logic. Suppose that price gouger S holds a monopoly on good G in a given area. And suppose further that the lowest price that S would be willing to accept for G is X, whereas the highest price that buyer B would be willing to pay for G would be Z (where $Z > X$). In the absence of anti-gouging restrictions, the market-clearing price will be very close to Z. With carefully crafted anti-gouging laws, however, it is possible to set the maximum legally permissible price at something closer to X. The law would simply need to know the value of X and set the maximum legal price of G at X. Since S is still willing to sell G at X, and B of course is willing to buy G at X, such laws could conceivably reduce the price that B must pay for G, without destroying S's incentive to supply B with G. Anti-gouging laws could thus, at least in principle, function as strategic mechanisms for reducing disparities in the distribution of cooperative surplus.[47] But while this result is possible in theory, in practice the epistemic hurdles involved arriving at knowledge of X for all goods G and all sellers S seem utterly insurmountable. As a result, I doubt that this argument could do much to support any actual legal regulation.[48]

In summary, the last two sections have argued that laws against price gouging are subject to several important objections. First, anti-gouging laws face a dilemma in the way they define the offense. Laws that define gouging in terms of "unconscionable" or "exploitative" prices do a good job capturing the nature of the moral opposition to price gouging, but are so vague that there is little chance that market actors will be able to predict which prices would be illegal and which would not. This is both unfair and inefficient. On the other hand, laws that seek to resolve this vagueness by setting clear limits on permissible price increases wind up being excessively rigid and prohibiting not only morally objectionable increases (say, those due to pure greed) but morally unobjectionable ones as well (those due to the supplier's attempt to recoup increased costs due to risk or opportunity costs). Finally, even if anti-gouging laws could be crafted in such a way as to avoid this dilemma, they would still face a decisive objection insofar as they prohibit mutually beneficial exchanges between sellers and buyers, and moreover prohibit them for buyers who stand in desperate need of precisely this kind of beneficial exchange. Anti-gouging laws thereby cause great harm to precisely the people who can afford it least. For all these reasons, I conclude that even if price gouging is in some way immoral, laws against the practice ought to be repealed.

7. MARKET FAILURE AND THE PRIMA FACIE PERMISSIBILITY OF PRICES

I argued in the previous section that there is a strong moral case to be made against the legal prohibition of price gouging, that this argument holds even given the assumption that price gouging occurs in the context of serious market failure, and even given the further assumption that price gouging is wrongfully exploitative. In this section, I will shift from arguing about what the law regarding price gouging ought to be, to a direct moral evaluation of the practice of price gouging itself. Specifically, I will argue that the problems of market failure discussed in Section 4 do not undermine the prima facie permissibility of price increases defended in Section 3.

7.1 The Concept of Market Failure Re-Examined

Before embarking on a point-by-point examination of how the concept of market failure applies to the context of price gouging, it will perhaps be worthwhile to try to get a little clearer on the concept of market failure itself. As we defined it in Section 4, a market failure occurs whenever the market fails to produce an efficient outcome, where an efficient outcome is understood as one in which the total benefits produced could not be produced at a lower cost. Another way of thinking of market failure (and success) is in terms of Pareto Efficiency. An efficient market could be defined as one that produces Pareto-Efficient outcome, and a Pareto-Efficient outcome is one in which no person could be made better off without somebody else being made worse off.[49] Markets fail, on this model, to the extent that they fail to produce Pareto-Efficient outcomes.

Now, the fact that actual markets routinely fail to produce outcomes that are efficient in either of these senses is hardly surprising news, least of all to economists. Economic theory only supports the claim that markets produce efficient outcomes on the condition that certain assumptions are satisfied, and these assumptions are extremely unrealistic.[50] In real markets, transaction costs are never zero, information is never perfect, and our actions often affect the welfare of third parties. Such shortcomings do not require any great ingenuity to discover. A world in which the assumptions of so-called "perfect" competition were actually satisfied would be *radically* different from the one that we currently inhabit. It would, to highlight just one startling fact, be a world in which it would be impossible for anyone to discover any product or service that they would like and be able to buy or sell! For if a product existed for which you would be willing to pay a certain amount, an amount that the owner of the good would be willing to accept, then that would be sufficient to show that the market is not efficient. This is because in an efficient market, all mutually beneficial trades have already been made. Nor could a market be efficient if there were new discoveries of resources or opportunities waiting to be made, nor if people's preferences ever changed. A world of perfect efficiency would, in other words, be entirely static.

Thus, if we are to understand the charge of market failure as a claim that markets fall short of the theoretical ideal of perfect efficiency, then such claims are neither terribly interesting nor a good basis for a moral criticism of the market or of market behavior. For all that such claims show is that the conditions under which we can demonstrate theoretically that the market will produce perfectly efficient outcomes have not been met. But demonstrating this is *not* the same as demonstrating that markets will *not* produce perfectly efficient outcomes. It is not the same as demonstrating that markets produce no *tendency* toward efficiency, even if it is a tendency that is never perfectly realized. And, perhaps most importantly, it is not the same as showing that any other practically realizable institution could do a *better* job.

To take the first of these claims first, the fact that markets fail to meet the conditions of perfect competition only removes one reason we might have for thinking that markets will yield perfectly efficient outcomes. It shows that we cannot demonstrate that markets will yield such outcomes with our theoretical models, but this leaves open the possibility that actual markets will bring about such outcomes in ways our models could not have predicted. As an analogy, consider cooperative behavior in one-shot prisoner's dilemmas. Most game theoretic models predict that in such conditions, cooperation will not emerge. Rational, self-interested players will see that defection yields a payoff superior to that yielded by cooperation no matter what the other player does, and will therefore defect. However, when we leave our theoretical models behind and observe how real people behave, we see that cooperation in one-shot prisoners dilemmas is not only possible, but is in fact quite common.[51] The fact that we cannot use our game theoretic models to prove that players will cooperate, in other words, does not show us that they *will* not cooperate. Similarly, when we look at the artificial but imperfect markets created by experimental economists, we see that very often perfectly efficient outcomes will emerge even under conditions of imperfect information and irrationality. Such an outcome could not have been predicted—at least not by the model of perfect competition—but it arises nevertheless, and economists have developed and are developing alternative theoretical models that explain why.[52]

Second, even if the fact of market failure demonstrates that market mechanisms will not produce perfectly efficient outcomes, this is still compatible with the possibility that they produce a *tendency* toward efficient outcomes. And this, probably, is all we should expect from them. Market competition is best thought of as a process by which we move from less efficient states to more efficient ones. This is one of the important insights of the Austrian School of economics, summed up nicely in Israel Kirzner's definition of competition as the "rivalrous activities of market participants trying to win profits by offering the market better opportunities than are currently available."[53]

Competition, for the Austrians, is a kind of discovery procedure whereby new opportunities for mutual benefit are sought out.[54] And there are two things worth noting about this discovery procedure. The first is that it only works if there actually exist unrealized opportunities for mutual benefit to discover. Competition in the Austrian sense is thus not only compatible with the fact that markets are not perfectly efficient; it actually *presupposes* it. The second thing to note is the role of profits in this process. Entrepreneurs in a nonperfectly efficient market reap what Kirzner calls "pure entrepreneurial profit," a return above and beyond their marginal cost of production which would not exist in an environment of neoclassical perfect competition. Such profit can, then, be thought of as a kind of inefficiency. But in reality, it is precisely the opportunity for such profit that spurs entrepreneurs to discover new opportunities for mutual benefit. If it is an inefficiency at all, it is an inefficiency that drives the creation of wealth in an economy.

Even granting all this, however, the fact that markets contain the possibility of negative externalities and monopoly power, and the fact that extreme inequalities of wealth exist, means that the tendency of markets to discover and exploit new opportunities for mutual benefit will be very imperfect indeed. Still, the relevant question is not whether some theoretical construct could produce better results, but whether any *actually possible* alternative institutional mechanism could. The literature of public choice economics suggests that we have at least as much good reason to suppose that government intervention in the economy will fail to produce efficient outcomes as we do to believe that unregulated markets will.[55] Whether these government-created inefficiencies are more or less tolerable than the market-created ones is something that must be demonstrated by empirical analysis and argument; the superiority of government regulation does not follow logically from the fact of market failure. In addition, in those cases where price gouging produces something short of a morally ideal allocation, the best response might not be to try to *prohibit* price gouging, but to alter the institutional rules under which it takes place. That is, if the reason we object to price gouging is the context of market failure in which it occurs, then the natural solution seems to be to correct the market failure, rather than to ban price gouging altogether. If, for instance, one's concern with price gouging is that antecedent inequalities of wealth will lead to the rich getting the goods and the poor being left with nothing, then one could address this by either attacking the inequality of wealth directly through social welfare policies or, perhaps more plausibly, having governmental agencies purchase scarce and necessary goods at market prices and provide those goods at a subsidized rate or free of charge to those in need. This latter approach was taken by the city of Boston, with apparent success, during a shortage of flu vaccines in 2004.[56] By setting up clear "rules of the game" and allowing market actors to operate freely within those rules, these approaches take advantage of market efficiencies while avoiding some of the concerns over distributional inequality raised by the unchecked operation of the market.[57]

7.2 The Moral Implications of Market Failure in Cases of Price Gouging

With this clearer understanding of the nature of market failure under our belt, we can now turn to examining what the implications of market failure are for our moral evaluation of the practice of price gouging. The first point to note is that in spite of whatever market failures may exist in situations of emergency, price increases nevertheless have a tendency, albeit an imperfect one, to produce the beneficial outcomes discussed earlier in Section 3.

Take, for instance, the issue of allocative efficiency. A real-world example of the tendency of price increases to promote the efficient use of resources can be seen in the example of Florida hotels after Hurricane Charley in 2004. According to charges filed by the state attorney general, one hotel in West Palm Beach charged three individuals a rate of over $100 per night for a room, more than double their advertised rate. The owners of hotels like this one were charged with price gouging under Florida's anti-gouging statute. "Families putting their lives back together," the attorney general wrote, "should not have to worry about price gouging."[58] But it is not clear that hoteliers' price increases actually gave families anything to *worry* about, at least in comparison to what their worries would have been in the absence of a price increase. After all, price increases do more than line the pockets of hotel owners. They cause consumers to make different decisions about how to satisfy their demand for a place to stay. As one commentator pointed out, a family that might have chosen to rent separate rooms for parents and children at $50 per night will be more likely to rent only one room at the higher price, and a family whose home was damaged but in livable condition might choose to tough it out if the cost of hotel room is $100 rather than $50.[59] Higher prices for hotel rooms lead consumers to think twice about how much they really need those rooms. Those whose need is great—perhaps those whose homes were completely destroyed and who have no friends or relatives with whom they could stay—will in general be willing to pay the higher price. Those whose need is less will be more likely to stay with a friend or neighbor instead or simply to forgo the hotel room altogether and put up with the inconveniences of a damaged home. The result of this is that the scarce and vital resource of a hotel room is conserved, and more rooms are kept available for those who need them most.

Of course, allocating resources like hotel rooms by price only serves to conserve them for those who are willing and able to *pay* the most, and the connection between willingness and ability to pay and need is contingent and imperfect. Someone who is extremely wealthy might be willing to purchase multiple hotel rooms even though her need for them is small in comparison with that of a much poorer person. To the extent that a moral case can be made for distributing scarce goods by price, then, it will be on the grounds that such distribution serves as a kind of heuristic for distributing according to what we think is *really* morally important, such as need or desert. Like all heuristics, it is imperfect. But it is not clear that we have any alternative mechanism that will do better.

Before turning to look at one alternative mechanism that *might* do better, it is worth noting one additional virtue of distribution according to price. Beyond promoting allocative efficiency by signaling to consumers to re-examine their need and look for substitute goods if possible, price increases also send a signal to potential suppliers. When the price of a good like electrical generators goes up in the wake of a disaster, this sends a signal to *potential* suppliers of generators—say, people who own generators in nearby towns unaffected by the disaster—that there is a profit to be made in bringing that supply to where it is needed.

Prices thus serve not only to allocate an existing supply among consumers, they also serve to increase the supply available for allocation. This is a crucially important point regarding the dynamic nature of markets, one that we often fail to appreciate in forming our moral intuitions about specific economic transactions. When we think about price gouging, we often imagine a small, fixed supply of resources being distributed among a group of people. If a high price is charged, the rich will get the goods, and the rest won't. From all appearances, the potential customers of price gougers are in a zero-sum game with each other—one could win only if another loses—and the price gougers take advantage of this vulnerability. This seems to violate the most basic of moral standards—if *we* were desperately in need of some good, we would not want others to profit from our misery. In a static world, price gouging seems to be a clear-cut violation of the Golden Rule.

But here, as with many other cases involving markets, our intuitive moral response is driven too much by what we can visualize, and not enough by what is harder to see.[60] It is easy for us to visualize the zero-sum relation between the individuals fighting over a small immediate supply of food or ice. It is more difficult for us to see the way in which the market forces at work in that scenario operate to increase supply and to spur the discovery and improvisation of substitutes, such that what is zero-sum in the microcosm is positive-sum in the macrocosm. The quantity of a resource available in a market can shrink or grow, and the most important factor in effecting this change is the resource's price. Indeed, the fact that a resource commands a high price in a market is an *essential step* in bringing additional supply to that market. Holding prices low, voluntarily or by regulation, may seem to achieve justice in the microcosm, but it does so at the cost of keeping the microcosm static, and preventing the influx of supply that would alleviate concerns about unfairly high prices in the market as a whole. Market competition is a process, and the high short-term prices charged by gougers are just one step in that a process—a step that is indispensible to the incentives for discovery and entrepreneurship which move markets closer to a state where people's needs are more widely met.[61]

Still, it might seem that there is one obviously superior alternative to allocating resources by ability and willingness to pay. That alternative is making individualized judgments about the need and/or desert of prospective buyers, and selling to those who measure highest on those morally relevant characteristics. Since the argument for relying on prices is simply that ability to pay *correlates* with what we take to be a morally significant characteristic—the extent to which an individual values the good—we could do better by assessing the morally relevant characteristic directly and distributing on that basis.

There is more than a grain of truth to this argument, and I suspect it underlies much of our discomfort with price gouging and, more generally, the use of prices to allocate scarce resources. No parent would distribute food to his children—even in an emergency—on the basis of ability to pay. I doubt that most people would treat even their neighbors this way. Why, then, should it be acceptable as a system of distribution more generally?

The answer has to do with several important differences between these kinds of relationships and the kinds of relationships usually involved in price gouging. First, most plausible moral views hold that we have special duties toward our families, friends, and neighbors. We might have imperfect or perfect duties of care, for instance, which conflict with and override our liberty to profit from selling them scarce resources. Furthermore, and more significantly for this argument, we are in a better position to *know* the morally relevant characteristics of those with whom we are in close association. This sort of consideration is easy for us as philosophers to lose sight of. After all, in philosophic arguments and thought experiments we can stipulate the morally relevant characteristics and take them as a given. In practice, however, discerning which characteristics are morally significant and which are not is considerably more difficult. And our ignorance of moral significance is itself morally significant, for it suggests that one of the criteria by which our actual practices should be evaluated is how well they work in a world where we do not operate with all the relevant moral knowledge. In some contexts our ignorance will be less of a factor than it is in others. It is relatively easy for me to know my neighbor's needs, character, and so on. But even with my neighbors my epistemic state is significantly inferior to that which characterizes my relation to my family. And a seller who has come to town for the first time in the wake of a disaster has essentially *no* way of knowing anything about the people to whom they are distributing their goods. Furthermore, if we are to take recent evidence from moral psychology seriously, it appears that individuals are not as skilled or consistent in assessing the morally relevant characteristics of others as we might like to believe. We are often swayed by what in a more objective light we would view as morally irrelevant characteristics, such as race, sex, or affective display.[62] The choice, then, is not between imperfect allocation by prices versus perfect allocation by moral merit. All our distributive options are imperfect. Sometimes the imperfections of market prices will be more significant than those of individualized judgment, and sometimes the opposite will be true. The point of this section is not to argue that price gouging is permissible in all cases. Rather, it is to argue that in many cases of price gouging, charging the market-clearing price will tend to allocate goods in a way that tracks (albeit imperfectly) what we think are morally significant characteristics like intensity of need. When it does, and when we have no alternatives available that better satisfy our moral obligations,[63] we have good reason to view price gouging as morally permissible.

While I think this kind of argument provides a good defense of the moral permissibility of price gouging in a wide range of cases, I should be clear regarding what I see as its main limitation. That limitation is that the argument I have given will not provide a justification of price gouging in cases where the features that normally justify price increases in a free market are entirely lacking. In some kinds of emergencies, for instance, the notion of a "market" seems entirely misplaced. Take the simple thought experiment often used to illustrate the nature of wrongful exploitation. *A* is drowning in a lake, and *B* rows by on the only boat in sight. *B* offers to give *A* a ride to shore *if A* is willing to sign a contract (which *B* has brought along in anticipation of just such an occasion) pledging to sign over the deed to his house in exchange. In this example, it is clear that *B*'s price does little to promote the value of allocative efficiency. There is no one else fighting for a spot in *B*'s boat. If *A* doesn't get in, *B* will simply leave it empty. Moreover, in this case, there is no doubt in *B*'s mind about which allocation of resources would best promote overall welfare or moral goodness however defined. *A* needs the extra seat more than *B* needs to keep it empty, and there is no need to rely on the information-conveying function of prices to tell him this. And, finally, although it is logically possible to make the argument that *B*'s exploitatively expensive rescue will lead others to increase the supply of rescues over the long run (*C*, *D*, and *E*, upon hearing the story behind *B*'s fancy new house, invest in houseboats and start patrolling nearby lakes looking for drowning victims to exploit), the appeal to the signaling function of prices in this context seems rather pathetically thin. In this kind of emergency, then, none of the standard moral justifications of market processes are present, and the worry about morally objectionable exploitation looms large. Price gouging in this sort of situation, then, ought to be regarded as morally impermissible—what is clearly morally required in this situation is rescue at a fair price, even if what exactly constitutes a fair price is not itself entirely clear.

Some cases of real-world price gouging may be like this. But most, I think, will not. First, natural disasters produce large numbers of victims, not a single victim like the drowning case above. This large number of victims means that there is both a need to allocate scarce resources among different individuals and a need to attract increased supply to the affected persons. Market prices can serve both of these functions. Second, natural disasters typically cause harm to victims over a long period of time compared to the drowning case. This length of time means an opportunity for market processes to work to serve both their allocative and signaling roles usually exists. Finally, natural disasters and the needs to which they give rise are, at least to some extent, predictable. In Philosophy-Land, we never know when we're going to come across an infant drowning in a shallow pond or a horde of faceless victims tied to trolley tracks. In the real world, however, individuals and organizations have some insight into what sort of natural disasters tend to affect which areas, when the threat is imminent, and what type of response will be needed. Market prices provide such market agents with an incentive to *anticipate* these problems and respond to them quickly or perhaps even preemptively.[64]

CONCLUSION

This chapter has examined the claim that price gouging is a morally objectionable practice that ought to be legally prohibited. This claim, I argued, is often grounded on the belief that price gouging occurs in the context of one or more market failures. However, even if we grant the existence of market failure in cases of price gouging, it does not follow that price gouging is something that ought to be legally prohibited or morally condemned. First, I argued that even if price gouging is immoral, it ought not to be prohibited by law. Existing laws against price gouging either fail to provide clear guidance to sellers or fail to take account of all the morally significant reasons that could justify a price increase, and it is difficult to see how laws could be reformed to avoid this dilemma. Furthermore, any legal prohibition of price gouging will create disincentives for individuals to engage in economic activity that helps those made vulnerable by emergencies. Because laws that prohibit price gouging harm vulnerable buyers and are unfair or unclear to sellers, they are immoral and should be repealed. Second, I argued that price gouging is, at least oftentimes, morally permissible. Price gouging can serve morally admirable goals by promoting an efficient allocation of scarce and needed resources and by creating economic signals that will lead to increases in the supply of needed goods, both of which can do much to help improve the lot of people in desperate need. When it does so, I have claimed that we have good reason to think of price gouging as morally permissible.

NOTES

Portions of this chapter draw heavily on my paper, "The Ethics of Price Gouging," *Business Ethics Quarterly*, 18, no.3 (2008): 347–78.

1. This number is derived from records of weekly average gas prices taken from the webpage of the Energy Administration Association, http://www.eia.doe.gov/oil_gas/petroleum/data_publications/wrgp/mogas_history.html, accessed April 2, 2009.

2. I do not claim that most people who object to price gouging would explain their objection in terms of market failure. I suspect the standard condemnation of price gouging is much more visceral than that. Rather, my claim is that standard condemnations of price gouging only make sense—or at least, they make as much sense as they can—on the assumption that markets are failing in certain ways.

3. See, for instance, J. Otteson, *Actual Ethics* (Cambridge: Cambridge University Press, 2006); and Horacio Spector, *Autonomy and Rights* (Oxford: Oxford University Press, 1992).

4. See Jan Narveson, *The Libertarian Idea* (Philadelphia: Temple University Press, 1988); and M. N. Rothbard, *The Ethics of Liberty* (New Jersey: Humanities Press, 1982).

5. See Milton Friedman, *Capitalism and Freedom* (Chicago: University of Chicago, 2002); and D. Friedman, *The Machinery of Freedom: Guide to Radical Capitalism* (La Salle, Ill.: Open Court, 1989).

6. I say "about" because it is unclear whether we should count certain statutes that are narrowly construed to prevent charging too much for certain very specific goods alongside the more common, general anti-gouging laws. Indiana and Massachusetts, for example, prohibit post-disaster price increases on fuel only, while Colorado restricts its coverage to medication. See IND. CODE ANN. §§4-6-9.1-1 to -7 (West Supp. 2007) and 940 MASS. CODE REGS. 3.18 (2007). Although these states might plausibly be excluded for being too narrow, Michigan might plausibly be excluded for being too broad. Its law prohibits charging an excessive price for any good and does not require any disaster or emergency to trigger the law's activation. See UDAP Statute MCL 445.903(1)(z). The number 34 is arrived at by adopting the most liberal criteria for determining whether a statute is an anti-gouging law. For a more complete analysis of state laws, see D. Skarbek, and B. Skarbek, "The Price is Right!: Regulation, Reputation, and Recovery," *Dartmouth Law Journal*, 6(2) (2008).

7. Anti-gouging statutes are generally triggered by an official proclamation of emergency and last either the length of the emergency or for some specified time—Kansas, for instance, specifies that its law shall be in effect for either the time during which the declaration of emergency is in effect, or for a period of thirty days after the event that triggered the declaration, whichever is longer. See KSA 50-6,106. Michigan is an exception to this general rule, as it requires no triggering event and simply has general prohibitions on excessive price increases or profits. See UDAP Statute MCL 445.903(1)(z).

8. Cal. Penal Code §396. The District of Columbia, Hawaii, and Mississippi, however, are among the states which have laws that are not limited to necessary or disaster-related items but extend to any good and/or service. See D.C. Code §28.4101-4102, Haw. Rev. Stat. §209.9 and Miss. Code Ann. §75-24-25.

9. Massachusetts, Virginia, Florida, Indiana, and New York are among the states that prohibit the sale of goods at "unconscionably high prices" or "grossly excessive prices" in the wake of an emergency. See 940 Mass. Code Reg. 3.18, Va. Code Ann §59.1-526 (Supp. 2005), Fla. Stat. Ann §01.160(2) (West 2002 and Supp. 2005), Ind Code Ann. §4-6-9.1-2 (West 2005), and N.Y. Gen. Bus. Law §396-r(1) (McKinney 1996 & Supp. 2005). Arkansas and California are examples of states that set a percentage cap (both use 10%) on price increases in the wake of a disaster. See Ark. Code Ann. §4-88-33 (2001 & Supp. 2005) and Cal. Penal Code §396 (West 1999 & Supp 2006). Most states that use a percentage cap also allow that cap to be exceeded if the cause of the price increase can be directly attributed to increases in cost to the seller.

10. Georgia, Louisiana, Mississippi, and Connecticut all have laws prohibiting any price increase for certain goods in the wake of a disaster. See Ga. Code Ann. §10-1-393.4(a) (1995), La. Rev. Stat. Ann. §29:732 (2005), Miss. Code Ann. §75-24-25 (2003), and Conn. Gen. Stat. §42-232 (1991). Louisiana's code is, for reasons that are at least understandable if not correct, one of the harshest laws on the book, stipulating that criminal gouging offenses that result in property damage in excess of $5,000 can be punishable by up to five years imprisonment at hard labor.

11. ee, for instance, the short list of rules governing the Ultimate Fighting Championship at http://www.ufc.com/index.cfm?fa=LearnUFC.Rules, accessed March 2, 2009.

12. See UDAP Statute A.C.A. 4-88-301 et seq. and Cal. Penal Code §396.

13. This definition is slightly different from that which I proposed in "The Ethics of Price Gouging" and seems to me to be superior to it in several respects. First, the sense in which a good is "necessary" is clarified somewhat, without being overly restrictive. Second, saying that the price of a good is "set" at an unfairly high level rather than "raised" to an unfairly high level allows for the possibility that price gouging can be done by individuals who, prior to the emergency in question, did not sell the relevant goods at all. Finally, "unfair or exploitatively high level" has been replaced by "unfair" level, since it seems to me that exploitation, to the extent that it is wrong, is simply a specific instance of unfairness.

14. The definition refers to necessary or extremely useful goods, rather than just necessary goods, since there is probably nothing that is strictly speaking *necessary* for coping with any particular emergency. For simplicity's sake, however, I will just use the term "necessary goods" in this chapter, with the understanding that this phrase should be interpreted quite broadly.

15. I will have more to say on how this bears on real-world, nonperfectly competitive markets later in the chapter.

16. See F. A. Hayek, "The Use of Knowledge in Society," *American Economic Review*, 35 (1945): 519–30.

17. F. A. Hayek, "The Use of Knowledge in Society," *American Economic Review*, 35 (1945): 526.

18. See, for instance, C. Wolf, *Markets or Governments: Choosing Between Imperfect Alternatives*

(MIT Press, 1993). As Wolf notes, this is only one of a number of possible ways of understanding the kind of efficiency involved in market success or failure. As the broadest and least technical such definition, however, the definition above will be most useful for the purposes of this chapter.

19. Accounts of exploitation vary. The present account has some similarities with those presented in R. E. Goodin, *Reasons for Welfare* (Princeton: Princeton University Press, 1988); and A. Wertheimer, *Exploitation* (Princeton, N.J.: Princeton University Press, 1996), but is meant to serve as a general concept of exploitation compatible with a range of competing conceptions.

20. See, for a discussion, Wertheimer, *Exploitation*, chap. 1. Most extant accounts of exploitation are compatible with the possibility that mutually beneficial exploitation can exist, and that it can be morally wrong. See, for instance, C. Meyers, "Wrongful Beneficence: Exploitation and Third World Sweatshops," *Journal of Social Philosophy*, 35 (2004): 319–33, where "exploitation" is defined as unfairly taking advantage of an individual, benefitting from her misfortune, and benefitting disproportionately relative to one's contribution. Robert Mayer, similarly, argues that the essence of exploitation is a failure to benefit the victim *as much as fairness requires*, and hence that even mutually beneficial transactions can be exploitative and wrong. See his "What's Wrong with Exploitation?" *Journal of Applied Philosophy*, 24 (2007): 137–50.

21. This, I should stress, is true of my own position as well, contrary to what at least one critic has suggested. See Jeremy Snyder, "Efficiency, Equality and Price Gouging: A Response to Zwolinski," *Business Ethics Quarterly* 19, no. 2 (2009): 303–304.

22. See, for a discussion, Matt Zwolinski, "The Separateness of Persons and Liberal Theory," *Journal of Value Inquiry*, vol. 42, no. 2 (2008): 147–65.

23. For a critical discussion of this type of argument, see D. Schmidtz, *The Limits of Government: An Essay on the Public Goods Argument* (Boulder, Col.: Westview, 1991).

24. If we define an inefficient outcome, as we have, as one in which it is possible to produce equal benefits a lower level of cost, then it does follow from the fact that a market outcome is inefficient that *some* institution could do better. But that institution need not be government. There are numerous examples where nonmarket but voluntary, nongovernmental institutions have provided the kinds of public goods that markets by themselves are unable to provide. See, for example, S. N. S Cheung, "The Fable of the Bees: An Economic Investigation," *Journal of Law and Economics*, vol. 16(1973): 11–33 on the provision of pollinating bees in apple orchards; and R. Ellickson, *Order Without Law: How Neighbors Settle Disputes* (Cambridge: Harvard University Press, 1991) on the provision of rules and enforcement mechanisms of property and liability in Shasta County cattle country.

25. See Henry Sidgwick, *Principles of Political Economy*, 2nd edition (London: MacMillan, 1887), p. 414.

26. Jeremy Snyder has proposed one such alternative regulatory scheme in Jeremy Snyder, "What's the Matter with Price Gouging" *Business Ethics Quarterly*, 19, no. 2 (2009): 275–93. See Matt Zwolinski, "Price Gouging, Non-Worseness, and Market Failure," *Business Ethics Quarterly*, 19, no. 2 (2009): 295–306 for a critique.

27. See, for instance, Idaho's regulation at Idaho Code Ann. §48-603 (2003 & Supp. 2007).

28. See, for instance, Kan. Stat. Ann. §50-6,106 (2005).

29. Virginia Post-Disaster Anti-Price Gouging Act, Va. Code Ann. §§59.1-525 to 529.1 (2006).

30. Fla. Stat. §501.160 (2008).

31. N.C. Gen. Stat. §§75-37 to 38 (2007).

32. Illinois, for instance, allows *no* price increases regardless of whether the increase can be attributed to additional costs faced by the seller. See Illinois Emergency Services and Disaster Agency Act of 1988, 20 Ill. Comp. Stat. 3305/7 (2007).

33. Alabama, for instance, allows a 25 percent increase plus an additional allowance for increased costs. See Alabama Unconscionable Pricing Act, ALA. CODE §§8-31-1 to 6 (2002).

34. The Federal Trade Commission, in its report on possible gasoline price manipulation in the wake of Hurricane Katrina, notes that "Unconscionability cases have been particularly difficult for courts to analyze because there are no clear criteria as to when a price term is unconscionable" Federal Trade Commission "Investigation of Gasoline Price Manipulation and Post-Katrina Gasoline Price Increases" (2006). Retrieved August 29, 2007, from http://www.ftc.gov/reports/060518 PublicGasolinePricesInvestigationReportFinal.pdf. The report goes on to quote several legal sources in support of its claim, such as E. Allen Farnsworth, who writes in his respected book on contracts that "unconscionability itself is incapable of precise definition." E. A. Farnsworth, *Contracts* (Boston: Little Brown and Company, 1982). The Uniform Commercial Code's test for unconscionability, on the other hand has been described as "unintelligible or abstract," Sitogum Holdings, Inc. v. Ropes, 800 A.2d 915, 919 (N.J. Super. 2002) (quoting Arthur A. Leff, "Unconscionability and the Code: The Emperor's New Clause," *University of Pennsylvania Law Review* 115, no.4 (1967): 485–559, and "an amorphous concept," Kugler v. Romain, 58 N.J. 522, 543-44 (1971).

35. In 2008, South Carolina's anti-gouging laws, which employ an unconscionability standard, were triggered after Hurricane Ike struck the area. In response, some gas stations refused deliveries of fuel from their suppliers. According to Michael Fields, executive director of the South Carolina Petroleum Marketers Association, "if they knew their next load would cost $5.50 (a gallon), they knew they would be accused of gouging. . . . They knew no one would believe, 'I gotta charge this because this is what it costs.'" The South Carolina attorney general, Henry McMaster, noted that price increases could be allowed under the anti-gouging law if stations were "able to explain it." Presumably, the gas station owners in question were not willing to risk steep fines on their ability to explain their price increases to McMaster's satisfaction.

36. Indeed, Lon Fuller has argued that the desirableness of clarity is not merely an external standard by which we can judge laws to be either good or bad, but an *internal* standard of legality itself. Laws that are basically unclear fail to achieve an essential purpose of law and hence, in a way, fail to be laws at all. L. Fuller, *The Morality of Law* (New Haven, Conn.: Yale University Press, 1964). Fuller, however, is more optimistic about the ability of the law to rely on imprecise standards such as 'fairness' without running afoul of the requirement of clarity than is F. A. Hayek, who writes that "one could write a history of the decline of the Rule of Law . . . in terms of the progressive introduction of these vague formulas into legislation and jurisdiction, and of the increasing arbitrariness and uncertainty of, and the consequent disrespect for, the law and the judicature." F. A. Hayek, *The Road to Serfdom* (Chicago: University of Chicago Press, 1944).

37. See the discussion of an alternative proposal at the end of Section 7.1.

38. In May of 2009, for instance, a state of emergency was declared in West Virginia due to heavy flooding. The floods triggered the state's anti-gouging laws, which limit price increases to 10 percent above cost. Shortly after this declaration, Marathon Oil Corporation announced that it would temporarily halt delivery of fuel to West Virginia because, in the words of its spokesperson, "We can't raise our rack price above the 10 percent threshold that West Virginia has set in their laws during a declared emergency. We can't raise our rack price to reflect the current cost of product in the market, so it isn't prudent to continue to supply a customer that doesn't have a contract at a price that is below the market price." From Greg Lindenberg, "Manchin vs. Marathon," *CSP Daily News,* June 1, 2009. http://www.cspnet.com/ME2/Audiences/dirmod.asp?sid=&nm=&type=Publ ishing&mod=Publications::Article&mid=8F3A7027421841978F18BE895F87F791&tier=4&id=95 CE97EF1B7A4A0987982F8D3DF3A244&AudID=CBA745B91AFB44FA923476ACBBD040A5. Accessed, November 19, 2009.

39. Louisiana is the only state of which I am aware to explicitly include increased risk as one of the costs that sellers can legitimately recoup by increasing their prices. See LA. REV. STAT. ANN. §§29.732.

40. See J. Buchanan, *Cost and Choice: An Inquiry in Economic Theory* (Indianapolis, IN: Liberty Fund, 1999).

41. On the subject of mutually beneficial exploitation, see note 20 above and accompanying text.

42. Alan Wertheimer and Robert Mayer reach the same conclusion, though via slightly different argumentative routes. See A. Wertheimer, *Exploitation* (Princeton, N.J.: Princeton University Press, 1996), and R. Mayer, "What's Wrong with Exploitation?" *Journal of Applied Philosophy* 24, no.2 (2007): 137–50.

43. The result of a shortage, in turn, is to effectively set the price at which goods can be obtained at infinity. Consumers' willingness to pay, on the other hand, is very high in the wake of an emergency, though well short of infinity. Since goods could be brought to market for a cost lower than consumers' willingness to pay, a potential consumer surplus is destroyed by anti-gouging laws and the shortages they create. The amount of consumer's surplus, if the demand curve slopes up steeply near the origin, is enormous, and is in fact arbitrarily large in terms of measurement.

44. Both the theoretical relationship between price caps and shortages and a discussion of the gas shortage of the 1970s can be found in many economic textbooks, including the leading textbook, P. Samuelson and W. Nordhaus, *Economics* (Boston: Irwin McGraw-Hill, 1998).

45. Or, rather, that they will be unable to do so *legally*. To the extent that anti-gouging laws limit supply while doing nothing to reduce demand, it is not unlikely that a black market will develop for the relevant goods. In such a market, we can expect prices to be even higher than they would in a market with no legal restrictions, due to the increased transaction costs necessary to avoid the law. We can also expect the likelihood of fraud and outright coercion to be greater due to the inability of consumers to appeal to the law to resolve whatever disputes might arise regarding their illegal transaction. See, for a related discussion of the economic effects of drug prohibition, M. Thornton, *The Economics of Prohibition* (Salt Lake City: University of Utah Press, 1991).

46. I address the comparative moral wrongness of neglect and exploitation in Zwolinski, "The Ethics of Price Gouging," *Business Ethics Quarterly* 18, no.3 (2008): 357-60.

47. See A. John Simmons, *On the Edge of Anarchy* (Princeton, N.J.: Princeton University Press, 1993), and Brian Barry, "Lady Chatterley's Lover and Doctor Fischer's Bomb Party: Liberalism, Pareto-Optimality, and the Problem of Objectionable Preferences" in *Foundations of Social Choice Theory*, ed. J. Elster and A. Hylland (Cambridge: Cambridge University Press, 1986).

48. Indeed, the hurdles seem very much akin to those faced by market socialists in setting prices in the absence of market signals. On the connection between the problems of market socialism and certain forms of economic regulation, see Irving Kirzner, *The Perils of Regulation: A Market Process Approach* (Coral Gables, Fla.: University of Miami School of Law, Law and Economics Center, 1979).

49. See, for a discussion, A. Buchanan, *Ethics, Efficiency, and the Market* (New York: Rowman and Littlefield, 1988).

50. See, for a discussion, F. M. Bator, "The Anatomy of Market Failure," *Quarterly Journal of Economics* 72 (1958): 351–79.

51. See, for a discussion, A. Roth, "Introduction to Experimental Economics," in *The Handbook of Experimental Economics*. ed. J. K. Hagel and A. E. Roth (Princeton, N.J.: Princeton University Press, 1995), 3–109.

52. See, for instance, A. Mas-Colell, A., M. Whinston, et al., *Microeconomic Theory* (Oxford:

Oxford University Press, 1995); V. Smith, "Markets as Economizers of Information: Experimental Examination of the 'Hayek Hypothesis'," *Economic Inquiry*, 20 (1982): 165–79; and Gode, D. K. and S. Sunder, "Allocative Efficiency of Markets with Zero-Intelligence Traders: Markets as a Partial Substitute for Individual Rationality," *Journal of Political Economy* 101, no.1 (1993): 119–37; all cited in D. Skarbek, "Market Failure and Natural Disaster: A Reexamination of Anti-Gouging Laws." *Public Contract Law Journal* 37, no.4 (2008): 709–18.

53. See Israel Kirzner, *The Perils of Regulation: A Market Process Approach* (Coral Gables, Fla.: University of Miami School of Law, Law and Economics Center, 1979), p. 9.

54. See Hayek, "Competition as a Discovery Procedure" in his *New Studies in Philosophy, Politics, Economics, and the History of Ideas* (Chicago: University of Chicago Press, 1968).

55. See, for a summary of this literature, W. Mitchell, and R. T. Simmons, *Beyond Politics: Markets, Welfare, and the Failure of Bureaucracy* (Boulder, Col.: Westview Press, 1994); G. Tullock, *Government Failure: A Primer in Public Choice* (Washington, D.C.: Cato Institute, 2002).

56. See "City Seeks to Buy Excess Flu Vaccine," (2004, October 15), *Boston Globe*, p. B2 from http://www.boston.com/news/local/massachusetts/articles/2004/10/15/6_accused_of_rmv_permit_scheme/, , accessed March 2, 2009.

57. Or, at least, they can take advantage of *some* of the efficiencies of a market pricing system. See, for a critique of the second kind of approach discussed above, part six of Frederic Bastiat's "What is Seen and What is Unseen" in G. B. de Huszar, ed., *Selected Essays on Political Economy* (Irvington-on-Hudson, NY Foundation for Economic Education, 1995).

58. Crist, C. (2004). Attorney General Charges Two Florida Hotels With Price Gouging Retrieved November 27, 2007, from http://myfloridalegal.com/__852562220065EE67.nsf/0/A15CA108ECBF1DDE85256EF30054D0FC?Open&Highlight=0,gouging,palm,beach.

59. Sowell, T. 2004. "Price gouging" in Florida. *Jewish World Review*, September 28. Retrieved November 15, 2007, from http://www.jewishworldreview.com/cols/sowell091404.asp.

60. This was one of the key insights of the nineteenth century French political economist Frédéric Bastiat, most famously expressed in his "What is Seen and What is Not Seen" in G. B. de Huszar, ed., *Selected Essays on Political Economy* (Irvington-on-Hudson, NY Foundation for Economic Education, 1995).

61. See, generally, Irving Kirzner, *The Meaning of Market Process: Essays in the Development of Modern Austiran Economics* (New York: Routledge, 1996).

62. D. Kahneman and A. Tversky's famous work in D. Kahneman, and A. Tversky, *Judgment Under Uncertainty: Heuristics and Biases* (Cambridge: Cambridge University Press, 1982), for instance, contains many examples wherein moral reasoning is improperly swayed by the language or order in which information is presented. More recently, Jonathan Haidt has shown that much of our moral reasoning is driven by, and tailored to fit, emotional reactions such as disgust. See J. Haidt, S. H. Koller and M. G. Dias, "Affect, Culture, and Morality, or Is It Wrong to Eat Your Dog?," *Journal of Personality and Social Psychology*, 65(1993): 613–28, and J. Haidt, "The Emotional Dog and its Rational Tail: A Social Intuitionist Approach to Moral Judgment," *Psychological Review*, 108(2001): 814–34.

63. Note that this is a significantly weaker condition than saying that there must be no alternatives available that produce morally better results. An act can surely be morally permissible even if it is not morally optimizing.

64. I can only speculate that this is sometimes true of the behavior of private individuals. No such speculation is necessary regarding the behavior of private firms. Steven Horowitz has documented the response of the private sector to Hurricane Katrina, noting that in the two weeks following the disaster, Wal-Mart shipped over 2500 truckloads of needed goods to Louisiana, a

substantial portion of which was given away free. This quick response time was made possible by
Wal-Mart's elaborate mechanisms for tracking storms before they hit in order to ensure that its
stores are well stocked prior to the time that demand increases. In the case of large firms, the ability
to increase price is often unnecessary in order to provide an incentive to engage in such anticipatory
behavior, since the economic success of such firms depends less on the profits made by any single
sale or set of sales and more on the long-term goodwill and repeat business of customers. See Steven
Horowitz, *Making Hurricane Response More Effective: Lessons from the Private Sector and the Coast
Guard During Katrina*, Washington D.C.: Mercatus Center (2008); and "Wal-Mart to the Rescue:
Private Enterprise's Response to Hurricane Katrina," *The Independent Review*, 13, no.4 (2009).

INDEX

The authorized representative in the EU for product safety and compliance is:
Mare Nostrum Group
B.V Doelen 72
4831 GR Breda
The Netherlands

www.ingramcontent.com/pod-product-compliance
Lightning Source LLC
Chambersburg PA
CBHW021845020426
42334CB00013B/198